M000314436

Everybody's Family Romance

Reading Incest in Neoliberal America

Gillian Harkins

University of Minnesota Press

Minneapolis • London

Chapter 3 was previously published as "Seduction by Law: Sexual Property and Testimonial Possession in *Thereafter Johnnie*," in "The Future of Testimony," special issue, *Discourse: Journal for Theoretical Studies in Media and Culture* 25.1–2 (Winter–Spring 2003): 138–65; copyright Wayne State University Press. Chapter 4 was previously published as "Surviving the Family Romance? Southern Realism and the Labor of Incest," *Southern Literary Journal* 40.1 (Fall 2007): 114–39.

Copyright 2009 by the Regents of the University of Minnesota

All rights reserved. No part of this publication may be reproduced, stored in a retrieval system, or transmitted, in any form or by any means, electronic, mechanical, photocopying, recording, or otherwise, without the prior written permission of the publisher.

Published by the University of Minnesota Press
111 Third Avenue South, Suite 290
Minneapolis, MN 55401–2520
http://www.upress.umn.edu

Library of Congress Cataloging-in-Publication Data

Harkins, Gillian.
    Everybody's family romance : reading incest in neoliberal America / Gillian Harkins.
        p. cm.
    Includes bibliographical references and index.
    ISBN 978-0-8166-5347-8 (acid-free paper) — ISBN 978-0-8166-5348-5 (pbk. : acid-free paper)
    1. American literature—20th century—History and criticism.
2. Incest in literature. I. Title.
    PS228.168H37 2009
    810.9′3538—dc22

2009027312

Printed in the United States of America on acid-free paper

The University of Minnesota is an equal-opportunity educator and employer.

20 19 18 17 16 15 14 13 12 11 10 09   10 9 8 7 6 5 4 3 2 1

Everybody's Family Romance

Nationalism is our form of incest, is our idolatry, is our sanity.

—ERICH FROMM, *The Sane Society*

Contents

Preface: Nobody's Home   ix

Introduction: Everybody's Family Romance   1

1. Laying Down the Law: The Modernization of American Incest   26

2. Legal Fantasies: Populist Trauma and the Theater of Memory   69

3. Seduction by Literature: Sexual Property and
   Testimonial Possession   114

4. Surviving the Family Romance? Realism and the
   Labor of Incest   152

5. Consensual Relations: The Scattered Generations of Kinship   188

Conclusion: Beyond the Incest Taboo   228

Acknowledgments   239

Notes   243

Bibliography   265

Index   299

Preface

Nobody's Home

I've been watching *Capturing the Friedmans* lately, Andrew Jarecki's 2003 documentary about childhood sexual abuse allegations in the late 1980s United States. Set at the height of what some critics have called child sexual abuse hysteria, *Capturing the Friedmans* tells the story of one family "captured" in a moral panic about the end of childhood innocence at the end of the century. Arnold Friedman was caught in a police sting for purchasing and sending child pornography in the mail. He had been under surveillance between 1984 and 1987, before the Internet transformed the policing of child pornography into a major component of new virtual surveillance tactics. By Thanksgiving 1987, the Nassau County sex crimes unit had begun investigation into Arnold's contact with children, focusing in particular on his relationships with children enrolled in after-school computer classes in his home. A prize-winning former high school science teacher, Arnold taught preadolescent boys how to use new computer technologies with the help of his son Jesse. During investigative interviews that allegedly included leading questioning, veiled threats, and hypnosis, children testified to nearly a hundred counts of forced sodomy along with more elaborate stories of group sex games and an extended sex predator ring.[1] Following a series of indictments based entirely on child testimony, in 1988 Arnold and Jesse Friedman were accused of sexually abusing multiple male children in their care. Arnold pleaded guilty,

resulting in his incarceration from 1988 to 1995 (when he committed sui-
cide in prison); Jesse also pleaded guilty and was incarcerated from 1988
to 2001, when he was released on parole as a registered sex offender
under Megan's Law.

Jarecki's film presents the Friedman case as a litmus test for changes
in what many have called the cultural zeitgeist. In 1988, the film suggests,
the United States was caught up in a sex panic of massive proportions. In
the aftermath of second-wave feminism and women's speak-outs about
incest and childhood sexual abuse, the public became convinced that child
sexual abuse happened frequently and that it was often largely repressed
from the conscious mind. New public awareness of child sexual abuse and
the possibility of traumatic forgetting and delayed recall prompted what
some have called a climate of hysteria or panic, a "witch hunt" for sexual
predators in sheep's clothing. By 2001, when the talking-head interviews
for Jarecki's film were conducted, interviewees showed a new, nervous
awareness of what psychologist and cultural critic Janice Haaken, in her
book *Pillar of Salt,* calls "the perils of looking back." Over the course
of the 1990s, the "memory wars" (as Frederick Crews called them) had
been fought over the possibility of traumatic forgetting and delayed recall. A new consensus emerged for a new century: children (and many
adult women) were highly suggestible and could be persuaded to "remember" sexual events that had not occurred. As the film *Capturing the Friedmans* demonstrates, looking back on 1988 from 2003 allowed viewers
to see how paranoiac fantasies about sexual victimization captured the
Friedmans, and to learn how to be a more reasonable audience in future
cases of child sexual abuse allegations.

It seems now, gazing retrospectively from the present all the way
back to the 1970s of the Friedmans' earliest home movies, that "something wrong" indeed happened in the closing decades of the twentieth
century. It is not clear, however, what exactly this "something" was. In
the film, the Friedman case stands in for complex historical phenomena
that are never fully explicated. Rather than treat the historical emergence
of child sexual abuse concerns, the film begins in medias res with the two
discourses of child sexual abuse that dominated popular culture: pedophilia and recovered memory. On one hand, the film raises questions
about how to interpret and respond to Arnold Friedman's admitted sexual interest in boys (which he says he had acted on at three different
points in his life) and his consumption of child pornography. This interest is described as "pedophilia," a clinical term describing serial sexual

interest in children that may be nonviolent or even loving. On the other hand, the film resolves questions about how to interpret and respond to recovered memory. Memories that emerge after the fact are depicted as fantasy, the result of a retroactive panic instilled in children by adults who fear the unusual or the unknown. These adults are easily swayed by fears that nonfamily members seek out contact with children to sexually abuse them, fears that are exploited to maintain the rationale for normative families: they protect children against dangerous outsiders. In its mediation of these two discourses, *Capturing the Friedmans* suggests that recovered memory discourse made it impossible for the public to "reasonably" assess and address the question of pedophilia. If hindsight is 20/20, *Capturing the Friedmans* uses this backward look to help us move forward, to correct the misperceptions of the past with more skeptical perceptions, new cultural habits for a new century.

This brief discussion of the Friedmans case seems to skirt the central problematic of this book: the rise of father-daughter incest as the zenith of child sexual abuse panic in the 1980s and 1990s. On the surface, *Capturing the Friedmans* has little to do with father-daughter incest. The film's treatment of pedophilia and recovered memory remains focused on the threat (real or perceived) of extrafamilial, same-sex contact. So how does the Friedmans case relate to this book's central focus on father-daughter incest? This book argues that father-daughter incest dominates the unexamined historical background of the Friedmans case, providing the secret connection between those discourses of pedophilia and recovered memory the film chooses to explore. The so-called memory wars of the 1990s were fought primarily over adult women's memories of childhood incest, with a special focus on allegations of father-daughter incest. Without a close and thorough examination of the emergence of father-daughter incest in this period, phenomena like the Friedmans case will remain a mystery, as the film *Capturing the Friedmans* suggests, whose only resolution is reification into the frozen images of mistakes past. My aim is to interrupt such reification by introducing a range of historical counterpoints that have appeared under the sign of "incest." This focus on incest, and more specifically on the turn from a narrowly construed father-daughter incest to the seemingly broader category of child sexual abuse, provides a framework to explore historical conjunctures otherwise lost to hindsight.

This leads us to two major questions that structure this book: Why did incest become the flashpoint for these debates about child sexual abuse? And why did this happen in the last decades of the twentieth century? The first question is fairly easy to answer. Many critics have argued that incest was used to mobilize cultural resources over the course of the 1980s, forging new connections among different domains of popular culture, state law, and jurisprudence. The particular power of incest to remake these connections in the late twentieth century stemmed from its history as a concept linking sexual regulation and normalization. To begin with, incest has long symbolized sexual taboo; the word "incest" has been used to denote any and all inappropriate or unsanctioned sexual liaisons. Culled from a prohibition on marriage between close kin (a definition with seemingly innumerable variations), "incest" has signified everything from same-sex sexual practices (likened to incest's presumed desire for something similar to oneself) to sexual practices within any collective unit (such as liaisons within a friendship circle, apartment complex, or academic department). Understood as taboo, incest represents both regulation and normalization. It prohibits some acts, but it does so in ways that establish norms for sexual conduct. And yet precisely because it establishes regulatory norms, the concept of incest can produce a pleasurable frisson. Transgressing the incest taboo is *jouissance* for psychoanalyst Jacques Lacan, but even in the mundane world of popular psychology the experience of rubbing up against cultural strictures is understood as titillatingly seductive. For some this transgression even has a left radicalism, refusing to obey a rule designed to reproduce stable governing hierarchies.

Since at least the early twentieth century, however, incest has also denoted sexual practices within a household kin group, especially between a parent and child or between age-differentiated offspring. This latter significance lends the term "incest" its unique traumatic force. Because it is a sexual practice between closely bound kin (here meaning economically and physically interdependent), its impact on the more vulnerable party is understood to be grave. The presumed desire for the act and potential mutuality of its pleasures is called into question, since incest exploits and tacitly reinforces structural hierarchies. In the 1970s second-wave feminists argued that patriarchy precipitated child sexual abuse. Girls (or sometimes children in general, who are accorded a subordinate and therefore "feminized" position in patriarchal households) were subject to exploitation by men, particularly those who lived in proximate reach or perceived women and girls to be their "property." This analysis led to a renewed interest in incest as childhood sexual abuse, as well as the extension of this analysis to explain child sexual abuse more broadly (as patriarchal exploitation of a structural condition). Incest was an abuse of power, not a challenge to it.

These legacies give incest its powerful symbolic resonance. Since it exemplifies both sexual taboo and sexual trauma, it is an enormous resource for both self-representation (sexual renegade/trauma survivor) and representation of "others" (demonic pedophile/seductive child). In the 1980s, popular forms of self-help culture, coupled with the confessionalism of television talk shows and new interest in post–traumatic stress disorder, placed child sexual abuse at the forefront of public consciousness. The 1980s saw a split in the public responses to the presentation of this issue: a voracious interest in consuming stories of incestuous trauma (minus the feminist analysis), and an equally voracious interest in persecuting perpetrators of child sexual abuse. Conveniently, these two interests found very different mechanisms for their pursuit. The public consumed stories of childhood incest, but sought justice for incidents of stranger molestation. The result was a truly odd and disjunctive organization of two discourses forged through an interest in child sexual abuse: pedophilia and incest (quickly taken up and discarded through the logic of recovered memory). While incest became an object of consumption, pedophilia was the *cause célèbre* of prosecution.

To return to the Friedmans case once again, we see these two discourses working together in the prosecution and resolution of the case. Arnold Friedman was initially investigated as a suspected pedophile on the basis of trafficking in child pornography. Extended investigation pursued his contact with children (boys) outside his own family, in keeping with the discourse of pedophilia. Once Jesse was also accused as party to the child sexual abuse, police investigators in the case questioned the "normalcy" of the Friedman family. As Detective Frances Galasso from the Sex Crimes Unit explains in one interview, she felt the family was "not exactly Fred MacMurray and *My Three Sons.*" Jesse Friedman then used this tacit presumption of incest in order to mitigate his own alleged culpability for sexual predation. Jesse claimed that his father had sexually abused him as a child in the hopes of expatiating the public's perception of his presumed "guilt." He later retracted this claim, explaining in one film interview that he had only made this statement because sex panic had made a fair trial impossible, and he had decided to exploit that panic to create some sympathy for his position. Meanwhile, Arnold confessed to a multiyear sexual relationship begun with his brother, Howard, when Arnold was thirteen and Howard eight; Howard repeatedly states that he has no memory of such events. *Capturing the Friedmans* shows the discourses of incest, repressed/recovered/false memory, and pedophilia being played off one another, blurring the distinctions between the object of consumption and prosecution, the subject of fantasy and of memory.

The second question—why the late twentieth century?—is much harder to answer. This is a historical question I have puzzled over for some time. The answer takes me back quite a ways, deep into historical arguments about the intimate imbrication of family and nation, and I offer the most extended response across the introduction and first chapter of this book. In this preface I address only those most recent arguments about historical causation that focus on the macrostructural changes in U.S. culture and political economy from the 1970s onward. There are two main lines of thought about why pedophilia and incest became dominant preoccupations in the 1980s and 1990s. The first is that child sexual abuse happens. This response often cites statistics on the frequency of childhood sexual abuse in the home or at the hands of trusted authority figures: the most often cited statistics state that one in three girls and one in seven boys experience some form of sexual abuse before the age of eighteen.[2] These are real forms of violence and/or exploitation, impacting large numbers of subjects, and as a society we are now ready to listen to and believe the victims. The 1970s and 1980s merely provided the right historical conditions to acknowledge this reality. According to psychologist Judith Herman in her 1992 book *Trauma and Recovery,* societies go through historical processes of acknowledging and then denying traumatic events. But the trauma exists regardless of these changing historical processes. A trauma like father-daughter incest, the subject of Herman's first book, was acknowledged by Freud, only to be quickly denied due to the threat of social scandal. Incest resurfaced in the later twentieth century when women's movements created the conditions to acknowledge violence against women, only to be denied again by false memory advocates. In this approach, the incidence of child sexual abuse is relatively persistent across time, only shaped by the social and political economic conditions of childhood and householding family life in a given moment.

This argument has some roots in second-wave feminism but is not necessarily continuous with those analyses. More recent advocates of this approach include the famous self-help authors Ellen Bass and Laura Davis, whose 1988 book *The Courage to Heal* has been both lauded for empowering women to address their sexual abuse histories and lambasted for falsely persuading women to imagine themselves victims of abuse. Bass and Davis explain that their decision to write the book came out of women's consciousness-raising and writing groups, where they first realized child sexual abuse was a bigger problem than often acknowledged. For Bass and Davis, as well as for other advocates, historical changes such as second-wave feminist movements, the "discovery" of post–traumatic stress disorder, the increasing entry of women in the helping professions, and greater popular access to mainstream media altered the conditions of reception for women's speech about sexual violence. In addition, new scientific knowledge about trauma and its impact on memory enabled more and more women to interpret a range of symptoms as the aftereffects of child sexual abuse. These changes gave women increased opportunities to talk about their early experiences of sexual abuse, which in turn increased opportunities for women to recall previously disavowed or forgotten experiences of childhood molestation. This approach views the historical changes of this period as largely positive, at least in terms of women's self-discovery and self-representation. The focus tends to be on the experiential and the subjective, with evidence drawn from the quotidian representations of everyday life or what sociologist Vikki Bell, following Michel Foucault, calls "subjugated knowledges" (*Interrogating Incest*, 89).

The second line of thought about why incest and pedophilia became a dominant preoccupation in the 1980s and 1990s differs from the first in almost every respect. Here the claim is that child sexual abuse is socially constructed. While this approach is careful to affirm the reality of child sexual abuse, its proponents tend to be far more skeptical that it is a widespread social crisis. Instead, they see changing historical conditions from the late 1960s onward as precipitating moral panics that distract the public from larger crises of political economy. The radical movements of the 1960s and 1970s had begun transformations to the racialized and class-restrictive norms of sexual conduct and formal kinship. While second-wave feminism challenged unequal pay and restricted access to the workplace, civil rights and labor radicals challenged the exploitative conditions of racist organizations of surplus labor. Diverse feminists struggled for women's self-determination over their bodies, from the right to choose abortion to the right to economic and social support to bear and raise children, from protection against sexual harassment to liberation from systemic sexual coercion and racist population control. In the Reagan years, these struggles over family and sexuality as zones of self-determination were retrenched into new norms of familial and sexual conduct. The slogan "family values" called for a return to heteronormative sexual and marital relations: private relations that would provide moral guidance once assigned to the state. This retrenchment was achieved largely through the use of moral panics, predominantly focused on the threat of a black underclass (the "welfare queen"), illegal immigrants (coming to "steal our jobs"), and child sex predators ("homosexual pedophiles"). Across these sites, discourses of child sexual abuse enabled a sex panic that refocused state protection on white middle-class families and state policing on racially criminalized others.

This particular panic focused on changing social practices of reproduction, child-rearing, and sexuality. As new technologies of reproduction transformed the nature of families, more middle-class women simultaneously reentered the workforce during childbearing and child-rearing years. Transformations attendant to second-wave feminism made public day care a necessity, although not a state-funded entitlement during the Reagan retreats from 1970s radicalisms. The fostering out of middle-class children to privately purchased "public" care made day care sexual abuse a locus of child sexual abuse panic.[3] Meanwhile, the state used its symbolic protection of (mostly white, middle-class) children from sexual abuse to mask its simultaneous downsizing of child welfare provisions and dismantling of service sectors for the poor. According to cultural studies scholar James Kincaid, "the child-molesting Gothic story" distracted Americans from more "structural social problems" such as poverty, lack of educational opportunity, and failure to provide basic services for children (*Erotic Innocence*, 12). The panic about children's vulnerability to sex created its own technologies of surveillance and supervision (remember Arnold Friedman's three-year mail sting) without substantively impacting the social conditions in which the majority of children lived. The boom of interest in childhood sexual abuse—galvanized by the symbolic power of incest—merely provided a screen for the more structural social problems of the period.

Everybody's Family Romance argues that neither answer is entirely satisfactory. Yes, sexual exploitation by intimate caregivers occurs and is often extremely damaging (although debates rage about how to measure frequency and harm). And yes, hyperbolic and panicky responses to sexuality (both childhood and adult) are often mobilized to stigmatize populations and reorganize the state's police powers. But each approach misses some of the key insights of the other: namely, how the emergence of women's stories about father-daughter incest in particular were coopted by—and yet retained resistant strains against—the dominant political and popular culture described here. This will be the main argument of *Everybody's Family Romance*: that new cultural forms articulated through father-daughter incest emerged across the 1970s, 1980s, and 1990s, and that these new forms were sometimes coopted by and sometimes resisted what I will be calling cultural logics of neoliberalism. This book takes up neoliberalism as a historical concept, attempting to read what political theorist Wendy Brown calls an emergent political rationality in relation to changing cultural logics of the family ("Neo-Liberalism"). Across the chapters that follow, I will argue that incest provided a key resource for neoliberal transformations in the political economy and cultural articulation of "America." But I will also argue that the articulation of incest as child sexual abuse through neoliberalism was not entirely successful. Cultural logics of the family provided occasions for both absorption and resistance to emerging forms of national neoliberalism. Resistant and radical counterarticulations continued to intervene in the work of this transformation, and much of the analysis that follows is dedicated to culling such resistance from the neoliberal archive.

Neoliberalism is most frequently used to describe the economic policies of free-market liberalization in ascendancy since the 1970s, spawned by transformations in international lending and interstate sovereignty. As theorized by Latin Americanists and social justice activists across continents, neoliberalism described the policies implemented through U.S. financial institutions, the World Bank, and the International Monetary Fund (IMF) during the transition from the cold war's three-worlds system to the allegedly one-world system of globalization (in reality a bifurcation of global North and South).[4] In 1990, the U.S. economist John Williamson coined the term "Washington Consensus" to describe these institutions' collective response to the financial crises of the 1980s in Latin America.[5] Williamson outlined this response in ten principles allegedly guiding international monetary relations aimed at "macroeconomic discipline, trade openness, and market-friendly microeconomic policies" (252). Within countries of the global North, and particularly within the United States, these transformations were described positively as liberalization and globalization. Discourses associated with neoliberalism—liberalization, globalization, market freedom, individual rights—rationalized rapid changes to political economic practice as a form of social liberation.

This book's subtitle, "Reading Incest in Neoliberal America," is meant to capture the odd conjuncture of "reading," or literary practices of interpretation, and "America," or political practices of U.S. nationalism, in the historical context of neoliberalism.[6] Within the United States, the allegedly economic policies of neoliberalism shaped new political discourses of nationalism and cultural logics of identification. During the 1990s, neoliberal policies sought to downsize the distributive functions of the U.S. welfare state while maintaining a strong security apparatus and close connections between corporate capitalism and political governance (often called the military- or prison-industrial complex). This required new cultural logics that would hail "citizens" on the grounds of national identification while retooling nationalism for neoliberal use. Neoliberal cultural logics often turned to the family to achieve this goal, hailing a vehemently "American" public by celebrating the end of unwanted state intrusion into citizens' "private" lives while valorizing family membership as the sine qua non of national belonging.

I read the two discourses of child sexual abuse outlined here—incest (with its correlate, repressed/recovered/false memory) and pedophilia—as part of neoliberalism's emergent political rationality and cultural logic. Together these two discourses provided a resource for governmental transformations of relations between family and state, welfare and risk, sex and crime as well as for the cultural representation of these relations as progressive, libratory, and beneficial. This book argues that 1990s incest discourses mark one very particular conjunction between the tactics of governance and the arts of nationalism. In the transformation from mid-century welfare governmentalities to a neoliberal "state" predicated on security, incest was transformed into child sexual abuse through specific surveillance rationales and funding chains figured as child protection. But at the same time, feminist struggles to refigure incest as sexual exploitation remained a strong counterpoint to governmentalized child protection. These cultural reconfigurations opened up terrain for social struggle over incest's proper referents. Across the diverse pedophilia and recovered memory discourses of the 1990s, incest marked a peculiar meeting point between nationalism and neoliberalism for a new era's family romances. "Reading incest" provides one way to trace these struggles over the meaning of culture and to discern the potential radicalism of representations otherwise lost to history.

My overarching argument is that reading incest is far more important to the historical understanding of the 1980s and 1990s than previous approaches have fully captured. *Everybody's Family Romance* argues that reading incest can provide an opportunity for, rather than merely an obstacle to, insight into the complex transformations of this period. In the emergent family romances of U.S. neoliberalism, I argue that images of incest can be read as forging connections between legacies of America's older family-nation couplets and emergent forms of ambiguously national family life. These so-called family romances interrogate the relation between the pasts of U.S. chattel slavery and the distributive impasses of the welfare state, between 1950s labor migrations and those of the 1980s and 1990s, and between decades-distant childhoods and emergent memories of an adult present. In so doing, they situate neoliberal America "historically," or as a crossroads between prior forms of national family life and emergent forms associated with neoliberalism. My goal in making this argument is to center women's self-representational agency in the era's broader left politic in order to reconsider the politics (rather than merely the perils) of looking back. This book therefore takes a backward glance, looking at how incest was plucked from its longer genealogy in literary culture and political economy to serve as a trope recoding family-nation relations across the mid- and late twentieth century. This backward glance then returns us to women's incest narratives of the 1990s, when a series of novels about the 1950s, 1960s, 1970s, and 1980s developed a politics of retrospection that interrogated the unfinished imbrication of the past in the present.

I hope that this book builds on and enhances existing approaches to reading incest. But some responses to its arguments have at times concerned me. Some readers have expressed concern that the analyses do not attend adequately to real survivor experience, or to the impact of sexual abuse allegations on actual people (including the Friedmans). This comment seems to target the book's prose more than its argument: the writing style is theoretical, some might say "jargony," and the overall stakes can seem abstract. I might reframe this comment as a third, unspoken question that haunts this book: Why me? What makes me write this book? Am I merely exploiting a controversial phenomenon for professional gain? Or do I have personal stakes? As Andrew Jarecki asks in his article "Secrets and Lies," voicing his dawning sense that the celebrity birthday clown David Friedman had a secret history, "What's this clown's story?" There is simply no way to answer this question without seeming to reveal the secret truth behind the professional clown's paint. Any answer is likely to locate the book within the terms of already existing debates. And since *Everybody's Family Romance* attempts to shift the terms of those debates, it avoids making such empirical or personal claims. This book is nobody's story.[7] And yet it examines how such queries and the stories intended to answer them have been broadly construed as everybody's family romance. This book therefore traces the dialectic between nobody's and everybody's story as it has been used to restructure U.S. relations between family and state. As such, the book is a domestic allegory, but one that interrogates the domestic for its odd national and familial hauntings and insists upon telling an unfinished story of resistance to the encroachments of neoliberalism.

Despite the theoretical language of the book, however, I want to state clearly that *Everybody's Family Romance* is committed to registering the impact of sexual violence on those who experience childhood incest. Its use of theoretical sources to investigate the dynamics of reading incest are genuinely intended to help us understand the impact of sexual violence more fully. To that end, the readings that follow are deliberately speculative, exploratory, and imaginatively robust. I am not seeking to document a historical period or establish empirically verifiable truths, nor am I claiming to develop a new method of reading or new theory of the novel as such. Far more compendious studies than mine have performed much of this important work while examining the emerging incest canon, including the recent monographs *Telling Incest* (Doane and Hodges), *Worlds of Hurt* (Tal), *Shattered Subjects* (Henke), *Trauma and Survival in Contemporary Fiction* (Vickroy), *Literary Trauma* (Horvitz), *The Politics of Survivorship* (Champagne), and *Trauma Cinema* (Walker). Thanks to the publication of these excellent studies, my project is able to focus more specifically on the detailed examination of a few, neither exemplary nor representative novels, read in relation to a broad swath of interdisciplinary arguments about incest and its taboo. I hope that this book offers some illumination of these broader dynamics, and that future scholars expand upon and challenge the terrain I chart here. Feminist work on incest is in my opinion an act of critical filiation: I therefore seek to reflect upon and energize the debates that precede and will invariably surpass me, even as I hope to encourage seemingly disinterested critics to reckon seriously with this all too often marginalized family affair.

Introduction

Everybody's Family Romance

> While the ancient Greeks used incest narratives to talk about the merciless
> vagaries of fate, the incest story as we tell it (a parent, usually the father,
> molesting the protagonist, usually a girl) flexibly lends itself to two of
> America's favorite plots: the gothic and the rags-to-riches Horatio Alger
> inspirational. . . . As a plot device, therefore, incest is both venerable and
> versatile, and until the recent glut of incest fiction it still had the capacity
> to shock.
>
> —LAURA MILLER, "But Enough about Us: Incest and the
> Memoirization of American Fiction"

Incest has a long and distinguished career as a literary figure marking relations between the family and the polis. Incest has figured prominently in
arts and letters since at least *Oedipus the King,* and scholars of emergent
English language literature have traced its use from medieval allegory to
Shakespeare's comedies, from sibling incest in late eighteenth-century
romanticism to paternal incest in women's writing from the nineteenth
century onward.[1] In the United States, incest played a particularly important role in early efforts to consolidate an Anglo–U.S. national literature.
Incest was used to figure a nation whose family matters were in crisis,
whose racial and territorial boundaries were perceived to be terrorized by
dangers from within and without. Twinned with "miscegenation," incest
figured the dangerous intersection between family and nation across literary genres and periods, signaling the spectre of scarcely intelligible
threats to social order. This incest figure has been picked up and recoded
across quite diverse narratives of national family romance, from Charles
Brockden Brown's 1798 *Wieland* to Herman Melville's 1852 *Pierre,* from
Pauline Hopkins's 1903 *Of One Blood* to William Faulkner's 1929 *The
Sound and the Fury,* and from Ralph Ellison's 1952 *Invisible Man* to
Vladimir Nabokov's 1955 *Lolita.* But according to Katie Roiphe in her
1995 *Harper's* article "Making the Incest Scene," at the end of the twen-
tieth century the role of incest in American literature suddenly changed.

Whereas once the specter of incest was used to figure a crisis in national family life, it was now the reality of incest that captured the national imagination. As Roiphe quotes from Sapphire's then forthcoming incest novel *Push*, "We is a nation of raped children." "Whatever the truth of that," Roiphe quips in response, "we are certainly a nation that wants to read about them" (68).[2]

Everybody's Family Romance asks how "reading about incest" reveals changing cultural and political forms of U.S. nationalism. In the 1980s and 1990s, a seeming boom in autobiographical novels and memoirs about incest emerged at the center of new literary markets, making incest one of the hottest topics to connect the daytime talk show circuit, the popular self-help industry, and the elite literary publishing circuit. Incest stories appeared in every medium from Pulitzer Prize–winning fiction and drama such as *The Shipping News* (Proulx), *A Thousand Acres* (Smiley), *How I Learned to Drive* (Vogel), and semiautobiographical novels such as *Bastard out of Carolina* (Allison) and *Thereafter Johnnie* (Herron), to popular memoir such as *The Kiss* (Harrison) and the celebrity narratives of Oprah Winfrey, Roseanne Barr, and Marilyn Van Derbur.[3] This surge in incest representation generated enormous scholarly and popular interest from cultural and literary critics, sociologists and psychologists, and political pundits left and right. The seemingly unexpected explosion of incest onto the literary scene raised a number of pressing questions about national culture at the end of the twentieth century. How precisely should we read incest in these texts? Was it merely one more titillating disclosure in the school for scandal allegedly transforming national culture? Or was it a real social problem that revealed the nation's households riddled with patriarchal sin? Did incest truly lie at the heart of everybody's family romance, and if so how should critics decipher its "secret" meaning?

Literary and cultural critics have differed widely in their interpretation of the new incest narratives. For some, these narratives expressed the empirical reality of women's lives. Incest literature documented widespread sexual violence against children too long left unrecorded. In this account, incest narratives revealed what feminist sociologists and psychologists called *The Best Kept Secret* (Rush) or *The Secret Trauma* (Russell). Incest had been represented as a spectral threat or a symbolic taboo only because women's narratives about incest had been repeatedly silenced. So many incest narratives emerged in the 1990s because second-wave feminist and civil rights movements had transformed cultural expectations about literary subject matter and opened new venues for the publication and reception of "alternative" literature. The rise of small feminist and lesbian presses made publication accessible for women who had previously been excluded from mainstream presses, and the success of a few best sellers made even mainstream publishing possible for a select group of women. Once the publishing industry grasped the possibilities of this new market, more and more women were empowered to speak out and contradict the masculinist silencing of incest in print. In addition, across the 1980s and 1990s popular media developed an intense interest in women's experiences of trauma. The celebrity icon Oprah Winfrey, self-identified as a child sexual abuse survivor, developed a major daytime talk show circuit for survivors and their advocates, as well as a book club that made incest literature into popular culture. The discussions that arose out of these initiatives read 1990s incest narratives as part of a broader social change in which hidden realities of violence were now being documented, and women's voices, previously unheeded, were now being heard.

For others, these incest narratives were indeed part of a broader social change, but not one intended to reveal the real violence of women's lives. While women's voices might be heard, what they documented was the process of a culture turning in on itself, more willing to hear stories of sexual scandal than social inequality. This account links incest literature to what it sees as the problem of self-help culture more generally, in which discovering one's "inner child" was part of a general climate of wounded self-knowledge (as Marilyn Ivy points out in "Have You Seen Me?"). Writing for Salon.com, Laura Miller argues that 1990s incest narratives exemplified a broader literary transformation she calls the "memoirization of American fiction." And in contemporary reviews like "Almost Famous: The Rise of the 'Nobody' Memoir" (Adams) and "Blab, Memory" (Yardley), critics lament the surfeit of self-referential literature in American letters. Incest narratives merely typified the sexually shocking, tabloid-style revelations of the new culture industry. Critics suggested that the popularity of incest literature in particular reflected a national turn "inward," a domesticating narcissism designed to shield readers from the broader social and political realities of the period. These discussions suggest that Americans produced and consumed a large number of incest narratives in order to translate the discomforts of the present into more familiar, familial form—incest narratives created a world in which readers could be first shocked by the revelation of incest, then soothed by its resolution through traumatic testimony.

In both accounts, incest narratives were implicitly understood as a continuation of the national family romance tradition. These narratives seemed similar to previous U.S. family romances that used incest to figure a crisis in the nation. According to both accounts, the 1990s family romance had captured the lives or imaginations of a good portion of the citizenry, making them national in scope. But the 1990s family romance also seemed different from its predecessors, telling a new story about the nation as a family riddled with sexual secrets and literal rather than symbolic unrest. Critics could agree that these 1990s narratives signaled a transformation in the referents of the nation's family romance. But what this transformation signified, whether these narratives redressed the sexual violence of U.S. girlhood or merely exploited it as hegemonic spectacle, remained under debate. *Everybody's Family Romance* enters this debate by revising some of its fundamental assumptions, reading incest against the grain of the national family romance tradition. The book reads incest as a trope bridging changing formations of U.S. nationalism, one that exploits the modern coupling of family and nation to recode violence and hegemony in formations of emergent social life. Thus I argue that incest both reveals hidden forms of gendered violence and lends itself to new hegemonic forms of domestic consumption. But this book also reads incest as a trope able to interrupt this revelatory hegemony, stealing away from the enclosures of either residual forms of nationalism or emergent forms of social organization.

This argument is developed across the five main chapters of this book, which chart the rise and fall of incest across the late twentieth-century United States. Historically, incest played an important role in narratives about the family-nation couplet: family romances. Emerging in the so-called era of revolution in Western Europe and across its "new worlds," bourgeois nationalisms used the family as an ideological resource for their struggles against monarchism and landed aristocracy. According to theorists of nationalism such as Benedict Anderson and Etienne Balibar, the family became a key element in the new fabric of national identity. The nation at once referenced deep historical origins and emergent horizontal ideas of membership. The family could encompass these two temporal demands, serving as genealogical matrix for local descent as well as an imaginary matrix for new translocal identifications (often based on shared language and what Balibar calls "fictive ethnicity" ["The Nation Form," 96]).[4] Coming out of romanticism and the rise of the novel over the late eighteenth and early nineteenth centuries, incest synthesized the contradictions of emergent sovereign individualism (with its willful break from the tyrannies of patriarchal rule) and the arational tendencies of spontaneous and untamed imagination.[5] As a romantic symbol, incest promised to reveal, if not revel in, the archaic forces of the ineffable and the unconscious. But it also presaged the social recodification of the "ineffable" in new modes of social constraint: the nuclear family.

Incest emerged as a dominant trope in the late twentieth-century United States as part of the breakdown of residual forms of the family-nation couplet. In the aftermath of the cold war, the 1990s have been described breaking with the historical and political systems of the past. With the fall of the Berlin Wall, "history," as Francis Fukuyama famously announced in 1989, was over.[6] This period was said to mark the end of the three major ideologies of modernity—communism, liberalism, and fascism—and the emergence of a single world ideology. Globalization emerged as the discourse of this new horizontal present, a break with the world history of modernity and the entry into a hegemonic world system (defined by political liberalism and economic liberalization). For its proponents, a new era had begun, in which the triumph of liberalism signaled the end of classical liberalism and the dominance of "neoliberalism," understood as a political rationality aimed at replacing closed markets, national protectionism, and state sovereignty with social privatization, trade deregulation, and state security apparatuses.[7] Neoliberalism named the political rationality of an allegedly new world order, one whose "globalization" of cultures and markets would be matched with transformations in the political rationalities of classical sovereignty, state power, and social authority. As many critics have noted, the discourse of globalization neutralized the impact of neoliberalism: inequitable international divisions of labor, growing exploitation of racialized and feminized labor exacerbated by these liberalized "flows," and rapid refunctioning of sexuality and gender for hierarchical secularisms as well as fundamentalisms.[8]

Within the United States, neoliberalism was linked to increased privatization, the dismantling of welfare state distributions, and the elimination of trade barriers across national borders. It was also linked to a series of federal provisions dismantling existing family law and refiguring "privacy" for new relations of race, class, and gender. This rapid transformation in political economy and its traditional rationales—and the equally rapid emergence of a new discourse to conserve meaning in the wake of change—seemed for some to call for radically new methods of scholarly inquiry and radical resistance. While there was little agreement about the nature of these changes among scholars in the social sciences or humanities, many agreed that the concepts of political sovereignty, national territoriality, state economies, and the rule of law were no longer adequate to address existing power relations.[9] The concepts used to describe mass and popular struggle within these systems also seemed sadly outdated, as the discourses and ideologies mobilized to legitimate neoliberalism absorbed many elements of traditional left critique. As Michael Hardt and Antonio Negri declare in *Empire,* their epic memorial to this transformation, the classical theories of modernity "cannot account for the real novelty of the historical processes we are witnessing today" (8). While Hardt and Negri's "Empire" has not proven the final word on the topic, numerous critics engaged with processes of globalization, neoliberalism, or various forms of imperialism seem to agree that radical resistance will require new analytic tools. That is, new epistemologies and aesthetics are needed to interrupt the uncertain hegemony promised by neoliberalism.

In the 1990s, some critics formulated an epistemology and aesthetics of "trauma" to capture the nation's legacies of racial, sexual, and gendered violence. "Trauma" was used to describe the ongoing effects of modernity's earlier epistemes, encompassing everything from the aftermath of enslavement, racial terror, and capitalist alienation to patriarchal violence, sexual subordination, and gendered normalization. According to Cathy Caruth, a premier theorist of trauma studies, "trauma" describes an experience of belatedness, a crisis in historical time that renders the subject a living symptom of as-yet-unarticulated historical truth. "Trauma" promised to register the violence of previous eras by articulating new forms of historical testimony, testimony that would bear witness to this past and redress its ongoing effects in a belated present. According to Caruth, "Traumatic experience . . . is an experience that is not fully assimilated as it occurs," such that "trauma" signifies a "crisis that is marked, not by a simple knowledge, but by the ways it simultaneously defies and demands our witness" (*Unclaimed Experience,* 5). This crisis in the experiential—by which Caruth also means the historical—can only be rendered legible through figurative language rather than epistemological claims. Thus testimony to trauma "must, indeed, also be spoken in a language that is always somehow literary: a language that defies, even as it claims, our understanding" (5). Following Caruth's books *Unclaimed Experience* and *Trauma: Explorations in Memory,* as well as Shoshana Felman and Dori Laub's groundbreaking volume *Testimony: Crises in*

Witnessing, a burgeoning field of trauma studies attempted to describe the aftermath of modernity's violences by critically recognizing literature and other cultural forms as world-historical testimony.[10] But even as such treatments of trauma promised to register and redress the violence of previous eras, some elements of trauma discourse were quickly incorporated into emerging cultural logics of neoliberalism.[11] As the mid-century U.S. welfare and warfare state were eroded, the "social" theorized and quantified by sociology and welfare policy research no longer seemed to be the most useful tactic of governmentality. The use of "culture" as a potential tactic of population management and social control became dominant; so too did its refashioning of aesthetics for both libratory and conservative ends. Culture became the terrain of social struggle, as witnessed in the culture wars and various strains of popular and radical multiculturalism.[12] In its conservationist mode, culture became a tactic for incorporating and neutralizing historical struggle as "difference." Neoliberalism seemed poised to absorb historical struggle by recognizing difference and even celebrating it, using the logic of cultural difference to incorporate the past into the present. Some understandings of trauma lent themselves to this emergent cultural logic, marking a break between past and present that enabled late twentieth-century societies to witness the aftermath of modernity's violent past. These new cultural logics exploited the so-called end of history to differentiate present social conditions (the growing gulf between rich and poor, the dramatic destruction of postcolonial states, the health and resource disparities of global North and South) from what could now be viewed as historical tragedies (modern colonialism, territorial expansionism, openly declared world wars). Even as neoliberalism and trauma announced a break with the past, neoliberal narratives of trauma and recovery seemed poised to reproduce the past in the present tense.

Everybody's Family Romance contends that neoliberal trauma used the language of family to achieve key elements of this cultural incorporation. Narratives of such trauma exploited the legacies of national family romance to reproduce familiar social relations within new cultural logics. These logics refunctioned family to do the work of neoliberalism in three ways. First, they made the family into the synecdoche for all broader social relations. Society was ultimately determined by family life, or "family values," even as it represented itself as an extended family. Second, these logics used culture to describe the family's social existence. Family values were cultural, not economic or political per se, determined by habits and beliefs rather than historical conditions. And third, these logics sought to resolve social struggle through the cultural representation of family trauma in journalistic media, novels, television, and film. Families riven by problems became the mainstay of both elite and popular culture, often represented in narratives of historical violence and its contemporary overcoming. In the most extreme form of these cultural logics, economic injustice, racial enslavement, and ethnic genocide became family traumas whose dissociating legacies might be healed by finding one's cultural voice and telling a public story.

The general effects of these logics can be traced across various cultural media of the period. The cultural studies critic Lauren Berlant has made one of the most concerted efforts to catalogue the effects of such logics across visual culture, new media, and novels. Berlant summarizes these effects as having created a new form of "infantile citizenship" (*The Queen of America*, 21) based on a sentimental politics of childhood and family. During the 1980s and 1990s, a shared sense of national belonging was articulated through what Berlant calls the "intimate public sphere" (5), "the expansion of a mass-mediated space of opinion formation that positions citizens as isolated spectators to the publicity that claims to represent them" (3). Citizens would come to accept this position through "the marketing of nostalgic images of a normal, familial America that would define the utopian context for citizen aspiration" (3). While visual culture and the new media arguably dominated this transformation, the novel could also be read as a "mass-mediated space of opinion formation" marketing images of a "familial America." In the 1990s, novels were often marketed on the basis of their ability to provide "nostalgic images" of families past. New media and technologies of instantaneous representation transformed the aesthetics of contemporaneity. The novel, arguably a residual genre, might therefore be seen as a uniquely retroactive medium. Like trauma itself, novelistic narratives were by definition belated. Capitalizing on the paradoxical nostalgia of print culture, the novel could be revived through a new "ideology of form" that sutured older modes of family romance to refashioned modes of social realism.[13] These neoliberal family romances articulated nostalgia as trauma, marketing a utopian promise for a wounded nation to transcend its violent past.

Incest provided one way to synthesize neoliberal logics into a new family romance, refunctioning residual elements of the family-nation couplet to better serve the contemporary United States. In this moment of alleged epistemological and historical novelty, it seemed that the incest taboo was also sadly out of date. From the 1970s to the 1990s, incest was transformed from taboo to trauma, recoded through new narratives by and about women. Concurrent with social movements against racism, sexism, and the exploitative class politics of U.S. society, what was later called the "survivors movement" emerged in the 1970s through the mobilization of seemingly disparate individuals into an unlikely interest group. There is little agreement about the origins of this collective identity, ranging from radical consciousness-raising groups (political culture), self-help support networks (therapy culture), women's writing groups (print culture), and inpatient treatment and criminal processes (psychiatric and medical culture). But regardless of its origins, by the 1990s survivor politics had definitively changed. Over the course of the 1980s and 1990s, incest survivors became a medicalized population, the exemplars of a culture of childhood trauma. Incest survivors were targeted by various state and extragovernmental agencies as the traumatized population par excellence, used to legitimate major governmental transformation yielding new funding protocols linking the Centers for Disease Control (CDC) to Child Protective Services (CPS), new federal resource sharing across antiterrorism security and child abduction policing, the quantification of racialized youth at risk and growing prison populations in new scales of child sexual abuse etiology, and the formation of white middle-class women as the statistical basis for a proclaimed epidemic of psychological unrest.

In the era of neoliberal privatization and the downsizing of the welfare state, the incest trope performed a particular turn, transforming the social relations of political economy while maintaining a symbolic focus on the national family.[14] Incest came to represent the politics of the nation as a culture of the familial subject, or, even more specifically, of the vulnerable child. No longer a symbolic taboo in the nation's family romance, incest had officially become the traumatic truth of a population (in Foucault's sense of the term; *The History of Sexuality*, 137). A new cultural idiom was articulated through incest, one that refashioned the dysfunctional family as the center of collective identification. New incest narratives transformed the role of the novel in citizenship training without fundamentally changing the novel's presumed nationalism. In place of training in the abstractions of national citizenship, incest narratives seemed to promise their readers a world of privatized citizenship in which consuming sexual trauma forged shared cultural identifications. Incest forged the lineaments of a new mode of national self-representation:

intertextual literary and popular media collapsed all familial referents into a therapeutic zeitgeist, whose belated revelation of sexual scandal and retroactive infantile citizenship could be embraced even by those disenfranchised from systems of political and economic entitlement. By the 1990s, incest seemed to be at the heart of "everybody's family romance," a narrative of family violence and survivor transcendence that turned the belated effects of patriarchal domination into the promissory future of neoliberal hegemony. Everybody's family romance enclosed elements of earlier novelistic radicalism—from the collective autobiographies of Gertrude Stein to James Baldwin's critique of protest fiction—into a sentimental melodrama in which "everybody's" neoliberal subjectivity could be incorporated.

But this story is much too simple. While some publishing and popular culture industries did package and market incest for easy consumption, reading incest narratives was never quite the national pastime Katie Roiphe described. *Everybody's Family Romance* argues that many 1990s incest narratives retain a radical edge, working against both emerging logics of neoliberal trauma and nostalgic remembrances of liberalisms past. Following 1970s and 1980s incest fiction by Maya Angelou, Toni Morrison, Gayl Jones, and Alice Walker, 1990s fiction by Dorothy Allison, Katherine Harrison, Carolivia Herron, Annie Proulx, Sapphire, and Jane Smiley contested this novelization of social relations as mere personal and familial trauma. These texts each take a retrospective look at the major transformations of the late twentieth century. The flexibilization of labor, the dismantling of heteronormative kinship, massive geographic displacement, the rise of the black middle class, the turn from welfare to workfare, and private land consolidation are all treated by the six writers I name here. These 1990s incest narratives refuse their documentary function for the present, insisting instead upon the genealogies of welfare state liberalism that inflect the supposed liberalizations of the century's end. Each novel interrogates the fusion of race, class, and gender commonly covered over by neoliberal idioms of incest, offering potentially radical contributions to left politics of the period. The problem is how to read them.

This book works to resuscitate the aesthetics of "shock" by reading for the latent radicalism of 1990s incest narratives. In the epigraph to this introduction, Laura Miller suggests that incest no longer has "the capacity to shock." In its new blend of American gothic and Horatio Alger myth, everybody's family romance told predictable and now multicultural stories of incest inflicted (gothic) and survived (pulling oneself up by the bootstraps). Here I would like to use Walter Benjamin's definition of shock as counterpoint to the unshocking "glut" described by Miller. In "A Berlin Chronicle" Benjamin argues that memory articulates a shock to dominant systems of representation. Memory unfolds "not in the manner of general representations, but of images that . . . constantly detach themselves from things and determine our perception of them" (29). This book gleans "images" of incest, what I call the tropological work of incest, from the generalized representations in which they have been repeatedly situated. My argument is that incest has *not* lost its capacity to shock, but rather critics have insisted upon their indifference to its banality, its generalization as representation. My approach insists upon this shock, encountering the images of incest as they "detach themselves from things and determine our perception of them." The goal here is to develop a shared methodology through which more readers will be capable of experiencing this shock. As a result, the incest trope will be released from its seeming banality and allowed to take a different turn at the end of the century.

This methodology reads neoliberal trauma against the grain, raising the following questions about incest's generalized representation: Why is the nation posited as the territorial or imaginative limit for these allegedly new relations of reading? How might incest narratives be read to challenge the nation form as their implicit referent? And how might reading incest against the American grain work to resist the hegemony of neoliberalism? The answer to these questions draws on materials from previous studies of the nation-state and modern family life, reading them alongside recent feminist publications about incest and sexual violence as well as literary studies of genre and form. Throughout, I attend closely to particular images of incest as they perform what Benjamin calls "the mysterious work of remembrance—which is really the capacity for endless interpolations into what has been—but also, at the same time, the precaution of the subject represented by the 'I,' which is entitled not to be sold cheap" ("A Berlin Chronicle," 16). This book traces incest across both its cultural generalizations and its autobiographical specificities, attempting to value the subject represented by the "I" as much as the social conditions that "I" seems to occlude. As such, the chapters that follow strain to reveal incest as both social and subjective, as the interpenetration of past and present that opens up "the capacity for endless interpolations into what has been."

National Family Romance

Everybody's Family Romance takes reading incest as its central task, but in order to read for incest's shocking memories we must first clear some familiar ground. Incest is multiply determined by methods of reading and analysis, already "read" by Freudian accounts of taboo and literary critical accounts of family romance. These existing approaches make it difficult to read incest against the grain, since they point incest's referents in particular directions (family and nation) and away from others (race and capitalism). This introduction briefly outlines the limits of these approaches to reading incest, spelling out how these familiar determinations make it difficult to see incest's potential determination otherwise.[15] In this approach, fantasy becomes a mode of articulation, one that uses incest to forge connections between domains (family and nation) while maintaining those domains' seeming autonomy from broader social relations (race and capitalism). The purpose of this approach is twofold: first, it composes an interdisciplinary incest archive from writings in anthropology, psychoanalysis, law, sociology, psychology, and political science as well as literature; second, it offers a new account of the daughter's representational agency as a vehicle for social struggle. Michel Foucault argues that "a historical knowledge of struggles" can emerge from genealogical methods combining scholarly research on the disciplines with what have previously been "disqualified knowledges" (*Society Must Be Defended*, 8). He calls this genealogy "a combination of erudite knowledge and what people know," which "allows us to constitute a historical knowledge of struggles and to make use of that knowledge in contemporary tactics" (8). Reading fantasy as articulation situates interdisciplinary scholarship in relation to the "disqualified knowledges" of so-called incest survivors (a task begun by early feminist researchers and sharpened by Vikki Bell's 1993 book on this topic). In particular, I undertake this genealogy in order to reveal "the daughter's self-representation" as the tactical form of a particular historical struggle.

This approach requires me to work within, and at times against, the tradition of family romance criticism developed across literary and historical studies of the nation form. The term "family romance" is frequently attributed to Sigmund Freud, the coiner of so many popular phrases marking the transition from Victorian ideologies of kinship to modernist sciences of the family. Immediately following the formation of the Vienna Psychoanalytic Society, in 1909 Freud published a brief essay entitled "Der Familienroman der Neurotiker."[16] Translated into English as "Family

Romances," this essay tells the story of bourgeois childhood—Freud's typical subject matter—by tracing one particular set of childhood fantasies, that of replacing one pair of parents with another. In its broadest claims, the essay presents the modern European child emerging into a new order of scientific rationality and normative socioeconomic and aesthetic relations. As the essay begins, "The liberation of an individual, as he grows up, from the authority of his parents is one of the most necessary though one of the most painful results brought about by the course of his development" (298). This necessary and painful liberation occurs through the complex process of fantasy, the form of quasi-agency though which the "individual" emerges into bourgeois realism. Fantasizing that its own bourgeois parents have replaced parents of aristocratic lineage, the "normal" child comes to accept the reality of its own situation by learning the facts of sexual science: namely, the facts of (hetero)sexual reproduction. Leaving behind its aristocratic longings and bourgeois *ressentiment*, the child is normalized through sexual differentiation from both its flawed ancestors and its neurotic contemporaries.

But Freud's coinage merely condensed three major threads of the nineteenth century: changes in the forms of family, novel, and nation. Several literary critics have argued that Freud's notion of family romance is lifted straight from the bourgeois novels of the nineteenth century, simplifying these narrative relations into a triangular psychic myth.[17] These family romances tracked a transition from earlier forms of aristocratic alliance and inheritance to the modern nuclear family's dominance in Western Europe. Changing labor and land use practices during industrialization and colonial expansion consolidated the European wage-earning unit and divided reproductive and productive labor in new ways.[18] During this same period (roughly the eighteenth and nineteenth centuries), the family also became a dominant symbolic and governmental resource for the new nations of Europe and its colonies. As Lynn Hunt argues in her study of the French Revolution, the "family model of politics" used the changing historical and aesthetic significance of the family to legitimate new bourgeois claims about individual freedom from patriarchal tyranny, even as emerging republican governments maintained strict control over family life and limited individual rights to white propertied men. According to scholars of the period's print capitalism, both newspapers and novels trained citizens in the imaginative relations of nationalism. Family romances provided a key medium for such readerly training, linking the Freudian "liberation of the individual" to the emergence of individualism, the delineation of public and private spheres, and the naturalization of gender difference in ideologies of white domesticity.[19]

"Family romance" provides a shorthand way to describe the historical coemergence of the bourgeois nuclear family, the modern democratic nation-state, and literary romanticism and realism. The problem remains how to read such national family romances. Following Benedict Anderson and other scholars of imagined communities, some critics have read for "imaginary" relations forged among disparate peoples. In his groundbreaking study of incipient nationalisms, Anderson offers "the following definition of the nation: it is an imagined political community—and imagined as both inherently limited and sovereign" (*Imagined Communities*, 5–6). This imagined community is a political entity, a new form of collectivity that abstracts a large variety of social relations and practices into the "nation." The political form of this new collectivity depends upon creating abstract images and concepts through which to produce collective identification. In his essay "The Nation Form" Etienne Balibar explains that "the naturalization of belonging and the sublimation of the ideal nation are two aspects of the same process" (96), which depends upon the production of ethnicity as a form of collective identity. Together, "language and race" coconstitute "fictive ethnicity" as the imminence of "national character" and the "means of transcending actual individuals and political relations" (96). This means of transcendence typically linked "fictive ethnicity" with genealogical descent: the family became the locus of this transformation, a new ground for the lived abstractions of national life.[20] In other words, the imaginary in this account may be a mode of abstraction, but its social effects are quite material. As the postcolonial theorist Ann McClintock puts it, "Nations are not simply phantasmagoria of the mind; as systems of cultural representation whereby people come to imagine a shared experience of identification with an extended community, they are historical practices through which social difference is both invented and performed" ("No Longer in a Future Heaven," 89).

Everybody's Family Romance pursues these questions into new domains, asking: How should we read the relation between "phantasmagoria of the mind" and "historical practices" in the late twentieth-century United States? How might the alleged national interest in reading about incest reveal a key turn in this relation? On one hand, the Freudian discourse of fantasy posited psychic relations (coded through gender and sexuality) as the origin of social relations. A fundamental oedipal struggle determined subsequent displacements, substitutions, and sublimations transcoding gender and sexuality onto class and race. On the other, the Marxist discourse of articulation (coded through class and race) posited social relations as the origin for psychic relations. A fundamental capitalist struggle determined subsequent ideologies, imaginaries, and hegemonies transcoding class and race onto gender and sexuality. I read fantasy and articulation together, arguing that fantasy is a historically specific practice of articulation organizing relations between domains of power. In the United States, fantasy appears to connect family to nation, sometimes through the individual lives of subjects and sometimes through the general practices of the state. But this seeming work of fantasy covers over its more complex articulatory power, which both differentiates and naturalizes relations of property and possession from relations of intimacy and kinship. I turn to the incest trope to reveal how fantasy's articulatory power works, and how this power of articulation could be put to different uses.

Fantasy as Articulation

Incest has not drawn significant attention within Marxist cultural studies, despite its significance to feminist readings of the political economy of family life.[21] This is due to incest's historical location at the juncture of Marxist theories of "articulation" and Freudian theories of "fantasy." In Marxist cultural studies, the concept of "articulation" has been used to describe connections between different domains of practice. Articulation is what Stuart Hall, in his essay "Race, Articulation and Societies Structured in Dominance," calls an "analogy" (326), a way of figuring connections between "(a) institutions; (b) forms of consciousness; [and] (c) political and cultural practices" (Williams, *Marxism and Literature*, 77). The analogy of articulation expresses the work of joining, of enjambment, as a physical and linguistic connection of different parts. It also expresses the disjunctiveness of such connections, their failure to suture different parts into a complete and seamless unity. The analogy of articulation allows critics to study points of connection, junctures where multiple determinations come together, where relations of cause and effect can be read as "indices of *effectivity*" (Althusser, "Ideology and Ideological State Apparatuses," 134). Stuart Hall argues that race is an "articulating principle" for societies structured in dominance, in which different modes of economic and political life must be linked in ways that make domination invisible or illegible as domination ("Race," 309). Several critics have argued that the articulating principle of race is often hidden in plain sight by specific historical tropes, words that perform this linkage while passing as race-neutral everyday speech. These tropes bespeak the particularity of specific historical and social conditions, precisely because they disappear among the common figures of their times. David Kazanjian and Brent Edwards have recently added "graft" and "translation" as tropes specific to the historical and social conditions of their archives.[22] The tropes mark both the locus of combination, what Kazanjian calls "forced imbrication" (*The Colonizing Trick,* 22), as well as its disjunction, what Edwards calls the "removal of . . . an added prop or wedge" (*The Practice of Diaspora,* 14).

Incest adds "fantasy" to this lexicon, using it to capture the imbrications and forced removals articulated through the Freudian familialism of the twentieth century.[23] This requires me to read fantasy within the logic of psychoanalysis, as a join and disjoin within the oedipal family, as well as through cultural studies of Freud, which situates this figure in the broader social relations described above. Freud used the German word *Phantasie* to describe a range of processes in which the subject transposed one desire, image, or signifier on another. In *The Language of Psycho-Analysis,* Laplanche and Pontalis define phantasy as an "imaginary scene in which the subject is a protagonist, representing the fulfillment of a wish (in the last analysis, an unconscious wish) in a manner that is distorted to a greater or lesser extent by defensive processes" (314). Phantasy represents a spectrum of representational options. At its two main poles, phantasy could be a conscious projection, the creation of "imaginary scenes," or a largely unconscious one, in which those scenes are projected on the theater of the psyche. Coming from the Greek word "phantasia," meaning "to make visible," the German term combined both conscious and unconscious processes in a single concept, emphasizing the process of signification (making visible) rather than the authorship or audience of such a process (differentiated by conscious or unconscious practices).[24] This process is less definitive than the scene itself, which is at times conscious, an active practice of imagination, and at other times unconscious, a more passive reception of phantasy or the fantasmatic.

Freud's conception of phantasy provides a very particular link to the "imaginative" relations of print culture and its "indices of effectivity." Freud himself used the concept of phantasy to describe the processes of creative writers, likening them to the processes of oedipal wishes more generally. Freud describes the temporality of phantasy in his essay on "Creative Writers and Day Dreaming," explaining:

The relation of a phantasy to time is in general very important. We may say that it hovers, as it were, between three times—the three moments of time which our ideation involves. Mental work is linked to some current impression, some provoking occasion in the present which has been able to arouse one of the subject's major wishes. From there it harks back to a memory of an earlier experience (usually an infantile one) in which this wish was fulfilled; and it now creates a situation relating to the future which represents a fulfillment of the wish. What it thus creates is a day-dream or phantasy, which carries about it traces of its origin from the occasion which provoked it and from the memory. Thus past, present and future are strung together, as it were, on the thread of the wish that runs through them. (439)

Phantasy is a temporal articulation, connecting three times through "the wish that runs through them." The scene of the daydream is itself the effect of an unconscious wish (implicitly an oedipal wish). The "day-dream" is the writer's fancy, that which articulates a future scene in which the "memory of an earlier experience" becomes an imaginary reality. Though imaginary, this reality is realized in the juncture of literature. The creative writer makes the time of phantasy the time of the now. But this now is constituted entirely by the effectivity of a past realized through it. "Past, present and future" are articulated by the "wish" that runs through them. And this wish is the origin of a later expression of phantasy as literary imagination—an articulation. Thus it is no surprise that phantasy in particular has been encoded as a kind of textual unconscious, one that also connects the novel form to the family romance. Here "creative writing" does in the world what phantasy does in the family: remakes original referents in the image of a more desirable outcome.

Many critics have used the English translation of this concept—fantasy—to capture the peculiar articulation of the imaginary in family romance fictions. Fantasy becomes a specific formation of the imaginary: it captures the material indices of effectivity not fully expressed in the concept of ideology, connecting the family as institution (or even ideological state apparatus) to other "institutions, forms of consciousness, and political and cultural practices" more carefully described by Williams (among other Marxist cultural critics). As articulation, fantasy promised to render the family a constitutive element of these broader social, economic, and political processes of historical materialism. But if fantasy has the extensive capacities of imagination, it also has the delimiting capacity of regulation, reifying "real" relations among the population in the image of bourgeois family life. To return to Freud's "Family Romances," the

translated "fantasy" does two kinds of work: first, it locates a tacit familial structure of desire and sexual science; second, it sutures the aesthetic
and the political into a bourgeois realism cleansed of its familial "others."
Freud calls the fantasies "works of fiction" (300) and explains that "if
there are any other particular interests at work they can direct the course
to be taken by the family romance; for its many-sidedness and its great
range of applicability enable it to meet every sort of requirement" (300).

But the "interests" that "direct the course" of the family romance's
potentially itinerant referents are very specific, and they absolutely determine its "range of applicability." These interests are determined "in the
last analysis" (Laplanche and Pontalis) or the "final instance" (Engels,
The Origin of the Family) by the methodologies that read them. For classical psychoanalytic interpreters, the last analysis is oedipalization, the
fundamental role of incestuous desire in forming the unconscious as the
repository of repressed material. What Freud elsewhere calls "primal
phantasies" are in the "last analysis" the primary form of the "unconscious wish": the wishes of oedipal processes refracted in imaginary
scenes that never become conscious. These primal phantasies are then the
fodder for a range of more or less conscious imaginary scenes, which are
"distorted to a greater or less extent" depending on the translations they
endure to become conscious. The acts of translation "remove an added
prop or wedge," the modes of repression that disavow oedipal wishes, by
imbricating oedipal elements with more socially acceptable or common-
place figures. The phantasy itself functions as articulation, with the subject appearing visible on the stage of its "imaginary" scenes. For classical
Marxist interpreters, the final instance is the mode of production, that
which defines the historical materialism articulated in all social or imaginary relations. Where classical Freudians posit the fragmentary signs of
the unconscious, classical Marxists posit the "fetishism of the commodity and its secret" (Marx, *Capital,* 163). "Real" relations among men lie
beneath both formations of conscious life. The difference is whether these
relations are driven by oedipal desire mystified as phantasy, or by relations of production mystified as ideology.

Making the Incest Scene

The break between last analysis and final instance indicates how the
"interests" that are expressed (or articulated) in the family romance are
delimited by the methodologies used to reveal them. The "scenes" phantasies render visible are determined by their temporal unfolding, the only

way we locate their presumed or retroactively posited origins. What is at stake here is how something invisible is translated into a "scene." Or, rather, what is at stake is how this seemingly visual translation depends upon a linguistic turn. This brings us back to the problem of the incest trope. *Everybody's Family Romance* reads fantasy as a key twentieth-century figure of analogy (articulation), while incest serves as its articulating principle. Incest provides the tropological turn through which fantasy becomes scene, which encodes its "secret" as an aporia of what can be spoken. The appearance of incest *as image,* as I discussed in relation to Benjaminian shock, renders its determination in language impossible. Either its image is secret, or its language is. If this scene could speak, however, it is unclear what it would reveal in the last analysis or final instance: the hidden history of the subject, or that of the commodity. Read as imagination, fantasy condenses different formations into a single image, incest, that symbolizes a problem of unconscious sexual desire initiated within the nuclear family. Read as articulation, however, fantasy is shown to (a) mystify the "secret" relation between commodification and subjection within (and as) the family form, and (b) maintain incest's force as a trope connecting sexuality, race, family, and nation as the limit of language itself.

This conjunction of language, commodification, and subjection has been of abiding interest to critics of U.S. racial formations and of African American cultural history in particular.[25] Several critics have recently offered contestatory readings of these relations of fantasy and commodity, focusing in particular on the role of "speech" in Marx's theorization of the commodity form. Marx's formulation of the commodity's "speechlessness" directly abuts U.S. legal efforts to delineate the properties of personhood from the personification of property. As critics such as Saidiya Hartman, Stephen Best, and Fred Moten have shown, the speech of the commodity is central to histories of racial capitalism, in which the concept of "property" is itself articulated through a racist logic of personhood.[26] Marx's implication that the commodity cannot speak adumbrates the racial formations of chattel slavery in the Americas. Tracing this question across formations of chattel slavery, U.S. Reconstruction, early twentieth-century music and literature, and contemporary fusions of alienability and fungibility in new forms of posthumanist property, this recent work has radically transformed readings of the commodity form as distinguished from other formations of propertied personhood and personified property.

My book adds an additional problematic to this genealogy of property: the incest trope. From the inception of the United States, incest has been used to differentiate propertied persons from personified property. Across many of England's white settler colonies, incest's extensive capacities have been bound to the reproductive logics of racial nationalism. In the U.S. context in particular, the "fictive ethnicity" described by Balibar became whiteness, a specific racial formation structured as a family tree.[27] Whiteness as a ruse of racial purity was intimately connected to the romance of incest, domesticating propertied personhood as the territorial genealogy of white settler nationalism. Incest and its twin figure, "miscegenation," marked the two symbolic limits of the familial nation: the dangers of endogamy posed by the demand for racial purity, and the dangers of racial impurity posed by the demand for exogamy. U.S. laws defining race as "blood quantum," restricting state-sanctioned couplings and delimiting properties of inheritance, made incest and miscegenation a representational index of racialized citizenship and privatized property relations. Carving the United States out of broader new world romances of racial métissage, incest established a specifically national romance that guaranteed the racial purity of the family through the regulatory mechanisms of the state. Paired with miscegenation, incest symbolized a threat to the racialized economic, political, and social order of the nation as a threat to the family.[28]

Reading the incest trope in relation to fantasy as articulation reveals the otherwise "secret" conjunction between economic relations, racial formations, and sexual regulation. Fantasy therefore does a similar work to "graft" or "translation," common-use terms that secretly turn as a trope of articulation. In the U.S. context incest has a peculiar relation to race as an articulating principle. Incest seemed to point to the opposite danger from so-called miscegenation. By appearing to signal the dangers of racial purity, incest turned away from the sexual violence that named interracial reproduction a relation of property rather than kinship. Incest therefore screened the imbrications of sexual regulation, racial formation, and economic relations. And fantasy installed these relations as the limit of familial (and national) life, recoding incest as a racializing and racist fantasy of purity and endogamy.[29] By adding the incest trope to this genealogy of property, *Everybody's Family Romance* aims to reveal how fantasy works to suture some domains of power (family and nation) while denying their imbrication with others (race and capitalism). This method will hopefully make incest available for alternative articulations, able to do the work of remembrance for those interested in turning the incest trope to different ends.

Neoliberal Family Romance

This returns us to the "glut" of incest narratives allegedly flooding the literary market of the 1990s. Much like Freud's turn-of-the-twentieth-century family romance, this turn-of-the-twenty-first-century family romance centered on a fantasy of parental substitution: this time, of bourgeois parents turned into sexual predators. Incest was now available for everybody's family romance, a trope for all peoples within the newly liberalized nation. Contesting this reading of national fantasy, the following chapters ask how "everybody" becomes the neoliberal subject of this American family romance. Why are women's narratives of incest so quickly read as symptoms of *national* trauma? Does the popularity of incest fiction signal a more imaginatively expansive kinship, perhaps even denationalizing the borders of "American" family romance?[30] Or does it merely localize sexual violence within the homogeneous seriality of U.S. families? Picking up the question posed by Louise Armstrong about the seeming devolution of incest politics in the subtitle to her book *Rocking the Cradle of Sexual Politics, Everybody's Family Romance* asks: "What happened when women said incest"?

To answer these questions, I read incest narratives written by women in the late twentieth-century United States. In keeping with the genealogy traced here, the focus remains on black/white racial formations as they emerge within and against a U.S. frame (cf. Cherniavsky, "Subaltern Studies in a U.S. Frame"). Several critics have pondered the absence of a broader range of racial formations within the incest canon. Certainly a wider range of narratives can be read through the analytic of incest, and unwitting sibling incest recurs as a theme in stories demarcating territorial borders or the violence of colonial contact and conquest. Here I choose to retain a narrow focus in order to reflect one peculiar genealogy of incest in the United States, where father-daughter incest has been embedded in specific racial projects of the nation-state, leading at times to the exclusion of a broader consideration of childhood sexual abuse across diverse literatures and cultural works. In the case of 1990s incest narratives, the peculiar dyad of black/white daughters has often been read as the instrument of national self-recognition and reproduction. Regardless of the aesthetics or politics of any given text, these particular incest narratives have become generalized as part of an unshocking glut of daughterly complaint. In the context of neoliberalism, this composite daughter marks the limit of fantasy as articulation.

The chapters that follow attempt to return an aesthetics of shock to these narratives. Chapters 1 and 2 explore the dominant articulation of incest, the attempted enclosure of incest within emergent cultural logics of U.S. neoliberalism. The first chapter charts the itinerary of the incest taboo across diverse theories of kinship and tactics of U.S. governance. Putting the ideas of Sigmund Freud and Michel Foucault in conversation with studies of U.S. governmentality, the chapter locates incest at the heart of the nation's ideological and social reproduction. I begin by reading Freudian accounts of incest and Foucauldian accounts of political sovereignty alongside welfare state experiments in child protection and sexual regulation. I then explore feminist efforts to remake relations between service provision, law enforcement, and patriarchal privacy in the name of combating incest. These feminist arguments made the sexual abuse of female children exemplary of state-legitimated patriarchal domination in the home, symptoms of gendered property relations first introduced by state law, then normalized by the formal gender-neutrality of welfare governmentalities. In closing I explore how these feminist approaches were taken up in new governmental efforts to recode incest as child sexual abuse, part of a broader transformation of family and governmentality for neoliberalism. As a result, gender paradoxically became a discourse of neoliberalism, used to separate family and sexuality from broader relations of race and capitalism.

My second chapter plunges into the controversies over recovered and false memory pervasive in 1990s popular and legal culture. Using Walter Benjamin and Guy Debord to frame the traumatic memory debates, this chapter queries the "legal fantasies" used to rationalize changing family forms in the 1990s. During this decade the publishing boom in incest-themed memoirs and novels provoked widespread accusations of crass commercialism, aesthetic devaluation, and literary literalism. This literary decline was later twinned with memory's fall from grace attributed to false memory syndrome. In the rise of the "memory wars" and legal cases adjudicating the referents of traumatic memory, incest accusations gave the state force to recraft relations between the family and ideologies of risk, harm, and national futurity. In this chapter I read popular media and U.S. legal proceedings to explore how ideas of scientific expertise and survivor testimony broke with prior understandings of the family romance, and yet maintained some of its major presuppositions.

Reading across debates about fantasy in recovered memory, I suggest that neoliberal rationalities of psychic life articulate a new form of "legal fantasy," which transfers patriarchal authority from father to state while maintaining the daughter's reification as evidence of an authority that is always beyond her.

The next two chapters explore alternative articulations of incest across two major novels of the 1990s, pursuing very close textual analysis to reveal the aesthetics of shock in two sample texts. My third chapter, on Carolivia Herron's wildly nonlinear 1991 novel *Thereafter Johnnie*, explores the potential liberation of the daughter's agency after the "fall" of the nation-state. Herron's tale of father-daughter incest in a black middle-class family living in 1970s Washington, D.C., renders incest into an allegory of nation and empire. Tracing disparate episodes of racial and sexual terror across two hundred years of national history, the novel narrates the apocalyptic end of the U.S. nation-state destroyed by its legacy of forced incestuous reproduction. Herron's novel returns over and over again to historical scenes of inter- and intraracial incest that at first seem to freeze the black daughter's body into the sign of an "X." This X translates the daughter's body into the signature and reified evidence of the nation's history of racial slavery and sexual violence. But the book does not ultimately make the daughter into the sign of her own victimization. Instead, I argue, the daughter exploits the fungibility of the X to steal her own representational agency back from its nationalist instrumentalization. Putting recent work on race, capitalism, and kinship in conversation with theories of trauma and testimony, in this chapter I ask how *Thereafter Johnnie* interrupts theories of traumatic transmission and the historical foreclosures imposed by their ideologies of form. I show how, in their place, the novel develops an allegory of daughterly agency that radically challenges the racial formations of national family romance.

Chapter 4 continues the study of daughterly agency, but in this case the work of Dorothy Allison situates incest in the context of white working-class narratives about family violence. This chapter stages the possibility of the "white trash" daughter's confrontation with social realism, exploring how the daughter's incest fantasies interrupt the aesthetics of violence attributed to the gritty realism of white trash novels. My consideration of Allison's 1992 novel *Bastard out of Carolina* pursues two key issues in order to demonstrate the specific entanglement of social realism with incest. First, I explore theories of social and working-class realism to demonstrate the novel's critique of masculinist figures of white labor. Second,

I examine Freud's essay "A Child Is Being Beaten" to argue that the novel's depiction of the beating fantasy provides a critique of bourgeois family romance. By bringing these two lines of inquiry together, I am able to show how *Bastard out of Carolina* stages within its pages a collision between social realism and bourgeois family romance as competing modes of representation. These two modes of representation are often synthesized in readings of the novel that focus on the daughter's survival of both poverty and incest as evidence of a transformative aesthetic. But in my reading I argue that the tensions between these two modes of representation are not resolved. Rather, the novel pits these modes against each other to reveal how their synthesis threatens to make the working-class daughter the instrument of her own commodification as traumatic subject. Situated in studies of labor, social realism, and psychoanalysis, this chapter reads the metonymy of "laboring hands" to show how the daughter steals self-representational agency from the codes of national family romance.

The fifth and final chapter then looks toward the future of incest writing, exploring how dominant and oppositional readings of incest are entwined in new forms of political fantasy. The chapter rounds out this study by returning to the most classic symbol of father-daughter incest: the "phallus." I explore feminist discourses of sexual harm, cultural discourses of sexual consent, and 1990s policy initiatives on family violence to explain how the phallus is allegedly demystified and then reimagined as part of more populist patriarchalism—one that incorporates the agency of the daughter through the rubric of consent. I ask how psychological studies of intergenerational consent such as the 1998 Rind study, memoirs such as Kathryn Harrison's 1998 *The Kiss,* and popular novels such as Sapphire's 1996 *Push* use neoliberal discourses of consent to reframe the generational borders of the national family romance. By reading two novels and a psychological study that link sexual consent to changing representations of the phallus, I explore the relationship between the economics of publication and allegations that incest literature has become too "pornographic." The study, memoir, and novel each offer radically different accounts of phallic authority, revealing latent gendered and racialized hierarchies lurking within new populist paradigms of consent. Situating accounts of neoliberal sovereignty in relation to queer theory and popular fiction, this final chapter captures and critiques the insidious remainders of violence lurking within new idioms of consent.

The book concludes by considering the implications of my argument for broader scholarship on childhood and sexual justice. Looking at questions of cultural imperialism in the study of child sexual abuse, the conclusion asks how diverse approaches to sexuality and violence impact transnational projects to amend and redress the social suffering of childhood. Incest provides one way to understand the role of Americanized childhood in the supposedly inevitable spread of neoliberalism. I explore how these consolidations of U.S. childhood provide a limit for new neoliberal hegemonies, in particular thinking about the historical function of incest in marking the break between old and new regimes of U.S. governmentality in relations of international power. Resisting the politics of that break, I close with alternative approaches to childhood dependency that might work against the neoliberal exceptionalism of the "American" 1990s.

One

Laying Down the Law:
The Modernization of American Incest

I know as well as anyone how "thankless" such research can be, how irritating it is to approach discourses not by way of the gentle, silent, and intimate consciousness which expresses itself through them, but through an obscure set of anonymous rules.
　—MICHEL FOUCAULT, *"Politics and the Study of Discourse"*

We believe that there is not a taboo against incest; merely against speaking about it.
　—TONI MCNARON and YARROW MORGAN, *Voices in the Night*

These epigraphs illuminate a central paradox of modern incest: the ubiquity of its discourse, and the elusiveness of its taboo. On one hand, incest discourse is everywhere. Rising to prominence in early twentieth-century Europe and the United States, incest discourse emerged from new disciplines of anthropology, psychoanalysis, and sexology. These new disciplines used the incest taboo to explain the telos of modernity, a movement from "elementary structures of kinship" to the modern bourgeois household. On the other hand, the incest taboo appears nowhere. Despite the ubiquity of its discourse, the incest taboo never takes positive form. Its ineffability, its elusiveness becomes the key to the taboo's power. Sometimes posited in the recesses of history, sometimes in the imperial peripheries of "savagery," sometimes in the modern patriarchal household, the elusiveness of the incest taboo allows it to be posited wherever it is needed. In the elusiveness and ubiquity of incest—its representational paradox— lie the key to its power. By being locatable nowhere, the incest taboo could be found everywhere. It was merely a matter of developing new disciplines whose mandate was to search for and research this elusive origin of modernity.

　　Across these domains, a new "archaeology of knowledge" produced anonymous rules of discourse as well as a unique hermeneutics of law.

This chapter undertakes a difficult task—to read the archaeology of incest and develop an alternative hermeneutics of its taboo. In *The Sane Society* (1955), Erich Fromm declared: "Nationalism is our form of incest, is our idolatry, is our insanity" (58). Here I argue instead that incest is our form of nationalism. In the United States, incest was plucked from its genealogy in European psychoanalysis and political economy to serve as a trope reorganizing family-state relations for mid-twentieth-century welfare governmentality. In this U.S. adaptation of the Freudian taboo, incest enabled ongoing strategies of population management that avoided the language of race in ways that still produced racist effects. Incest was then recoded once again during neoliberal restructuring at the end of the twentieth century, when a retreat from social welfare was coupled with the state's retrenchment of forced labor (workfare), militarization (warfare), and population control (new logics of family). Women's speech and writing about incest were central to this last transformation, which used the experiential discourses of incestuous trauma to animate new regimes of child protection and sexual offense law. My focus in this chapter is trained on those disciplines that allowed incest to do such profoundly political work—first psychoanalysis, then sociology, criminology, and psychology. Reversing Fromm, I will show how positing incest as the irrational idol underlying nationalism fostered a peculiar form of twentieth-century U.S. governmentality.

This chapter traces incest in its movement from taboo to trauma across the twentieth century. This involves two moves: first, to constitute an archive of incest; second, to develop a method of reading it. I begin by drawing together Western European incest discourses of the early twentieth century, exploring how structural theories of the incest taboo emerged from anthropology, sexology, psychoanalysis, and the racisms and nationalisms of modern empire. This structuralist incest taboo did not refer to any specific system of kinship or sexual exchange but instead symbolized a universal law governing human entry into culture. Historical studies of incest contradict this structuralist account, positing the modern nation-state as the origin of this allegedly universal law. This incest taboo was an effect of modern power, consolidated across statutory and case law, the traditional monikers of the state, as well as more diverse governmental, disciplinary, and nonstate formations. In the 1970s and 1980s, feminist researchers reversed both accounts of incest by claiming, with McNaron and Morgan, that "there is not a taboo against incest; merely against speaking about it" (15). With evidence that incest actually takes place, and not infrequently, feminist researchers argued that its "taboo" was merely on women's discourse. While the incest taboo may enact structural rule over kinship and sexuality, and political rule over family life, it fundamentally guarantees patriarchal rule over women.

Despite their seeming differences, however, these three accounts share a common use of incest to figure the limit or vanishing point of modern rule. Across this archive, incest establishes relations within and between six orders of modern rule: (1) a biological or genetic order of "natural" kinship, often coupled with ideologies of racial hypo-descent; (2) a social order of kinship premised in alliance, inheritance, and exogamous exchange, often used to elaborate "ethnic" collectivities; (3) a sexual order governing proper gender identification and object choice, often naturalizing hetero- and repronormativity; (4) a paternal order legitimating coercion and sexual violence, predicated on a system of patriarchy; (5) an order of subjective injury signified by psychological harm and trauma, frequently gendered; and (6) an order of political right through which the preceding orders are regulated and legitimated, often modeled on modern ideas of the state. From this archive, I develop an alternative method of reading incest. Across these six orders of modern rule, incest functions as a principle of articulation that forges connections and manages disruptions in changing relations of rule. At each juncture, incest "appears" as a specific rhetorical figure: as analogy at points of connection, as paradox at points of disjunction. These figures appear at key junctures of knowledge and power across the twentieth century, articulating new relations of rule even as they appear at (or as) the seeming limit of every specific historical formation. This chapter traces the appearance and disappearance of incest across these junctures in order to demonstrate its centrality to twentieth-century cultures of governmentality. It does so in order to open incest to alternative and potentially more radical articulations. Anticipating the hegemonic "memory wars" of the late 1980s and 1990s, this chapter reads incest as the form of an unfinished struggle over the "appearance" of power across the twentieth-century United States.

Incest as Taboo

Genealogies of the modern incest taboo abound. Typical sources include studies of hysteria and European bourgeois gender relations; racial projects emergent with struggles over nationalism and empire; nineteenth-century raciology and racial science; legal developments adjudicating competing forms of state sovereignty; ethnological research into the social life of indigenous peoples in the Americas, Africa, and Australia; Darwinian ideologies of natural and sexual selection; and industrialization's turns to privatized relations of production (and reproduction) under capital.[1] By the end of the nineteenth century, these threads were brought together in two emerging disciplines studying kinship and sexuality: anthropology and psychoanalysis. In anthropology, early work by E. B. Tylor, James Frazer, R. R. Marett, and Émile Durkheim was slowly consolidated into systematic and synthetic approaches to the so-called basic units of culture: religion, kinship, and exchange. In psychology, nineteenth-century work on hysteria was taken up in Jean-Martin Charcot and Pierre Janet's experiments at the Salpêtrière.[2] But where Charcot and Janet experimented with ideas of genetic degeneracy as the explanation for hysteria, Sigmund Freud theorized an incest taboo explaining hysterical symptoms through childhood sexuality rather than racialized kinship. Freud's incest taboo blended anthropological and psychological insights to form a widely influential account of deracinated kinship and atavistic sexuality in need of a modern father's law.

Freud developed his theory of the incest taboo after several "failed" attempts to locate the secret causes of hysteria. Freud first departed from Charcot and Janet by claiming that hysteria resulted from childhood sexual experiences.[3] He initially posited actual episodes of intergenerational "seduction" or sexual contact between young girls/women and men significantly their seniors (including fathers, uncles, or family friends) as the root of hysteria. He only later decided that hysteria did not require such an episode of seduction; it could rather be induced by any type of experience perceived to awaken and distort an already extant childhood sexuality (I treat the "seduction hypothesis" at length in chapter 2).[4] In this shift, Freud became more interested in the role of the unconscious in sexual life. According to Freud, psychoanalysis provided the insight that human consciousness was structured through fundamental unconscious prohibitions, "repressions" that guarded the subject from true realization of his or her deepest, most fundamental desires. These prohibitions took many forms, some more or less translatable into conscious thought. But underneath all these conscious prohibitions lay one, fundamental prohibition governing all social life: the prohibition against incest. Freud's incest taboo condensed these prohibitions into a single (unconscious) sexual rule, the most well-known formula forbidding the child from pursuing a (presumed) desire for the opposite-sex parent. While this is most familiar in the male form, as a prohibited desire for the mother and forced acceptance of female substitutes, all children go through the process of finding substitute satisfactions of being like the same-sex parent and thereby later having opposite-sex partners like the prohibited parent.[5]

This prohibition ensures subjection takes place through "civilization": indoctrination into the gender norms of family identities, the libidinal production and repression of intrafamilial desires, and ultimately the realization of civilized sexuality through exogamous marital ambitions. But this modern Oedipus complex also hides a complex racial logic in its story of gendered sexual subjection. According to scholars such as Sander Gilman, Anne Pellegrini, and Alys Eve Weinbaum, Freud's incest taboo bears the traces of at least two major discourses of racial difference: the era's dominant discourses of anti-Semitism, and the counterdiscourses of young Jewish women revealed in the case studies.[6] In her book *Wayward Reproductions,* Weinbaum suggests that Freud exploited incest's association with Jewish sexuality in turn-of-the-century Western Europe in order to universalize what were denigrated as Jewish particularities: "Not only were Freud's findings audaciously sexual, but incest, far from being regarded as a 'universal' experience, was within the scientific and medical literature of the period invariably cast as a Jewish racial trait characteristic of a people who were thought to be mired in tribal exclusiveness" (165). Through a reading of Darwin and contemporary racial sciences, Weinbaum argues that Freud uses the particularities of the case studies and of anti-Semitic raciology to universalize the "wayward female passions and reproductions [that] were specifically stereotyped as Jewish in character" (159). Freud's use of "genealogical metaphors" (164) reconstitutes his patient's discourse as a resource for his new universal science, one that would replace—by reproducing and supplementing—the anti-Semitic discourses that permeated anthropology and raciology of the time. Incest became universal through Freud's theory of its taboo.

One of the problems facing Freud, however, was the taboo itself: how could he prove the universality of incestuous desire if civilization made it taboo? According to his own theorization, the incest taboo by definition could not be known by its subject. The problem lay then in how to translate patient speech-acts into the professional discourse of psychoanalysis. This required an excursion into speculative metapsychology, specifically the ontogeny-recapitulates-phylogeny argument most clearly outlined in *Totem and Taboo: On Some Points of Agreement between the Mental Lives of Savages and Neurotics* (1913).[7] Here Freud explains that "taboo prohibitions have no grounds and are of unknown origin. Though they are unintelligible to *us*, to those who are dominated by them they are taken as a matter of course" (25). Prohibitions defined as taboo have three main qualities: they have no known explicit rationale (via grounds or origin); they are unintelligible to those outside their social reign; and they are naturalized by those who live under them. Precisely because the taboo lacks conscious rationalization (grounds or origin), it is only visible to the outsider, and then only as a series of unintelligibilities demanding explication. *Totem and Taboo* uses this definition to develop an origin story—from allegorical state of nature to Western European civilization—that establishes the rational grounds of psychoanalysis as the modern science of self-knowledge. Taking inspiration from Charles Darwin and James G. Frazer, Freud creates his own "state of nature" tale in which humans develop a social contract expressed in familial taboo (rather than state law).

Freud's parable begins by explaining the seemingly groundless "horror of incest" (3) as rooted in a lost, prehistoric origin. This requires him to chart the transformation of primitive totemism into "taboo" (24). Freud recasts the story of Darwin's "primal horde," a group organized around a "violent and jealous father" (175) whose monopoly of women and other goods leads the sons to kill him. This act of patricide issues in a new sense of guilt in which "the dead father became stronger than the living one had been" (178). In order to protect themselves against the symbolic authority of the dead father, the brothers "created out of their filial sense of guilt the two fundamental taboos of totemism, which for that very reason inevitably corresponded to the two repressed wishes of the Oedipus complex" (178): the murder of the father and the appropriation of the mother. According to Freud, what was once an action becomes a repressed wish. And what was once a real prohibition, represented in the person of the father, became over time an "unconscious" taboo. This movement involves a necessary forgetting, historically, and a necessary repression, psychologically. What was once "impressed upon them violently" (40) becomes an internalized taboo that persists "from generation to generation, perhaps merely as a result of tradition transmitted through parental and social authority" (40). Taboo crafts "ambivalent" (38) obedience, making history into psychology (199). "Civilization" (92) requires the relegation of such active wishes to the unconscious, manifested in fantasies and symptoms rather than explicit and self-conscious behavior. Thus for obsessional neurotics, struggling with the mandates of civilization, "the prohibition is noisily conscious, while the persistent desire to touch is unconscious" (38).

This origin story allows Freud to constitute civilizational difference, rather than biological race, as the rationale for the psychoanalytic method.[8] First, *Totem and Taboo* posits an invisible and unconscious prohibition as the defining trait of modern civilization. If violent and incestuous acts mark the atavism of precivilizational rule, incest fantasy (as the unconscious "persistent desire to touch") is all that remains in the aftermath of the father's symbolization in (and as) an unconscious incest taboo. Modern neurotics reveal the trace of such prohibition in their ambivalent vacillation between "thinking and doing" (200). Second, Freud's account differentiates the ambivalent and introjective function of taboo from the express mandate of state law. According to Freud, the taboo is an "unwritten code of laws" (25) whose power to protect civilization from sexual primitivism depends upon its effective binding of the unconscious. Civilization is predicated on the ability to *internalize* an unwritten taboo rather than *obey* a written law. Thus "the beginnings of rituals, morals, society and art converge in the Oedipus complex" (194). This detaches sexual normalization from state law and relocates it within the family (thereby short-circuiting the state's alleged interest in protecting citizens from biological degeneration). Third, psychoanalysis becomes (tacitly) more important than the state in protecting civilization from its threatened degeneration. The only way these unwritten laws (taboo) become intelligible is through the "knowledge of concealed mental impulses which we have acquired from the psycho-analytic examination of individual human beings" (20). Only the new modern sciences—such as psychoanalysis—are suited to cultivate the civilized and protect against sexual atavism.

Freud's account has been surprisingly influential across the twentieth century, shaping subsequent understandings not merely of the unconscious but also of civilized repression and the necessity of heteronormative gender and marriage arrangements to protect society from "primitive" unrest. Left here, Freud's theories of totem and taboo might be easily dismissed on the basis of their overt civilizational racism, if not their presumptive sexism. But Freud's phylogenic explorations of the ontogenetic incest taboo have remained a useful counterpoint to subsequent efforts to rewrite Freudian philosophy as ontology. In later interpretations of Freud, this messy civilizational telos is transformed into a more structuralist (or synchronic) account of the incest taboo. After the psychoanalytic movement had suffered several splits and regroupings, one thinker in particular announced a "return to Freud" to clarify the relation between history and ontology in the incest taboo. Jacques Lacan resituated Freud's arguments about an "unwritten code of laws" in the context of the aesthetic movements of surrealism, the linguistic theories of Ferdinand de Saussure, and the structuralist anthropology of Claude Lévi-Strauss.[9] Fighting the positivist turn to ego psychology and libido as sex drive, Lacan insisted upon reading Freud textually, imitating Freud's own method in *Totem and Taboo* to discern the "unwritten code of laws" within the text. In so doing, Lacan transformed the Freudian incest taboo into a structural "Law of the Father" that opened *the family* to historical change, yet maintained *structural kinship* as the basis of universal subjection.

Lacan's incest taboo makes a linguistic model of kinship the structural precondition of all subjection. Called at different times the Law of the Father, Name-of-the-Father, and the Father's No (the latter two playing off the shared pronunciation of *Nom-du-Père/Non-du-Père*), this incest taboo joins language and kinship in a tripartite system: the Real, the Imaginary, and the Symbolic. A basic overview (taken primarily from *The Seminar of Jacques Lacan, Book VII*) could be summarized as follows. When the subject first enters into language, it imagines that some fullness or plentitude has been lost. This originary loss is called the Real, and it can only be retroactively posited as that which came before language, before words barred the subject from its full reality (alternative terms include Lack, the Other, the Phallus, the Thing/*das Ding*). Imaginary relations are all the subject really knows (as an ego). They are the signifiers (my things/*meine Sache*) through which the subject attempts to fill up its lack (the Real) or through which it tries to represent its desire (inaugurated by the cut of the Real). Kinship then provides the Symbolic order through which subjects interpret this sense of loss. The lost Real comes to seem like the lost Mother (which is the Other-become-Thing or vice versa, or the *petit objet a* or Phallic representative), and the Father comes to represent the Law against life's full satisfaction (through the symbolic threat of castration, *Nom/Non-du-Père*). Thus Lacan formulates a Law of the Father as the bar through which the subject enters culture. The father's sovereign prohibition on the mother constitutes an incest taboo for the child, but one through which the father becomes Symbolic, the mother comes to signify the domain of the lost Real, and all signifiers of the gap between these two orders are Imaginary (which Lacan also calls "discourse" [63]).[10]

This Law of the Father has proven a double-edged sword for feminists and other critics interested in alternative approaches to family and sexual life. On one hand, this structural formulation seems more open to alternative articulations than Freud's account of the incest taboo. The Law of the Father describes the subject's *mistaken* search for a lost fullness. No particular father or mother really represents the terms of this loss. Because the Law of the Father is Symbolic, and predicated on a fundamental misrecognition, many feminists have argued that it can be dismantled, replaced by alternative arrangements of kinship and sexuality. It describes rather than prescribes a given social order, and as such can be a useful tool for critical analysis.[11] On the other hand, this structural formulation can be more closed to alternative articulation than Freud's messy civilizational logic. Because the Law of the Father is Symbolic, and predicated on a fundamental misrecognition, it is not necessarily dismantled when replaced by alternative arrangements of kinship and sexuality. Many have argued that labeling this regulatory matrix the Law of the Father establishes phallologocentrism as a universal structure, which can absorb alternatives to the symbolization of "Law" and "Father" regardless of its changing forms (thus, all lesbians become phallic, while not all phalluses become lesbian).[12] Whereas Freud's incest taboo is predicated on a civilizational telos and embedded ideologies of racial difference, Lacan posits a blank slate for his ontology of language and kinship. Incest becomes a structural absence, rather than a genealogical presence. In other words, Freudian incest registers the ghost of racisms past, while Lacanian incest seems to render such hauntings incidental, misrecognitions along the path to Symbolic order. For Lacan incest appears as the conceptual limit of signification: "The prohibition of incest is nothing other than the condition sine qua non of speech" (*Seminar, Book VII*, 69).

Incest as Power

Both Freud and Lacan make the incest taboo into a new universal for specifically modern societies. This universal taboo has found its most influential critic in the French philosopher Michel Foucault, whose *History of Sexuality*, volume 1, can be read as an extended rebuttal of both Freudian and Lacanian psychoanalysis.[13] In this sweeping survey of modern power, Foucault argues that discourses of the incest taboo are indeed part of new technologies of power, but not in the way psychoanalysis suggests. Foucault asserts instead that the incest taboo must be understood in the context of a massive transformation in European social structures from the seventeenth century onward. Foucault argues that this transformation involves a shift from a model of political right based on sovereignty to a model based on power. For Foucault, the incest taboo must primarily be understood as a ruse of power, a figure of law used to articulate kinship, sexuality, and political economy as distinct but overlapping domains. I will, in this section, briefly survey Foucault's major arguments about incest in modern formations of power, focusing in particular on the paradox of incest as an "orthogonal articulation" (*Society Must Be Defended*, 253) connecting disciplinary and state power. This reading of incest brings Freud into new relief, revealing how incest's taboo articulates—as paradox—relations between seemingly private sexual normalization and ongoing forms of state racism.

Foucault's account of power, while widely known, deserves to be recounted here in order to clarify its significance for reading incest. According to Foucault, "Power is everywhere; not because it embraces everything, but because it comes from everywhere" (93). Power is the "multiplicity of force relations" (92) that constitute a specific sphere or domain. But these force relations do not come from above (or from below for that matter). They are constituted instead by "ceaseless struggles" (92) whose points of contact yield both connections (forging what he calls "a chain or a system") and "disjunctions and contradictions" (92). Across the first four sections of *The History of Sexuality*, volume 1, Foucault focuses on two specific modes of power that he calls "deployments": the deployment of alliance and the deployment of sexuality (106). The deployment of alliance operates primarily through laws governing the legitimate use and transfer of property and social status, what Foucault calls "a system of marriage, of fixation and development of kinship ties, of transmission of names and possessions" (106). But in modernity, Foucault argues, "economic processes and political structures could no longer rely on [the deployment of alliance] as an adequate instrument or sufficient support" (106). The deployment of alliance was then supplemented by a deployment of sexuality. Unlike the deployment of alliance, this mode was constituted primarily through disciplinary institutions (medicine, psychoanalysis, sexology) and their normalizing discourses. Through the deployment of sexuality, disciplinary norms of sex produced an "intensification of the body—with its exploitation as an object of knowledge and an element in relations of power" (107).

These two deployments intersect in a new sphere of force relations: the modern family. The deployment of alliance still reproduced existing social relations through the careful management of inalienable "names and possessions"; marriage and inheritance were still regulated by law.

But the deployment of sexuality simultaneously worked against this system of social reproduction, constituting the sexed body as the enumerative site of more decentered, discursive, and fungible forms of power. At the intersection of these two deployments, the family became both "an agency of control and a point of sexual saturation" (120), a locus for "techniques for maximizing life" (123) that made subjects self-disciplining. And what was the name of this locus, the precise point of intersection for the deployment of kinship and the deployment of sexuality? Incest. According to Foucault, incest named the principle of articulation for these two deployments. As such, incest is a pivot at the heart of the modern family:

> In a society such as ours, where the family is the most active site of sexuality'. . . [incest] occupies a central place; it is constantly being solicited and refused; it is an object of obsession and attraction, a dreadful secret and an indispensable pivot [*joint* (144)]. It is manifested as a thing that is strictly forbidden [*interdict* (144)] in the family insofar as the latter functions as a deployment of alliance; but it is also a thing that is continuously demanded in order for the family to be a hotbed of constant sexual incitement. (109)

Incest is a "pivot," that upon which a related part depends or turns. But it is also a "secret," that which cannot be disclosed or known. As a pivot, incest seems to connect patriarchal systems of property and language to the biological reproduction of children and social reproduction of norms. As a secret, however, it harbors potential disjunction, a break in the normalizing society that allows power to continue developing imminent force relations in new spheres (homosexuality, gender inversion, sexual dysfunction, promiscuity, polyamory).

For this to work effectively, however, incest had to be represented as "*interdit*," prohibited or forbidden. Incest must appear neither as pivot nor secret but instead as a form of sovereign right (which he mostly terms *droit*, using *loi* in specific instances). As Foucault explains, incest marks the "paradox of a society which, from the eighteenth century to the present, has created so many technologies of power that are foreign to the concept of law [*droit* (144)]: it fears the effects and proliferations of those technologies and attempts to recode them in forms of law [*droit* (145)]" (109). Incest's work as pivot and secret is recoded into a form of right (here translated as law): the prohibition of incest (which he calls *l'interdiction de l'inceste*). This recoding (signified in the translational slide between interdiction, taboo, law, and right) was undertaken by the emerging disciplines of the eighteenth and nineteenth centuries and consolidated in late nineteenth-century anthropology and psychoanalysis. For Foucault, the modern incest taboo—Freud's specific formulation of "taboo" for interdiction or prohibition—is born of these new mechanics of power: "By asserting that all societies without exception, and consequently our own, were subject to this rule of rules, one guaranteed that this deployment of sexuality, whose strange effects were beginning to be felt— among them, the affective intensification of the family space—would not be able to escape from the grand and ancient system of alliance. Thus the law [*droit* (144)] would be secure, even in the new mechanics of power" (109). The incest taboo conflated law (*loi*) and right (*droit*) within new mechanics of power, even as it mystified how state laws of alliance used it to guarantee social reproduction.

Psychoanalysis plays a very specific role in this history of sexuality, entering late in the elaboration of incest as prohibition and incitement (the "rule of rules" in the form of interdiction). Freud had comprised his incest taboo from the raciology of his times, crafting a universal prohibition from what Foucault calls "state-directed racism" (119). This new form of racism, "a dynamic racism, a racism of expansion" (125), correlated a "concern with the body and sex to a type of 'racism'" (125) such that "the concern with genealogy became a preoccupation with heredity" (124). At the end of the nineteenth century, psychoanalysis emerged to create "a dividing line [*ligne* (169)]" (128) within this expansive domain of racialized sexuality. Where the deployment of sexuality had first emerged to differentiate the bourgeoisie from the nobles, the psychoanalytic incest taboo acted as "a bar running through that sexuality [*une ligne qui . . . la barre* (169)]" (128). This taboo elaborates what Foucault calls "secondary mechanisms of differentiation" (129) which use "repression" differentially: first, to distinguish between civilized and atavistic peoples on the grounds of practice; second, to transfer legitimate knowledge about atavism from racial science to psychic classification.[14] Psychoanalytic technique is legitimated "by its analysis of the differential interplay of taboos according to the social classes" (128). The so-called incest taboo symbolizes "law" (*loi* throughout this section) as a form of representational ambivalence, an "interplay of taboos" that cannot be represented but that determines all representation—what Lacan called the "sine qua non of speech."

The book's final chapter, "Right of Death and Power over Life," returns then to the concept of political right (*droit*). Here biopower is the main analytic concept, used to explain the shift from the sovereign's right of death to the government's power over life. Biopower also has two modes: *an anatomopolitics of the human body* (associated with the disciplines) and *a biopolitics of the population* (associated with regulation) (139). Where the state once performed its sovereignty as a right (*droit*) to put citizens to death, modern governance gains legitimacy by maximizing the life of its population. Regulation must be aimed at improving the life of a population, which in turn binds regulation to new disciplines dedicated to measuring and evaluating the health and happiness of populations. This era marks the "entry of life into history" (141), as Foucault famously asserts, and "the biological existence of a population" (137) becomes the means and ends of governance. While in his separate essay "Governmentality" Foucault asserts that the state is merely a "mythicized abstraction" (103), at the end of *History of Sexuality* he asserts that the "state" appears as a sovereign actor through its biopolitical agenda. According to Foucault, biopower defines the remaining sovereignty associated with government as "the right to kill those who represented a kind of biological danger to others" (138).

Across *History of Sexuality,* volume 1, "race" connects and disjoins disciplined bodies and regulated populations. In his final chapter Foucault provides his fullest account of how reproductive racism becomes "state-directed" (119), tying it to the emergence of "sex *as a political issue*" (145, my emphasis). This politicization of sex situates it in the domain of regulation, which Foucault associates with the management of populations (or "species body" [139]). We see the "entry of life into history," and sex into politics, through the production and management of racialized populations. Foucault explains that sex was "at the pivot [*charnière* (191)] of the two axes along which developed the entire political technology of life" (145), the hinge or turning point of "disciplines of the body" and "the regulation of populations" (145). It is through the pivot or hinge of sex that we move from a mode of power in which "blood was *a reality with a symbolic function*" (147) to one in which sexuality is "*an effect with a meaning value*" (148). Once, power "spoke" (147) through blood's irrefutable reality, symbolizing power through sanguinity. But blood's material existence has been replaced with sexuality's immaterial meaning. Political right (*droit*) that was once grounded in sovereignty (speech as symbolization of blood right) was now the effect of meaning collation (right as the maximization of discursive effects). Thus we move from a "*symbolics of blood* to *an analytics of sexuality*" (148), creating a "new concept of race" (148) associated with the "controllable effects of sex" (148), but retaining "the mythical concern with protecting the purity of the blood and ensuring the triumph of the race" (149). This recombination constitutes the biopolitics of population, or "racism in its modern, 'biologizing,' statist form" (149).

The account of racism developed in this chapter, "Right of Death and Power over Life," is amplified in the lectures collected in *Society Must Be Defended*. In his lecture of March 17, 1976, Foucault clarifies some of these claims as they relate to changes to political right (*droit*). Here Foucault explores the limits of biopower, which has drawn life into history and sex into politics in what he calls the "normalizing society" (253). In such a society, the only real limit to biopower is death. And the only way to inflict death is through biopolitical logics: those subject to death are no longer political adversaries, but biological threats to the population. According to Foucault, racism is "a way of introducing a break [*coupure* (227)] into the domain of life that is under power's control: the break between what must live and what must die" (254).[15] Not only does race provide "a way of separating out the groups that exist within a population" (255), it also provides "a way of establishing a biological-type caesura [*césure* (227)] within a population that appears to be a biological domain" (255). Foucault argues that the biopolitical function of race, its use for regulating populations through the norm, also constitutes it as a biological precondition for letting die. As he goes on to argue, "In a normalizing society, race or racism is the precondition that makes killing acceptable. . . . Once the State functions in the biopower mode, racism alone can justify the murderous function of the State" (256). Here Foucault offers his clearest formulation of racism in such a normalizing society, explaining that "paradoxes that appear at the points where the exercise of this biopower reaches its limits" (253) tend to emerge as "racism" (256).

Yet a key difference can be sifted from these texts, one I will draw out here to resituate incest in relation to biopower and its paradoxical limits. In *Society Must Be Defended*, Foucault explains that biopolitics and anatomopolitics meet in the norm, in what he calls an "orthogonal articulation" (253) or what he elsewhere describes as a "grid pattern . . . articulated, in a sort of perpendicular way" (251).[16] This orthogonal articulation works as the juncture for discipline and regulation. He states that "sexuality exists at the point [*au carrefour* (224)] where body and population meet" (251–52), a crossroads like the pivot, joint, or hinge described in the "Right of Death" chapter. Sex is the (main) historical example of the force relations of the normalizing society. And within the operations of biopower, race (or a symbolics of blood) is encoded in sex (an analytics of sexuality). Sex is a pivot (*joint, charnière*), implying some potential movement or swing to its turn. It is only fixed into an orthogonal articulation (as *carrefour*) in the normalizing society, which depends on sex to articulate race within both discipline and population. When all is working well, (sexual) norms (which express norms of race) mark the orthogonal articulation of discipline and regulation, their crossroads (*carrefour*).

But biopower expresses itself as a paradox in two places in Foucault.[17] The first paradox is death, the limit to biopower that appears as racism: "Paradoxes that appear at the points where the exercise of this biopower reaches its limits" (253) tend to emerge as "racism" (256). This is the caesura of biopower, a break in its articulation, its paradoxical limit. The articulatory paradox of mortality *appears as* racism, articulated through sovereignty as the right to kill or let die. This is where race exceeds sex in Foucault's account, where race is desexualized and left remaindered, beyond history (where life is). The second is "the paradox of a society which, from the eighteenth century to the present, has created so many technologies of power that are foreign to the concept of law [*droit*]: it fears the effects and proliferations of those technologies and attempts to recode them in forms of law [*droit*]" (109). This second paradox leads to Foucault's discussion of incest. A parallel formulation to the paradox marked by racism might be that the paradox of natality appears as "perversion-heredity-degenerescence" (118), articulated through the incest taboo as the pivot and secret of biopower. This would suggest that the paradox of natality is also . . . racism. But it does not appear as such. The paradox of natality is a limit to biopower which *does not seem to appear at all*. Thus racism only "appears" (as such, race *as desexualized racism*) in death, where biopower meets its limit.

What about in life? What is the "appearance" of racism in life? One might clearly argue that "letting die" marks natality for populations of color, as Dorothy Roberts argues in *Killing the Black Body*, and that even this limit appears as racism. But instead we find at this second paradoxical limit Foucault's discussion of the incest taboo: *la droit* (political right) figured as an interdiction that is both pivot (*joint*) and secret between alliance and sexuality; the dividing line (*une ligne de partage*) that acts as a bar (*une ligne qui . . . barre*) running through sexuality; the interdiction whose meaning effects (whether repression or action) consolidate its symbolic sovereignty. Hence the problem: the incest taboo is formulated to make biological racism disappear. The biopolitical agenda toward life *as natality* is placed behind the "line" of incest's pivot, which "appears" as a "bar" to a secret that will out: the secret of sexual desire. That is the impact of the Freudian turn.

Incest appears as a break with what Weinbaum calls the race/reproduction bind by inaugurating a line or bar (interdiction) that incites discourse about "secret" sexual desire, inciting a new set of relations through which social difference (now recoded as class) will be managed. Incest appears as an intimate articulation (*joint*, pivot) that harbors a secret (which must come out). Meanwhile, race appears as a disjunction (*coupure, césure*) that divides populations and lets die or legitimately kills. As a result, we have an account of racism that refuses to recognize natality at all. Race as racism "appears" at a distance from reproduction, barred at the "crossroads" figured as sexuality. And incest "appears" as an articulation that bars natality from race/racism while inciting sexual discourse about its taboo. Thus incest marks a central paradox of power as articulation: incest figures the impossibility of "representation" (speech, language, image, figuration as such) when power takes representation—discourse about symbolization as state (*droit*) and father (*loi*)—as its mode.

Incest as Law

The historical archive of incest law in the United States traces the contours of a "secret" coded and recoded as incest. For Foucault, incest lies *within* biopower, symbolizing the limit to power (taboo) even as it generates relations of force (pivot) and productive meaning-effects (secret). Incest in Foucault's account, as well as in Freud's, traces this edge of biopower as taboo, pivot, and secret. Incest provides the occasion to insist that biopower has maximized the field of life, seizes life from before inception, and regulates and disciplines life from the copula to the grave through the mechanism of family. It also acts as a tropological turn between race and class, recoding biological racism articulated through reproduction as class difference articulated through behavior (which codifies the very concept of incestuous "practice" in civilizational terms). But here I want to avoid a too-quick synthesis of Foucault's arguments about the deployments of alliance and sexuality and those pertaining to the two modes of biopower (discipline and regulation). The following sections explore if and how regulatory and disciplinary norms meet in an "orthogonal articulation," with sex/uality as its crossroads, and racism and incest as its limits. A distance still exists between the incest taboo as the "rule of rules" and the incest taboo as it relates to the "orthogonal articulation" of norms. And it is not clear where—or if—these two formations touch. Does incest figure the paradoxical limit of biopower? Or does it in fact constitute biopower's orthogonal articulation as paradox? If so, how can we better track the force relations that appear through this paradox, in order to wrench incest from its biopolitical moorings and wield it for more robustly feminist antiracist and queer politics?

In this section, I focus on U.S. laws prohibiting incest, culling from this record a partial account of how power has been recoded as political right in and through the law itself. One of the findings of such a method is that race seems to drop away. The discourse of incest across U.S. law, from colonial common law to recent Supreme Court jurisprudence, makes bare mention of race, although the racial and racist effects of incest law can be discerned across scholarship on sex law more generally. The role of incest law—or its regulatory means for the state—directs attention explicitly to sexuality, or sex as a pivot. Incest law at first appears to operate through sovereign interdiction, what Vikki Bell terms the "thou shalt not" (*Interrogating Incest,* 29) of prohibited incest. But this sovereign interdiction immediately gives way to what Courtney Megan Cahill calls linguistic preterition ("'What Is Our Bane,'" 7), unable to say what state secret it so carefully guards. Laws against incest are notoriously vague. They offer inconsistent definitions of the acts prohibited, frequently proffering in their place declarations of the legitimacy of the law itself. In her 1998 survey of laws against incest, Leigh Bienen argues that despite a wide range of stated prohibitions, the definition of incest remains inconsistent and unclear. There are numerous formulations of incest as prohibited behavior and as crime, but there is no consensus regarding the meaning of this offense.

Incest law developed unevenly across United States history. The early British colonies in America created their own statutory law but also adopted meanings from English common law, creating a complex system of statutory rape and incest codes. In medieval England, as Elizabeth Archibald explains in *Incest and the Medieval Imagination,* incest was originally treated as a sin by the ecclesiastical court. It did not explicitly become part of English common law until the Punishment of Incest Act of 1908, which focused primarily on the poor. Until this point, incest with a child was not distinguished from statutory rape as defined by the

1275 Acts of Parliament, Statute of Westminster I (which defined sex with a child under the age of twelve as rape, regardless of whether or not force was used or consent was obtained) and the 1576 Statute 18 Elizabeth (which lowered the age to ten).[18] American colonial law followed the definition of statutory rape based on 18 Elizabeth (although they did not maintain this age limit), slowly developing its own statutory code during early Republican debates over the status of feme sole and family dependency among legal whites.[19] In the nineteenth century, some U.S. states adopted the example of England's 1861 Indecent Liberties offense for children under sixteen, creating new discourses about the chastity of the victim and the power and property relations of seduction.

Incest emerged independent of statutory rape unevenly across American legal traditions. Bienen summarizes early incest laws as creating primarily "a crime grounded in principles of morality, property, and the laws governing inheritance" ("Symposium," 1504). Colonial and early state legislatures negotiated the linkages between Christian, civil and criminal definitions of incest in various ways. The 1650 Connecticut General Court (operating as colonial legislature), for example, first made incest a criminal offense as "carnal copulation" based on Leviticus, but in 1715 incorporated it under a marriage statute ("Symposium," 1529).[20] The Massachusetts Colony, on the other hand, codified capital criminal laws in 1660 that did not include Incest ("Symposium," 1521), following what it perceived to be British canon law. And in 1779, a Vermont statute mixed civil and criminal approaches creating "An act for the punishment of incest, and for preventing incestuous marriages" that prohibited inheritance and required the offender to wear a capital letter "I" ("Symposium," 1524–25). By the late eighteenth and nineteenth centuries, incest prohibition still focused on the "regulation of marriage and prevention of inbreeding," with uneven focus on intent or consent ("Symposium," 1532). By 1908, every U.S. state had the statutory crime of Incest.

But despite the stated prohibitions against statutory rape and incest, the historical record reveals few prosecutions of cases of intrafamilial assault or marital incest. In their survey "Prosecution of Child Sexual Abuse in the United States," John Myers, Susan Diedrich, Devon Lee, Kelly Fincher, and Rachel Stern point to the difficulty of locating actual cases tried successfully under these statutes. For Myers and his collaborators, the gulf between legal prohibition and jury prosecution can be traced from the inception of English common law through the case law of what Henry Luce called "the American century." The definitional statement on the ambiguity of case law can be found in the 1736 treatise *The History of Pleas of the Crown*, where the chief justice of the Court of King's Bench in England, Sir Matthew Hale, remarks: "It must be remembered, that [rape] is an accusation easily to be made and hard to be proved, and harder to be defended by the party accused, though never so innocent" (quoted in Myers et al., "Prosecution of Child Sexual Abuse," 35). This phrase is cited repeatedly in U.S. case decisions, including as recently as the 1997 *State v. Chamley* South Dakota Supreme Court decision overturning a prior child sexual assault conviction with the warning "allegations of sexual misconduct are easy to allege and difficult to disprove" (quoted in "Prosecution of Child Sexual Abuse," 35).[21]

This difficulty grows exponentially when researchers seek out cases focused specifically on incest. As Bienen points out, "Incest turns up rarely in decisional law" ("Symposium," 1502), to the degree that "well into the middle of this century some states have not one reported case annotated under their traditional incest statutes" (1546). Some exceptions to the rule against prosecution can be found in infamous incest trials of the nineteenth century. Louise Barnett for example analyzes the 1879 accusation of father-daughter incest within a military family in *Ungentlemanly Acts: The Army's Notorious Incest Trial,* while Daniel Moon explores an 1894 incest prosecution in "'Unnatural Fathers and Vixen Daughters': A Case of Incest, San Diego, California, 1894."[22] The "Un-" opening of both analyses indicates the negative form through which prosecution did take place. Incest was prosecuted as a negation of proper role, either of the army gentleman or the natural father. Across statutory and common law, the meaning of incest seems far less important than the rationale for its prohibition and prosecution. This break between the stated aims of incest law and its prosecution, between what Vikki Bell calls the "thou shalt not" (*Interrogating Incest,* 29) of incest law and the messy dicta of decisional jurisprudence, is part of the power of incest to recode what Foucault called biopower's "meaning value" in legal forms. These exceptional cases prove rather than disprove the rule of incest law, which has historically demonstrated more interest in specifying the domains of the unnatural, the ungentlemanly, and the unacceptable than in alleviating conditions of sexual subordination or structural dominance.

Incest law might best be understood as a series of statutory proclamations about the dangers of errant meaning effects. As Courtney Megan Cahill argues, in her essay "'What Is Our Bane, That Alone We Have in Common,'" the sovereign prohibition against incest consistently refuses to specify the referents of its prohibition. Laws against incest often fail to define their object, elaborating instead the just grounds for the state's interest in regulating kinship roles, sexual choice, and the natural relationship between them. Despite the fact that "courts use so-called rational analysis to justify the distinctions they make between legitimate and illegitimate desire" (Cahill, "'What Is Our Bane'" 5), this "rationality" in fact produces the grounds (as well as the vehicle) of legal legitimacy as shifting and ambiguous. Legal justifications for the incest prohibition are contradictory and changeable, at times claiming to protect against the possible genetic defects caused by incestuous reproduction, at times to protect against the social defects caused by role reversals inside the family, and at times against the sexual defects caused by age-inappropriate sexual relations. [23] Cahill points out that justifications for incest's legal prohibition are either "overly general or far too specific" (37), since the logic of the prohibition works to exclude a range of unions not directly relevant to incestuous relations and in effect allows a range of incestuous unions to go unregulated.

Legal reasoning legitimates political right by making incest into a fungible concept determined by legal rhetoric. Incest is endlessly inscribable with new meaning, yet never grounded in any particular relations of representation (other than those between law [*loi*] and state [*droit*]). The justification for incest law rests not on any consistent body of doctrine but rather on constantly shifting claims about the state's legitimate interest in using law to protect nature, culture, family norms, and public health. In upholding the 1983 Washington state conviction of Marvin Kaiser for incest committed against his sixteen-year-old stepdaughter, for example, Acting Chief Justice Munson points out that "the statutory schemes differ; some states prevent illicit intercourse by consanguinity while others also include relation by affinity" (*State v. Kaiser*, 884).[24] He goes on to list other potential rationales as "prevention of mutated birth," "to promote and protect family harmony, to protect children from the abuse of parental authority," and to protect society because "society cannot function in an orderly manner when age distinctions, generations, sentiments and roles in families are in conflict" (844). After evaluating the statutory role of incest law, Justice Munson concludes that "the statute bears a rational relation to a legitimate governmental objective. . . . The legislation bears a reasonable and substantial relationship to the health, safety, morals or welfare of the public. We hold the statute is therefore constitutional" (844).

This arbitrary and conflictual set of justifications articulates state interest in the prohibition of incest through the rhetorical forms of taboo. Courtney Megan Cahill argues that these laws derive their legitimacy from the force of an unstated, and unstatable, taboo, grounding legal prohibition less in logical argumentation than in linguistic and discursive acts of negation. Cahill claims that U.S. courts use what Eve Kosofsky Sedgwick, in *Epistemology of the Closet,* terms an "erotic negative" (202), which Cahill summarizes as the "rhetorical act of preterition: the act of assigning an unspeakable act a negative value and thereby obliterating (though simultaneously reifying) its existence" (7). While the laws themselves repeatedly justify the state's interest in prohibiting incest, these justifications articulate disjunctions as much as connections. Laws against incest emphasize the legitimacy of the state's intervention into otherwise consensual sexual choice, while at the same time insisting that sexual choice is defined by its distance from the family. What can be represented before the law as a sexual choice comes to depend upon the legal definition of kinship, which in turn is defined through its opposition to unsanctioned sexual practice. But, through the preterition of incest law, the definition of kinship relies precisely upon the ambiguous referents of erotic negation. As a result, kinship is naturalized as prior to and precipitating norms of sexual choice, even as sexual choice reinstitutes the priority of kinship norms.

To truly grasp the paradox of incest's "orthogonal articulation," however, we must move away from the "thou shalt not" of incest law and turn instead to the "thou shall" produced by the disciplines and governmental processes associated with the welfare state. If incest statutes articulate "a rational relation to a legitimate governmental objective" (*State v. Kaiser,* 844), child protection systems enact governmental rationality through the welfare provisions of the state. On one hand, laws against incest emphasize the legitimacy of the state's intervention into family and sexuality in order to protect them from irrational eroticism (which cannot be named). Both children's sexuality and adult sexual activity between legally recognized kin are regulated by laws against incest. On the other hand, emerging institutions of child welfare and child protective services seemed to extend this legal strategy to the domains of the social, without in any way resolving the linguistic paradoxes of rationality articulated in law. The state's alleged interest in such diverse objects as "health, safety, morals, or public welfare" (*State v. Kaiser,* 844) inaugurated what Foucault terms "the birth of a new art" of government, "or at any rate of a range of absolutely new tactics and techniques" ("Governmentality,"

100).[25] This takes us into the anatomopolitics of the body and the making of disciplinary childhood.[26] Child protection operates through a disciplinary injunction more akin to the sovereign utterance "thou shall." But this performative seemed to emerge from nowhere, a bureaucratic and managerial tactic locating "responsibility" within the family domain. The family became its own self-normalizing social unit, merely "governed" by the new professional classes populating juvenile courts, family services, child protective services, and the welfare system.

Incest and Disciplinary Childhood

This section departs from previous sections by using "and" rather than "as" in its title. The study of child welfare takes us on a brief excursion *away* from incest, only to demonstrate its haunting centrality to child welfare practices. In *The Will to Empower,* Barbara Cruikshank provides a pithy summary of welfare studies: "The practices of welfare do not lend themselves to analytical precision" (17). This comment is particularly resonant for studies of child welfare. The cluster of governmental and nongovernmental organizations managing child welfare and child protective services is immense, underfunded, and largely ineffective. Here, I will draw out an imprecise picture of the child welfare complex as it emerged through the early and mid-twentieth century, in order to clarify how the preterition of incest law is rationalized (and locally naturalized) in its disciplinary languages of harm. During the development of child welfare within the greater policy initiatives of the U.S. welfare state, the child—as we shall see—provides a key instrument for what Foucault calls the "'governmentalization' of the state" ("Governmentality," 103) as well as the disciplining of society. This shift occurred through the partnership of the state and a new twentieth-century extragovernmental discipline: sociology and its empirical study of social problems. The measurement and statistical calculability of childhood provided one key mode for the arrangement of norms and the distributions of social welfare around and through the governance of those norms. This ever changing calculus was then used to equate "public welfare" with "public safety," linking childhood normalization with the biopolitical security aims of the state. In this era the child becomes, in ways still somewhat baffling and resistant to synthetic analysis, a key to national security.

The "modernization" of incest was realized only in its nationalization, or, in this case, its federalization of child protection and family responsibility. This nationalization came through the production of "harm" as a standard of care, intervention, and prevention. If Fordist production and Keynesian economics marked mid-century efforts to federalize the nation, child welfare and family responsibility reveal its local coordinates—the social as a domestic national enterprise. Building on Jacques Donzelot's *The Policing of Families*, Cruikshank's study of welfare regimes argues that the "social" developed out of nineteenth-century and early twentieth-century reform strategies: "The social emerged as (1) an object of scientific knowledge (statistics, surveys, the census, and political economy), (2) a set of techniques for indirectly intervening in the lives of the dispossessed (social work, social service, social welfare, economy), and (3) the object of reform movements" (6). The production of the social transformed the sovereign fiction of politics, elaborating a new managerial tactic joining the governmentalized state and its disciplinary institutions. As Cruikshank goes on to explain, "Once the social became the object of reform, agitation, and science, the political lost its spatial association with sovereign power and the state" (7). Seeming to echo Foucault, this governmentalization of the state wrested the political from its sovereign state moorings. The determination of "politics" now emerged from multiple zones, including the social science studies that secured the social as the primary domain of welfare governmentality.

This change in the spatialization of politics depended, at least in part, on producing new spatial relations of power described as "parental rights." The institutionalization of child protection services articulated a series of legal relations between parent and state through the body of the child. This was not the end of classical structure in political economic thought. Rather, new formations created new centers of power and lines of authority. The parent-child relation provided a key articulation for these orthogonal structures, allowing more abstract legal language to be localized in the management of family health. This occurred primarily through the language of harm. If incest law created multiple links between public welfare and sexual regulation, child welfare constituted a unified concept that was generalizable (if equally vague). According to Cruikshank, harm prevention largely provided the units of evaluation, measurement, and quantification of social welfare policy. Moving away from the sovereign ideology of a right to punish, mid-century welfare governmentality focused on the strategy of harm prevention. Harm localized legal forms within the family and provided an increasingly race-neutral rhetoric to evaluate and organize social life. This process constrained the possibilities of social forms emerging in opposition to the legal forms of the state (first, using class rather than race rhetoric and then, ultimately developing rhetorics of sex that "appeared" race- and class-neutral). This was largely achieved by representing governmental tactics as protective responses to harmful family relations. The social became determined by these familial relations, constrained by the legal forms of appropriate parent-child emotional and physical duties of care subsequently realized in the social study of family.

The governmentalization of harm protection took place across three major periods of what Hamilton Cravens, in his essay "Child Saving in Modern America," calls "organized child saving" (4).[27] Cravens defines this project as "institutionalized concern for children as members of, and participants in, the social order, regardless of personal relationships of one sort or another" (4). Following general periodization in child welfare scholarship, Cravens breaks U.S. child saving behavior into three distinct eras, each articulating the moral, social, and political status of children in different ways. Cravens argues that "organized child saving" has strong roots in the Progressive era (1870s–1920s), the first era to institutionalize social concern that children needed to be properly trained as future citizens. While linkages between state interests and children as future citizens had been central to a broad range of regulatory reforms prior to the twentieth century, a consistent discourse relating child welfare to the interests of a bureaucratic state was first articulated in Progressive-era reform.[28] Progressive-era child saving consistently linked the overall social and familial conditions of children's lives to public health and welfare, focused in particular on the improvement of populations perceived as deviant (primarily new immigrants and the urban poor). Progressives also sought to strengthen the state's right to save children (as future citizens) from perceived family maltreatment. In their book *Helping Children*, Murray Levine and Adeline Levine point to this era's "shift in public attitudes toward the rights of government vis à vis the rights of parent" (211), articulated through a series of legal rulings that eventually emphasized the state's *parens patriae* rights to secure the welfare of the child.[29] By 1910, most states had passed laws enabling private societies to bring child maltreatment before the courts, but the circumstances of those interventions and the systems through which alternative care were mandated remained haphazard and governed by informal—often biased—procedures.[30]

The second era, from the 1920s through the 1950s, saw increasing investment in the normalization of childhood (Cravens, "Child Saving,"

12). Child-saving activity shifted from interventions targeting deviant populations—and emphasizing child maltreatment as endemic to those populations—to one focused on normalized childhood itself. The "normal child" became the center of concern in child protection discourse. New government agendas were created to establish childhood norms and legal standards of preventive intervention in family life. Child protective services were moved from the private to the public sector and centralized, and in the process their aim was shifted from intervention on the grounds of child maltreatment to providing support for family welfare.[31] According to Stephen Antler, the early child protection movement that had focused on "the investigation, prosecution, and punishment of those guilty of physical abuse" ("The Rediscovery of Child Abuse," 40) turned in its federal form into an anticruelty movement reliant on social work more than police activities. Protecting children from maltreatment was linked to a variety of policies, from child labor regulation to support for normative family roles and targeted focus on "neglect."[32] Foster care and adoption replaced institutional care as the response to child maltreatment interventions, with an emphasis on the importance of having a "normal" family life. As Marguerite Rosenthal and James A. Louis explain, in an essay titled "The Law's Evolving Role in Child Abuse and Neglect," public relief and welfare systems instituted local controls for recipients, including "'suitable home' criteria" (61) that included standards in sexual behavior, morality, and housekeeping. Interventions now targeted "'unfit' parents" (62) as guilty of child maltreatment, allowing for state-by-state interpretations of "fitness" based on unstated regional norms of racism and class discrimination. Following from the early articulation of states' rights, the "unfit parents" designation was used disproportionately against black families in the South and poor families across state lines (62).

The third era marked a turn toward and then ultimately away from broader social and economic approaches to childhood and into the ideology of child abuse (Cravens, "Child Saving," 20). In the 1960s, a series of social and political upheavals impacted the disciplinary approach to child saving. According to Levine and Levine, "in the 1960s, mental health professionals rediscovered poverty, child abuse, birth control, and abortion" (*Helping Children,* 179). Child welfare resurfaced as a primarily social and economic, rather than strictly familial, problem. Poverty, neglect, and unequal opportunity were reinterpreted as impediments to child welfare and dealt with through federally mandated programs.

Through the War on Poverty and Great Society programs, community mental health centers were established along with Medicare and Medicaid, supplemental security income, and Headstart.[33] But the 1960s, despite its apparent commitment to addressing the socioeconomic contexts of child welfare, was also the decade in which medical models were popularized as the rational tools for measuring and evaluating what came to be the exemplary figure for child maltreatment—physical violence against children. In 1962, Dr. Henry Kempe and his associates published an article on "battered child syndrome" that presented their findings of physical abuse in a Denver hospital. This medical "discovery" of physical violence against children became rapidly popularized not only as the key to child protection, but also increasingly as the means to combine child welfare and childhood normalization.

The 1962 discovery of child abuse reduced what had formerly been known as child maltreatment—which included a range of practices—to the synecdoche of physical violence. Harm outcomes were inferred from the physicality of the force used against children. The violence standard of childhood normalization rendered parental force corporeal, delineating neglect and other forms of status abuse from the legal limit of proper parental conduct—physical abuse. While states implemented mandatory reporting laws that would ultimately contribute to the present crisis in the provision of services, the publicity and call for universal state responsibility for child protection from *physical* violence made child abuse "a national issue" (Antler, "The Rediscovery of Child Abuse," 42).[34] Thus even as the 1960s concern with broader "social problems" affecting child welfare came to address a range of kinship and sexual norms, including problems posed by out-of-wedlock pregnancy, birth control, and abortion along with child abuse and neglect, these problems were increasingly seen as medical in etiology and in expression.

In the era spanning from the 1970s to the present, a new focus on child abuse took the goals of the previous eras—intervention into families on the basis of maltreatment, prevention as the aim of federal bureaucratization and normalization—and combined them into a discourse on childhood individualism that condensed social and economic relations into a rationalized, medical etiology of the "child at risk." Children became isolated and individualized risk-assessment cases, decoupled from social and familial context even as that context was used to determine risk factors. Child welfare services were dedicated not to ensuring the aim of overall child welfare, but rather to protecting children from isolated abuse. This practice maintained parental responsibility to provide basic needs while separating parental responsibility from socioeconomic contexts. According to Neil Cohen, in his article "Child Welfare History in the United States," child welfare services normalized what counted as "essentials" that parents usually provide and then set standards for state responsibility in the absence of parental provision. These norms excluded broader social provisions such as "health, nutritional, educational, and recreational services" that were considered separate from essentials required for parental childrearing (14).

The transition begun in the 1970s was not merely the outgrowth of changing rationales for child protection and public safety. This period has also been identified as the dawn of neoliberalism, the shift from mid-century welfare state mandates to new regimes of governmental regulation, security, and control. The retreat from economic subsidy for family discipline and normalization was partnered with growing commitments to policing and criminalization as a tactic of population control. This broader turn toward declaring social "war" as the logic of public welfare—from the war on poverty to the war on drugs—was partnered with a transformation in proposed governmental solutions.[35] The rapid growth of the prison-industrial complex and military-industrial complex occurred simultaneously with the transformation of child welfare into protection from parental child abuse and neglect. An active process of redefining and recrafting the meaning of "family" occurred simultaneously with this 1970s shift. Moving away from rhetorically racist articulations of hierarchical family difference, exemplified by the 1965 Moynihan report, Ashraf Rushdy argues that in the later 1970s "the discourse of the 'family' . . . assumed a form in which the intended racial referent was hidden in the coded transracial language of social science and public policy" (*Remembering Generations,* 13). This new discourse of family "appeared to be race-neutral but [was] read as racialist discourse" (13).

The 1970s witnessed a transition from programs targeting "social problems" to those targeting the child as a victim of a pathological family. The "disease model" of physical child abuse came to stand in for the range of issues previously articulated in child welfare and child protection discourse, producing an account of the pathological family behind the abnormal child (Antler, "The Rediscovery of Child Abuse," 47).[36] Statutes perpetuating what Leroy H. Pelton calls the "myth of classlessness" sought to protect children from the harm imposed by physical violence, even as the definitions and disciplinary criteria for evaluating and measuring such violence exhibited the very "preterition" Cahill describes in incest law.[37] Definitions of abuse were left deliberately vague to allow the greatest latitude of interpretation, although the express aim was to also make such definitions specific enough to limit discretionary abuse. While this approach reflected some early concerns with pathological social behavior, the privatized, medicalized, and individualized approach in the 1970s spawned a new social service industry consumed with "professional" knowledges of individual pathology.[38] Such a statutory aim resulted in an increased state role in the normalization of discipline, if not in the definition of proper family roles.

"Child abuse" then is in some ways the latest coinage in state vocabularies used to articulate norms of care and family role as well as norms of violence and discipline—in the latter case, norms of both legitimate state intervention and legitimate parental authority. This moral legitimation links state governance with the diffusion of disciplinary norms. Normalization, however, was achieved not through standardized norms of parental care but rather through the subordination of parental norms to the authority of state agencies. The vagueness of the statutes and the vagaries of cross-state implementation and institutionalization resulted not only in "considerable leeway for intrusions on family life" (Rosenthal and Louis, "The Law's Evolving Role," 67), as is commonly asserted, but more for the legitimacy of "intrusiveness" to structure the norms articulated through childhood harm. As Rosenthal and Louis state, "A more universal consequence of the legislation was to increase the scrutiny of individual behaviors by citizens and state agents" (68), a mode of surveillance that produced normalizing effects distinguishing the defining legislation of, for instance, incest and marriage law, from the "intrusive" legislation of child abuse law. While the "making and molding of child abuse" (as Ian Hacking calls it, in an article of this title) seemed merely to absorb dominant ideologies of child saving, it also delegitimated nondominant approaches to social justice and economic equity for children, including efforts to provide for and protect children from the state.

In place of these imminent social practices and other potential formations, institutions of child protection, funded by the federal government but often regulated locally in state and city bodies, produced their own baroque knowledge out of ill-funded, undertrained, and often mismanaged engagements with family life. Partnered with official social science knowledges and policy statements, the implementation of child protection was a mess. This binary of order and chaos is, I would like to suggest, part of the operation of power across these domains. Its impact is on the seeming isolation and naturalization of "family" as the proper arrangement of kinship structure, and the alienation of kinship structure from other social forces (such as economics, politics, or more specifically racial formations and gendered structures of access and power). According to Cruikshank, the social sciences masked the overtly racist and classist modalities of governmental biopolitics: "The ways poor people are governed very often have little to do with state power except when, for example, the national guard is brought in. More often, poor people are governed at the level of the social through case management, empowerment programs, parenting classes, and work training" (*The Will to Empower*, 40). Thus "social scientific knowledge is central to the government of the poor" (40) precisely because it provided new statistical and empirical tools to translate the racial mandates of "security" into the positive goals of public welfare.

Incest as Patriarchal Right

To examine the relation between incest discourse and its taboo as an orthogonal articulation for securitized governmentality, we move, also, into new disciplines: the uneasy alliance between psychology and sociology in the remaking of criminal justice. If "social scientific knowledge is central to the government of the poor," the supplement of psychological knowledge provided leverage for neoliberal transformations of the rationale for state policing. As we turn to the role of sexual abuse within broader child protection regimes, incest appears as a pivot for the transformation of welfare's isolation of the family from the social, to warfare's extension of the family to encompass the social entirely. So what happens to incest in these accounts of statutory regulation, on the one hand, and disciplinary normalization, on the other? As Mary McIntosh argues in her introduction to a 1988 special issue of *Feminist Review* titled "Family Secrets, Child Sexual Abuse," child sexual abuse does not fall squarely in the historical purview of child protection services, with its emphasis on state intervention in the home. According to McIntosh, "The concern with child sexual abuse lies, in a sense, at the confluence of two distinct historical streams, one of them concerned with cruelty to children, mainly within the home or the family, and the other concerned with sexual relations with children, mainly outside the family" (7). The first stream, concerned with cruelty to children within the home or the family, has historically shown little ability—and perhaps interest—in developing protocols and techniques to assess and intervene in familial child sexual abuse. The second stream, concerned with sexual relations with children outside the family, has shown the same lack of ability or interest in developing protocols and techniques to assess and intervene in familial child sexual abuse. These efforts have focused more on identifying and publicly stigmatizing non-normative sexual conduct on the part of adults and adolescents, using children as a ready instrument for "detecting" and disciplining deviant adult sexual behavior. As McIntosh goes on to remind her audience, "There is, of course, a very venerable *name* for this point of confluence—incest— but it is a name that has become almost empty of social content" (7).

How does incest provide a "venerable name" for the point of confluence between these two historical approaches, even as it is evacuated of what McIntosh aptly summarizes as "social content"? How do the theorizations and instrumentalization of the "social" described in the previous section evacuate incest of anything but rhetorical force? What kinds of force relations does this delineation of language—from unwritten code of laws to written preterition, from articulatory paradox to catachresis of harm—establish in the governmentalization of the state and the bureaucratization of the social? And how does the family conjoin biopower and neoliberal political rationality through the orthogonal articulation of incest? In order to grasp this process, we must return to the questions with which this chapter opened: how disciplines of knowledge shape incest's fungibility as a regulatory trope. Prior to the 1970s, studies of incest had tended to insist upon its low incidence and minimal impact. Studies that did discuss childhood sexual experience more generally tended to suggest it had neutral or perhaps positive outcomes, or that young children (particularly girls) desired sexual contact and therefore behaved in flirtatious or overtly seductive ways, bringing the experience upon themselves. Incestuous experience was considered more rare, but also more likely to be the instigation of the female child, whose oedipal desires guided her search for paternal love and affection.

Among the most famous studies of incestuous experience are K. Abraham's 1927 essay "The Experiencing of Sexual Traumas as a Form of Sexual Activity," L. Bender and A. Blau's 1937 study "The Reactions of Children to Sexual Relations with Adults," and L. Bender and A. E. Grugett's 1952 "Follow-up Report on Children Who Had Atypical Sexual Experience." Alfred Kinsey and his research group did report on childhood sexual experience, including incest, in their 1953 *Sexual Behavior in the Human Female,* but it was not really until S. Kirson Weinberg's landmark 1955 study, *Incest Behavior,* that a full-blown study of empirical incest appeared. Weinberg famously stated that there were less than two incest perpetrators per million people in the United States, a statistic widely cited until the early 1970s.[39] According to several studies on prosecution and juvenile courts, the centrality of Freudian explanations did indeed determine the interpretation of child sexual experience. But this determination did not necessarily predict legal outcomes; as Rachel Devlin points out in "Acting Out the Oedipal Wish," "Psychoanalytic and legal ideas were, if anything, somewhat at odds with one another on this question, a fact which implies that postwar society was conflicted about the issue of father-daughter incest, rather than simply bent on wholesale denial" (610). Reading case records and criminological studies alongside psychoanalytic case histories, Devlin suggests, along with Lynn Sacco and Beryl Satter, that the pre-1970s responses to allegations of incest were far more complex that these few oft-cited studies suggest.[40]

By the late 1970s, scholars strongly influenced by second-wave feminism had made significant entry into the domains of sociology and psychology. Fed by popular initiatives such as women's consciousness-raising groups and the movements toward public disclosure about formerly privatized experiences, feminist researchers who had entered the social sciences advocated for research on women's experiences. Several sociologists and psychologists worked in particular to change the statistical knowledges about incest as a measurable, and therefore empirically validated, experience. Feminist sociologists and psychologists such as Sandra Butler, Diana Russell, Florence Rush, and Judith Lewis Herman all argued that earlier statistical analyses of incest had been predicated on a disciplinary understanding of childhood that was complicit with patriarchal belief systems.[41] These researchers criticized earlier studies of incest for emphasizing its infrequency, its benign or even beneficial effects, or its manifestation of extreme family problems linked to class and racial pathologies. As Sandra Butler pointed out in her 1978 book *Conspiracy of Silence,* those cases of incestuous assault that *were* documented "were seen primarily in the hospitals and police stations of the inner cities across our nation. . . . Incestuous assault was seen as being endemic to seriously disrupted groups of people who display massive pathology in their interpersonal relationships" (9). The close-knit relationship between sociological research and the disciplinary institutions of the state had, Butler and others contended, biased research on incest to support dominant ideologies of family deviance and individual pathology.

Feminist researchers pointed out that the bulk of mainstream socio-logical data on incest weighted statistical accounts of incestuous assault in those families highly policed by the criminal justice and social service system. In her efforts to discredit this type of research on incest, Butler pointed out that these research protocols in effect participated in state efforts to criminalize "lower-class families" as the source of incestuous pathology. As Butler explains this union of sociology and criminology:

> Many studies that have focused on the lower-class families in our pop-ulation have highlighted the numbers on public assistance, the children within them born out of wedlock, the degree of drug and chemical dependency of the parents, the high incidence of wife-beating, violent behavior, child abuse and neglect, promiscuity and crowded living quar-ters. All of these behaviors were seen as corresponding to the incidence of incestuous abuse within these families and many as having precipi-tated the assault. (9–10)

Discriminatory practices of criminal reporting weighted statistical ac-counts of incestuous assault in families already likely to be highly policed by the criminal justice system. These statistics were then circulated as evidence that aberrant kinship was the cause of criminal incestuous behavior. Empirical research on incest had been complicit with the patri-archal bias of psychoanalytic and structural accounts of the incest taboo. These accounts, as Foucault pointed out, used the taboo against incest as the hallmark of civilized entry into the householding practices of the state-secured middle class. Actual practices of incest appeared in the atavistic and criminally racialized families of the lower classes. Such statistical research legitimated a disciplinary approach to the family in which state intervention into kinship was articulated as child protection against the danger of nonnormative domestic arrangements.

Early feminist research was dedicated to disproving such a discipli-nary bias toward the father's structural role as family sovereign, argu-ing that incest was not a symptom of the failure of a patriarchal law, but rather of its success. If prior research on incest upheld a structural account in which a strong paternal role in the family protected *against* the disruption of incest, feminist researchers argued precisely the oppo-site: "Turning the earlier sociological discussions on their head, there-fore, feminists argue that it is not the incest prohibition but, rather, the actual occurrence of incest which provides a key to a sociological under-standing of social structure and culture" (Vikki Bell, *Interrogating Incest*, 3). As Sandra Butler summarized her own findings:

The true range of families dealing with incestuous assault has little to do with class, race, economic status or social background. Were it possible to provide a more realistic profile of a typical family in which incestuous abuse occurs, it would more likely be a middle-class family composed of a husband, wife, and children living together in a nuclear situation. (11)

Feminist sociological and psychological research claimed to uncover a new empirical truth: that incest was a common occurrence. Even more controversially, this research argued that while incest took place across race and class configurations of kinship, its most "typical" and "realistic profile" was of the middle-class nuclear family. These feminist studies of incestuous abuse focused on demonstrating that sexual abuse was in fact a *gendered* norm of patriarchal child-rearing practices (a father-headed nuclear household). In Elizabeth Ward's 1984 summary of *Father-Daughter Rape*: "Most Daughters are being prepared, overtly or covertly, for stereotypical femininity. . . . Father-daughter rape is merely a phenomenon at one end of the spectrum of the means by which this construction is achieved" (196–97). These studies broke what many researchers referred to as a gendered "conspiracy of silence" connecting the structural theory of the incest taboo, sociological studies of incest, the social welfare policies of child services, and the preoccupations of statutory rape and incest law.

Many feminists saw these four domains as participating in a patriarchal conspiracy, in which women's voices were not heard and their ideas not respected in shaping the meaning of state protection and parental rights. Toni McNaron and Yarrow Morgan captured the most powerful claim made by these early initiatives when they stated: "There is not a taboo against incest; merely against speaking about it" (*Voices in the Night*, 15). Laws against incest and child protective service disciplines were considered complicit with the ongoing patriarchalism of the state-family relationship. It was paternal, not parental, rights that were protected by *parens patriae* doctrine. It was fathers, not daughters, who benefited from the separation of incest and rape laws. Together, incest law and child protective services created a loophole for the permitted use of female children in the home. In *Rocking the Cradle of Sexual Politics*, Louise Armstrong summarized this early analysis: "Even comparing the father-child relationship to that of master-servant would be inadequate, since the child had none of the rights of a servant. Within a total patriarchal structure, sexual use of children was permitted and presumed. Not only had children, like women, historically been chattel—male property—but there had always been a greedy interest in sex with children" (14–15). So long as they were filiated dependents of a legitimate, legally recognized patriarch, girl children were a form of "chattel" in the eyes of the state.

Second-wave feminist psychological and sociological analyses of incest returned it to the domain of political right (*droit*). Many of these feminist researchers were working in the same historical moment as Foucault when he delivered his lectures on biopower and political right in 1975–76. During this period they too queried psychoanalytic discourses of incest, and they too launched an analysis that took new axes of power as central to the workings of contemporary state and society. But their account focused primarily on gender to analyze force relations within the family and between family and state.[42] While not explicitly making recourse to Lacan, second-wave feminists tacitly reinforced the idea that modern U.S. society was governed by a "law of the father." But what Lacan viewed as symbolic, many second-wave feminists viewed as socially constructed and politically determined. Judith Herman echoes this idea in her 1981 book *Father-Daughter Incest,* in which she says, "The asymmetry in the observation of the incest taboo makes sense psychologically only in one particular kind of family: a father-dominated family, with a rigid sexual division of labor, in which mothers care for children of both sexes, and fathers do not" (54). The "secret" of incest was that it was the outcome of father-dominated families. If incest had been theorized as the "limit" to biopower, feminist researchers argued that the paradox of this limit appeared as sexism (*rather than* racism). Gendered force relations explained the discourse of the taboo as much as the practices it covered over. Feminist researchers broke "the silence" of this patriarchal conspiracy when they documented incest as a common form of child sexual abuse, a privilege accorded fathers within this legal and disciplinary system. The next step then was to use this research to intervene in the criminal justice and child-protective domains that served as gatekeepers for this regulatory silence. The "social content" of incest needed to be restored.

Incest as Child Sexual Abuse

Coming out of second-wave feminisms, a range of efforts was made to restore the social content of incest, including disciplinary and legal reform as well as more popular and cultural work. None remained completely faithful to the second-wave feminist analyses, but together they recoded incest in state law and child protection. State reform efforts took two major modes, both of which used the rhetorical figure of analogy to forge new connections between political right and gender. The first mode addressed state law using the analogy of rape; the second addressed the disciplinary institutions of child welfare using the analogy of child abuse. In the first mode, feminist advocates attempted to recode incest as analogous to rape in order to expand the meanings of sexual assault. In the late 1970s, feminists sought to reform the Model Penal Code statutes related to sexual offenses.[43] Their overall goals included rewriting the meaning of sexual assault to include sexual conduct (like incest) previously disqualified as rape. This required them to explain how incest (and other seemingly nonviolent offenses) were "like" rape, a violation of the person and a serious crime. Previously, incest had been treated as an isolated breach of proper alliance and normative conduct. Feminist reformers therefore had to recode incest, moving it from a marital or sexual prohibition to a criminal form of sexual violence. To return to Bienen's summary of incest law, "Placing the redefined crime within the rape reform statute, as a subcategory of the most serious sex offense, was a symbolic declaration that Incest was an abusive crime against the person deserving a harsh penalty not a statute regulating marriage" (1534). Recoding incest as a form of rape was intended to clarify the harm of the act as well as legitimate the overall reform effort. Assuming that child protection would be hard for most political representatives to oppose, feminist reformers recoded incest as child sexual abuse to lead the more general charge at overall rape law reform.[44]

Reformers used new medical terminology for child sexual abuse to replace the moral terminology of incest, seeking to make legal code sexually explicit rather than leave reform statutes vacillating in a logic of erotic preterition. Reform became a battle over the linguistic domain of the law. Feminist advocates "were talking about penises, anal intercourse, oral genital acts, breasts, vaginas, and sexual penetration. The male legislators were the ones who were embarrassed. This was a brilliant preemptive strike in the battle for control of the discourse" (Bienen, "Symposium," 1567). Childhood incest was to be shifted from a highly gendered discourse about feminine seduction and seductiveness into a gender-neutral discourse of harm to persons, always including examples of the sexual abuse of boys. This reform effort succeeded, Bienen suggests, in characterizing incest as "an assault upon the person, capable of being verified by case reports and systematic data collection and defined in precise medical diction. When this language was written into the statute, it was emblematic of the philosophical and doctrinal changes embodied in the redefinition of the offense" (1568). While this language was not always written into the statutes (as we shall see momentarily), the over-all aim of such reforms did succeed in redefining incest as a form of child sexual abuse. It also succeeded in explaining how child sexual abuse might be understood in terms of sexual assault, even when it did not meet the penetration or physical force standards often applied in adult rape cases. Feminist reformers helped to redefine sexual assault against children by creating a more specific taxonomy of acts, which might include both "oral/genital acts and acts defined by sexual contact or touching" (Bienen, "Symposium," 1501). This language of "graded offenses" was intended to broaden the definition of childhood sexual abuse, assist with preventative intervention, and keep judges from dismissing all charges in plea bargain situations.

The second effort articulated incest as analogous to physical child abuse. Over the course of the 1970s, psychiatric and psychotherapeutic clinicians, social workers and child protective services personnel, and federal and state criminal justice officials began to collaborate on new protocols for the identification and response to child sexual abuse. Professionals in the mental health and child protection fields developed an interest in child sexual abuse as a subset of child abuse over the course of the 1970s, triggered by client disclosure, public mobilization of adult survivors, and second-wave feminist support for tackling the issue (Corwin, "An Interview with Roland Summit"). In 1978, a Washington, D.C., consultation conference was gathered by Kee MacFarlane of the National Center on Child Abuse and Neglect, drawing together people from across the helping and policing professions who shared an interest in child protection. The majority of the helping professionals gathered had learned about child sexual abuse through exposure to incest, but the incest paradigm was also challenged by participants working with street youth and male survivors. This conference helped broaden the existing incest analysis to include nonfamilial forms of child sexual abuse and exploitation, including the pedophiliac abuse of boys and the exploitation of children by strangers and through commercial trafficking. The child abuse analogy located incest within the domain of child protective services, even as it extended its reach to a broader nonfamilial social domain.

This landmark conference also marked a shift in the methodology of child sexual abuse, from a clinical paradigm to a criminal one. As Roland

Summit, author of "The Child Sexual Abuse Accommodation Syndrome" and a conference attendee, notes: "The people who were making gains in this field were people outside of psychiatry and often outside of the mental health professions altogether. The cops and the vice officers knew more about this field than we did, and we needed to learn from one another" (in Corwin, "Interview," 7).[45] This produced a tension between those "who saw child sexual abuse as a pure analog of stranger rape" (Summit, in Corwin, "Interview," 21) and those who wanted to situate it within the domain of traditional child welfare. The question was, in other words, whether child sexual abuse would be treated as a sex crime or as a form of child abuse, whether it would be criminalized or relegated to the disciplines attached to child protective services and family courts. "We began to split on the relative emphasis of prosecution at about that time" (in Corwin, "Interview," 9), Summit explains, because of the dilemmas of identification and assessment already befuddling child abuse agencies and the problems posed by increasing criminalization without increasing ability to identify and respond to this specific form of abuse. Police officers and social workers became partners in the detection and prosecution of child sexual abuse, leading to an array of problems with differential ideas of evidence, verifiability, and impact. It also lent itself to the growing police function of child protective services in general. Partnered increasingly with the Immigration and Naturalization Service, criminal justice, and other forms of state policing and penalization, the child protective service was recoded as an arm of the security apparatus more than a helping hand, even if it had often been an empty one.

The problem with both these modes of reform was the constraint of analogical legal thinking. Stephen Best calls this law's "agency of form," arguing that "analogy can of itself function as a kind of causality" (*The Fugitive's Properties*, 24). Thus analogy as "a legal metaphor provides both a speculative possibility [tenor] and a specific embodiment, or limitation on the breadth of possibilities [vehicle])" (24). Figuring child sexual abuse as analogous to rape as well as to child abuse extended the possibilities as well as embodied the limits of this recoding. As Best explains the constraint imposed by analogical legal forms: "Causation inheres within form when a culture finds within it space to constrain expectations, to organize uses, to channel meaningful purposes" (25).[46] One of the more dramatic limitations, indeed, was its practice of linguistic and discursive embodiment. Feminist legal reformers analogized various forms of sexual misconduct as rape, attempting to delegitimate homophobic persecutions and paternal exploitation in the same statutes. Age and consent were to determine legitimate sexual conduct, while gender and sexual orientation were to be barred from legal determinations. Disciplinary reformers to the child protection systems analogized various forms of sexual contact with children as incest, making all forms of child sexual abuse the domain of child protective services. This provided a new articulation of sex that worked orthogonally to family: incest as child sexual abuse. This manifested in several ways. As Bienen points out, legal reforms included three main recodings: gender neutrality, new age limits, and redefinition of sexual conduct ("Symposium," 1508). The age limits attempted to universalize a gender-neutral "age of consent," applied equally to boys and girls.[47] This was intended to remove "statutory rape" as a gender-biased protection of adolescent girls from influences outside the family and level prosecution bias and the sexist interrogation of women and girls' sexual history. What it also allowed, however, was the alleged protection of "boys from homosexual assaults by adults" (1513). Partial and uneven incorporation of feminist reform initiatives, coupled with diverse interpretations of their intent, lead to greater protection for some status groups against particular offenses while further jeopardizing or isolating others. And these conditions changed from state to state and context to context, as official legal reform was not always matched by investigative and prosecutorial reform. The result was an increase in discourses, taxonomies, and penalties related to sexual conduct with children without any consistent application or evaluation of their effects. One uniform response focused on the clarification of the sexual status of the "child," which grafted rape law reform onto child abuse codes. This required elaboration of the peculiarity of sexual harm for children as a status group, leading to an increased focus on the unique sexual susceptibilities of children *in general* (as an essential trait of the category "child"). As the California Supreme Court explained a state statute "prohibiting lewd and lascivious acts with children," the law "recognizes that children are uniquely susceptible to such abuse as a result of their dependence on adults, smaller size, and relative naïveté. The statute also assumes that young victims suffer profound harm whenever they are perceived and used as objects of sexual desire" (*People v. Martinez* 1995).[48]

Reformed laws often rely on studies of psychological harm to uphold their claim that children must remain a protected class of sexual minors, often equating physical size, sociopolitical dependence, and cognitive development. But despite this seeming uniformity, child sexual abuse laws vary widely in their definition and application of age differentials, levels of harm, and prohibited conduct. According to Charles A. Phipps, writing in "Children, Adults, Sex and the Criminal Law," across statutes three core components are typically used to define childhood sexual abuse: conduct, mental state, and age of the victim (41–42). The declaration "children cannot consent to sex" has a variety of meanings depending upon the conduct described by the word "sex"—penetration offenses often carry stricter punishments and age guidelines than contact offenses or the vague offense "indecent liberties." It is in fact often the conduct that determines the meaning of the word "child," although some states deliberately leave conduct definitions nebulously worded in order to ensure that children are protected from all forms of "offensive" contact. Paradoxically, the language of "graded offenses" can allow more judicial discretion in finding a variety of acts "indecent" that may or may not be legible as explicitly "sexual" in nature. As a Massachusetts appellate court explained in defense of its "indecent assault and battery statute": "A touching is indecent when, judged by the normative standard of societal mores, it is violative of social and behavioral expectations in a manner which is fundamentally offensive to contemporary moral values and which the common sense of society would regard as immodest, immoral, and improper" (*Commonwealth v. Lavigne* 1997).[49] Statutes regulating sexual contact with children produce new forms of erotic preterition, now explicitly focused on the normative forms of childhood sexuality.

While the results of child sexual abuse statutes are nearly impossible to discern, some broad brushstrokes can trace the general contours of the contemporary scene. According to many critics, new child sexual abuse legislation and case law actually end up replicating the split between incest (sexual contact with family members or intimate caregivers) and stranger danger (sexual contact with anyone outside the family circle). These laws claim to universalize standards for sexual contact with children, creating a facially neutral approach to the sexual abuse of all children as children (rather than as daughters, sons, students, innocents, delinquents, and so on). But by placing the definition of sexual normalization squarely within the child itself, a new array of social, political, economic, and disciplinary relations is born. On one hand, such statutes have the potential to render almost all activity between adults and children potentially sexual, violative, and harmful. This leaves detection, verification, and prosecution at the discretion of various state and social actors. As a result, even facially neutral legislation has been perceived as targeting "sexual relations with children, mainly outside the family" (McIntosh, "Introduction to an Issue," 7), with special emphasis on what David Evans, in *Sexual Citizenship,* calls the focus on "male masculine sexuality as the main threat not only to children, but also to parental, in effect paternal, authority" (214). By policing sexual relations between children and nonfamilial adults, many applications of such laws actually legitimate parental (perhaps paternal) rule.

On the other hand, these statutes make it difficult to detect, verify, and prosecute sexual acts within the domestic household or family unit. So-called incest cases are notoriously difficult to detect and verify in preadolescent children, whose total subordination to adult caretakers blocks detection and whose testimony after detection is considered highly unreliable and unverifiable. In addition, the pedagogical authority of the parent over the child means physical force is not necessary to coerce "willing" behavior, since the body of the child is defined by its dependence on parental affection and care. As Phipps once again points out, in the case of morally legitimate parental care it becomes impossible to distinguish between a parent's digital penetration of a daughter with "sexual intent" and one legitimated as "teaching her proper hygiene or applying medication" (53). The normalcy of the parent-child relation becomes the yardstick for measuring potentially inappropriate sexual contact. A child can report parental sexual abuse, of course, but child reporting is often interpreted as age-appropriate acting out against parental authority or the effect of one parent's vindictive influence during strife or divorce. Cases of continuous incestuous abuse are therefore more likely to surface during adolescence. But the seeming complicity of female adolescents with the sexual demands of parents or guardians has often made prosecution more vexed. These cases fall into a discretionary loophole, somehow not discernible as rape, statutory rape, child sexual abuse, or incest.[50] Legislation that bars inquiry into sexual history, motivated by feminist law reform, can paradoxically silence juvenile victims whose sexual history would contextualize non-resistance or active compliance in a history of childhood abuse (Bienen, "Symposium," 1573).

As a result of the grafting of incest law and child sexual abuse reform, the sexual violability of the child becomes an articulatory paradox of political right. Sexual harm is defined as outside the domain of parental relations with children, even as incest is nominally prohibited to structure legitimate forms of kinship. This nominal prohibition—granted the new force of law—is part of a broader recoding of what Best calls the agency of form (*The Fugitive's Properties*, 24), or the potential transformation through legal analogy. It delimits, even as it promises to extend, the force of law in the affairs of family life. But now it is not exactly the family, but rather the entire apparatus of the social, that is being reformed through the discourse of incest. The status category "child" becomes an overdetermination of new tactics that make children simultaneously violable and inviolable, outside the interpretive acts of subjective agency but central to their interpretation and rule by others. The child becomes an overdetermination of new tactics and technologies of power—like Lacan's child of *méconnaissance* or the protected child of welfare discipline, the sexually vulnerable child becomes an instrument of new relations of power. In this recoding, the agency of legal form reconstitutes the dismantled incest taboo as a tactic of national security, with children as the special object and instrument of new tactics of governmentality and state-directed racism (incorporating new logics of the racialized criminal, including the serial pedophile or sex predator). The child is reassembled as the site around which legitimate discourses of security are produced for the national safety. This becomes then the key outcome of the recoding of incest as child sexual abuse in legal forms: "That same argument said that men like that ought to be put in prison, but men like that aren't going to go to prison unless a child can testify" (Summit, in Corwin, "Interview," 21). Incest provided the grounds for new governmental rationality with the child as its instrument. While it was prohibited in new and ever more complex ways, nowhere was it empirically verifiable.

An amazing sleight of hand had been accomplished.

Mistaking the Harm of Incest

I keep a small pile of found items on my upper bookshelf, mostly debris from the maelstrom of mid-twentieth-century U.S. governmentality, among them a stack of books related to my subject matter: *Oedipus: Myth and Complex*, by Patrick Mullahy (1948); *Children in Focus: Their Health and Activity*, from the American Association for Health, Physical Education and Recreation (1954); *The Police and the Underprotected Child*, by C. J. Flammang (1970); and *The "New" Police*, by J. F. Elliott (1973). Piled one on top of the other, they now seem to physicalize the orthogonal articulation of incest I have traced in this chapter. I began by arguing that Oedipus turned myth into complex through Freud's universalization of the incest taboo. In his attempt to legitimate psychoanalysis as the new science of modern subjection, Freud insistently reformed the origin and grounds of regulation to assure sexual normalization. Foucault's rejoinder to this project insisted that sexual normalization was in fact the grounds of the incest taboo; the origin was itself a myth, a ruse of new forms of biopower and racial governmentality. And yet this myth is written into and across the legal and disciplinary forms of incest prohibition and child protection. That is, I suggested in my reading of the linguistic preterition of incest law, very much the force of its power. But the myth of incest, or even its Oedipus complex, does not fully explain what happened in the late twentieth century when "women said incest," as Louise Armstrong puts it. This requires a new analytic insight: that the empirical affirmation of incest as a practice of child sexual abuse paradoxically reinforced its mystifying power within legal forms. Or, I should say, this empirical turn, coupled with new formations of emergent neoliberal governmentality, recoded and reproduced incest as an "orthogonal articulation" for contemporary biopower.

Incest provided an odd, and for many feminist activists quite unexpected, resource for the transformations of governmentality in the later twentieth-century United States. Foucault theorizes governmentality as a "form of power, which has as its target population, as its principal form of knowledge political economy, and as its essential technical means apparatuses of security" ("Governmentality," 102). What interests me here is not the role of incest in discourses of political economy—nil—but rather the awkward fit between popularized discourses of psychology and the specific political economies of neoliberalism. By establishing new analogies linking sexuality, family, and state, incest recoded the "social" as the last safeguard of national security. The figures that emerged from this recoding criminalized new populations through the discourse of child sexual abuse, as we see in Roberta M. Berns's 2001 textbook *Child, Family, School, Community*, subtitled *Socialization and Support*: "A high percentage of drug users, juvenile runaways, and prostitutes have been sexually abused as children" (173). Child sexual abuse becomes a resource for new social etiologies of populations "at risk," even as the threat of the serial pedophile legitimates ever increasing monies for police powers and incarceration. As the late 1970s turned to 1980s, these reformations recoded the law as the benevolent arm of the state, even as that reach increasingly extended surveillance and policing rather than safeguarding and protection.

This returns me to the problem of "terms of analysis" with which I opened. But now my problem is redoubled: after second-wave feminism, how to maintain a commitment to gendered analyses of power, or gender as a relation of force, without using gender as the neoliberal index of liberation? How can we read incest as articulation without giving in to its social formalization? Here I would concur with Raymond Williams that "it is the reduction of the social to fixed forms that remains the basic error" — "the mistake, as so often, is in taking terms of analysis as terms of substance" (*Marxism and Literature*, 129). But even the nuanced theories of articulation found in Williams and Hall are not entirely attuned to the fungibility of incest, with its habits of dissemblance and resemblance in the face of more seemingly powerful and generalizable analytics. Searching for an analytic better attuned to the peculiar illegibility (or multilegibility) of incest, the next chapter explores the "mistakes" of 1990s incest discourse. In particular, the chapter reads popular debates about recovered and false memory—the "memory wars"—in relation to neoliberal discourses of risk and liability. There I happily consider the popular claim that women's incest memories are a form of mistake. But chapter 2 reads mistake as both error and theft, a form of articulation that "determines otherwise" the fantasy form of familial memory. Looking at Freud's alleged mistake in the seduction hypothesis alongside the much decried mistakes of recovered memory, I will explore the dilemma of daughterly agency within neoliberal rationalities—the mistake of her wayward fantasies. Whether, in the course of the decade's events, she proves to be mistaken or not will have to await the deliberations of that chapter.

Two

Legal Fantasies: Populist Trauma and the Theater of Memory

It is precisely the sense of language as an *indissoluble* element of human self-creation that gives any acceptable meaning to its description as "constitutive." To make it *precede* all other connected activities is to claim something quite different.

—RAYMOND WILLIAMS, *Marxism and Literature*

Language shows clearly that memory is not an instrument for exploring the past but its theater.

—WALTER BENJAMIN, "A Berlin Chronicle"

If chapter 1 explored the modernization of incest, chapter 2 explores what some might call its "postmodernization." In the late 1980s and 1990s, incest became a dominant trope for a national culture in crisis, without its moorings in cold war security rubrics or the rationalities of welfare statism. While neoliberal economic transformation had been under way since the 1970s, its cultural and political transformations of U.S. nationalism only fully emerged in the aftermath of the three-worlds system. Looking at the role of incest in these transformations, this chapter asks: How can 1990s incest be read as part of new technologies of representation under neoliberal governmentality, specifically as it is refracted through the United States? How does neoliberalism set the scene for the "memory wars" over traumatic recall and testimonial self-representation? Answering these questions will take us through the looking glass of the popular media, the therapist's office, and the courtroom. What will be produced across these sites is a spectacle, from Freud's early departure from state law to his contemporary return in the court of popular judgment. From Freud to federalism and back again, this chapter charts the wake of the 1990s "witch hunt" to manage American temporalities.

In 1993, the November 29 cover of *Time* magazine asked the question: "Is Freud Dead?" Paralleling Nietzsche's famous declarative, this interrogative asked the reading public to meditate on the end of modernity's great theories. According to Paul Gray's cover story, "The Assault on Freud," Freud was among the major modern theorists of "the world's vicissitudes" (47), providing "this troubled century's dominant model for thinking and talking about human behavior" (47). But like God before him, Freud now appeared subject to doubt. A new skepticism emerged as the twentieth century ended, a skepticism arising from what Gray describes as "a coincidence of developments" (47): the rise of pharmaceutical treatment, Clinton-era health-care reform proposals and their predicted insurance impact, and the phenomenon of repressed memory syndrome. These three developments raised doubt not only for psychoanalytic practitioners and their elite clients, but also for a general public seeking explanations of their status in a new world order. As Gray explains these popular fin-de-siècle anxieties: "The collapse of Marxism, the other grand unified theory that shaped and rattled the 20th century, is unleashing monsters. What inner horrors or fresh dreams might arise should the complex Freudian monument topple as well?" (47). It was the end of the cold war, the end of ideological conflict, and the end of Marxism. Perhaps Freud's time had come as well.

Newsweek, in its March 27, 2006, issue, took up the thread of *Time*'s inquiry, but with a significant difference. In "Freud in Our Midst," Jerry Adler (writing with Anne Underwood) repeated the question, but only in order to challenge its tacit finality: "Is Freud still dead? And if not, what is keeping him alive?" (44). The answer focused once again on the so-called postideological moment of the early 1990s. The "death" of Freud was announced during neoliberalism's seemingly unchecked ascendancy, when the promise of technological mastery, increasingly speculative financial capital, and regulatory panaceas such as the Violence Against Women Act (VAWA 1994), the Personal Responsibility and Work Opportunity Reconciliation Act (Welfare Reform 1994) and the Immigration Reform and Control Act (1996) signaled a laissez-faire national individualism tapped into the free play of "open" markets.[1] In this 1990s, Freudian hermeneutics seemed relics of an earlier era of social and psychological struggle. The zenith of U.S. world power relied instead on the strength of psychological empiricism, the power of measurable and marketable goods, and new technologies of pharmaceutical self-mastery. Situating the *Time* article in its historical context, Adler writes: "It is no accident . . . that Freud's reputation reached a low point in the early 1990s, which was not only the height of the recovered-memory hysteria, but also of the post-cold-war optimism that made a best seller of Francis Fukuyama's book 'The End of History'" (49).[2] This chapter explores the tacit connections between what Adler calls "recovered-memory hysteria" and "post-cold-war optimism," or between the sociohistorical struggle of the memory wars and the neoliberal ascendancy of the Clinton years. According to the Adler article, the 1990s were a peculiar historical moment, one in which the transition from cold war to infinite war on terror was marked by a temporary optimism for U.S. supremacy and a disdain for the ideological excesses of the last era's theories. If Marxism was dead, "recovered-memory hysteria" clearly signaled a need to terminate Freud's legacy as well. In this historical account, the recovered memory movement was primarily a regrettable, but perhaps necessary, mistake, one that enabled society at large to repudiate the worst of Freudian-tainted hermeneutics and embrace nascent models of medically diagnosable and pharmaceutically treatable well-being. Once the memory wars had been conclusively fought and won, Freud's ghostly remains could be reformed to supplement neoliberal rationality and soothe the anxieties of life in the new security state. Unlike Marx and Darwin, Adler's article implies that Freud is still an important and necessary supplement to twenty-first-century neoliberalism. Freud lives on in the popular imagination not as an intellectual scientist, but as a specter almost synonymous with, yet a panacea to, the security apparatus of U.S. late capitalism.

Against this particular reading of the memory wars as a historical juncture between consumer and militarized neoliberalism, I would like to read the memory wars as an alternative account of 1990s transformations. In 1994, Fred Crews coined the term "memory wars" to describe the popular and legal debates over the legitimacy of women's claims to have "recovered" memories of childhood sexual abuse. Crews's claim, like claims by Elizabeth Loftus, Richard Ofsche, and Ethan Watters, was that overzealous therapists and primarily nonprofessional self-help cultures were inducing women's "false memories" of sexual abuse.[3] The memory wars marked a break with retroaction, a refusal of the past-looking glance of memory and a turn to future-oriented risk management. They also participated in a new mode of national familialism. The memory wars were part of a broader regulatory and popular recoding of family in relation to the national interest. The 1990s acts alluded to above transformed the governance of family without taking the family as its explicit point of intervention. Together these acts created a tighter network of security and enforcement through households, a network in which the public risk of sexual abuse played a key role.[4] This 1990s turn departs from the ideas of the last chapter—the modernization of incest through the social and governmental management of harm—to remap familialism as an ideology of risk.

This chapter looks at the 1990s memory wars as the theater of power-in-transition, in particular as the theater for ideological and social struggle over the relation between family and state. The memory wars were only one small part of this broader transformation, and I do not mean to use incest to explain the broader rationales and effects of these changes. Rather, I will use the memory wars to clarify how public debates about recovered and false memory participated in the reconstruction of popular culture as a tactic of neoliberal governance. To make this argument, I take up what Raymond Williams calls "the stress on language as activity" (*Marxism and Literature,* 31). Williams's materialist approach to language dovetails with Walter Benjamin's discussion of the theater of memory, in which the performative qualities of language also constitute the enigma of performance itself. For my argument the "language" of memory is always already its theater, a performance that places "emphasis on consciousness as inseparable from conscious existence, and then on conscious existence as inseparable from material social processes" (as Williams puts it, in *Marxism and Literature,* 59). I will use this approach to ask the following questions: How are the "material social processes" of memory articulated in this historical moment? What is the role of "recovered memories" of father-daughter incest in shaping these processes? To address these questions, I argue that certain ideologies of trauma and new technologies of the security state go hand in hand, joined by those Freudian universalities now particularized as an American traffic in risky memory.

The Universal Particular, or The Emergence of Incest Survivorship

This statement by "Survivors of Child Sexual Abuse," read at the first International Conference on Incest and Related Problems, Irchel University, Zurich (August 10–12, 1988), captures much of what was exciting as well as debilitating about early experience-based activism:

> Incest is not a THEORY—it is FACTS
> DON'T give us pills—give us alternatives
> Punish the CRIMINAL—NOT the victim

DON'T tell us what to do—GIVE US THE MONEY TO DO IT
Whilst the victim needs a witness—INCEST REMAINS LEGAL
Make homes SAFE—REMOVE THE ABUSER
STOP Incest—START telling the TRUTH
Blaming MOTHERS is too easy—BLAME THE ABUSER
Incest is a Life Sentence for US—It should be FOR THEM
Rape a Child—YOU RAPE YOUR FUTURE. (3)

The incest survivor movement, as it is sometimes called, emerged alongside other women's movements of the 1970s.[5] While sexual abuse experiences were documented prior to the 1970s, an identity and a political
platform were only consolidated in the context of other identity political agendas. Early consciousness-raising and writing groups surfaced a
range of experiences, from gendered labor exploitation to routine sexual
violence. Women who told stories of childhood sexual abuse in the home
found they were not alone, and the experience rapidly became a symbol
of women's plight in "patriarchal society." Incest survivorship emerged
as part of broader feminist efforts to politicize the personal, to locate
political agency in the everyday experiences of women. Incest survivorship in fact exemplified this effort, taking the most "personal" and secret
experience and making it the rationale for political mobilization. The
title of a 1983 conference, "Pulling Together II: Surviving and Stopping
Incest," clarified this rationale, linking collective mobilization to stop
incest with the ongoing experience of "surviving" it.[6]

While no real collective platform ever emerged, within the context
of second-wave feminist movements of the 1970s and 1980s efforts were
made to organize survivors and seek changes to the legal system or raise
public consciousness. Public "speak-outs" and artistic projects aimed at
ending "secrecy," raising public awareness of the harm of incest, and
improving access to mental health and support services for survivors.
"Telling the secret" is perhaps the most common euphemism-turned-
strategic-speech in survivor activism. As Linda Alcoff and Laura Gray
remark in their article "Survivor Discourse," "This strategic metaphor of
'breaking the silence' is virtually ubiquitous throughout the movement:
survivor demonstrations are called 'speak outs,' the name of the largest
national network of survivors of childhood sexual abuse is VOICES, and the
metaphor figures prominently in book titles such as *I Never Told Anyone,
Voices in the Night, Speaking Out, Fighting Back,* and *No More Secrets*"
(261).[7] "Telling" is a significant trope in survivor self-representation—it
is, in fact, *the* trope of survivor self-representation. Speaking out about

incest became political empowerment for its survivors and purported to debunk the myth of the taboo and testify to the real social content of gendered violence.

Print culture seemed at first to be the key to social actualization for survivor politics. Publication, first through small feminist and lesbian presses (e.g., *Voices in the Night,* Cleis Press, 1978) and subsequently through major mainstream publishers (e.g., *The Courage to Heal,* HarperCollins, 1988), promised the publicity that speak-outs sought. Early autobiographic and novelistic treatments of intimate child sexual abuse such as Maya Angelou's 1970 *I Know Why the Caged Bird Sings,* Toni Morrison's 1970 *The Bluest Eye,* and Alice Walker's 1981 *The Color Purple* all retroactively seemed of a piece with emergent survivor discourse of the 1980s. More explicitly survivor-identified volumes such as Louise Armstrong's 1978 anthology *Kiss Daddy Goodnight,* Katherine Brady's 1979 *Father's Days,* Charlotte Vale Allen's 1980 *Daddy's Girl,* and Michelle Morris's 1982 *If I Should Die before I Wake* solidified the sense of a structure of feeling emerging into popular culture.[8] The tension between these two bodies of texts has often been overlooked, however, in the effort to consolidate (and, for some, dismiss) the emergence of a singular "voice" of survivorship. The first set of texts, all authored by African American women, explicitly focus on the racial formations that structure family life. Often eschewing dominant ideologies of public and private spheres, these texts interrogate the use of race and racial hierarchies to devalue black female children in ways that subject them to increased sexual vulnerability. In contrast, the second set of texts, all authored by white American and Canadian women, tend to focus on the dynamics of privacy and domesticity shaping white middle-class family life. These texts produce a more limited scene of family violence, isolating sexual vulnerability in the home and minimizing the broader social relations and racial formations that produce domestic privacy.

The semantic figures emergent across these 1970s and early 1980s texts were subsequently consolidated into a unified "voice" of incest survivorship. In a chapter ("It's about Patriarchal Power") in their book *Telling Incest,* Janice Doane and Devon Hodges point out that African American women's incest fiction provided at least a partial origin for this voice, which then retreated from their broader antiracist critiques to articulate a normative "multicultural" incest narrative. These texts were cited as the foundation of a new recovery or survivor genre, even as their aesthetic politics were reduced, misdiagnosed, or ignored. The new recovery or survivor genre tended to replicate the analyses, tropes, and plot points of white middle-class narratives, even as it claimed a new multicultural representativeness.[9] This multicultural incest paradigm is exemplified by *The Courage to Heal* (1985) and *I Never Told Anyone* (1991), both edited by Ellen Bass (the first coedited with Laura Davis, the second with Louise Thornton). *The Courage to Heal,* sometimes called the incest "bible" (Haaken, *Pillar of Salt,* 180) or "the incest book for all people" (Doane and Hodges, *Telling Incest,* 68), boasts a broad cultural range of anecdotes, sprinkled throughout the self-help projects of the main text and offered again at the end in a series of first-person narratives. A careful representativeness became the hallmark of survivor discourse in the mid- to late 1980s, an effort to demonstrate the universality of incest and child sexual abuse without, fundamentally, changing its script. A certain uniformity came to define the recovery or survivor genre, despite the diversity of its cultural, racial, and class representatives.

By the late 1980s, "survivors of child sexual abuse" had certainly found an audience. To cite Louise Armstrong once again: "However little the social response to the issue of incest improved anything for children and women, it held astonishing promise as spectacle" (*Rocking the Cradle,* 80). An Orwellian 1984 witnessed a *Life* magazine article titled "The Cruelest Crime, Sexual Abuse of Children" (McCall) and *Newsweek*'s "Sexual Abuse: The Growing Outcry over Child Molesting" (Watson), while in the same year "Something about Amelia" became the first television movie about paternal incest to include the point of view of the daughter.[10] But Armstrong's comment is also instructive: "social response" in the 1980s was closer to reader response than social activism. Audiences were developed, who developed a taste for incest and child sexual abuse and seemed unsparing in their attention to the "spectacle" of self-disclosure and intrafamilial confrontation. But with mass audience came a mass loss of control over the institutions and domains of interpretation. The public telling of incest became part of what Guy Debord describes as "the society of the spectacle" (in his book of that title), in which "the basically tautological character of the spectacle flows from the simple fact that its means are simultaneously its ends. It is the sun which never sets over the empire of modern passivity."[11] Telling, with its overtones of both reporting to and reporting on, had become linguistic figure without any force: a present participle used as a gerund. It went nowhere. Like Debord's spectacle, it existed as a tautology, remaking articulation into repetition.

The political mobilization of incest survivors had seemed potentially promising. As a "class" without clear determining interests, survivors seemed poised to translate a key structure of feeling imminent in the radicalisms of 1970s. They were not determined by any preestablished social processes or political analytic; Marxist accounts of historical materialism, liberal accounts of rights-bearing individuals, even emergent feminist accounts of sexual or domestic violence did not fully capture the potential radicalism of incest survivor articulation. But this imminent articulation was rapidly absorbed into the hegemonic processes of the 1980s. The so-called survivor movement never fully consolidated as a social formation; instead, the dominant social order refunctioned subjective speech about incest to incorporate new regimes of the private, the aesthetic, and the natural. In finding useful analytics for the social, Raymond Williams argues in *Marxism and Literature* that "a distinctive and comparative feature of any dominant social order is how far it reaches into the whole range of practices and experiences in an attempt at incorporation. There can be areas of experience it is willing to ignore or dispense with: to assign as private or to specialize as aesthetic or to generalize as natural" (125). But in the dominant social order of the 1980s, this process of incorporation had extended its reach in new and surprising ways. As was the case with other potentially radicalizing movements of the 1970s, over the course of the 1980s multiculturalism and a more discursive than materialist identity politics absorbed much of the energy of these incipient struggles.

The structure of feeling that became incest survivorship was rapidly taken up and incorporated in new formations of the spectacle which bolstered emerging federal and nongovernmental administrations of the private, the aesthetic, and the natural. As the 1970s turned to the 1980s, conservative and liberal agendas were joined in a new mode of governmentality administering cultural technologies of the self. Neither a radically democratic nor a socially redistributive project, cultural logics of "empowerment" focused on improving the "self-esteem" of target populations in order to enhance their sense of agency.[12] Across the 1980s, self-esteem movements made the dismantling of the welfare state seem like social justice. Developing and affirming self-esteem required the state to cease providing benefits and services, since its citizens would fare far better by standing on their own two feet (when not pulling themselves up by their bootstraps). The 1983 California Task Force to Promote Self-Esteem and Personal and Social Responsibility sought to demonstrate how welfare use, substance abuse, crime, academic failure, teen pregnancy, and child abuse could be solved by policies targeting "self-esteem" (Cruikshank, *The Will to Empower,* 92). This dovetailed with a declared "war on drugs" that allegedly fought substance use but effectively increased incarceration of blacks and Latinos, introduced new federal controls on judicial discretion in sentencing, and created a dominant popular discourse on crime and safety.[13] Being "tough on crime" meant maximizing the well-being of the population, who would be freed from the confines of state management and left to their own devices (so long as they were not criminally racialized or illegally migratory).

If the 1960s war on poverty appeared as tragedy, its 1980s counterpart was a spectacular farce. Across the changes of Reaganomics, militarized social security, popular xenophobia and racism, this 1980s war on the poor created a culture of "personal responsibility" that would reach its popular and policy zenith in the 1990s. The individual became the locus of new forms of agency, by which I mean both bureaucratic entity and subjective activity. As Barbara Cruikshank elaborates in *The Will to Empower,* "Self-esteem is a technology in the sense that it is a specialized knowledge of how to esteem our selves, how to estimate, calculate, measure, evaluate, discipline, and judge our selves. It is especially, though not exclusively, a literary technology: 'self' emerges out of confrontation with texts, primarily, or with the telling and writing of personal narratives" (89). The self-help movement generalized technologies of self-esteem to populations beyond the scope of explicit governmental intervention. The potential radicalism of incest survivorship within broader social processes had been transformed into the *vanguard* of a dominant ideological project. In the 1980s, breaking the silence had been produced and marketed for easy consumption: incest disclosure was the most private speech-act possible, and its mass production made telling secrets a form of willing self-commodification. Incest survivors became a spectacle, that which "presents itself simultaneously as all of society, as part of society and as *instrument of unification*" (Debord, *The Society of the Spectacle,* thesis 3). The spectacle offers a particularity, a "part of society," as the instrument of its unification or horizon of universality. The spectacle of incest in the 1980s and 1990s constituted one such instrument, illuminating a new dominant "literary technology" based on the rationalization of the self, the ability to "estimate, calculate, measure, evaluate, discipline, and judge our selves" (Cruikshank, *The Will to Empower,* 89).

The country had indeed entered the decade of "the big-time incest narrative" (Doane and Hodges, *Telling Incest*, 68). The survivor "voice" gained "enough institutional authority to shape a persuasive discourse about the links between patriarchy, incest, and women's social subjugation and psychological distress" (*Telling Incest*, 61). But this voice no longer served as an agent of social change. It was merely the instrument of collective self-fashioning in a larger market of technologies of the self. As Louise Armstrong laments this shift, when women spoke out about incest, "it was not our intention merely to start a long conversation" (*Rocking the Cradle*, 7). According to Armstrong, the rise of the "incest *industry*" (77) commodified and thereby depoliticized incest survivor discourse. But I would add that this "industry" was more of a monopoly across networks of production and distribution, synthesizing very different "literary technologies" across news media, popular journalism, memoir, the novel, television, and movies as part of a new spectacle of culture. This did not depoliticize incest survivor discourse, however. It actually *politicized* it, in the classic sense of the term—it made it a participant in state regulatory discourses. This spectacularization of print and self-narration made subjective testimony the instrument of the state, and new regulatory efforts to increase monies for domestic and sexual violence grounded their legitimacy in survivor testimony.

It is no surprise then that these new cultural technologies recrafted racial formations as the locus of governmental power. Despite claims for a new universality of incest discourse, its role in popular and regulatory media reproduced racial difference as the grounds for intervention. As Kimberle Crenshaw points out in her discussion of intersectionality and violence against women of color ("Mapping the Margins"), governmental apparatuses tend to use statistics about violence against women of color to ground legislation fundamentally oriented to protecting white women. This resulted in increased statutory interest in hearing incest testimony from women of color as proof of regulatory necessity, without interest in transforming the aims and effects of statutes on child sexual abuse on the basis of that testimony.[14] In her essay "Brixton Black Women's Centre," Marlene T. Bogle points out that "all the myths, stereotypes and racism that surround child sexual abuse have portrayed incest as problematic only for white women and children. Black women did not have a place in this because of the racism inherent in explanations of child sexual abuse. Incest has been seen and believed to be the norm within the Black culture and way of life" (134). According to Bogle, many British black sexual abuse survivors feel "that statutory bodies use us at their convenience and when it suits them" (133), a concern echoed in the U.S. context.[15] Incest had come full circle. From the antiracist artic- ulations of early black women novelists through the "voice" of the public survivor, incest recoded subjective experiences of incest as the universal particular of the late twentieth-century United States. Its particularity absorbed experiential differences based on race and racism and repro- duced them in the spectacle of "universal" father-daughter incest. Sur- vivors had become a cultural prosthesis of neoliberal governmentality.

But was this truly the end of incest as the scene of historical struggle? I would like to suggest instead that "conjuncture," in Althusser's sense of the term, was simply on the move. The locus of political, economic, and cultural force relations that might precipitate the antagonisms of social struggle was difficult to locate, but signs of its presence could still be dis- cerned. In *The Society of the Spectacle* Debord reminds us that "the spec- tacle is not a collection of images, but a social relation among people, mediated by images" (thesis 4). This materialist approach demands re- newed attention, allowing us to see how "the spectacle grasped in its total- ity is both the result and the project of the existing mode of production. It is not a supplement to the real world, an additional decoration. *It is the heart of the unrealism of the real society*" (thesis 6). We must return the spectacle to its conditions of production, the social relations among people mediated by images. This requires a journey into the "heart of the unrealism of the real society." In the sections that follow, this jour- ney traces a dialectic between social relations among people mediated by images (spectacle) and imaginary relations among people mediated by society (fantasy). This relation between the society of the spectacle and the subject of fantasy will be the locus of conjuncture I explore here. Across the trajectories of new technologies of the self, I will show how incest survivorship introduced a break in the culture of the spectacle through the scenes of its mistaken memories.

Trauma

If the 1980s were the era of Reaganite transformations, they were also the era in which trauma became the dominant discourse of incest survi- vorship. Lauren Berlant's astute summaries of this era make *The Queen of America* persuasive reading, particularly as a current review only con- firms its prescient sense of trauma culture's encroaching impact. Berlant's effort to track the popularization of trauma and recovery extends well into the 1990s, as does Ann Cvetkovich's development of an *Archive of Feelings* to situate trauma in relation to new sexual publics. As Berlant extends her own arguments in "The Subject of True Feeling," the figure of the "exploited child" (128) provided the key to "national sentimentality, a rhetoric of promise that a nation can be built across fields of social difference through channels of affective identification and empathy" (128). Through the figure of the child, and the new figuration of all subordinated subjects as quasi-children, "sentimental politics generally promotes and maintains the hegemony of the national identity form, no mean feat in the face of continued widespread intercultural antagonism and economic cleavage" (128). Berlant's key insight is that trauma produces a new articulation of "national-popular struggle," one "now expressed in fetishes of utopian/traumatic affect that overorganize and overorganicize social antagonism" (132). These summaries of what Ann Kaplan calls "trauma culture" in her book of that title synthesize the changes emergent in the late 1970s, during the clinical diagnostic crises of the post-Vietnam era in the United States, and dominant in the 1980s, during the academic attention to Holocaust trauma and testimony in the humanities and the popular awakening of the inner child across mass market media.[16]

If the exploited child became the figure of suffering in the 1980s, sexual abuse became the paradigm of such exploitation. Complex lexicons and histories of suffering, exploitation, and violence were conflated in new understandings of trauma.[17] The first three terms marked the major analytic traditions of modern Western political economy: suffering as a sentimental discourse of social relations, exploitation as a Marxist discourse of economic relations, and violence as a liberal discourse of political relations. Each of these analytics proposed a causal relation imminent to modern society and sought to capture it in an analytic term, prioritizing either the social, the economic, or the political as the major domain of causality and material effectivity. Trauma condensed these three traditions and displaced them from any of their major domains. In their place, trauma referenced a new domain of culture, one that could articulate the *effects* of social, economic, and political relations without dwelling on any particular domain of causation. Clinical and theoretical writings have insisted that trauma is defined by its form, not its content.[18] Trauma shifted discussions of violation to the aftermath, rather than the cause, of violating events and circumstances. Social antagonism was defined not by causes (determination) but by effects (symptoms). This shift moved social antagonisms from the analysis of social relations to that of social feelings, making contradiction into ambivalence (or even ambiguity).

This was a potentially radical move, synthesizing residual analytics into an analysis of emergent conjunctures. Trauma demarcates a particular conjunction of subjectivity and biopower at the end of the twentieth century. In *Trauma: Genealogy of a Concept,* Ruth Leys points out that while trauma has been declared a central concept of the twentieth century, it was only consolidated *as* a concept in 1980 by the American Psychiatric Association definition of post–traumatic stress disorder (PTSD) in the third revision of the *Diagnostic and Statistical Manual of Mental Disorders* (DSM-III). According to Leys, PTSD rationalizes and provides coherence to disparate fields of study, including the physiology of shock, psychic stress, hysteria, and hypnosis (3–5). The earliest genealogies of trauma hearken back to the mid-nineteenth century, when "the structure of the modern sciences of memory came into being" (Hacking, *Rewriting the Soul,* 4). Trauma only became associated with a psychic, rather than a physical, wound between 1874 and 1886.[19] By the early 1900s, Jean-Martin Charcot, Pierre Janet, Morton Prince, Josef Breuer, and Sigmund Freud were more interested in the "wounding of the *mind*" (Leys, *Trauma,* 4) than in physiological shock. Together, these early twentieth-century theorists suggested that what "disturbed the integrity of the individual under the stresses of modernity" (Leys, 4) could best be described as a "memory crisis," to use Richard Terdiman's phrase (*Present Past,* 3). Such a memory crisis seemed to describe an interruption provoked by the encroachments of modern technologies. The train accident, urbanization, industrialization, and the growing conflicts of empire and domestic race relations all impeded the traditional temporality of subjection.

But in the late twentieth century, this "memory crisis" had become a medicalized norm. No longer the crisis of an individual more broadly construed as the subject of modernity, trauma now reduced modernity to the scale of the individual subject. This new, late twentieth-century model of trauma became PTSD, a subjective time disorder involving what Allan Young called the "*medicalization of the past*" and the "*normalization of pathology*" (*The Harmony of Illusions,* 39). After World War I, Leys notes a return to Freud's interest in externally induced trauma, elaborated through the treatment of shell shock and war neurosis rather than the hysterical symptoms of unresolved oedipal trauma.[20] The early Breuer-Freud cathartic method was reexplored by William Brown, William McDougal, and Charles S. Myers, who worked toward cognitive recovery and integration of traumatic memories. Work on combat fatigue from World War II and the potential restorative qualities of the cathartic-abreactive cure made the final turn toward contemporary accounts of trauma that focus on its aftermath, PTSD.[21] These approaches emphasized the healing possibilities of remembering, privileging the response to trauma over earlier twentieth century interests in its cause. According to Allan Young, in the DSM-III definition "PTSD's defining feature is its etiological event. Evidence of a traumatic experience is adduced from the patient's *active memory* of the event; from his *embodied memory* of it (consisting of traces of the event, mirrored in symptoms); and from *collateral information* that places the patient in circumstances severe enough to qualify as traumatogenic" (*The Harmony of Illusions*, 120). The etiological event renders the temporal paradox of trauma in diagnostic terms: the defining event of PTSD is its emergence in individual memory. Memory is the location of pathology as well as healing, and PTSD becomes the (blunt) medical instrument for retrieving "history" and normalizing it.[22]

The transformation of early twentieth-century trauma to postmodern PTSD had three major touchstones: U.S. soldiers' struggle to readjust to U.S. society after their experience of war in Vietnam, Jewish survivors' testimony about the horrors of the Shoah or Nazi Holocaust, and adult women's delayed recall of childhood events involving sexual abuse. In the first instance, U.S. involvement in the wars of Southeast Asia rendered a generation of young American men incapable of "normal" life in the imperial metropole upon their return. The treatment of U.S. Vietnam war veterans led to the proposal of a PTSD definition to be included in the 1978 DSM. Diagnostic criteria have changed repeatedly across the 1980 and 1987 revisions, but their main effect was "to further unify the PTSD diagnosis" (Young, *The Harmony of Illusions*, 115). The second instance, work on survivor testimony about the Holocaust, was initially described as "concentration camp syndrome" and "survivor syndrome" (Leys, *Trauma*, 5) without developing a new medical terminology or generalized theory of trauma. Only after the Vietnam War did a full codification of PTSD emerge (1980), and over the course of the 1980s and 1990s the Holocaust became more central to the ideology of PTSD (Leys, 15). Between Vietnam and the Holocaust, however, a third major coordinate of trauma culture appeared on the horizon: incest as a form of child sexual abuse. Judith Lewis Herman's 1981 treatise *Father–Daughter Incest* was a breakthrough book based on clinical work with incest survivors.

Soon professional and popular psychology volumes on incestuous abuse came to dominate media representations of "trauma." Post–traumatic stress disorder may have emerged into the DSM lexicon following work with U.S. Vietnam veterans; it emerged into the popular print and tele-visual lexicon following work with U.S. incest survivors.

By 1992, Herman's *Father–Daughter Incest* had given way to her more synthetic work on *Trauma and Recovery*, and the particularities of incest had become part of a new unity of correspondences (between war and domestic violence, genocide and incest) through the concept of trauma. The problem with incorporating incest and child sexual abuse into PTSD diagnoses, however, was the legacy of Freudian theories of incest. Freud developed several different trauma concepts across his work. In early explanations of hysteria in adult female patients, Freud first posited and then retreated from the "seduction hypothesis" that the majority of his hysterical female clients had been "seduced" by an adult male (father or father figure).[23] Freud published "The Aetiology of Hysteria" in 1896, explaining his hypothesis that patients had experienced early sexual contact with male authority figures and that their adult hysterical symptoms were the displaced remainder of this earlier childhood trauma (awakened by subsequent events in their sexual development). Freud subsequently changed his mind about the etiology of adult hysteria, as he explained in a famous letter to his friend and confidant Wilhelm Fliess, written on September 21, 1897. According to this letter, "the father" would need to be almost universally "perverse," and hysteria widespread, for the seduction hypothesis to be valid, "whereas surely such widespread perversions against children are not very probable" (quoted in Jeffrey Moussaieff Masson's edition of *The Complete Letters of Sigmund Freud to Wilhelm Fliess*, 264). Freud goes on to explain that the problem with this first hypothesis is its failure to look at the fantasy structure of the "etiological event" of memory. Freud argues that he should have taken into consideration "the certain insight that there are no indications of reality in the unconscious, so that one cannot distinguish between truth and fiction that has been cathected with affect" (264).

Some critics claim that Freud retreated from the so-called seduction hypothesis because his theorization of childhood violation at the hands of senior male authority figures, primarily known to his clients and often in the immediate household circle, would be considered scandalous. In his book *The Assault on Truth*, Jeffrey Moussaieff Masson argues that the 1896 paper affirms that such "early experiences were real, not fantasies, and had a damaging and lasting effect on the later lives of the children who suffered them" (3). Masson suggests that Freud deliberately retreated from his discovery of widespread child sexual abuse because the incestuous nature of this abuse caused a scandal, which forced Freud to recant his theory and posit instead the reality effects of fantasy. Masson laments this choice: "By shifting the emphasis from an actual world of sadness, misery, and cruelty to an internal stage on which actors performed invented dramas for an invisible audience of their own creation, Freud began a trend away from the real world that, it seems to me, is at the root of the present-day sterility of psychoanalysis and psychiatry throughout the world" (144). Freud's initial hypothesis—what Hall Triplett in his article "The Misnomer of Freud's 'Seduction Theory'" calls the "infant genital trauma theory" (660)—would certainly have been considered scandalous.[24] So too, however, would Freud's subsequent suggestion that childhood sexual desire was the real source of these seduction "fantasies."[25] If the first theory emphasized childhood purity, contaminated from the outside by sexual predation, the second emphasized childhood agency, its forceful desire for oedipal resolution thwarted merely by paternal prohibition.

Both of these options drew a strict line between fantasy and reality, or between an "actual world of sadness, misery, and cruelty" and "an internal stage on which actors performed invented dramas for an invisible audience of their own creation." But there is still a third option, the one most popular with readers of the Freudian oeuvre as a whole. This reading indicates that Freud did not retract his earlier hypothesis as a complete mistake; he rather supplemented it with the discourse of "fantasy." Freud renounced his claim that *all* instances of hysterical neurosis were *caused* by infant genital trauma. Both of these emendations require explanation. First, Freud no longer felt that a childhood sexual experience needed to have occurred in the real life history of every hysterical client. Second, he no longer felt that such experiences always caused subsequent hysteria. So some hysterical clients might not have experienced explicitly sexual events in childhood, and not all people who experienced such events turned out hysterical. What explained the etiology of hysteria then? For Freud, it was the supplemental force of fantasy. An event might have taken place without any particular significance attributed to it. Only in the aftermath of the event, once sexual significance could be attached to the event retroactively, did it become a psychological "scene," one riddled with anxiety and guilt and thereby managed through repression. This fundamentally transformed the determinative difference between the "actual world" and "an internal stage." Both these worlds were a stage, and fantasy projections "of sadness, misery, and cruelty" were no more or less "invented" depending on their referents in historical fact.

If, as Freud lamented in his retraction of 1897, "there are no indications of reality in the unconscious," this does not mean that nothing is real. It means rather that reality is striated with fantasy, so that "one cannot distinguish between truth and fiction that has been cathected with affect" (in Masson, *Complete Letters*, 264). This shift in the presumed imbrication of real and fantasized events made the status of social reality less easily determined. One had to look at fantasy *as a process of articulation,* one that referenced the structures of the unconscious (both Oedipus complex and potentially repressed childhood seduction) through condensation and displacement, or through various procedures of overdetermination. For my study, what is most significant about Freud's two theories is the production of etiology as a kind of hermeneutics of the mistake. Freud's mistakes forge fantasy as an open-ended process of articulation, despite his own "correction" of oedipal desire. Fantasy described both the process and effects of retroaction and repression. A strong attempt to determine fantasy emerges across Freud's work, an effort to make oedipalization the foundation of all fantasy processes (what Laplanche and Pontalis, in *The Language of Psycho-Analysis,* call the "last analysis"). In this determined account oedipalization precipitates fantasies as the aftermath of incestuous repression, the masked condensations and displacements of oedipal desire, even as oedipal fantasies can then retroactively be used to manage and make sense of any earlier childhood sexual experience. But despite the effort to make incest determinative, the hermeneutics of the mistake leaves fantasy constitutively open to alternate articulations.[26]

This opportunity was seized by feminist clinicians and theorists interested in using trauma to reconstitute the meaning of women's sexual abuse memories. The aim was to create therapeutic scenes where female clients could reconstitute the material effects of language about incest, to articulate incest as an etiology of mistaken memory from which women gained agency. One problem however was with PTSD's difference from the etiologies of fantasy. In the late twentieth-century United States, trauma was a medicalized concept that rendered symptoms into material indexes of harm, organized by bureaucracies of the American

Psychological Association and the American Medical Association. PTSD resulted from events whose violence or inassimilability caused the subject to dissociate, to "split" from normative reality and repress elements of the event from experiential incorporation. These events then returned in flashbacks, intrusive phenomena whose literality materialized the initial event in the present (as posttraumatic memory). In attempts to posit incest in legitimate etiologies of traumatic memory (rather than fantasy), feminist psychologists developed lists of symptoms to literalize the aftereffects of incest trauma. In her book *Secret Survivors: Uncovering Incest and Its Aftereffects in Women,* for example, E. Sue Blume includes an "Incest Survivors' Aftereffects Checklist" citing thirty-four posttraumatic symptoms common to incest survivors, including symptoms such as: "3) Alienation from the body—not at home in own body," "5) Wearing a lot of clothing, even in summer," "6) Eating disorders, drug or alcohol abuse" "20) Pattern of being a victim (victimizing oneself after being victimized by others), especially sexually," and "27) Sexual issues: sex feels 'dirty'; aversion to being touched . . . compulsively 'seductive' or compulsively asexual . . . conflict between sex and caring" (xxvii–xxx).[27] Checklists such as Blume's sought to formalize the process through which previously disconnected symptoms could be linked together to authenticate the reality of childhood incest.

The problem was that incest trauma did not seem to produce symptoms distinguishable from some versions of normative womanhood in the United States. There was no way to distinguish trauma from fantasy, at least in purely psychological terms. According to critics of the itemized PTSD symptomology, it was difficult to lay claim to an event-specific etiology when the symptom lists seemed to describe "normal" feminine behavior. Janice Haaken argues such symptom lists minimize the presenting similarity between the effects of sexual abuse and fantasies produced by more general experiences of patriarchy (including women's potentially erotic responses to such a system). Despite its good intentions, the traumatic turn threatened to reify all gendered expressions of ambivalence or harm as signs of buried sexual abuse. Based on her interviews with forty-four feminist therapists near Madison, Wisconsin, Jeanne Maraecek claims that therapeutic "trauma talk" "subsumes the particularities of a woman's experience into abstractions (e.g., 'trauma,' 'abuse') and reduces experience into discrete, encapsulated symptoms (flashbacks; revictimization)" ("Trauma Talk in Feminist Clinical Practice," 165). In part, this approach used trauma to render incest equivalent to other, more socially recognized forms of traumatic event. "Trauma talk identifies clients as injured rather than sick" (168), Maraecek explains, positioning "women clients as the victims of catastrophic events that are undeserved and beyond their control" (163). This approach creates a narrative structure in which women become the heroic victors over external events, paralleling the gendered experience of childhood sexual abuse with more culturally valorized experiences of gender-neutral catastrophic events or gender-specific masculine events of war or public violence.

Trauma thereby sets up a logic of equivalences between socially recognized events, creating new figures (now symptoms) through which exceptional experiences become part of common speech or the knowledge of everyday life. These figures do not connect new domains of practice (tropes linking formations of violence and experiential subordination), but rather sever those domains one from another and link them only through traumatic signifiers, "terms such as *trauma, wound, injury, emotional pain, brokenness,* and *damage*" (Maraecek, "Trauma Talk," 162). The signifiers are "like" one another, but they cannot articulate one to another in any more powerful or determining way. By making language "merely" metaphorical, trauma talk evacuated the specificity of familial politics and rendered symptoms into signifiers of postmodern equivalence. Incest comes to constitute memory as nonperformative language, not theater. It separates the original event from its subsequent symptoms, making incest into an originating trauma whose historical reality is realized through a specific PTSD narrative: once she recognizes her prior victimization by external forces, the "survivor" finds redemptive liberation from internalized blame, ambivalence, or erotic response. This is why, according to Janice Haaken, "the dysfunctional family was now cast as a battlefield, with women and children as the traumatized survivors of domestic wars" (*Pillar of Salt,* 3).

Where incest had provided an orthogonal articulation for welfare governmentality, trauma created new correspondences between forms of social experience. These correspondences lost their articulatory power; unlike fantasy, they were not tied to determination. PTSD provided a language that "unified" the articulatory potential of fantasy, with its avowed mistakes, and the medicalized determinations of trauma, with its literalizing memories. And incest became the perfect vehicle for this illusory unification. With its grounds in modern family life as the definitional fantasy, and its new incorporation of war, battle, and social struggle as cultural signifiers, incest was the trope of a society on the move. It signified a new social real, the "unrealism at the heart of the real society": women incest survivors whose traumatic memories would help remake popular culture and governmental practice over the 1990s, without seeming to touch down on any specific social conditions or materialist histories. If trauma allegedly "honors women's reality" (Maraecek, 178), Haaken is right to suggest that "the real issue involves the nature of remembering. Further, it involves contestation over the role of women as credible observers and chroniclers of the social terrain" (2). But this contestation rapidly became a "war" that articulated monopolies over the society of spectacle, one that would establish new relations between what Doane and Hodges call the "credibility of narrators and the credulity of audiences" (*Telling Incest*, 3) in emerging cultures of neoliberalism.

False/Memory/War

By 1992, the scene was set for the memory wars. Rising skepticism about traumatic memory and the high incidence of child sexual abuse produced what some have called "the great incest backlash" and others "a return to sanity." This issued in a two-sided popular and legal struggle, what Frederick Crews dubbed the "memory wars" in 1994. More successful as public theater than any of the scenes that came before, this struggle over the difference between "true" recovered memories of child sexual abuse and "false" memories implanted by therapy made history. This was done deliberately, performatively, and with much care: the constant refrain of "witch hunt" paralleled the 1990s to the 1640s, and references to Salem and the Spanish Inquisition continually used historical analogies to differentiate persecutory mass culture and rational common sense.[28] Popular representations of the "memory wars" made history itself analogical, using the instrument of memories true and false to restage the changing historical conditions of the 1980s and 90s as spectacle. Even the coinage "memory wars" replicates this strategy; if militarism typically projects a "theater of war" in addition to its material forces, to call the 1990s public debates about memory "wars" is to indicate the theatricality of language marking social contestation in this period (already under way since the war on poverty, war on drugs, and war on crime). This theater linked nongovernmental organizations and popular media as major territories of public spectacle. Skirmishes across these territories focused increasingly on control over representation, more and more frequently leaving aside struggle over the conditions governing the territories themselves as domains of production and circulation.

The "false memory" rhizome can be teased carefully into three main responses: first, the formation of the False Memory Syndrome Foundation (FMSF); second, the shift in popular media representations; and third, the funding and advancement of research initiatives to test and measure the accuracy and reliability of recovered memory (if there was such a thing). The first response, the FMSF, was founded by Pamela Freyd in 1992 after her daughter, Jennifer Freyd, accused Pamela's husband (Jennifer's father) of sexual abuse. Jennifer Freyd had recalled memories of sexual abuse by her father which she discussed in her therapy sessions before confronting her parents.[29] This resulted in Pamela Freyd's attempts to organize what Ian Hacking calls an "action group" (*Rewriting the Soul*, 14) to demonstrate the potential falsehood of recovered memories of child sexual abuse. This group coined the phrase "false memory syndrome" to describe the retrieval of child sexual abuse memories in therapy. This syndrome explained how so-called recovered memories were in fact iatrogenically induced, "false" memories produced by overzealous therapists seeking increasingly literal histories of violation to explain their patients presenting symptoms. Hacking describes the foundation as "a banding together of parents whose adult children, during therapy, recall hideous scenes of familial child abuse" (121). The FMSF immediately garnered widespread attention in the popular media, beginning with an article in the *Toronto Star* in May 1992 and an immediately subsequent article published in the *San Francisco Chronicle*. This war was frequently cast as a battle between families and therapists, with survivors sidelined as the dupes of these two institutional formations. The FMSF and "false memory syndrome" rapidly grew in media and cultural presence to completely overtake public interest in incest survivors.

In the public representation of the FMSF, primarily white, heterosexual, middle- and upper-class women have been "seduced" into having false memories of incest by popular representations and therapeutic suggestion.[30] As Frederick Crews argues in *The Memory Wars*, "false" memories are induced in these female patients as part of the transferential economy of the therapeutic scene—the only historical reality they represent is the "event" of therapeutic transference. Allan Young suggests this is the result of therapeutic processes popularized in the late twentieth century: "Claims about repressed memories and neurological processes notwithstanding, abreactive therapy operates, like any other successful cure, through a *generic* mechanism, namely, countersuggestion. If patients and their doctors believe otherwise, and if their beliefs result in a remission of symptoms, then this merely underlines the power of suggestion" (74). If abreactive therapy creates a generic traumaticity to women's speech acts in the clinical scene, this is in part due to the generic quality of the therapist's countersuggestion. The cure is itself a genre, an anticipated closure of a preconstituted script. The "remission of symptoms" or seeming cure is simply a part of this therapeutic theater. This contrasts with Young's summary of Breuer and Freud's approach to the talking cure: "For them, the traumatic memory is not *a prop in the theater of countersuggestion* but a system of connected images, associations, and emotions—simultaneously a psychological and neurological reality" (74, emphasis mine). False memory syndrome posited a form of psychic anarchy for otherwise privileged white women; they were particularly susceptible to the "propping" up of their psychic life by the theater of countersuggestion.[31] The fantasy scenes that result are then vested with the reality of childhood sexual abuse, even though they do not "connect" images in any systematic way accorded to the determinations of psychological reality.

This was a dramatic reversal of the popularly lauded "recovered memory" discourse of incestuous trauma. Recovered memory was shorthand for a variety of approaches to delayed recall of traumatic content, linked to the flashback and intrusive phenomena of PTSD as well as the specific phenomena of delayed recall on child sexual abuse. False memory discourse exploited the simultaneous nebulousness and literality of recovered memory as a concept, on the one hand critiquing its lack of empirical specificity and on the other its restrictive focus on empirical events.[32] The rationale for memory's legitimacy was up for grabs, and a simple binary—true or false—reigned as the mode of popular adjudication on this issue. For the memory wars, as Crews called them, were fought primarily in the court of popular opinion. By the time these debates reached state courtrooms, the battle was almost entirely won. This popular victory for false memory syndrome was achieved by presenting recovered memory as an alibi for privileged women whose failures were otherwise inexplicable (or more accurately their own fault). Here is a typical account, offered in 1993 by Richard Gardner, a Columbia University professor of child psychiatry notable for his invention of parental alienation syndrome and his service on the board of the FMSF: "The simple solution is very attractive. . . . You're thirty-five or forty and your life is all screwed up, and someone offers this very simple solution. 'Ah, I never realized that I was sexually abused. That explains it all!'—it's a simple answer for the therapist as well as the patient" (quoted in Watters, "Doors of Memory," 77).

False memory advocates scored a relatively easy victory by recoding populist ressentiment as commonsense rationality. Recovered memory discourse made female patients and therapists the "heroes of their own lives" (Linda Gordon, in a book of that title). But false memory discourse made the commonsense everyman the hero of a new age of populist reason. This discourse consistently positioned white middle-class women as the representatives of recovered memory. As one typical source explains, "Recovered memories had emerged from America's golden communities" (Johnston, *Spectral Evidence*, 4), "prosperous families" (4) or "the perfect family" (10). These privileged women struggled with a vague malaise and sought a legitimate etiology for their own discontent. This made them engage in transferential identifications with other women's stories of victimization (first lifted from television or print narratives and then personalized in expensive therapies).[33] In other words, white middle-class women consumed popular stories of child sexual abuse and made them their own. If the spectacle of the survivor voice had promised universality through the particularities of incest, new formations of blackness and whiteness disallowed women's participation in this new cultural universalism. Black women were positioned once again as the insignificant real of sexual violence, while white women were the hyperreal of narcissistic sex panic and self-aggrandizement. Privileged (coded as white) women took over the more legitimate stories of child sexual abuse among the poor and populations of color (where it really happens but doesn't really matter) and used them to theatricalize their own middle-class angst on the stage of world historical suffering.

The popular media quickly took up this account of privileged malaise and hysterical blame.[34] In the same 1993 *Time* issue that boasted "The Assault on Freud," Leon Jaroff's companion essay, "Lies of the Mind," offers a brief synopsis of this familiar story. Subtitled "Repressed-memory therapy is harming patients, devastating families and intensifying a backlash against mental-health practitioners," Jaroff's article opens with the requisite anecdote: "Melody Gavigan, thirty-nine, computer specialist from Long Beach," suffered from a lengthy depression and entered a psychiatric hospital, where her therapist suggested she had repressed a sexual abuse history, which she then recovered as memories of father-daughter incest (52). Then the third paragraph begins: "But she remained uneasy. Signing up for a college psychology course, she examined her newfound memories more carefully and concluded that they were false" (52). After she "begged her father's forgiveness" and sued the hospital (52), we leave Melody behind to focus on the scope of national victimization: "Gavigan is just one victim of a troubling psychological phenomenon that is harming patients, devastating families, influencing new legislation, taking up courtroom time, stirring fierce controversy among experts and intensifying a backlash against all mental-health practitioners: the 'recovery'— usually while in therapy—of repressed memories of childhood sexual abuse, satanic rituals and other bizarre incidents (*see box*)" (52).

The box, playfully titled "It Came From Outer Space" (McDowell, "It Came," 56) offers readers a brief insight into the kinds of otherworldly memories retrieved in the "thriving recovered-memory industry" (Jaroff, "Lies of the Mind," 59), including alien abduction and satanic ritual abuse. In contrast to such "fanciful" (56) material, Jaroff asserts that rationality does indeed recognize the reality of child sexual abuse: "No one questions that childhood sexual abuse is widespread and under-reported" (52), he explains. What rational people question is "can memories of repeated incest and other bizarre incidents be so repressed that the victim is totally unaware of them until they emerge during therapy or as the result of a triggering sight, smell or sound?" (52). What follows is what Kathy Woodward describes as the media's signature "statistical panic" of this period. Here Jaroff uses numeric probabilities to undermine the very possibility of recovered memory: "Across the U.S. in the past several years, literally thousands of people—mostly women in their 20s, 30s, and 40s—have been coming forward with accusations that they were sexually abused as children, usually by members of their own family, at home or, in many cases, at hidden sites where weird rituals were practiced" ("Lies of the Mind," 52). Apparently, "literally thousands" of women are accusing family members of ritual abuse. This rapid conflation of incest and Satanic ritual abuse was a unique achievement of the FMSF, who exploited the idea that (as Hacking phrased it in *Rewriting the Soul*) "Satan had become the star of American television talk shows" (114), "there was panic in the air" (115), and "rumors were flying" (115). This was indeed a "system of connected images, associations, and emotions" (Allan Young, *Harmony of Illusions*, 74), but it was not organic to the psychological reality attributed to Freud. This was a new articulation, one that exploited trauma's "removal of . . . an added prop or wedge" (Edwards, *The Practice of Diaspora*, 14) from incest and made it available for "forced imbrication" (Kazanjian, *The Colonizing*

Trick, 22) with new cultural forms. In other words, the memory wars exploited the removal of "fantasy" from incest's determinations in order to redetermine it for new uses, very much what I would call a prop in the theater of countersuggestion.

This theater however was not the therapist's office, but the pages of popular media. Across these pages audiences were asked to reimagine the real and to rationalize it through a commonsense understanding of statistical equivalences: panic is an overreaction, there is panic about Satan (witch hunt), Satan is part of recovered memories, recovered memories were started by incest memories, therefore incest memories are likely to be unfounded. Rational people recognize that incest happens, but rational people also recognize that it doesn't happen as much as people claim. The truth, as always in the 1990s, lay in the middle way. For if one backdrop for the memory wars was furnished by the Salem witchcraft trials, another appeared in the form of the Clinton health care reform proposals. Slightly unusual in Leon Jaroff's *Time* article is a passing comment about healthcare and the costs of insurance: "Some professionals are currently pushing for increased coverage of mental health in the President's proposed national health plan" (55). The proposed health care reform was expected to affect which medical and psychological treatments would be covered by insurance. Debates about how to resolve potential transformations in the state's provision of health care and/or regulation of the insurance industries formed another important setting for the theater of memory. The first (Salem) set the stage for new forms of popular rationality, the training of everyman's common sense. The second (legitimate health diagnoses mediated by state and insurance industries) prepared for the remaking of scientific rationality, the performance of the expert as rational gatekeeper.

These two settings were synthesized across the images in the 1993 *Time* and the 2006 *Newsweek* articles dedicated to the death and afterlife of Freud. This story of Freud's modernist death and neoliberal afterlife is visually dramatized in the artwork accompanying each article. In the 1993 articles, images by Matt Mahurin appear on full facing pages to the article text.[35] Coupled with the cover article's images of Freud as a puzzle coming apart from the head down and the famous long black Freudian couch hovering mid-air outside a shadowed skyscraper (Figure 1), the images for the Jaroff article emphasize the fetishistic quality of Freud as modern icon. The two images accompanying the Jaroff article isolate the human head and then render one feature as synecdoche

Figure 1. Illustration by Matt Mahurin for *Time*, November 29, 1993, 48.

of gendered consciousness according to Freud. The first features a pale woman's face emerging from the lower third of the page, surrounded entirely by darkness so that it appears to emerge disembodied from the shadows. A golden key hovers mid-air above a dark keyhole in her up-tilted forehead. The second image features a profile of a man's head against a flat grayish–pale green background, his elongated tongue circling up to dip into the bowl of his half-open skull (Figure 2). Across these images, the morphology of psychoanalysis is depicted in couch, mind, and tongue, all displaced from their routine settings and isolated in scenes of fragmentation and décalage. "Lies of the Mind" emphasizes the false logic of illumination attributed to Freudian ideas. Here the play of light and shadow distort and obscure the promise of realism. If the woman's face promises the perfect realistic objectification, stark revelation of her passivity awaiting the illuminated key, the man's full profile is illumination itself, a distorting realism that makes the entire image surreal, animated by an agency of self-knowledge in which his humanity becomes unrecognizable. The gendered differences between these images of white psychology mimic the ideologies of agency disseminated by Freud.

In Jerry Adler's *Newsweek* article of 2006, which celebrated the successful dismissal of recovered memory entirely and the potential for a Freudian comeback free from the taint of incest, the images changed dramatically. Here the glossy realist photographs by Chris Buck vary in size, from a single oversized image to a mid-sized series and small photo in closing. Each image features human bodies scaled in relation to major scenes of neoliberal culture.[36] In these photographs, a large leather couch appears alongside the humans in each picture, a fetishistic reminder of the institution of psychoanalysis now integrated in the popular imaginary of consumer comforts. The first image, also the largest, extends across its full page to include approximately one-eighth of the right-facing page where the article begins (Figure 3). This realist photograph depicts a generic mall scene, with an escalator in the foreground joining two floors visible in the upper and lower halves of the page. As is the case with most mall imagery, it is impossible to discern geographic or social specificity from the background itself. An Ann Taylor visible on the second floor and a Banana Republic on the first suggest at least middle-income shoppers, as do the attire and postures of the human bodies in the photo. But as the mall itself signifies a possible gap between status and class, emphasizing the consumer power to "appear" middle class through the accumulation of its status symbols, the signs themselves are not immediately

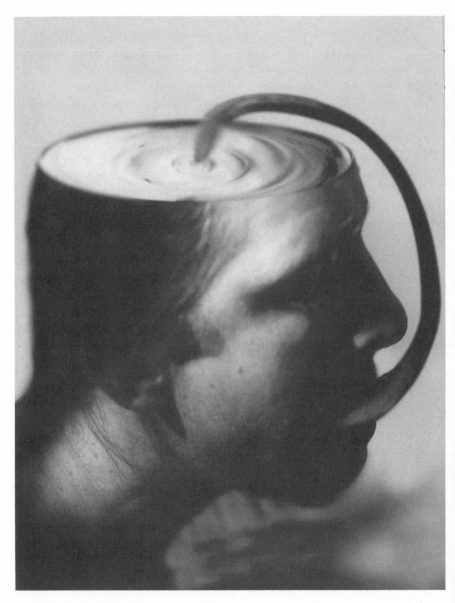

Figure 2. Illustration by Matt Mahurin for *Time*, November 29, 1993, 54.

Figure 3. Photograph by Chris Buck for *Newsweek*, March 27, 2006, 42.

referential. On the bottom left side of the main page, two conventionally gendered, white to light-skinned although racially indeterminate women stand riding the up escalator, facing away from each other but sharing the same stair. Their postures indicate bland indifference. In front of them is the Freudian long black leather couch, which they seem not to notice. One older, seemingly white man is almost unnoticeable at the top of the escalator, while two older, seemingly white men chat on a bench in the lower deemphasized third of the image; the right arm of another shopper is even less prominently figured behind the women.

Beside this image the article opens: "We stand now at a critical moment in the history of our civilization, which is usually the case" (43). The light but racially indeterminate women stand, it seems, in a critical moment in the history of civilization—the middle-class shopping mall. Moving-without-moving between floors, the women face away from each other and do not seem to recognize their situation (critical), their civilization (between Banana Republic and an imperial destination unseen), or even the link that promises to connect it for them (the couch). Instead, they are moved by technology toward the next level of consumption. The older men below will soon fade from view. This visual code registers a changing meaning for what Walter Benjamin describes as the allegorical work of the *flâneur*. In "Paris, Capital of the Nineteenth Century," Benjamin argues that Baudelaire's "allegorical genius" is "fed on melancholy," a combination that "estrange[s]" the city through the gaze of the flâneur; the allegorist sees as the flâneur does, poised on the "threshold" of both the city and the bourgeoisie of the nineteenth century, the "crowd" a "veil" that makes the "familiar city" a "phantasmagoria" (156). In this passage, Benjamin suggests that Baudelaire's *flâneur* seeks the new in death, which creates the "illusion of perpetual sameness" (158). Such an illusion—of novelty and perpetual sameness like one mirror reflected in another—produces "the phantasmagoria of 'cultural history,' in which the bourgeoisie savors its false consciousness to the last" (158). While Benjamin defines the nineteenth century through this aesthetics of novelty, his description can be usefully modified to describe the aesthetics of the memory wars at the end of the twentieth. Here the novelty of incest feeds the memory wars as a "phantasmagoria of 'cultural history.'" But in place of the city or its arcades, the shopping mall comes to represent the capital of new empires.

Across these two popular magazine cover stories, Freud's institutional death inaugurates his popular afterlife in the service of a happier, more diverse consumer capitalism and neoliberal subjects of commercial and domestic privacy. Freud as sociopsychological institution might have been a casualty of the early 1990s memory wars, but this death freed him from his modernist legacies and enabled U.S. neoliberalism to embrace his more "intimate" and interpretive technologies of the self as a useful supplement to the rationalities of capitalist governmentality. The 1990s memory wars salvaged Freud from incest's contamination, revaluing Freud-the-popular-icon to better service consumer citizenship. Freud provides the "illusion of perpetual sameness" for neoliberal culture, the illusion of history cleansed of its modern debris, freed from the determinations of now archaic political economic regimes in order to feed the "false consciousness" of neoliberalism. This requires one final move: the clarification of the "expert" who will help guide the commonsense every(woman) through the shopping mall of life. Who will have the expertise needed to decipher the role of the couch for this present? Once the witch hunt analogy has done its work of severing history from its means of production, who will help the populace see the correct path through this "critical moment in the history of our civilization"?

Trial by Testimony

These final questions lead the memory wars back into the courtroom, where a series of legal cases determined proper scientific expertise on the meaning of memory. In the early 1990s, recovered memory was put on trial. This turn to the courts was initiated by survivors themselves, seeking recognition and often recompense for their alleged experiences of childhood sexual abuse. Caught between the failures of collective activism and the punishments of the media, some U.S. survivors and their feminist advocates turned to the state to adjudicate the rationality of incest memory. Across these cases university-based researchers were pitted against clinicians who worked with survivors in routine practice. While seemingly adjudicating the domains of proper science, these cases also raised significant questions about the domains of proper agency for therapists, clients, and juries of popular culture peers. Like the young woman whose arrested face awaited Freud's golden key, female clients were found guilty of passivity. Their only agency came from the half-illuminations of their therapists, a play of light and shadow through which countersuggestion came to seem like their own idea. Over the course of these cases, as in the images of 2006, women survivors of child sexual abuse were successfully recoded as young ladies gone shopping. They had merely purchased the wrong brand of self-authentication. And it would cost them dearly. As women brought both civil and criminal suits before the law, the courts and the legislatures replaced the welfare state mandate to document and resolve "social problems" with new forms of governmentality designed to manage populations through the testimonial adjudication of the traumatic past.

In the late 1980s and early 1990s, delayed-discovery statutes were tolled to allow for civil and, eventually, criminal prosecutions of child sexual abuse cases based on recovered memory. In the late 1980s, efforts to toll statutes of limitations found their first victory in Washington state following *Tyson v. Tyson*.[37] The key issue of the *Tyson* decision was whether fairness required courts to toll the statute of limitations (allowing incest survivors in particular access to a fair trial) or uphold the statute (allowing the accused to stand trial only when evidence unsullied by time is available). The *Tyson* majority opinion held that fairness required protection of the accused. Writing for the majority, Justice Durham argued that child sexual abuse did not constitute an exception to the statute of limitations, since this cause of action posed the same problems of "objective, verifiable evidence" (78) that the statute protected against. The court stated that family or therapist testimony was not "empirical, verifiable evidence" (78), the former because of the possibility of bias and the taint of time over memory, and the latter because "psychology and psychiatry are imprecise disciplines. Unlike the biological sciences, their methods of investigation are primarily subjective and most of their findings are not based on physically observable evidence" (79). The dissenting opinion by Justice Pearson argued that "fundamental fairness" should grant alleged survivors access to courts, where their evidence could stand or fall on a case-by-case basis.

This disagreement reflected a broader philosophical argument about the relation between fairness (a balancing act between judiciary and legislative agencies) and empiricism (a balancing act between medical and psychological professions). While Justice Goodloe, concurring with the majority, felt that broader questions of fairness were "the exclusive province of the Legislature, and the judiciary must not invade it" (81), Justice Utter's dissent argued that "it is important for this court to adjust tort law doctrine in response to changes in social values and knowledge. Judicial action is especially appropriate when taken on behalf of individuals who are not organized as a political force and who cannot produce legislative solutions to their problems" (95). Justice Utter's dissenting opinion understood judiciary decisions as the last resort of those who had not formed a political bloc. Instead of placing the issue into the political arena, "increased knowledge and increased public awareness have produced the issue before us" (96). *Tyson* outlined the key issues of the recovered memory cases that would play out over the 1990s: first, whether memory repression and recovery were objective phenomena with professional validity (meeting criteria for the admission of scientific evidence); and second, whether child sexual abuse was an objective phenomenon with social validity (meeting criteria based on popular credibility and fairness).

These two issues met in the conjunction of incest. As the dissenting *Tyson* arguments made clear, incest exemplified the need for judicial activism in relation to accepted scientific knowledge. Incest exemplified the "breach of duty" and "breach of trust" properly addressed through the courts (as intentional torts) (92 [Pearson, dissenting]); it was also the most likely form of child sexual abuse to result in traumatic memory repression. This new knowledge *about incest*—emerging into scientific validity but still grounded in clinical experience and popular culture— necessitated judicial activism on behalf of alleged victims to ensure fairness, to toll the statute of limitations and allow specific cases to be tried on the basis of their evidence (rather than barred on the basis of presumed paucity of valid evidence). This conjunction was pivotal to the superseding of *Tyson* by 1988 Washington state legislation RCW 4.16.340, "Actions Based on Childhood Sexual Abuse," which specified detailed time frames for delayed discovery to toll the statute of limitations specifically in cases of child sexual abuse. By 1993, twenty-three states had changed the statute of limitations for civil suits on child sexual abuse (McNally, *Remembering Trauma*).[38] And by 1994, the Federal Minor Victim of Sexual Assault Law started running the statute of limitations at age twenty-five for minor victims of child sexual abuse.[39]

Following the movement tolling statutes of limitations for child sexual abuse, several successful civil and criminal cases were tried, often producing verdicts of guilty based on the recovered memory testimony of the plaintiff and expert testimony verifying the legitimacy of recovered memory as a scientific concept. These cases tended to affirm the validity of memory repression as a scientific theory and to leave the reliability of such memories to case-by-case evaluation.[40] But by the mid-1990s, the situation had dramatically changed. Through the advocacy of the FMSF, new "empirical" research experts on the falsifiability of memory battled with expert testimony (often clinical) about the legitimacy of recovered memory.[41] The trier of fact (an average juror) would no longer adjudicate memory's reliability in specific cases. Instead, the reliability of memory became itself a question of scientific theory (rather than practice). Beginning with the 1990, 1991, and 1994 *Ramona* cases in California and developing across the 1993, 1994, and 1995 *Sullivan* cases in Illinois, the 1996, 1999, and 2001 *Quattrocchi* cases in Rhode Island, and the 1995 and 1997 *Hungerford* cases in New Hampshire, a series of legal decisions overturned prior judicial acceptance of recovered memory as a legitimate scientific concept and invalidated both plaintiff testimony and the testimony of scientific experts on the topic. The doors of memory, as Ethan Watters termed it in a 1993 *Mother Jones* article, were officially closing.

How did this happen? What was articulated in the state-by-state reversals that spanned the 1990s? Several critics have registered the importance of these cases in relation to changing protocols of scientific evidence, remarking increasingly activist judicial constructions of science in the aftermath of the U.S. Supreme Court ruling in *Daubert v. Merrell Dow Pharmaceutical*.[42] *Daubert* amended the "general acceptance" standard for admissibility of scientific evidence from the 1923 case *Frye v. United States*, arguing that *Frye* has been superseded by 1975 Federal Rules of Evidence (specifically Rule 702, governing expert testimony).[43] As the protocols and procedures of "science" had undergone dramatic changes between 1923 and 1993, the *Daubert* Court argued a more complex rationale was better suited to the scientific technologies of a new era. *Daubert* created four new criteria to determine the admissibility of scientific evidence: (1) whether the scientific hypothesis can be/has been tested (594); (2) whether it has been substantiated by peer review and publication (594); (3) the known or potential rate of error of a particular scientific technique (595); and (4) the identification of scientific community to determine general acceptance of theory or technique (595). *Daubert* summarizes Rule 702 as enhancing flexibility, focusing on "the scientific validity—and thus the evidentiary relevance and reliability—of the principles that underlie a proposed submission" (595–96) with a focus "solely on principles and methodology, not on the conclusions that such principles and methodology generate" (596). This shift in focus—and the new four-prong test of testability, peer review, reliability, and general acceptance that guided this shift—would play an important role in the 1990s sexual abuse cases' transformation of memory in both science and law.

The key recovered-memory cases of the 1990s cited *Daubert* in their decisions, creating new imbrications of science and law in their determinations of admissible evidence. On a state-by-state basis, courts developed criteria for scientific evidence based on interpretations of *Daubert, Frye,* and state rules of evidence (often modeled on FRE 702 and 104). Across the recovered-memory cases, the trial courts exercised what *Daubert* described as their "gatekeeping function" (594) regarding scientific expertise and admissible evidence, denying the "general acceptance" of recovered memory due to a seeming contradiction between validity (testability, reliability) and relevance (helpfulness to a trier of fact). But the legal regulation of scientific protocol, standards of reliability, and assessment of generalizability is not my main concern here. For me, the key interest in these cases is their adherence to a new form of managed temporality. While the turn to law to regulate scientific norms is concerning, I find even more peculiar the turn to time management and risk assessment to adjudicate child sexual abuse claims on seemingly "scientific grounds." These cases reintroduced a new form of incest taboo, a bar to looking back that made only the future relevant to American jurisprudence. And this future was subject to new insurance imaginaries, articulated through protection against the risk that future recall might pose on an unfolding present.[44] Across four specific cases, *Hungerford, Quattrocchi, Ramona,* and *Sullivan,* I will explore how such risky memory came to bar the past and regulate the future in the name of a national public interest in the family.

The first two are criminal cases in which defendant appeals resulted in pretrial evidentiary hearings to determine the reliability of recovered memory as scientific evidence: *State v. Hungerford* and *State v. Quattrocchi.*[45] In 1994 in Rhode Island, John Quattrocchi was charged in a criminal case for child sexual abuse against a former girlfriend's daughter based on recovered memories. Found guilty, he appealed to the Rhode Island Supreme Court, which cited *Tyson* and *Daubert* in calling for a preliminary evidentiary hearing to determine whether or not "recovered memory" was admissible (*State v. Quattrocchi* [1996]).[46] Here the court specified that the preliminary hearing must determine whether such evidence is reliable and whether or not expert testimony is appropriate in this situation (including evaluating its relevance or helpfulness to a trier of fact). In 1995, meanwhile, the Joel Hungerford and John A. Morahan criminal cases of alleged child sexual abuse were combined in New Hampshire to enable a preliminary hearing on the same grounds.[47] The findings from this hearing, first summarized in *State v. Hungerford* (1995), were elaborated most fully in the New Hampshire Supreme Court *Hungerford* ruling against the State's appeal in 1997. The 1997 *Hungerford* ruling was then cited extensively in the 1999 *Quattrocchi* court's denial of the State's appeal on similar grounds. Together, these multiyear rulings significantly shaped what would on the one hand be awarded scientific recognition as empirical fact, and on the other what would be publicly disseminated as legitimate popular knowledge.

In the *Hungerford* pretrial hearings, experts on both sides of the memory debate argued about the general acceptability, reliability, and relevance of testimony based on recovered memory.[48] Unlike in earlier debates between memory experts within court testimony, here experts shared some agreement on the scientific theory of memory repression, but disagreed on the reliability of therapeutic processes through which memories are recalled. In the 1995 opinion following the preliminary hearing, the Hillsborough County Superior Court judge, William Groff, found that (1) the *Daubert* rule could be applied to both the concept of repressed memory and its retrieval in therapy; (2) there was no general acceptance of scientific processes of memory retrieval; (3) the process of memory retrieval in the instant cases violated generally acceptable scientific practice; and, (4) memories retrieved through these processes were thereby inadmissible. As a theoretical principle, the scientific concept of repressed memory met the criteria of general acceptability. And as a scientific concept, expert testimony on recovered memory was deemed relevant to assist a trier of fact, who otherwise would lack specialized scientific knowledge on this subject. But the *processes* of memory retrieval—or recovered memory—did not find general acceptability, because these processes were deemed unreliable and failed to meet criteria of testability and falsifiability. This meant that no acceptable expert testimony existed on the subject of recovered memory, or the reliability of memory retrieval. Precisely because repressed memory was a scientific concept, and because its retrieval could not meet criteria of scientific reliability, all testimony (expert or plaintiff) on the topic was inadmissible.

On appeal, the State insisted that processes of memory repression and retrieval are not special scientific concepts, but rather normal processes within the understanding of the average juror (142 N.H. at 120). This allowed the 1997 *Hungerford* court to spell out this logic even more clearly. As Justice Clifton summarizes these arguments in his 1997 affirmation of the 1995 decision, "Although there are skeptics, it does seem to be accepted in the psychological community that people are capable of repressing or dissociating conscious recollection of all or part of certain traumatic events. . . . There is, however, a vigorous debate on the questions of how the process of repression occurs, how the process of retrieval occurs, and indeed if in fact retrieval is possible at all" (121). The logic in *Hungerford* shifts the terms of general acceptability from empirical research to clinical practice: recovered memory may be generally acceptable in the abstract (scientific community), but the process of its retrieval is contested (clinical methodologies and clinician intrusion) and therefore unreliable. The court's decision not to admit repressed memory testimony focused on the therapeutic processes through which memories were "recovered," including "visualization" techniques that the court described as a self-induced trance or a "loosely analogous circumstance" to hypnosis (123).[49] But the process alone was not the only problem. The agency of the therapist in providing the "prop" of countersuggestion was the final disqualifier for therapeutic reliability. The therapist in this case was accused of affirming belief that "visualization" revealed veridically accurate memories for her client.

Over the course of these decisions, the "gatekeeping function" of the trial court moved from determining what was legitimately generalizable as a scientific concept to what was legitimately particularizable in a therapeutic process and, thereby, in plaintiff testimony.[50] Therapists could not be overly particular with their clients—they could not suggest that images and ideas created in suggestive therapeutic circumstances were specific to the lives of the clients, were "real" in their psychological reality. Echoing the *Tyson* decision from the 1980s, the 1997 *Hungerford* court verified that psychotherapy did not provide reliable testimony by definition, since the goal of therapy to cure the patient "tends to distort the 'historical truth' of events in the patient's life" (123). Thus *Hungerford* affirmed the four-part *Daubert* criteria, but added an additional four criteria specific for trial courts to use in evaluating reliability in recovered memory cases: (1) the plaintiff's age at the time of the event's alleged occurrence; (2) the length of time between the alleged event and its recovery as memory; (3) the availability of objective, reliable corroborative evidence; and (4) the process through which the memory was recovered (psychotherapy, hypnosis, sodium amytal, etc.) (127). Based on these eight criteria, the cases in *Hungerford* were dismissed.[51] This dismissal focused specifically on the failure to establish scientific reliability for its relevant community, the "average juror": "The phenomenon of repressing recollection of a traumatic event, and subsequently 'recovering' it, may be familiar to or even accepted by parts of the psychological community, but it is far from being familiar to the average juror" (121).

The *Quattrocchi* pretrial hearings of 1998 offered two weeks of similar debates over the general acceptability, reliability, and relevance of recovered memory testimony, discussed at length in Justice Clifton's opinion in *State v. Quattrocchi* (1999).[52] This opinion reviewed the main arguments of both parties in the hearings, focused on the State's request for a "relaxed" *Daubert* standard tailored for the soft sciences and Quattrocchi's request for a strict *Daubert* standard plus *Hungerford*'s additional four criteria. The 1999 *Quattrocchi* Court reaffirmed the guidelines used in the 1996 *Quattrocchi* decision, finding that "repressed recollection" or "recovered memory" failed the first three of the four *Daubert* tests (citing *Hungerford* 1997 throughout). Not only did no "quantifiable error rate" exist, none was possible since ethics prohibited creating laboratory tests to standardize rates of error in delayed recall of known child sexual abuse.[53] The court then treated the question of general acceptance at some length, moving from the initial *Daubert* test to a lengthy exploration of the case through the additional four prongs of the *Hungerford* test. The *Hungerford* test suggested that the reliability of specific recovered memories was dependent upon the therapeutic processes through which they were recovered. Regarding the case at hand, the court cited testimony by Richard Ofsche that Patricia Gavin-Reposa, the therapist who treated the child referred to in the case by the fictitious name of Gina, had "validated, and drew attention to, a relationship between Gina's symptoms and her repressed memories" (*State of Rhode Island,* Vol. 10 at 833) and Elizabeth Loftus that Gavin-Reposa had an "agenda" of finding memories. But the 1999 *Quattrocchi* court goes one step further, determining that the unique suggestibility of therapeutic settings makes *any* retrieval process unreliable. In this case, the particularities of therapeutic propping lead to the disavowal of recovered memory as a scientific concept in general (since the theory cannot be empirically tested otherwise), as the court concludes this section: "Therefore, under the additional criteria set forth in *Hungerford,* repressed recollection as a scientific knowledge is unreliable."

Across *Hungerford* and *Quattrocchi, Daubert*'s reliability and relevance standards are remapped onto *Frye*'s general acceptability, only the community of application has changed. The cases have moved from the scientific community in general, to particular problems of therapeutic methodologies, to the generalized problem of therapeutic methodology, to the generalized unreliability of recovered memory as a scientific concept. On appeal, the 2001 *Quattrocchi* court reaffirmed this logic: since recovered memory is a scientific concept distinct from normal memory (therefore relevant), and since there is no testable/falsifiable expert testimony on this concept (therefore not reliable), the court cannot allow Gina (the percipient witness) to testify: "She is precluded from testifying about these repressions that fall outside the purview of the common juror" (10). Scenes of judgment had come full circle, with the court's "gatekeeping" responsibility remaking the general knowledge of an "average juror." Science is judged in the court of popular opinion, with trial justices as mere "gatekeepers." The average juror—or the court's representation of the average juror—comes to determine the meaning of science, the figure propping the court's gatekeeping function in this little theater of countersuggestion.

In other words, the case reversals of the 1990s generalized their findings to recraft the courts as a point of social articulation. The move into courts is part and parcel with the 1990s return to Freud I described at the start, but it is a return that reverses the early twentieth-century articulatory work of Freud. If Freud's production of psychoanalytic expertise was a departure from regimes of state law and its recognized racial sciences, at the end of the century psychology's hermeneutics returned science to the courts. What is at stake in this return to and public dismantling of "Freud" is the connection between hermeneutics and scientific expertise. This connection was broken via the popular forms of the memory wars, then remade in the courts' gatekeeping *of the popular.* The news media could celebrate the return of a popular and unthreatening Freud, trundled about as a big leather couch from shopping mall to suburban home, precisely because the courts had barred Freudian "propping" from reliable therapeutic methodology. If on the one hand Freud's Vienna Society for Neurology and Psychiatry was largely unknown, "a microcosm of erudition arguing a theoretical point" (as Roland Summit described it, in his interview with Corwin, 24), the 1990s memory wars were on the other hand widely known, a macrocosm of common sense arguing an empirical point.

But this was not the culminating impact of the legal memory wars. Even as common sense shrunk the past into empirically recognizable forms, the future was expanded to protect public interests in family. In cases such as *Ramona v. Isabella* (1994), *Sullivan v. Cheshier* (1994), and eventually *Hungerford v. Jones* (1998), tort cases were brought against

therapists whose clients terminated family relationships on the basis of recovered memories. In these third-party liability suits, parents were granted
the right to sue therapists for affirming memories of child sexual abuse
(with a particular emphasis on incest). In 1990, Holly Ramona brought
civil charges against her father, Gary Ramona, on the basis of recovered
memories of child sexual abuse (*Ramona v. Ramona*).[54] Before that case
came to court, Gary Ramona countersued—but he did not sue Holly.
Instead, he sued Holly's therapist, Marche Isabella; Dr. Richard Rose,
Western Medical Center; and (briefly) her mother, Stephanie Ramona, for
three causes of action: slander per se (charged against Stephanie Ramona),
negligent infliction of emotional distress (against all), and reckless or
intentional infliction of emotional distress (all) (*Ramona v. Isabella*).[55]
In the "Verified Amended Second Complaint," without charges against
his former wife, Stephanie Ramona, Gary complained that therapist
malpractice caused the termination of his marriage, the loss of contact
with his children, his daughter's civil suit, damage to his reputation, the
loss of his job, mental anguish, and emotional distress. Gary Ramona's
countersuit was tried March 21–May 13, 1994. The jury ruled in Gary
Ramona's favor, finding that therapists do hold a third-party liability for
a duty of care and could be found guilty of negligent infliction of a tort.
Holly Ramona's suit was dismissed.

In this decision the *Ramona* court broke with emerging trends in
third-party liability under California tort law. Traditionally common law
only recognized a duty of care when a specific legal relationship existed
(such as privity of contract) or when a proximate physical relationship
could be established. As Cynthia Grant Bowman and Elizabeth Mertz
explain in their article "A Dangerous Direction," California extended
"duties of due care" (567–68) for third-party liability with specific con-
siderations, including "forseeability of harm to the plaintiff," "the moral
blame attached to the defendant's conduct," "the policy of preventing
future harm," and "the availability, cost, and prevalence of insurance
for the risk involved" (568). California also set precedents limiting third-
party liability in order to limit ever expanding networks of "risk" and
their attendant insurance costs. While precedents in *Dillon v. Legg* (1968)
and *Molien v. Kaiser Foundation Hospitals* (1980) moved California law
toward recognizing more intangible forms of injury (such as emotional
distress), this movement was restricted by policy demands for a "bright-
line rule" to help "avoid the social burden of multiplicative liability"
(Bowman and Mertz, "A Dangerous Direction," 570).[56] This posed the

problem of how to determine "forseeability of harm" without extending foresight to such a degree that insurance bore undue burdens (according to policy makers indebted to insurance industry lobbyists). The answer seemed to lie at least in part in moral conduct. This allowed risk-taking conduct to be assessed morally, as a form of intention rather than through its effects. Harm that resulted from moral conduct was not foreseeable, making negligence an effect of either immoral or irrational conduct. "Risk" was the calculated future-oriented conduct of moral or rational persons, therefore unlikely to result in "harm." Since harm is determined only after the fact, is in other words a retroactive category, risk and harm were organized into a new cultural logic of temporality.[57]

Through the third-party duty of care cases focused on recovered memory, therapists were found to have inflicted harm on a third party through morally irresponsible conduct. In the *Ramona* case and the *Sullivan* case that followed it, this new rationality of risk was used to affirm the public value of family relationship, or to imply rhetorically that family relationships are protected by a public duty of care. Family values would be vested in third-party duties of care, insured by state legislation as well as case-by-base decisions. Across *Sullivan v. Cheshier* (1993, 1994, 1995), Kathleen Sullivan's parents successfully brought suit against her therapist, William Lesley Cheshier, for malpractice on the basis of having damaged their family relationship. After Kathleen Sullivan accused her older brother of sexual abuse (without taking legal action), her parents brought suit against Cheshier, complaining that her accusations had ruptured the family and charging Cheshier with "intentional and reckless infliction of emotional distress and for the injury to their family relationship."[58] After a summary motion to dismiss several of the charges, the case was ultimately brought in federal court (under diversity jurisdiction) to determine whether third-party suits for malpractice could be permitted. The court upheld three counts: a public nuisance claim, in which action can be taken when injury results from practicing clinical psychology without a license (Count V); loss of consortium with a child (Count IV); and one according to Bowman and Mertz "labeled malpractice but contradictorily pleading intentional harm" (Count I) ("A Dangerous Direction" 565). As Justice Zagel summarizes these counts bluntly, "The injury is the excision of their daughter from their family" (*Sullivan v. Cheshier* [1994] at 662). *Sullivan v. Cheshier*, like *Ramona*, articulated family relationships as a valuable public interest, to be protected against rationally foreseeable infliction of harm.[59]

Together, these cases created new cultural rationales for the popular and the public based in neoliberal temporalities of harm and risk. As Moira Johnston explains in *Spectral Evidence,* her book documenting the *Ramona* cases, "It was in the fluid and fast-changing tort actions of the courtroom—not in the legislature's statutes—that these conflicts in social policy were being resolved and new law forged" (287). In *Ramona,* the therapist was found guilty of "negligence in reinforcing the memories, not in implanting them" (Bowman and Mertz, "A Dangerous Direction," 562). This affirmed a standard of rationality for therapeutic methodologies, one that defined moral conduct as conduct dedicated to foreseeing and avoiding possible harm to family relationships. As in *Hungerford* and *Quattrocchi* hearings, the therapist must not prop the patient's recall with validation, or else that therapist is guilty of moral misconduct against the public interest and subject to judicial censure. Meanwhile, women who become patients are by definition irrational, with no willed conduct of their own. As Holly Ramona asserted at trial, attempting to interrupt this assumption: "I'm the one telling him he abused me. He insists that it's everybody else talking. No matter how much I say it, he still insists that I'm not reporting these events to him. I wouldn't be here if there was a question in my mind. I know my father molested me."

Yet across these cases any scene in which a young woman severs family relationships is by definition scripted by another. Through the findings of these cases, women who recall sexual abuse mark the constitutive outside of popular, scientific, and legislative rationality. The very action of memory constitutes the daughter as irrational, because her agency is always mimetic and therefore propped by the analogies of the other. Her past remains outside representation, a danger to the future that serves (once again) as a transit point *between domains of representation.* As such, it provides a fungible resource for new relations of risk, figuring the "unrepresentable" within new relations of traumatic correspondence. Thus I would modify Berlant's observation that "utopian/traumatized subjectivity has replaced rational subjectivity as the essential index of value for personhood and thus for society" ("The Subject of True Feeling," 132) in order to propose that traumatized subjectivity has not replaced rational subjectivity, but rather *rationalizes the unrepresentable* for instrumentalization in policy and popular logics.[60]

This is the neoliberal recoding of incest described at the beginning of this chapter. In part, the findings in these cases can be linked to the threat of financial damages awarded in civil suits. The cases provoked furor when tort law established the economic liability of white middle-class men for "unprovable" allegations of familial or intimate sexual assault. But these cases are not only about the financial interests that accrue to specific persons within family roles (the protections of job, security, reputation, and parent-child relations whose financialization is recognized through tort reward). They are also about the financialization of social relations themselves, the management of public interests and common values through insurance imaginaries of foreseeable risk. The connection between these cases is in their transformation of harm into risk, their articulation of new rationales of "common" knowledge in the "public" interest. Public interest is rationalized as a third way, what Summit, in his interview with Corwin, calls the "sane and scientifically reasonable thrust" (25) of the middle ground disseminated to the wider populations: "We have stumbled in the dark toward a better understanding of something that's never been fully understood before. And in the midst of our stumblings we are passing a torch to a larger number of people who will take a less emotional view of it and turn it into common knowledge" (25). This stumbling toward a more rational and popularized third way is linked to new cultural formations of the state within neoliberal governmentality.

Private Properties in the Warfare State

As I mentioned at the start of this chapter, the broader legislative landscape of 1990s statecraft was transformed by a series of statutes targeting new financial relations of the social. These acts each focused on a different object of legislation—violence against women, immigration, and welfare—but together they acted in concert to restructure social relations according to new ideologies of the public interest. The recoding of federal legislation and bureaucratic regulation in the language of security and self-empowerment restructured the family as a target, object, and instrument of governmental power. This occurred at least in part through the changing figurations of the political, the clinical, the popular and the juridical traced here. If the harm of incest enabled its orthogonal articulation for welfare governmentalities, the risk of incest assisted its neoliberal transformation. Make no mistake, incest was simply one small element of numerous movements toward flexible familialism, taken up in much larger scale through the restructurings of family via welfare, immigration, incarceration, and terrorism. But incest did play a particular role in this larger restructuring of the security apparatus of the warfare state, providing one mechanism for recoding the family's domestic relations as new national relations of risk and security.

The memory wars were in effect one element of the changing apparatus of the security state. The war metaphor leaves the trace of incest as a tactic of the security state, particularly as it turns to its neoliberal formation. In *Society Must Be Defended*, Foucault suggests that war becomes a "struggle," a "striving toward the universality of the state" (225); "it will take place essentially in and around the economy, institutions, production, and the administration" (225). This war articulates race as the principle of social antagonism, such that war between races becomes "national universality." But in the late twentieth century, the "introduction of more subtle, more rational mechanisms" (244) transforms the security apparatus of racialized antagonism into new logics of futurity: insurance, risk assessment, and liability. These more subtle mechanisms include, paradoxically, the rationalization of trauma and the protection of citizens from future risk. In the United States, incest was used by such technologies to remake national security through the cultural logic of risk.[61] Across the 1990s, legislation inspired by child protection—from California's Three Strikes bill to Megan's Law, the Amber Alert, and Jennifer's Law—created new networks of information dissemination and increased monies for policing and overall criminalization of the public sphere.[62] By 2003, the Supreme Court finalized these processes by overturning retroactively applied delayed-discovery rules to recovered memory cases (as unconstitutional) and upholding that states had the right to determine whether or not convicted sex offenders had a right to additional risk assessment to ensure that public sex offender registrations did not extend "punishment" beyond the time of incarceration (constitutional).[63]

The apparatus of such protection emerges, once again, as what Foucault called the "mythicized abstraction" produced from processes of governmentality: the state. As Benjamin remarks in his essay on the illusions and imagery of Paris, "*Empire* is the style of revolutionary heroism for which the state is an end in itself" (147). As I have suggested, this "style" is part of the ever expanding relations of capitalist citizenship through which the state becomes once again an imperial sovereign. If Benjamin describes the late nineteenth-century imperial capital of Paris, Mohammed A. Bamyeh, in "The New Imperialism," reformulates this description for late twentieth-century empires: "This time around, however, history is repeating itself with all the trappings of tragedy: in its long journey back to where it came from, the state has also managed to accumulate much more instrumental power over society" (2). This instrumental power is in effect the power of tragedy. The state is a figure in the new drama of neoliberalism, reliant for its heroic role on its seeming ability to recognize the trauma of its subjects and insure them against future risk through its public security.[64] This combination of recognition and protection relies in part on the trope of incest, its ability to create new equivalences between various kinds of social suffering. As a universal particular of the 1990s, incest provides a system through which past and future, parent and child could become instruments of new systems of intelligibility.

In the next chapters, I explore how the managed temporality of trauma is taken up and contested in incest literature of the 1990s. Berlant makes an astute point in her clarification of new representational logics of trauma: "Subaltern pain is not considered *universal* . . . but subaltern pain is deemed, in this context, universally *intelligible,* constituting objective evidence of trauma reparable by the law and the law's more privileged subjects" ("The Subject of True Feeling," 144). This breach between the "real" and its intelligibility has been central to the arguments of this chapter. It also carries me forward into the next chapter, which analyzes a novel written to interrupt this breach between the particular pain of the subaltern and its universal intelligibility as representation. If this chapter explored how "the law and the law's more privileged subjects" repair pain through traumatic recognition, the next two chapters explore how "the literary and literature's more privileged subjects" attempt to do so as well. These chapters on literary incest explore how cultural logics of trauma have been instrumentalized to leave "pain" particular, even as its representation expands new terrains of the universal. Across these chapters I close read two incest novels written by women whose alleged histories of sexual abuse have been part of their work's critical reception. Reading literary production and literary criticism as distinct domains of disciplinary knowledge, I explore how the cultural logic of memory can be stolen by the daughter to remake an alternate history of the nation's changing family romance.

Three

Seduction by Literature: Sexual Property and Testimonial Possession

What happened? It was slavery. And white and black are so close.
And dark and light are so close. And someone's white grandfather
buried someone's black grandfather after those slaves sang that song and
died. Truth. Freedom. . . . It was slavery that happened and I read the
story in a book.
    Who buried whom? Is the story over?
                —CAROLIVIA HERRON, *Thereafter Johnnie*

In June 1991 the *Washington Post* printed three interconnected articles
responding to the publication of Carolivia Herron's experimental novel
Thereafter Johnnie.[1] The longest of these articles provided an in-depth
interview with Herron about the connections between her first novel,
her public disclosure of recovered memories of childhood incest, and her
announcement of a new work-in-progress documenting her personal
story of sexual abuse at the hands of an uncle. Over the course of her
interview with Donna Britt, Herron explained how she had recovered
memories of child sexual abuse by different members of her extended
family.[2] She explained how these memories had shaped her writing,
largely unconsciously in her first novel, *Thereafter Johnnie,* then more
overtly in her autobiography-in-progress, *An Instance of Holocaust.* As
Herron explained at a Washington book party for *Thereafter Johnnie:*
"There is a connection between this text and my own life" (Britt, D1).
What this connection is, however, remains unclear over the course of
the interview and its companion pieces. The problem presented by both
her first book and her manuscript-in-progress, these pieces suggest, is not
only the confusing relationship they present between "life" and "text."
It is also the confusion they introduce about how to interpret this relationship, soliciting and yet refusing psychological approaches to the novel
and literary approaches to incest survivorship.

Herron's comment reflects a broader turn in the production and reception of incest literature in the 1990s. Black women writers have been hailed as the first innovators to break with conventional uses of incest in U.S. literature.[3] Incest has most often been represented as either a symbolic prohibition or a specter of unrest, usually in the form of mistaken sibling romance. While this is arguably true of pre-1945 incest literature, in the 1950s some experiments with the tradition were already under way in Ralph Ellison's *Invisible Man* and Vladimir Nabokov's *Lolita*. Both texts depicted incest or adult-child sexual relations as real events with narrative consequences. But both of these texts maintained a male protagonist's point of view, registering the reality of intergenerational sex without reckoning with its gendered significance. It was only with the 1970 publication of Toni Morrison's *The Bluest Eye* and Maya Angelou's *I Know Why the Caged Bird Sings* that female experiences of unwanted adult-child sex were represented within twentieth-century domestic arrangements. *The Bluest Eye* was Morrison's first novel, a narrative exploration of incestuous assault and reproduction from the point of view of the daughter in a working-class black family. Incest provided an occasion to treat the denigration of blackness and female youth through white supremacist aesthetics, looking in particular at their impact on Pecola Breedlove's self-image. Angelou's first autobiography, *I Know Why the Caged Bird Sings*, includes episodes of childhood sexual abuse by her mother's boyfriend. And in 1978, the same year that Louise Armstrong published the first "survivor" anthology, *Kiss Daddy Goodnight*, novelist Gayl Jones published *Corregidora*, a narrative written in blues form to trace the genealogy of a Portuguese slaveholder who procreated with three generations of his daughters.

By the 1990s, these early novels and autobiographies by black women had been redescribed as founding a new tradition of incest literature, one more focused on the life experiences of women and girls across lines of race and class. Some critics called this a new multiracial or multicultural genre: survivor literature, incest literature, or trauma literature. These critics cast literature as an important vehicle for survivor self-representation, a claim that grew more urgent as the memory wars seemed to usurp all other forms of public self-representation. Literary representation might resist the populist empiricism of the false memory syndrome and its widespread reception as commonsense. This made the early literary work of black women writers all the more important as a historical record of incest survivor writing. Demonstrating origins prior to the popular spectacles of the memory wars seemed key to legitimating women's incest narratives in the 1990s.[4] While this research recast much historical writing in revelatory terms (Mary Shelley, Virginia Woolf, and Djuna Barnes, among others, became key literary foremothers), the 1970s writings by black women offered the most immediate forms through which to claim a legitimate past. The longer history of black women's writing on sexual abuse and exploitation, often coincident with analyses of racism and racially determined concepts of gender difference, legitimated the authenticity of these texts in ways claimed to symbolize the broader multiracial experiences of "women." Emphasis was placed on finding similar codes embedded in texts of the new genre. *Thereafter Johnnie* provided one key turning point in this effort, a novel that Kali Tal described in her mid-1990s *Worlds of Hurt* as the "one book-length example of sexual assault literature by a woman of color" (156).

This claim can only make sense if "sexual assault literature" denotes a very specific cultural and historical code, one focused as much if not more on the life of the author than the content of the book (Tal, 17).[5] This seems particularly odd in the case of *Thereafter Johnnie,* which is not self-evidently autobiographical and which primarily depicts father-daughter incest as a series of erotic encounters sought after by the daughter.[6] *Thereafter Johnnie* is a highly experimental novel, structured as twenty-four epic chapters written in free indirect discourse from multiple and embedded points of view. The characters created through these points of view are more allegorical than realist, types (the philosopher, the poet, the saint) who meditate on the philosophical, poetic, and religious connections between late twentieth-century incest and nineteenth-century racial slavery. The past haunts the present in *Thereafter Johnnie,* but its meaning eludes and vexes the main characters since it only appears through the tangled relationships between members of the Snowdon family. None of the main characters are able to grasp the meaning of the past any more than they are able to relinquish their insistence upon its hold over the present. As the epigraph suggests, the novel's central characters are haunted by an unfinished past—the generations-distant past of African American slavery, certainly, but also the contemporary past, when an episode of father-daughter incest destroyed the Snowdon family in the 1970s. Following an affair between daughter Patricia and father John Christopher Snowdon, the birth of a daughter, Johnnie, leads to the dissolution of the family and allows for the irruption of the past into the present. This recent episode of reproductive incest seems to call forth earlier episodes of incestuous reproduction, linking the two "pasts" of the Snowdon family through the repetition of incest. Figuring out the relationship between these two pasts becomes a kind of obsession for the novel's protagonists—particularly for John Christopher and Patricia, the father and daughter who find themselves drawn into an incestuous affair marked by its irresolvable roots in forgotten history. As John Christopher laments, "I don't, I don't, I don't, I just don't understand my daughters. What happened? Tell me what happened?" (66). Despite each character's obsession with finding out the story of "what happened," however, the novel is decidedly unclear about the relationship between the historical violence of slavery and the contemporary crisis of father-daughter incest. Even as each member of the Snowdon family blames the past for their present crisis, the status of "the actual past," as Stephen Knapp puts it in "Collective Memory and the Actual Past," remains highly indeterminate (123). Despite the fact that everyone in the family insists that "what happened" necessitates historical excavation and explanation, no one is able to agree on precisely what history is or how it might impact the errant desires of present-day kin. As Johnnie exclaims in frustration, "History doesn't help. Slavery won't go away" (174). Characters cannot figure out how the irruption of incest in their present lives plays out the historical violence of their past, and in the absence of knowledge John Christopher and his wife, Camille Snowdon, along with daughters Patricia, Cynthia Jane, and Eva, and (grand)daughter Johnnie, produce a series of stories about the unfathomable violence of history. In stories combining biblical, epic, and romantic parables traversing two hundred years of U.S. history, the Snowdon family narrates its genealogy as the inheritance of incest, from the rape of Patricia's great-great-grandmother Laetitia by her father/master during enslavement, to the childhood "seduction" or molestation of Patricia by her father John Christopher, to Patricia's adolescent and adult sexual pursuit of her father under the guise of biblical reenactment.

Thereafter Johnnie offers an important intervention into the popular and critical interpretation of incest literature described at the outset of this chapter. In its exploration of the connections between psychology and literature, history and memory, and slavery and incest, *Thereafter Johnnie* offers a powerful reinterpretation of 1990s "sexual assault literature" in relation to older forms of family romance. In this novel, specifically erotic depictions of incest present a puzzle in how late twentieth-century characters (and critics) come to terms with the legacies of chattel slavery in the racial and sexual formations of the contemporary United States. Returning to the specific problem posed by the two pasts of *Thereafter Johnnie*'s incest narrative, I ask (following Arlene Keizer, in her article "The Geography of the Apocalypse"): "What is the connection between the incestuous sexual abuse of black girls/women by their black fathers and the incestuous sexual abuse of enslaved black girls/women by their white father-masters?" (388) While both are "eroticized incestuous relationships" (387) Keizer explains, there is an important difference between the contexts of "incestuous sexual abuse" (388) in legal enslavement and liberal freedom. But what is this difference precisely? Is one rape, and the other seduction? If, as Keizer suggests, *both* instances represent "eroticized incestuous relationships," how can we interpret them as "sexual abuse" without either negating women's agency or making recourse to structural arguments about domination that collapse the difference between legal enslavement and liberal freedom, as well as between past and present, life and text? The answer to these questions lies in the daughter's sign of the "X," a literary and historical crossroads marking two distinct paths: one toward a future promised, the other toward a freedom yet to come.

The Absence of Trauma

Trauma theory offers one prominent hermeneutics through which to decode the literary and historical crossroads of *Thereafter Johnnie*. Different from 1980s psychological studies of trauma, trauma theory developed in the academic humanities during the 1990s to describe certain aporias in representation. Literary and philosophical approaches to trauma described a breakdown in the historical conditions through which subjects know and narrate their experience. Cathy Caruth exemplified this approach, writing in 1995 that trauma is defined "solely in the *structure of its experience* or reception: the event is not assimilated or experienced fully at the time, but only belatedly, in its repeated *possession* of the one who experiences it. To be traumatized is precisely to be possessed by an image or event" ("Trauma and Experience," 4–5). Caruth's approach extended the concept of trauma much further than its previous uses, building on poststructuralist theories inflected by psychoanalysis to construe trauma as a concept of history (more than merely a historical concept). Unlike Ruth Leys and others interested in the genealogical specificity of twentieth-century trauma, Caruth, Shoshana Felman, and Dori Laub, among others, speculated on the uses of trauma to rethink genealogy itself. In her reading of Freud's *Moses and Monotheism,* Caruth asks, "What does it mean, precisely, for history to be the history of a trauma?"(*Unclaimed Experience,* 15). In reply, Caruth suggests that history is structured as a kind of possessive belatedness. As she explains in the introduction to her edited volume on trauma, "The traumatized, we might say, carry an impossible history within them, or they become themselves the symptom of a history that they cannot entirely possess" ("Trauma and Experience," 5). History itself becomes both symptom and dispossession. The traumatized subject's belated effort to possess impossibility is what then drives history forward.

This summary makes trauma theory seem quite relevant to a text like *Thereafter Johnnie.* At its best, trauma theory helped destabilize the linkage between more positivist historical and literary studies and dominant formations of power. Many critics have argued that national and imperial projects legitimated monopolies on violence and unequal social relations through historical discourses of empirical verifiability and documentary realism (as Thomas Bender argues in his *Rethinking History in a Global Age*). Mainstream historicist approaches reliant on these discourses seemed likely to miss the crises of subjection marked by trauma. Even Marxian dialectics appeared wedded to modern teleologies and modes of subjection that could not recognize their own dysphoric effects. Trauma was initially offered as an intervention in such representational systems of domination. As Shoshana Felman and Dori Laub argued in *Testimony: Crises in Witnessing,* trauma marks "extreme limit-experiences" (xvi) that challenge conventional modes of historical representation. In so doing, it creates "a history which is essentially *not over,* a history whose repercussions are not simply omnipresent (whether consciously or not) in all our cultural activities, but whose traumatic consequences are still actively *evolving*" (xiv). This experience requires a unique type of historical agency, one that enables subjects to bring trauma *into* historical representation through alternative modes of representation. Felman and Laub, followed by others, theorized such a unique historical agency as "testimony." Testimony was articulated through modes of representation that are aesthetically rich, and often textual (whether print, photographic, or cinematic). Such alternative, more overtly aestheticized expression allows critics to discover "truths that are unspoken—or unspeakable—and that are yet inscribed in texts" (xiii–iv).

But this approach cannot fully grasp *Thereafter Johnnie's* hermeneutics of history. It also threatens, if used incautiously, to recuperate historical aesthetics into a newly restrictive "ideology of form" (to use Fredric Jameson's phrase, *Political Unconscious,* 76). Jameson uses elements of psychoanalysis to modify a Marxist dialectical approach to literary textualization, in which "various sign systems . . . are themselves traces or anticipations of modes of production" (76). Here he theorizes history as an "absent cause" (35), "unaccessible to us except in textual form, [so that] our approach to it and to the Real itself necessarily passes through prior textualization, its narrativization in the political unconscious" (35). Trauma theory also used psychoanalytic insights, often derived from poststructuralist interpretations of Lacan, to interrupt positivist historicism and new critical legacies of textualism that refused the "adventure of insight" (Felman, *Jacques Lacan*). But unlike Jameson's approach, in some studies of traumatic testimony textualization became almost wholly synchronic, not merely indexing the past to the symptomology of the present but identifying that past with it. Traumatic testimony seemed to remake historical form into almost pure articulation. Gone were the restrictive conjunctures of early twentieth-century "professional" psychoanalysis. Gone the confounding Oedipus complex with its intractable family formations, as well as the racial, national, and imperial struggles out of which this adventure began. While trauma's form might resemble Hutcheon's historiographic metafiction (*A Poetics of Postmodernism,* 5) or Jameson's socially symbolic act (*The Political Unconscious,* 104), it seemed at its most radical to supersede normative historical formations altogether. Trauma's textualization promised a more intimate dialogism of testimony and witness, relieving professional psychoanalysis of clinic and couch and reviving its insights for a more expansive literary criticism.

On one hand, the daring rootlessness of trauma theory might provide more mainstream critical reception for what Paul Gilroy in *The Black Atlantic* calls the "politics of transfiguration" in countercultures of modernity (37). Contrasted to the "politics of fulfillment" (37), which uses texts to secure the unfulfilled promise of modernity, the "politics of transfiguration" articulates askew to modernity's major modes of representation. Here "the willfully damaged signs which betray the resolutely utopian politics of transfiguration therefore partially transcend modernity, constructing both an imaginary anti-modern past and a postmodern yet-to-come" (37). Trauma theory might provide one idiom for such utopian transfiguration of modern criticism itself. On the other hand, trauma theory offered no specific conditionals on its interpretive dialogism.[7] There seemed to be no particular social, historical, or economic conditions that attuned critics to the transfigurative modes of traumatic testimony. And all too often, the insights ventured forth resembled those of Lacanian psychoanalysis, transfigured into more diverse social and cultural conditions of the late twentieth century. Traumatic "witnessing" seemed to valorize the synchronic absorption of diachronic difference into a present (in psychoanalytic fashion) while eschewing alternative modes of historiographic relation. Textualism (as dialogic with the critic) becomes the locus of historical recognition and redemption (if not automatically social transformation or justice).

Counterposed to this approach, literary critics of minoritized racial formations have insisted that print texts—particularly novels—traffic in both the politics of fulfillment and of transfiguration. As Lisa Lowe points out, Asian American cultural politics produce "novels" in quotations, texts that simultaneously interrogate the politics of fulfillment promised by "cultural institutions" of the novel and transfigure novelism into history "imagined otherwise" (to use Candice Chuh's phrase, in her book of that title).[8] African Americanist literary critics have generated voluminous scholarship on print culture as a mechanism of historical dispossession and a vehicle for transfiguring the "culture" of modernity. Testimony, public disclosure, print publication, and literary status have all historically been organized through white supremacy to disenfranchise and delegitimate subjects defined by law (and/or custom) as black. But even as print culture is theorized as the form of historical repression and denial (of literacy, of family, of recorded history), authority over print literacies and legitimacy through life's novelization are theorized as a key domain that might transfigure the politics alleged to fulfill modernity's promise.[9]

The novel marks a peculiar locus of this historical struggle, particularly in its association with family romance. In particular, African Americanist feminist critics have pointed out that using the family romance form presents particular genealogical problems rendering either fulfillment or transfiguration quite difficult (as Deborah McDowell notes in "Reading Family Matters"). Modern family romances have been predicated on a coherent family form codified by liberal legal systems. When self-determination is linked to particular legal and literary family formations, the genealogies of U.S. slavery only become legible as "a secret within a family, a secret about family, and a secret denying the possibility of family" (Rushdy, *Remembering Generations*, 29). The politics of fulfillment would disclose the secret and recover family as the proper domain of civil and sexual self-determination. As McDowell and others have pointed out, the fulfillment of this promise circumscribes black feminist (and queer) self-determination within the confines of the modern family.[10] The politics of transfiguration, however, remain radically delimited when such genealogy is the precondition of historical and literary legitimacy. As Elizabeth Yukins frames it in her article "Bastard Daughters and the Possession of History," "Kinship can neither authenticate nor secure memory" for African American women writers (222), leaving them with the literary problematic of "bastard consciousness" (226).[11] Without the ability to "claim proprietary rights to traumatic memories" of historically distant trauma, Yukins suggests, "historical trauma creates an insurmountable barrier to familial cohesion and inheritance" (222). This chapter argues that trauma marks a peculiar juncture in the politics of fulfillment and transfiguration for the 1990s. In particular, incest-as-trauma figures an impossible contradiction between the novel as fulfillment and the novel as transfiguration of the familial nation. Rather than use trauma to disclose this contradiction as a "secret," however, or resolve it as testimony about the nation's violent past, I read *Thereafter Johnnie* as inducing in its characters (and its readers) a form of genealogical shock.

Testimonial Possession

Set in the 1970s, *Thereafter Johnnie* explores the time of the familial nation as it is being contested by both black nationalism and second-wave feminism. A document of unfinished social revolution, *Thereafter Johnnie* uses incest to mark the fissures and demands of witness for black women writers. In black women's literature emerging across the 1970s to the 1990s, critical family romances challenged both black radical complicity with masculinist paradigms of hearth and home and white feminist disregard for racist genealogies of gendered domesticity. In *The Daughter's Return*, Caroline Rody describes these literary efforts as "vital and courageous daughterly labor" (6); here I explore how the daughter's representational labor transfigures these dual demands for filial testimony. In *Thereafter Johnnie*, the Snowdon daughters take on the duty to recall and transmit the past. But the more they try to "claim proprietary rights" to memory, the more they seem to go into shock. As Eva, the youngest daughter and prophetic observer of the Snowdon family's dissolution, puts it most presciently in the chapter "The Story of the Stone":

> At first we can trace the facts, identify all the forces and counterforces, and even assign blame, but it doesn't take long before the facts become lies, extensions of what we want and what we don't want to see, the facts are ourselves finally, and the more I focus on myself and the facts that mark out my life, the more pathetic I am, arbitrary in interpreting what happened, the mind is a stone running away with itself, a projectile incapable of perceiving the powers that propel it, it insists upon itself too much, it is hopelessly personal. The mind is incapable of fact. (103)

In a text obsessively concerned with locating origins, Eva's account of the "mind" offers one condensed formulation of the novel's narrative structure. In effect, the novel's protagonists do nothing *but* return to those scenes in which some "force" seems to have set the facts in motion—the time that Patricia seduces her father, the time that the father touches Patricia as a child, the time that John Christopher and Camille decide to marry, the time that the daughters dance together in the moonlight. But the characters' efforts to "trace the facts" only end up sending them into a kind of atemporal shock. As Walter Benjamin describes this process in "A Berlin Chronicle," "It is to this immolation of our deepest self in shock that our memory owes its most indelible images" (57). Such immolation makes the act of remembering both seductive and dangerous, since "with the joy of remembering, however, another is fused: that of possession in memory" (57). For the Snowdon daughters, this shock is inextricable from the "indelible images" of incest. The more they try to grasp hold of these images, the more "possessed" they become by memories that return them again and again to the "shock" of U.S. chattel slavery.

As Eva's statement suggests, this attempted "return" is always itself a moment of inauguration. The more characters seek the origin for their historical predicament, the more they are subjected through a compelling force they can no longer identify. Rather than producing more coherent generational transmission, the Snowdon daughters' passion for reference—and utter impatience with one another's interpretation of referents—radically isolates each family member and ultimately dissolves any sense of realist plot. In the desire for historical knowledge that drives them forward, the Snowdon daughters seem to chase the past "down the rabbit hole," as Patricia Williams describes such quests in *The Alchemy of Race and Rights* (5). Even as Patricia insists, "I remember. I remember. It happened. Once upon a time it happened" (32), Johnnie bemoans, "I have been telling and telling to you this story from Washington City and I don't know where I am. Where is Washington City? What has happened?" (23). What one character testifies to as fact, the next declares to be fiction; what one names, the other negates. One argues that Patricia seduced her father. Another insists that Patricia was raped. As Johnnie summarizes this problem of testimonial isolation: "I am telling a story the story of my mother's look and her loveliness and me. When she woke up to me for my mother it was like falling asleep" (23).

The Snowdon daughters become possessed by the goal of historical disclosure even as they endlessly, at times willfully, prove unable to fathom the dysphoric effects of their own compulsive narrating. This narrative temporality dispossesses the characters of their "now" and sets them adrift in time, compelled to narrate not history they possess but the very logic of "possession" through which they become kin. The time of the novel is always and never: "*when* and *if*" (154) as Johnnie insists; "while" (203), according to Patricia. While *Thereafter Johnnie* is ostensibly a novel about father–daughter incest in a middle-class African American family living in late twentieth-century Washington, D.C., the events that form the main plot of the novel remain maddeningly amorphous. Even the explicitly sexual encounters between Patricia and John Christopher are represented as poetic, philosophical, and religious meditations on the aesthetics of eros rather than formal realism (allusions include Yeats's "Leda and the Swan," Lot's tale from Genesis 19, legends of John the Baptist, *King Lear,* and painterly chiaroscuro). Broken into twenty-four chapters ostensibly focalized through different characters' point of view, the novel does not cohere as a realist narrative. Despite its inclusion of realist scenes of father–daughter incest, *Thereafter Johnnie* disrupts the location of these scenes in any specific narrative frame. Instead, the realist incest scenes themselves subtend a narrative time in which literary and historical testimony meet at the juncture of slavery and freedom, coercion and choice.

This narrative time refigures the progressive "history" of the nation-state in relation to the "memory" of its familial subjects. At first the novel appears to be narrated by an omniscient witness who watches the various scenes from the vantage point of divine authority. In "Vesperus," the opening chapter of the book, Johnnie is a disembodied light floating through the library. "Descend. Descend dear Johnnie, light-years away from us," the narrative voice intones, "Down. Johnnie, descend" (4). The narrator's biblical language sets the apocalyptic scene of a deserted Washington, D.C., where "Johnnie" is a grieving, mourning light moving through the empty monuments to national knowledge and power.

Over the course of the chapters, this omniscient narrator devolves into a series of character-specific points of view, until at the end these intersecting points of view constitute a collective "storytelling tribe" called "Diotima":

> And I, Diotima, learned this tale from Diotima, the one who long ago came to us from the north where she knew the black maiden, who is Johnnie, Diotima came here to Puerto Escondido telling this tale and creating the storytelling tribe of Diotima so that we may know what has passed in the north and why there is such great silence there . . . whispering into each window awakening the children—did she whisper these words? Is it true? Did it happen? (241)

Diotima is introduced earlier as Patricia's sometime lesbian lover and Johnnie's guardian after Patricia's death. By text's end, Diotima, Patricia, Johnnie, Eva, and Cynthia Jane (Janie) are all interwoven into the "storytelling tribe" of history's end.

In place of the subjective property of memory, the novel emphasizes the social conditions of storytelling, or the way that oral memory is past along through collective narration. Telling the story from Puerto Escondido in the third world territory that was once Mexico, "Diotima" marks the collective precedent (Greece) and antecedent (Mexico) to U.S. world power.[12] The United States as exemplary modern nation-state and cold war superpower emerges in the novel through a series of poetic, philosophical, and religious origin stories associated with the family romance of the West. Patricia's incestuous desire is figured as the narrative extension of national family origins. As Janie explains, "*Patricia, you may know from the Latin, is derived from the word for father, pater, patria, patrician*—father and nation. A name like that fit right into the myth she spun for herself and felt compelled to act out in her body" (187). Once John Christopher and Patricia have consummated their sexual relationship and Patricia has given birth to a daughter—"Kristen Dolores, meaning she before whom Christ sorrowed, that is to say, Johnnie" (133)—the nation itself begins to fall apart in a world war waged between the "third-world people" (170) and the United States. Patricia kills herself by dissolving into the air above the Potomac River, the remaining black population flees a burned-out Washington, D.C., for the protection of the Allegheny Mountains, and Johnnie, "the lost soul" (105) of the nation, is left a disembodied light haunting the Carnegie Library, mournfully pondering the national history that has brought her into such being at the end of the world.

Historical Violence

Thereafter Johnnie does not, in other words, tell a story of historical trauma recoverable through possession of (or by) memory. Rather, the daughters' "testimony" dissolves the subjective conditioning of memory and induces instead an alternative genealogy of national and narrative time. Within the novel, kinship marks two distinct but interrelated kinds of national time. In the first, kinship signifies the time of divine national origins. The family provides the symbolic foundation of the nation, a biblical iteration of God's will incarnate in patriarchal law. In the second, kinship signifies the historical time of national progress. Here the family provides a social index of changing political and economic organizations of conjugality and sexuality. In this second, progressive time of kinship, a particular norm of family life is installed as the "modern" achievement of the secular metropolitan nation.[13] What Hortense Spillers, in her essay "'The Permanent Obliquity of an In[pha]llibly Straight,'" calls the "one man, one woman" (158) dyad is legitimated as the apex of civilizational achievement, the modern family form against which all other kinship forms are measured. This nuclear family translates incest taboo into Law of the Father, localizing, as Spillers goes on to note, "these two—this law—in a specific locus of economic and cultural means" (158). This one particular form of family life articulates the Law of the Father as an index of modern progress, in which the nation moves from a past steeped in authoritarian domination to a present liberated by liberal (and potentially neoliberal) hegemony.

The divine origins of national kinship and the progressive history of family time are linked through their articulation of racial difference. In order to naturalize this modern account of secular national life—with its distinctions between civil society, domestic privacy, market agency, and political rights—kinship becomes a site of racializing knowledge-production in which the archaic "past" and the modern "present" are delineated through *The Elementary Structures of Kinship* (Lévi-Strauss). As Elizabeth Povinelli describes the imperialism of kinship studies, "Subjects of empire provided the site in which a family, a sexual form, and a governmentality based on them were naturalized" ("Notes on Gridlock," 219) even as they provided evidence for the "civilizational" supremacy of one familial form over another. This "modern" kinship becomes the apex of historical progress, while its particularity is retroactively universalized as the founding symbol of the nation. So-called anomalous kinship forms—those which appear to "lack" the Law of the Father—

then designate, in Spillers's words, the "vestibulary" of national culture ("Mama's Baby, Papa's Maybe," 207). African American kinship in particular becomes the atavistic threshold through which a Law of the Father is naturalized as the civilizing origin of the secular (white, bourgeois) U.S. nation. The abstracted "symbolic order" of the nation relies not merely on a particular representation of kinship, but on a particular formation of time through which secular history erases genealogies of racial terror and sexual violence as well as alternate forms of conjugality and pleasure.

Because kinship racializes both the divine time of national origins as well as the secular time of national progress, it is perhaps unsurprising that *Thereafter Johnnie* uses an apocryphal "curse" to figure African American kinship as a rupture in this double-time of the nation. After 240 pages of narrative exploring the impossibility of locating historical origins, and the impossibility of coherent characterization or plotting in the unmooring of narrative from historical time, in the closing chapter the storytelling tribe Diotima suddenly provides an exegesis of the national history that has come to an end. Articulating the "origins" of slavery in the end of the "world," Diotima narrates the time of the nation as a domesticating "curse" upon what Arlene Keizer, building on the House of Atreus, calls the "House of Africa" ("The Geography of the Apocalypse," 389):

> And from these origins has there come this great curse upon our house: "The females shall be raped and the males shall be murdered." And . . . to certain of the males born to the house but who nevertheless survive murder and slavery—to these shall be given the power of revenge upon the females of their own house who consented with the white males for their destruction, these males shall be given the female children of their own house, and these shall be raped. And raped again. (*Thereafter Johnnie*, 239–40)

In a novel that redounds in myths and epic structures, this "curse" articulated at the end of the novel has often been read as the exemplary myth of the narrative as a whole. As one of the most peculiar and politically discomfiting myths of the novel, this curse upon African American kinship is often read by critics to retroactively explain the compulsive incestuous relations between John Christopher and Patricia, providing a telescopic history of the United States as a story of incest.

There are two main temporal orders imputed to the novel through a reading of the curse: an order of causation, and an order of continuity.

In the first order, the sexual violence of enslavement is read as the cause of subsequent sexual violence in African American families. This order seeks to show that the sexual exploitation of white slave owners disrupted African American kinship systems and resulted in subsequent distortions of sexuality and the breakdown of the incest taboo. As Elizabeth Breau explains in her article "Incest and Intertextuality in Carolivia Herron's *Thereafter Johnnie*," the curse is used to "force an acknowledgement of how the sexual exploitation practiced by white slave owners distorted the sexuality of both master and slave and blurred the familial boundaries that ensure observance of the incest taboo" (92). The second order seeks instead to show that sexual exploitation by white masters during slavery is continuous with sexual exploitation by black fathers during freedom. This second order also attempts to assign liability for incest to racial terror and exploitation, but reads capitalism as the continuous underlying ground for sexual exploitation. In this second order, what Keizer calls "the continuities of racial oppression, the continuities of patriarchal oppression, and the continuities in victims' responses to sexual abuse and domination . . . are linked by being embedded in a capitalist framework" (389). Late twentieth-century incest, according to this second order, is an ongoing *effect* of those discourses of patriarchal property begun in slavery.

Neither of these readings fully interrupts the national kinship paradigm described above. By casting incest as the symptom of an apocryphal curse that seems to mark both the beginning and the end of history, critics read the curse "historically," or as an exemplum of narrative order that remakes the world that has gone before. The curse posits what I will call patriarchal materialism as the historical link between slavery and freedom, maintaining either causal or continuous identity between legal property and sexual possession across time. Such a model of patriarchal materialism emphasizes the prerogatives and privileges of possession over and against the changing conditions in which racialized property relations take hold. In other words, this reading implicitly upholds the symbolization of the incest taboo as a paternal right of property. Thus this chapter adds to Keizer's astute reading of the "subtle connection between the moral and economic values of patriarchal slaveholders and those of middle-class property owners" (390), one that translates, as she points out, into a geography establishing "continuities of patriarchal domination and female submission" (391). My concern is that such a "kinship" between fathers predicated on the historical continuity of property makes it impossible to think racialized kinship and capitalism together, a cate-chresis captured by Keizer in her summary: "John Christopher, the father in the novel, is connected to these Founding Fathers through his gender and his domination of the women in his domestic sphere. (He is sepa-rated from them by his racial subjugation.)" (399). The domestication of property as paternal right is divided from the ongoing "racial subjuga-tion" of the political and civil sphere. This division between *private* patriarchal domination—understood as an implicit liberal prerogative of paternal right—and *public* racial subordination—understood as a lapse in liberal promises of rights and entitlements—maintains a horizon of kinship as divisible and defensible from the state, even as it insists upon property as the primary mode of patriarchal domination in the domestic sphere.

In place of either a causal or a continuous mode of historical expla-nation, I would like to read this "curse" as an allegory of the violence performed by such historical narratives. Counterposed to the "story" of "Truth" and "Freedom" that Johnnie "read in a book" (173), the enun-ciation of this "curse" at the end of the novel does not retroactively order and explain its narrative confusions. Instead, like Walter Benjamin's famous angel of history, the curse resists the "homogeneous, empty time" of progressive history and its narrative forms ("Theses on the Phi-losophy of History," 261). As an allegory of history, the curse introduces a narrative time through which "the past carries with it a temporal index by which it is referred to redemption" (254). *Thereafter Johnnie*'s insis-tence on the indexical time of the curse seeks to "brush history against the grain" (257) in the Benjaminian belief that "*even the dead* will not be safe from the enemy if he wins" (255). This reading of the curse resists the heteronormative historicism that naturalizes patriarchal property, as well as the traumatic antihistoricism that often leaves it too fully behind.[14] In their place, the curse opens onto an alternative genealogy of national family romance, one that challenges both the rationality of sec-ular historical progress and the mystical breach it attributes to African American kinship. And in so doing, it opens up the daughter's agency to reveal history otherwise, to repudiate the curse of history possessing the Snowdon daughters through its indelible images of incest.

The Law of the Father

This reading of the curse prompts me to ask, following Hortense Spillers, how a "model" of kinship founded in the man-woman reproductive dyad produces African American kinship as the site of a specifically historical failure. As Spillers asks, "How does this model, or does this model, suffice for occupied or captive persons and communities in which the rites and rights of gender-function have been exploded *historically* into sexual neutralities?" ("'The Permanent Obliquity of an In[pha]llibly Straight,'" 158–59). This man-woman reproductive dyad hides the conjunction of race, natality, and political right at the heart of secular kinship. But what Freud and Foucault theorize as bar or limit, *Thereafter Johnnie* calls curse. And in the cursed time of *Thereafter Johnnie,* this limit appears again and again *as incest.* Thus while property is central to how we should read the novel's images of incest, my reading will resist the conflation of property and sexuality under the sign of patriarchy. Incest in the novel must be understood not as the exercise of patriarchal right (taboo) or abrogation of paternal responsibility (secret), but rather as a way of narrating liberal formations of sexuality and kinship as *historical inevitabilities.* What is at stake in *Thereafter Johnnie* is how secular family forms are fused to the liberal deployment of sexuality in ways that cover over alternative genealogies of national power. It is, in other words, the political articulation of the incest taboo *as* a Law of the Father that is under attack from the myth of slave origins to the apocalyptic war with which the narrative ends.

In the cursed time of *Thereafter Johnnie,* one might say that two types of incest appear: one that uses sexual property to define the political referents of kinship, and one that figures sexual choice as its political limit. In the first instance, that of incest in legalized enslavement, the novel depicts the father as both lawyer and master. The female line of the protagonist family comes generations ago from "the family of the masters, which a long time passing had been a family of lawyers, all the masters having been lawyers since the time of Elizabeth the First" (236). Kinship in this first instance is a genealogy of legal inheritance, in which the father is identified with the "law" governing forms of just force and possession. The proprietary "Law of the Father" in the context of enslavement is exerted through the commodification of humans and the delimitation of sentience and will. As Saidiya Hartman argues in *Scenes of Subjection,* property is distinguished from kin through "the difference between the deployment of sexuality in the contexts of white kinship—the proprietal relation of the patriarch to his wife and children, the making of legitimate heirs, and the transmission of property—and black captivity— the reproduction of property, the relations of mastery and subjection, and the regularity of sexual violence" (84). The system of enslavement operates through a law of the father that combines economic and legal domination, distinguishing between property and kin precisely by regulating the legal legibility of consent and its attendant assignments of culpability. Thus, in the legal terms of possessive enjoyment, incest clarifies by delimiting the relation between genealogy, property and subjectivity through the power of legitimate possession; "enjoyment registered and effaced the violence of property relations" (Hartman, *Scenes of Subjection,* 25).[15]

In *Thereafter Johnnie,* this first appearance of incest is defined precisely through the differential rights of enjoyment that distinguish property *from* kin. The unchecked erotic "enjoyment" of property becomes the linchpin of proprietal patriarchy, in which the father is both master and lawyer. Here the father/master/lawyer is depicted having sex and procreating with a subject who is both slave and daughter in a peculiar form of possessive self-extension, what Hartman calls "the extensive capacities of property—that is, the augmentation of the master subject through his embodiment in external objects and persons" (21). The great-great-grandmother of Johnnie is herself the victim of incest and progenitor of a kinship line founded in this fact: "Before her twentieth year had she received within herself the sperm of both her white father and of the white male child, her father's son, her half-brother. The child life of both had she held within herself" (236). Thus the illegibility of incest as a *violation* becomes the symbol of historical bondage by law:

> What happened? Slavery happened. Africans came into bondage to Europeans in a new promised land. And males with light, bright, white skin slept with the black females who had nursed them, and slept with their sisters, and slept with their daughters and nieces and cousins and begot children—and thus began a great crime of these contending peoples of one nation. (174)

According to *Thereafter Johnnie,* the "nation" is created through a slave system founded on incest—but a form of incest that is illegible within the legal definition of kinship and property relations. The so-called Law of the Father thus produces proper kinship by normalizing the enjoyment of property as distinct from and yet productive of the enjoyment of kin. He regulates the difference between commodified and domestic relations as itself the political right of a racialized and racializing patriarchal authority.

The second type of incest in *Thereafter Johnnie*—the rape/seduction that takes place between Patricia and John Christopher in the 1970s—

"thereafter" appears as a patriarchal failure to achieve proper freedom. Through a dominant historical narrative of the nation, familial subjects appear free from the domination of the past by expressing their liberty in particular forms of agency—intimacy, love, consensual sex, participation in the marriage contract, and voluntary reproduction.[16] As Spillers poetically names this transformation from the literal law of the father to the liberal incest taboo, "This universal prohibition involves us in a democracy of ancient scandal that must be related in some sense to the architectonics of domesticity" ("Permanent Obliquity," 160). Such an architectonics returns us once again to the modern secular form of family life in which, as Povinelli argues in "Notes on Gridlock," "love makes families elemental(ly). *Family Values,* for instance, hinges together family and nation through an argument about the value of intimate recognition" (228). As Povinelli summarizes this transformation most pointedly, "*Love* thematizes and indicates the affective site where choice and compulsion are blurred" (229). The "bondage" of the nation does not end, but is instead symbolized as an unmourned crisis in national history: the paradox of incest now embedded in liberal family love. This results in a story of political freedom with an inarticulable, subjectivating loss at its heart: "After the masters had gone was there not much weeping? did they not weep and mourn? mother and child, sorrowing over the sins of property rights, power and passion that had brought them both into life" (238–39).

Within such a "liberating" architectonics, new bonds of intimacy and love cover over the "sorrowing over sins of property rights, power and passion" that marks the legacy of unredressed enslavement. New deployments of sexuality strip "sex" from its historical moorings and universalize desire, consent, and love as the mechanisms of domestic "freedom." Sexuality becomes an index of new orders of public and private life, with sexual *choice* marking the political limit of kinship in the late twentieth-century chapters of the novel. This limit will be met and traversed time and again in John Christopher's fathering of his daughters, specifically in the incest that marks his relationship with Patricia. Four chapters in particular chart John Christopher's rise and fall as liberal patriarch: "Monopoly," "Three Witches," "The King of Hearts," and "Atlantis." These four sequenced chapters create a minor story arc within the book as a whole, tracing John Christopher's initial seduction of his future wife Camille, his absorption in managing the sexual desires of his daughters, his effort to seduce his seemingly wayward daughters back into paternal rule, and his memory of a childhood curse that echoes the "curse on the House of

Africa" (Keizer, "The Geography of the Apocalypse," 389). Across these chapters, property remains key to the relation between fatherhood and legal domesticity. But the property relations subtending the "law of the father" change considerably from those depicted in chattel slavery. As we shall see, the property relations subtending John Christopher's inhabitation of the liberal father's "law" will undermine rather than uphold his patriarchal rule.

"Monopoly" first introduces us to John Christopher as the liberal subject of the modern family. His deracination from racialized status and entry into economic agency is demonstrated through his ability to manage gendered difference in liberal systems of sexual exchange. In this chapter he is shown negotiating with his future wife, Camille, acting as a figurative "banker" who seduces his bride-to-be into giving herself to him according to the abstract rules of the market. As they play Monopoly, John Christopher controls "the rules" that determine values of exchange, figuring his seduction as regulating the conditions of her consent. "You have to play by the rules of the game," John Christopher insists (37). But the rules themselves are intangible, subject to his changing will. "You make up the rules, Chris, why can't I make up a rule?" (37), Camille laments. The rules of the market are necessarily both arbitrary and delimited, however, specified through the terms of value dictated by the "banker" and backed by the distributive justice of the police. John Christopher insists "kiss me or you forfeit the game" while he visits her in jail, and tells her, "It says here you owe me ten dollars" (37). Capturing the spirit of capitalism within their erotic barter, Camille replies, "That's not fair! I keep owing you everything" (37). Camille's unspecifiable debt constitutes liberal sexuality in a peculiar mode of exchange. Value is derived from Camille's willingness to barter certain acts—to forfeit a "kiss," to "lie down" before him and "open her legs" (37), and so on—without seeming to bestow a property right along with them.

In fact, liberalism depends upon the distinction between property right and gift, or between civil contract and sexual consent. Wendy Brown argues that liberalism as a political philosophy operates by distinguishing between the liberating effects of contract and the subordinating effects of consent: "Contract is a civil act abstracted from relations of power: it is expressive of, and performs, formal equality and relations of distance. Consent is a more intimate act implicating relations of power; it marks the presence of power, arrangements, and actions that one does not oneself create but to which one submits" (*States of Injury,* 162–63).

In describing "liberalism's family values," Brown writes, "Insofar as consent involves agreeing to something the terms of which one does not determine, consent marks the subordinate status of the consenting party" (163). Differentiating contract from consent separates economic from sexual exchanges, seemingly protecting against property rights in humans while in fact reifying specific modes of expropriation as private or noneconomic. As a result, the terms of liberal sexuality are produced through market logics ("Monopoly") but then displaced from legitimate forms of market agency (appearing as consent and desire). Camille's desire in particular is cast as a response, rather than as a form of potential agency. As John Christopher explains: "I'm moving toward you gently to get you, so that I can have you slowly, mylady. You'll be very sure that you want me" (38). John Christopher's liberal subjectivity is defined by his ability to produce Camille's "consent" as a private act—as gift—conditioned upon desire rather than coercion (or legalized force).[17] Through this process John Christopher seemingly realizes the role proffered by race-neutral deployments of sexuality and the rise of the black middle-class family enabled by post-1970s capital.

Domestic Possession

Once he fathers daughters, however, John Christopher finds his monopoly over the rules of sexual commerce shaken. The chapter "Three Witches" traces John Christopher's initial euphoria over the delights of liberal paternity and subsequent dysphoria over his daughter's seeming sexual waywardness. At first he experiences fatherhood as the apex of liberal subjectivity. John Christopher's task is to raise his daughters to become proper liberal subjects, each one "completely individual and so precious" (53). Their ability to become such subjects depends upon his performance of paternal duty, represented here as the ability to solicit and manage their desire (like the potential husband in "Monopoly") while displacing it from himself onto substitute objects (unlike the father/lawyer/master). Indeed, his initial description of fathering daughters shows him happily monopolizing their desire within the family in order to prepare them for liberal womanhood, defined by proper consumption of commodities and proper consent to sexuality:

> You thought their love for you would make it hard for them to grow up, because of their attachment to you, their father, you worked hard to be the best a father can be to his daughters when they are growing up and wanting things and you wanted so much to be the one giving

things to them so that they would know that their father is good and
you took good care of them. (45)

The daughters' "love" is both vehicle and obstacle to the normative
social relations of liberal subjectivity. According to John Christopher, it
is their "attachment" to their father that drives the daughters' desire, an
interiorizing desire that must be channeled into external "things." John
Christopher therefore identifies himself as the locus of desire as well as
the regulator of its displacements. He becomes "their father" through
his provision of material goods that satisfy desires that belong properly
to him. Thus he generously teaches them to seek satisfaction in civil society and commodities because he believes that these goods serve merely as
fetishized substitutions for him as "father" or secret monopolist of desire.

The discourse of love emerges precisely as the "domestic architectonics" distinguishing liberal father from legal master, children from commodities. John Christopher performs paternal authority as a pedagogical
duty to regulate his children's desire, rather than enjoying their sexual
appropriability. He becomes the monopolist of desirous consent rather
than the law delimiting those subjects capable of it. Thus John Christopher emerges as a loving, liberal father by representing himself as the
regulator of commerce and social status in the eyes of his children: "You
watched each one as she was growing up so you could be there tearing down barriers whether it was some racist teacher at school or if
they needed more money or clothes in a different style so they could be
unique" (45). He will equalize their relation to civil society by tearing
down "barriers" from racism to the lack of individuating commodities—
a system of "equality" formalized as a noncoercive equivalence between
economic freedom and social status.[18] The "democracy" of this incest
taboo structures familial affect and enjoyment through the formal equality of middle-class domesticity. John Christopher's status as liberal father
depends upon the power of his "love" to guarantee his children's equality. In other words, his ability to regulate his children's status is the key
to his own. Here his children's achievement of liberal subjectivity seems
to function "like" a commodity of the paternal order, exhibiting the fungibility of paternal inscription described by Saidiya Hartman and echoed
in legal scholar Barbara Bennett Woodhouse's suggestion "not that children *are* property but that our culture makes assumptions about children
deeply analogous to those it adopts in thinking about property" ("'Who
Owns the Child?'" 1042).[19]

Recent theorists of American childhood have attempted to understand liberal "patriarchy" as founded in such analogous or even metaphorical property relations. According to David Archard, Sanford Katz, and Barbara Bennett Woodhouse, parental rights legislation and rulings establish the father as liberal pedagogue who bears his duty to protect the interest of his children as a property right. As Woodhouse argues in "'Who Owns the Child?'" although "we live in a time that no longer formalizes ownership in human beings" (1041), "the Court's elastic construction of Fourteenth Amendment liberty to include parental control of the child served—just as in the economic due process cases—to defend traditions of private ownership, hierarchical structures, and individualist values against claims of collective governance" (1037).[20] What she calls "patriarchal property thinking" (1041) constitutes children as a kind of figurative property of parental rights, exhibiting the fungible capacity of the commodity in highly circumscribed domestic contexts. Fathers are mandated to instruct children in the proper desires of future subjects. Children are figurative property that extend the parent, rather than literal possessions who behave themselves as alienable commodities. But unlike Woodhouse's liberal critique of the white patriarchal household, in *Thereafter Johnnie* children are not rendered *analogous* to property but rather are used to figure a representational *crisis* in so-called property—one that reveals the genealogy of racialized kinship condensed in the discourse of love.

John Christopher's elegy to the joys of paternal possession comes to an abrupt halt when he sees his three daughters dancing together and singing an unfamiliar song in the moonlight. Coming upon them unexpectedly where they dance in the valley of Howard University, he becomes convinced that they are singing a song that perverts and distorts the proper relations of liberal family life. The song sounds to him like "mixed black poetry that mocked and teased regular poetry with black rhythms" (44), a sound they have not learned from him and that he associates with untamed public space or the streets of D.C., what he calls "a dirty black street song black children sing" (43). This "mixed" black sound registers for John Christopher as a kind of sexual waywardness, one that threatens his seductive powers as a liberal father: "You could tell they were doing something strange—you couldn't see well from where you stood but didn't they want to make love to one another in bed with their clothes off? You believe that's what they wanted, they were not innocent. Maybe they had already done it to one another, how could you know?" (45).

According to John Christopher, his daughters' failure to differentiate between social forms—between "black" and "regular" poetry (44), between male and female, and between sexuality and love—threatens the secular ideal of familial love. As he asserts in the shock of regulatory confusion: "I want them to forget heaven and love the earth but I don't want them to love the earth like that. . . . I don't want them to love poetry more than they love me. When I teach them to turn away from poetry to love the world I don't want them to go to bed with one another. They mix everything up" (65).

Stirred by watching his three daughters sing their song and dance together in the snow below him, John Christopher feels the return of "the ancient curse that follows you out of the south" (49), the one that follows him from the ocean "where so many of our ancestors lie fathoms deep. So many. Fifteen million black Africans undone by death" (48). We learn two chapters later that this curse comes to John Christopher most immediately from his childhood, when he was cursed by a vagrant after hearing a church sermon on the differences between carnal love (*eros*), brotherly love (*philos*), and divine love (*agape*) (80). In the chapter "Atlantis," a young John Christopher remembers hearing a sermon on "John, Christ's beloved disciple," in which "he had recognized his own name, John Christopher" (78). In the sermon, only John demonstrated divine love for Christ, and therefore only he witnessed "the end of all earthly things, the Apocalypse was revealed to him when he was chained to the island of Patmos" (80). Confused and lost after the sermon, John Christopher strays from his home and runs into an itinerant man with whom he discusses his fear of this ending. Asserting his panicked desire to survive the end, John Christopher cries out: "Please don't burn me, I want to be saved from the fire like Lot was saved" (82). "Like Lot? You're sure?" the vagrant asks, and like the emblematic Lot, John Christopher will mistake his paternal love as divine reward and fall into the curse of incest.[21]

It is the promise of survival, of becoming "like" a biblical patriarch, that seems at first to consolidate John Christopher as a masculine liberal agent. The chapters tracing John Christopher's childhood and young adult life follow his course from frightened child to complacently authoritative adult. But the daughters' song seems to return "the ancient curse" that follows him not merely from childhood but from generations past, from the ocean "where so many of our ancestors lie fathoms deep" (48). This curse—multiplied across textual iterations from beginning to end—

consistently appears in the novel as a haunting, unredressed public *sound*. Visiting a national museum at the novel's start, Patricia contrasts "the remnants of excluded black shadows the evicted dark peoples of George-town murmuring shadows, grieving, muttering" with the museum, where "each thing they have is set up all by itself alone" (11). Patricia perceives her father as like the museum objects: "All by himself. Alone. Holy Cup Vial Chalice Grail Urn Skull Cup. Alone" (11). But by the novel's end, Johnnie will describe John Christopher's plunge into the sound itself: "This mourner, my father" (233), Johnnie intones, explaining how John Christopher "mourned all that night and the sand that was the many voices of the annihilated village whispered and rustled and fell" (233).[22]

John Christopher's efforts to be a liberal pedagogue are haunted by what the novel consistently represents as an unredressed public sound. Sound returns what Fred Moten, in *In the Break,* calls "the inspirited materiality" of the black radical tradition, that which constitutes "a kind of temporal warp" (11) within national histories of progressive capitalism and liberal kinship. Moten theorizes sound as the "break" articulated by "the historical reality of commodities who spoke—of laborers who were commodities before, as it were, the abstraction of labor power from their bodies and who continue to pass on this material heritage across the divide that separates slavery and 'freedom'" (6).[23] Here the daughters' song interrupts John Christopher's flight across that divide, opening up "a temporal warp" in historical progress and its promise of fulfillment: metaphorical property relations within the liberal family, paternal rights to regulate proper alienability beyond that family. But what Moten de-scribes as "temporal warp," John Christopher interprets as historical breach. John Christopher becomes convinced that his daughters pervert his monopoly over deracinated identity instead of being seduced to the intimate bonds of loving family life. The "mixed black poetry" that returns in the song threatens the liberal incest taboo not only with les-bian incest, but also with historical "miscegenation" and the racialized property relations hidden in the genealogy of family. If, according to Benjamin, "the shock with which moments enter consciousness as if already lived usually strikes us in the form of a sound" ("A Berlin Story," 59), the shock of the daughter's song enters John Christopher's conscious-ness "as if already lived" in the return of the curse.

The daughters' song threatens to return genealogies of "inspirited materiality" to the liberal scene of race-neutral patriarchal property think-ing. John Christopher hears this song as his failure to adequately separate love from history, gift from utility. He cannot achieve democratic domesticity precisely because of the social utility of his love, its instrumentality to keep the history of property relations at bay. Listening to the daughters singing in the moonlight, John Christopher feels the curse return as a will to power: "You discovered that you feared something about them and you wanted power over them, you felt the terrifying warning of that power in the fire that stirred upon your thigh" (50–51). Declaring himself the "King of Hearts," in the next chapter John Christopher reasserts patriarchal power like a modern day Lot, transforming divine authority into biopolitical sovereignty. To recontain his daughters' wayward desire, John Christopher forces them to watch him perform open-heart surgery on a stray dog. Referring to the dog as a "stray bitch," he declares to his daughters: "This is life. She lies there spread-eagle on the operating table, unconscious, the mask of anesthesia tied around her nose" (59).

Throughout the procedure, which takes up the entirety of the chapter, John Christopher declares his power as the historical achievement of biopolitics. His fatherhood symbolizes biopolitical sovereignty, the juncture of deracination and sexual liberation he wishes his daughters to recognize and revere. As John Christopher declares during the surgery: "Where do you think your equal rights came from anyway? . . . Do you want to know who freed you? Shall I let you know who freed you? WE freed you, damn it, *we* freed you! Medicine! Doctors!" (70). Declaring "freedom" a "gift," John Christopher insists: "Your freedom is a luxury I give you, medicine has given you the right to your own life, your own body—I came that you might have life and that you might have it more abundantly" (70). As the aim of his surgery on the stray dog, John Christopher reveals the liberal, loving father as the "King of Hearts," the sovereign of progress who remakes the daughter's heart into proof of his dominion over life's properties: "Stray bitch. She is in my hands now. I will cut out her heart and strip it—I have to strip the heart and the pericardium in order to keep her body from rejecting her own heart. She won't even recognize her own heart when I am finished. But I'll give her heart back to her and she'll keep her heart and she'll live anyway" (58).

Desiring Daughters

But something goes awry after John Christopher's effort of claim patriarchal authority over "blood" in historical time. John Christopher asserts his power as the ability to give life itself as a "gift." Here the *bios* is defined as a heart stripped and returned to its body, a heart that will beat the time of "freedom" as a liberal "gift" from patriarchal sovereignty. Rather than realigning the daughters' recognition with liberal love, however, John Christopher's action seems to unleash Patricia as "stray bitch" whose heart she insists not only belongs to her father, but through this belonging renders "Daddy" her rightful possession. For it is only after she witnesses the open-heart surgery on the dog that Patricia becomes "possessed" by the aim of having sex with her father. Unable or unwilling to cede her desire or to substitute another object in its place, Patricia insists: "You are the father who gave me being. Whom should I desire but you? Whom should I possess?" (34). Patricia does seem to recognize the natural rights John Christopher seeks to bestow, but she insists that this "gift" undoes the secular property arrangements he has claimed. As Patricia hails John Christopher's penis: "It's a gift, it's a gift from god that cannot be refused and I will have god, I will have god I will have god within me for all time forever eternally completely absolute—I will have god and only god as my lover" (208).

Patricia's open pursuit of a sexual relationship with her father constitutes the heart of the novel's hermeneutic puzzle. *Thereafter Johnnie* is relentless, much like Patricia herself, in its depiction of her will to pursue and maintain this sexual relationship despite its power to dissolve herself (she evaporates as she jumps from the Potomac bridge), her family (whose broken bonds are mourned as the end of freedom), and the daughter of this union (turned into a light haunting the Carnegie Library). Patricia violates all norms of dignity and decorum in her pursuit of sex with her father; she lies down for him on the Washington Mall and begs "him to make love to her" (191), and following him ultimately to San Juan, she seduces him in the bath of a hotel room. Echoing the language of John Christopher's surgery, Cynthia Jane reports, "She told me she wanted to be his bitch" (191), while Eva speculates, "Maybe she's a complete fleshpoint of passion—the bitch like you said, a bitch in heat" (198). As Patricia herself laments, "What's the only thing that's hard in the whole damn world? What is hard, Janie, is to get your body laid, to be somebody's bitch" (208). What appears at the historical and literary crossroads of the late twentieth-century incest scene is Patricia's spectacularized expression of agency. Patricia does not consent to sex with John Christopher but seems rather willful to the point of derangement in her effort to have him. As John Christopher says during one of their sexual encounters, "You have chased me unmercifully. Aren't you the same child who has chased me unmercifully all your life?" (14).

The rest of this chapter dwells on the hermeneutic puzzle posed by the daughter's agency, specifically reading its enigmatic sign (the daughter's "X") as the crossroads of literary and historical representation in the 1990s. Saidiya Hartman has argued that black women's sexual agency was deliberately constituted as an enigma by antebellum discourses of seduction (*Scenes of Subjection*).[24] According to Hartman, these discourses of seduction constituted the "family romance" of chattel slavery: "Seduction erects a family romance—in this case, the elaboration of a racial and sexual fantasy in which domination is transposed into the bonds of mutual affection, subjection idealized as the pathway to equality, and perfect subordination declared the means of ensuring great happiness and harmony" (89). In order to decode the effects of this romance, Hartman asks the following questions: "How does seduction uphold perfect submission and, at the same time, assert the alluring, if not endangering, agency of the dominated?" (88); "How can rape be differentiated from sexuality when 'consent' is intelligible only as submission? How can we discern the crime when it is a legitimate use of property or when the black captive is made the originary locus of liability?" (85). This historical romance constituted black women's sexuality as the locus of both "perfect submission" and "alluring agency," will-lessness and willfulness. *Thereafter Johnnie*'s late twentieth-century incest scenes raise similar questions about the "locus of liability" for the daughter's seeming assertion of agency. But, in addition, we must also ask: What forms of family romance are constituted by 1990s discourses of seduction? And what new "scenes of subjection" are produced by the literary and historical connections drawn between family romances past and present?

Determining the "locus of liability" has been a key problem for critics writing on *Thereafter Johnnie*'s incest scenes. Several different scenes are presented as incest in the novel. These sexual scenes are narrated in reverse order, unfolding backward in time until they reach the generations-distant scene of enslavement. First, there are two chapters depicting incestuous sex between John Christopher and a young adult Patricia. These events are at least nominally presented as chosen or sought by Patricia. The first chapter in which they have sex is placed somewhat early in the text but is entitled "The Last Time." Patricia and John Christopher have already been involved in a convoluted sexual relationship at this point, and Johnnie has been born from their union. In this chapter, John Christopher participates actively in a sexual discourse resembling the chapter "Monopoly": "My girl, prettyPat, but come here to me a moment, I will do something for you" (13). His nicknames for Patricia in these incest scenes, "prettyPat" and "patPat" (12), mark her as his possession, the heartbeat of the stray bitch he has produced. His patter is entirely the discourse of possession, now realized in its sexual form: "I'll do what I want to do, sweetheart. I'll do what I like and you'll like it too, I promise you. Aren't you mine? I'll take care of you. Do what I tell you to do and undress sweetheart" (14); "But I own you my dear, I own you. I can do what I want with you now. Come here now and do what I tell you to do. Come. Stand over here with me right now my darling and take off all of your clothes for me so that I can see you" (14).

The next chapter treating their sexual relationship depicts the moment in Puerto Rico when Patricia and John Christopher have sex in a hotel room. This chapter, called "The First Time," arrives quite a bit later in the text. Here Patricia has followed John Christopher to San Juan in order to consummate their sexual relationship. This culmination of Patricia's pursuit of John Christopher takes the form of passive self-presentation; her behavior operates as passive seduction or seduction by passivity, forcing him to initiate sexual contact. Patricia follows John Christopher into the bathtub and places herself before him, where he begins to caress her body. But she panics when intercourse is about to begin: "She has never expected this. She has not imagined that something could happen" (119). Patricia struggles against him "and she means it" (119), but after he releases her she moves to be on top of him and they have sex. As she climaxes she cries out, "Daddy, Daddy!" (119) while her body makes an X shape:

> Then he is no longer her god, nor her king, nor her lover, nor her father, but he is an erected penis urging itself into a female hole, only that, he is a penis with a female hole to enter, and does enter it, expending itself himself within live female flesh, pushing and pushing and pushing in, without will or hope, only a risen penis inside a live female. (120)

This passage reverses the order of seduction traced across the chapters "Monopoly," "Three Witches," and "King of Hearts." Patricia hails him as "Daddy," but this hail occurs precisely as John Christopher is reduced from his various roles of "god," "king," "lover," or "father." At the so-called root of these ordinations, we find that John Christopher is simply an "erected penis," "without will or hope." "The First Time" that John Christopher engages in sex with his daughter, he is reduced to a penis entering a "female hole." John Christopher's penis no longer regulates figural and literal property as the standard of possessive exchange but rather becomes an "it" without agency or will: "It expends itself, John Christopher's penis in Patricia his daughter" (120).

After this sexual encounter, Patricia appears to regress into a childlike state: "Patricia, prettyPat, patPat, patPat, whispering possessed in her forgotten baby voice as her father sleeps" (120). "Patricia, prettyPat, patPat," echo of the dog's heartbeat and also John Christopher's nickname for her in these erotic scenes, returns as Patricia's "forgotten baby voice" to trace what appears to be the memory of a prior sexual event that took place when she was two. The novel reports: "Shaking and trembling and no one to hold her as she shakes and trembles in her first orgasm, not this time but the first time, the first time, hidden, forgotten, violated by a touch of her father's fingers upon her two-year-old clitoris" (120). In the lengthy sequence that follows the revelation of this "first" first time, "Daddy" is addressed over and over again as the agent of this foundational violation: "Whispering the words she had no words for in the beginning, during the first time, as he sleeps fifteen years later her body stiffens into a catatonic X of horror, violation violently enforced pleasure and pain, she whispers possessed by the words she did not have at the beginning, 'Daddy, Daddy, Daddy. I hate you, I love you, I hate you, I love you, I hate you, I love you, I love you, I love you, Daddy, Daddy, Daddy'" (121).

Across these three scenes, the X becomes legible as the mark of incestuous sex. And it clearly signals the enigmatic agency of incest within the liberal family romance. What is not clear, however, is how to read it. On one hand, Patricia's utterance of the word "Daddy," combined with the "X" her body makes, reveals to critics the "violation violently enforced pleasure and pain" of molestation at age two. This means that the X, while seemingly a sign of sexual agency, resituates that agency as merely the effect of an earlier moment of violation. The complex seduction of John Christopher's paternal authority would be revealed as, at root, the violence of "a male penis risen inside a female hole." But on the other hand, even as X seems to mark the spot of a hidden sexual violation, it does not exactly present clear testimony about what this violation entails. Patricia may be "possessed by the words she did not have in the beginning," but it is her body that memorializes that "violation violently enforced pleasure and pain" standing outside of time. Here Patricia is possessed in two different registers, that of a socially and historically seductive linguistic repetition and that of a dehistoricizing bodily arrest. Her words articulate the unrepresentable sequence of the father's rule, translated into a syntactic binary equalizing subject and object, love and hate: "I love you I hate you Daddy Daddy Daddy." But this grammar of subjection only reveals an inexplicable present constituted precisely through its ambivalent repudiation of an unknown past. And the daughter's body offers no further information about this past, offering only somatic memorializing—the bodily X—to reveal the history of sexual violation behind the daughter's seeming volition.

Literary Crossroads

This confusion is deepened by the repetition of the X across widely different contexts in the novel. The X appears again in the final scene of incest in the text, this one arriving at the very end of the text and occurring several generations previously. Here Johnnie's great-great-grandmother Laetitia has, like Patricia, already given birth to a daughter whose father is also her, the mother's, father. And, like the scene in "The First Time," this daughter (Rowena) will bear witness to a scene of incestuous sex between her mother and her father/grandfather. Echoing the literary style and plotlines of Reconstruction-era interracial romances, the narrative explains how Laetitia's daughter Rowena has been raised to believe she is white. While Laetitia lives in a cottage owned by her master and is made sexually available to the men of the master family, her daughter is kept unaware of her parentage or the situation of her mother. Entering the cottage one afternoon, Rowena witnesses Laetitia "held in the air in the shape of an X in order to be fornicated" (238) by two men: father and brother. Expressing her shock and horror, Rowena is told by the two men that they have the right to "sell you or rape you any day of the week" (238). Here the X seems to mark severe domination, the antebellum "romance" of chattel slavery revealed as the violation of forced incest.[25]

But to make matters even more confusing, the X does not remain at the scene of incestuous agency, violation, or reproduction. The X does not merely return Patricia's adult incest (producing her child Johnnie) to the scene of an earlier incestuous violation (Patricia's molestation at age two), nor both of these late twentieth-century scenes to an antebellum scene of forced incestuous reproduction (Laetitia and Rowena). For the X haunts Camille as well, who frantically crushes the X when it intrudes on her memory of the day she waited for John Christopher to marry her. Camille insists that "Chris saw her first and she is the only one Chris comes for" (227) as she "beats and screams and cries out and then beats in silence" (230) the "black thick heavy roach" (229) crawling across her white pillow. As the roach looks "to find a dark place and live there"

(230), she crushes it and leaves it alive "flightless wings and senseless antennae misshapen into a pulsing X unseen" (230). And the critical literacy demanded by the X plagues characters in the text itself. As Camille explains, "I still don't understand how Patricia became the way she was. I knew something was wrong when she was about two years old" (179–80) and was found catatonic against the window in a storm, turned into an "X shape." "It's as if she had been raped by a hurricane," Camille laments (180).

While it seems clear that the X signals an unknown meaning related to sexuality, it is not clear how to interpret it. The "hurricane" hypothesis suits one interpretation of the text; perhaps the X signals the modes of power through which patriarchy is described as a natural force. This reading would treat the father as a sovereign lurking in the heart of liberal freedom, one who continues to exercise something like absolute power over his female children as the final legacy of property rights in others. This family romance insists that the late twentieth-century discourse of seduction operates in similar ways to its antebellum predecessor (without the racial specificity). The key difference is in the expectation that family relations should be free from the taint of market relations, or at least should not treat daughters as exploitable property. As Judith Herman asserts in *Father–Daughter Incest*: "The father, in effect, forces the daughter to pay with her body for affection and care which should be freely given" (4). In trying to argue against the claim that children either desire or produce the conditions for father-daughter incest, some feminists have analogized children to "captives," as Herman does in her later volume *Trauma and Recovery*: "Political captivity is generally recognized, whereas the domestic captivity of women and children is often unseen. A man's home is his castle; rarely is it understood that the same home may be a prison for women and children" (74).[26] This account represents children as "captives" to suggest that their structural subordination negates a genuine capacity for negotiation, complicity, or pleasure that would render them liable for the incest.

This approach would return us to the identity of John Christopher with the "Founding Fathers" (Keizer, "The Geography of the Apocalypse," 399), in which the bundle of political rights signified by property extends the enjoyment of the commodity's fungibility to the liberal father's enjoyment of the child. The daughter's X becomes a form of testimony to the hidden patriarchal violence of kinship, which in turns allows it to index these different scenes to one another. Elizabeth Breau in her 1997

African American Review article argues that Patricia's pursuit of her
father is caused by a prior scene of childhood molestation, when John
Christopher commits "digital rape" (93) of Patricia at age two. Summa-
rizing this scene, Breau explains: "Patricia, possessed by paternally
implanted desire for her father, can do nothing but pursue him, and John
Christopher must live with the unrelenting repercussions of his own desire
as Patricia's aggression removes even the barrier of his self-control" (94).
Extending this reading to the scene of incest in racial slavery, we are back
to the curse as the exemplum of causative or continuous modes of patriarchal materialism. If the historical curse appears as sound, the X marks
its arresting function in contemporary print. The daughter's X testifies to
the workings of this curse, proof of the ongoing violation inaugurated by
the formations of racial slavery. Her semblance of sexual agency would
be merely the resemblance of the father's seduction, which in turn resem-
bles the patriarchal law of the masters.

Making this argument can be an important political project, and
demonstrating the ongoing sexual violability produced by sexism and
racism is a valuable goal. My concern however is with what might be
lost in this approach. This reading of the X forges patriarchal continuity
outside the political conditions of history. In other words, "patriarchal
kinship" becomes the referent of the daughter's seeming agency, translating the body of the daughter (its X) into the mark of its own sexual
violability. The daughter would be granted testimonial agency, but only
to the degree that she herself represented sexual property. As Deborah
McDowell elaborates this problem, "This attempt to control both black
women's written *bodies* and their *written* bodies must be read and its
service to the family plot interpreted, for that plot makes women permanent daughters content merely to transcribe their father's words"
("Reading Family Matters," 97). This would become the form of testimonial possession discussed earlier in this chapter, in which characters
could claim "proprietary rights to memories" only by taking on the roles
of liberal family life. Here, however, we see the delimiting effects of such
memorial rights. As a marker of the patronymic erased by the violence
of slavery and the denial of literacy exercised in its name, the X constitutes the black daughter's body as the testimonial cross of history. "History is your own heartbeat" (1), Ashraf Rushdy comments in his study
of palimpsest narratives, *Remembering Generations*. But here that heartbeat, patPat, prettyPat, signifies only the daughter's ongoing service to
the national family romance.

The question of *print* representation (rather than sound) is key here. *Thereafter Johnnie* draws attention to the historical erasure of alternative accounts even as it refuses to write an account revealing incest as a historical "secret." Instead, it situates incest as the mark of both a *historical and literary* "interdiction and denial": the daughter's X. As Spillers, in "'The Permanent Obliquity of an In[pha]llibly Straight,'" explains the problem posed by African American incest narratives, "if 'family,' on this historic occasion, describes, for all intents and purposes, a site of interdiction and denial, we could go so far as to say that the mark of incestuous desire and enactment—a concentrated carnality— speaks for its losses, confusions, and above all else its imposed abeyance of order and degree" (176). Such a "concentrated carnality" at the site of the black daughter's body comes to ground the "historic" familialism of the nation as itself outside time. As Elizabeth Yukins suggests, the testimony of what she calls "bastard daughters" (222) is burdened with the demand of "reproduction" (225)—a figure for the historical and contemporary "join" (to use Toni Morrison's words in *Beloved*, 213) at the site of family. What Yukins describes as the "capacity to claim propriety rights" to memory transmission across generations actually naturalizes kinship as the source of historical transmission—the daughter's violated body articulates a historic familialism linking kinship and nation ("Bastard Daughters and the Possession of History," 222). Patricia becomes the "ahistoric, reified female" (Spillers, 163) of the incest taboo, her representational agency under historical erasure. Patricia can only be possessor possessed (*Thereafter Johnnie*, 206), "deserter deserted" (7), as Johnnie describes her, "my mother. Monomaniacal" (21).[27] She is an instrument of history, surely, but never its agent.

The Ends of Freedom

In closing I would like to suggest that the X opens up the narrative time of the nation to alternative forms of political articulation. The daughter's X introduces a transfigurative gap—or temporal warp—in the historical and literary narratives that bind father and nation. The repeated sign of the X, as Saidiya Hartman argues regarding the "politics" of practice for the enslaved, exerts an "effort to wrench the political from its proper referent" (65). According to Spillers, through kinship "a social subject in abeyance, in an absolute deferral that becomes itself a new synthesis, is born: the African-American, whose last name, for all intents and purposes, becomes historically X, the mark of his or her borrowed culture's profound 'illiteracy'" (159). Because of this kinship formation, "African-American fiction show[s] father-daughter incest or its surrogate motions as an *absence,* not an overdetermination" (176). This marked absence, this X of borrowed culture, is the reason why African American *daughters* as Spillers puts it, remain "silent figures, like materialized vectors in a field of force, [they] are *interestingly* silent in the sense that incest fiction, even written by women, *never,* as far as I know, establishes the *agency* of the incestuous act inside the female character" (161).

But in the apocryphal time of *Thereafter Johnnie,* what "flashes up at a moment of danger" (Benjamin, "Theses on the Philosophy of History," 255) is precisely the *agency of the daughter.* The daughter's agency appears neither as absence nor overdetermination, but rather as a determination otherwise that discloses the ongoing literary and historical violence of national kinship. This sign of the X opens the space for what Houston A. Baker calls "critical memory" or "the very faculty of revolution"("Critical Memory and the Black Public Sphere," 3). Such critical memory is used to create the time of revolution in the novel, that which seeks to "bring about a real state of emergency" (Benjamin, "Theses," 257). But this state of emergency, that which interrupts progressive national time, is not brought about by an "angel" of history (257). Instead, the state of emergency is caused by an act of sexual theft. If the X is "borrowed" to mark the site of the African American father's murder in Spillers's "American Grammar Book," here the X is "stolen" to interrupt both progressive time and a revolutionary time predicated on the public sphere.[28] An astute observer of the historical relation between fathers, property, and freedom, Cynthia Jane cries out: "She's stolen our father from us, she's stolen him, we're all bastards now!" (197). It is *this* antihistoricist gesture, this stealing of the father, that Cynthia Jane recognizes as the end of a progressive movement toward freedom, lamenting: "She didn't have to do it, she didn't have to go after him, there was plenty of time and we could have all been free" (201).

This is precisely the point—she didn't *have* to do it; nor was it a choice. What the daughter's agency stages is the breakdown in will-lessness and willfulness, "perfect submission" and "alluring agency," desire and domination. And it is this sexual rupture that performs the theft of "freedom," the refusal that there will be "plenty of time." The X therefore does not mean that the daughter "has" agency.[29] Rather, X marks the representational crossroads through which agency becomes curse: either culpability (consent to her own exploitation) or erasure (reduction to her own victimization). As the novel draws to a close, the approaching apocalypse seems to offer a new path out of the crossroads. Counterposed to a public discourse of freedom — "We stood in the streets staring at police there later when the city burned. There was always whispering somewhere in the building. Someone was always high on something and someone always explaining freedom" (99) — the Snowdon women close the novel with a counterdiscourse of freedom based on the experiences of "black children" (48) and black women. On the night John Christopher and Patricia have sex in San Juan, Eva is raped by a white vagrant on a stone outside the Carnegie Library: "To me Washington is a stone, the particular stone upon which I was raped" (97); "Washington, my inheritance. Washington Roulette" (100). Patricia on the other hand identifies as Washington: "Patricia kept saying she was the sign of the fall of Washington, that her empty skull was the Capitol dome, and finally that you, her child, would restore the soul of the city, that you would be the light in the skull" (214).

The daughters mark "Washington" as the space of an unfinished revolution. This revolution must seize time in the name of the daughter, must wrench the political from its proper referent in order to transfigure the meaning of a world-to-come. This requires, however, an excavation of the past. The daughter at first seems to provide this join of past to present, to reproduce the enigma of sexuality as a romance for others to decipher. Of the night described above, Camille insists of John Christopher and Patricia, "He raped her. I discovered he had raped her. That first time. He finally told me. . . . She had tried to seduce him and after all did not want him. Not even once" (181–82). But Cynthia Jane insists that Patricia seduced him, and that "Eva had somehow guessed it too and dramatized it that way so foolishly, with rape instead of with seduction, as it truly was" (193). In place of reifying the daughter as the crossroads of this history, the sign of a repeated violation that totalizes her sexuality, the novel externalizes this crossroads as "Washington." As Eva dreams on the night of her rape and Johnnie's conception, a "black female child" will be "the awakener" (129) who will ultimately bury the Washington monument under a "field of sand" (130). A crowd of youths watch the black female child uncover a pointed object that they cannot lift from the sand: "It is a stone, the stumbling block, the beautiful smooth white piercing stone upon which my city has fallen, it is the Washington Monument that, in fulfillment of the dreams of the people, shall stand forever, covered under a field of sand" (130).

The X is a sign, then, but one that is not yet legible. It points toward an alternative future, a politics of transfiguration whose witnesses do not yet exist. This is why, despite numerous witnesses, no one seems able to articulate a definitive meaning for Patricia's spectacular and repeated gesture, the cross that marks for different characters and critics her childhood rape, her adult sexual compulsion to commit incest, the violation of enslaved rape, and the injured body of the captive: "her right hand rising in a gesture that is her signature, higher against that sky, no, no I won't have it I don't want it I shall not take it if you force me to live I will tear it down, that gesture of utter repudiation what does it portend my mother?" (27–28). This gesture of repudiation forms the X that signals to her family the presence of an inexplicable, mystified cause of distress. When Patricia performs the mark of the X, Camille recognizes that "she was trying to tell us something . . . and I guess that something stayed wrong because I was never able to figure out what she was trying to tell us" (183). But the illegibility of Patricia's testimony stems from Camille's refusal of its excessive meaning: "When I asked her why she felt that about life she would start talking about herself as if she were a myth, a myth of a falling city, or nation, or world, or god" (183).

In Patricia's gesture of repudiation, the X marks neither an origin (trauma) nor an endpoint (freedom) but rather a temporal counterpoint to the historical conditions through which trauma and freedom forge a national narrative. Through this representation of the X, *Thereafter Johnnie* asks: How can such routine violence, so routine in fact that it has the shocking effect of appearing as "curse," be the political exception to national time? How, to echo Benjamin in closing, can such routine violence be true and yet "*still*" be true? ("Theses," 257.) The X as Patricia performs it interrupts both this historical violence and the "curse" it produced:

> I look and see what is before me and see that it is large and grand and tragic and even the gods have known about it and see how hopeless it has been for me to shield myself or try not to fulfill what was spoken of me, because here it is, the moment that was foretold, the event of my life, the one trouble I was born to accomplish and not survive in this world, task of my life, the path I walk to complete the destiny of my life, calls down the curse of heaven through my hatred of this world. Repudiation. (33)

As a gesture of repudiation, the X does not only memorialize a historical event, a violated body, or a sexual secret—although it also does all of these things—but in addition renders visible the process of historical violence that conflates black women's sexual and representational agency with patriarchal possession. And so the X ends as a repudiation of this curse of history, one that marks a space of freedom as yet unarticulated. The X signals an urgent need to rewrite a literacy of freedom—a determination otherwise at the site of agency, a "revelation" that revolution demands another time.

Four

Surviving the Family Romance?
Realism and the Labor of Incest

That our true stories may be violent, distasteful, painful, stunning, and
haunting, I do not doubt. But our true stories will be literature.
— DOROTHY ALLISON, "Believing in Literature"

Declaring her commitment to literary radicalism, Dorothy Allison opens
her essay "Believing in Literature" (1994) by questioning the difference
between true stories and literature. In her usual aphoristic style, Allison
poses the difference between autobiography and literature as a question
of taste. It is taste, not truth, that has historically differentiated literature
from autobiography — particularly from the autobiographies of the poor,
the minoritized, and the oppressed. Allison's oeuvre offers a recurrent
meditation on the politics and aesthetics of taste, pursuing a "violent,
distasteful, painful, stunning, and haunting" aesthetics of working-class
life, domestic abuse, and queer sexuality (*Skin*, 166). For Allison, this
style is best described as "distasteful," an effort to use literary technique
to stun and haunt "belief" in the political aesthetics of literary taste.
This literature of distaste was the hallmark of her books *Trash* and *The
Women Who Hate Me,* the first a collection of short stories and the second a collection of poetry, published by the small feminist press Firebrand
in 1988 and 1991 respectively.[1] By 1992, however, Allison's aesthetic intervention shifted from margin to mainstream. With the 1992 publication
of her first novel, *Bastard out of Carolina,* by Plume, Allison's distasteful truths became the stuff of formal literature, vested with belief not
merely by her alternative or counterculture audiences but now by mainstream readers, reviewers, and scholars.

This chapter asks how Allison's previously distasteful truths were transformed into a mainstream literary taste. In the 1980s and 1990s United States, literary multiculturalism exhibited a new taste for truth, particularly for the true stories of violence and survival attributed to working-class or so-called minority realism. Following the canon wars of the 1980s, a multicultural approach to literature sought to include more "diverse" texts in venues from college classrooms to national bestseller lists. Original proponents of multiculturalism had criticized the canon for privileging white male authors, for creating narrow standards of value based on specific aesthetic principles, and for maintaining critical optics blind to queer, feminist, or antiracist strains in even mainstream texts. The call for a more multicultural canon was a critique of canon formation itself, intended to transform critical and aesthetic values into the terrain of contestation and struggle. In place of a canon—even a multicultural canon—these critics used "multiculturalism" to call for a more dynamic, open-ended approach to evaluating and interpreting literary work.[2] But this more critical multiculturalism rapidly gave way to institutional multiculturalism, which used diversity as the yardstick for emerging literary voices. The multiculturalism installed in many academic and popular fora simplified the initial agenda, transforming its explicitly antiracist, feminist, and queer critique into a positive embrace of depoliticized "difference." Literary texts were valued for their cultural difference and representativeness, producing wildly uneven debates about the aesthetic abilities of a successful, but at times denigrated, new generation of authors.

This chapter explores one subset of literary multiculturalism, what I will be calling "survivor realism." Survivor realism describes texts in which poverty, racism, or sexism is treated as trauma to be overcome by a surviving subject, frequently the protagonist if not the presumptive author of the book itself. *Bastard out of Carolina* exemplifies this genre for many, a novel whose realism is linked to its depiction of Southern white poverty and childhood sexual abuse. As a popularly acclaimed novel and a syllabus regular in English classrooms around the country, *Bastard out of Carolina* is attributed the "triumphant authenticity" often reserved for late twentieth-century texts that expose painful social realities and then transcend them through literary publication. The phrase "triumphant authenticity" comes from Elizabeth Young's review of Allison's second novel *Cavedweller* (1998), "Southern Cross," in which she observes: "In order to become the 'Dorothy Allison' that her readers know, she has been forced to excavate and display all the aspects of a past that might have impeded the progress of a less determined author—her poor, white-trash Southern upbringing with all its concomitant domestic trauma; her lesbianism and the struggles involving class and politics that accompanied this entire legacy" (124). Dorothy Allison's successful "crossover" (as Blanche McCrary Boyd calls it, in "Crossover Blues," 20) with *Bastard out of Carolina* has been repeatedly linked to where she crossed over from, both her personal history as well as her authorial history as a writer of autobiographical short stories and poems. As Young continues: "When a writer whose work has been almost exclusively confessional exchanges self-exposure for invention, she takes a giant step. She's leaving home" (124).

It is the spectacle of this departure, as a textual leave-taking from autobiographical "home" to what Henry James called the house of fiction, that marks Allison as what Michael Rowe calls "one of the most important new writers in American letters today" (5). Allison's move into the house of fiction is inevitably attributed to her own mastery of literary realism. *Bastard out of Carolina* garnered a good deal of popular and critical praise for what Sybil Steinberg in a review in *Publishers Weekly* calls "her distinctly rawboned style of Southern storytelling" (35) and Vincent King, in his essay "Hopeful Grief," labels "kitchen-sink realism" (123) and "gritty southern realism" (124). Critics have invariably applauded the way this style familiarizes and authenticates what are presented as otherwise shocking or unbelievable truths: namely, the reality of childhood physical and sexual abuse. The regional realism attributed to Allison's style—full of what Randall Kenan describes as "pecan pie and gospel music, snuff-dipping grannies and kissing cousins" ("Sorrow's Child," 816)—provides a familiar context for the allegedly shocking revelation of incest in particular. Thus even as Allison's realist style is hailed as a literary achievement, its window onto the horror of incest and the main character's personal journey toward survival seem to provide the real value of the text. As Renee Curry explains, "If you want to understand how a twelve-year-old girl survives incest, survives the mother who cannot love her, and develops masochistic sexual desires, then Bone can voice her truth" (102). *Bastard out of Carolina* is often read as a survivor story, one that documents and transcends the traumatic reality of family violence through the survival of its protagonist (and by virtue of its existence the survival of its author).[3] The real value of the text is its lesson in social justice, a lesson available to us paradoxically only through fiction, where the authenticity of literary realism authorizes the authenticity of the "minority" writer.[4]

In this political aesthetic, realism becomes the means (and ends) of social justice, linking author and protagonist as heroes who triumph over the social relations that precede and precipitate the text as the vehicle of redemption. In this way the literature of distaste articulated by Allison becomes a new politics of taste, a taste for trauma that consumes fiction as social redemption. The fact that survivor realism has populist elements, that it aims at an important corrective to bourgeois family romance, that it is often aligned with overtly feminist commitments—these are all welcome interventions. The danger of this formulation, however, as Walter Benjamin pointed out regarding social realism in the early twentieth century, is that survivor realism is presumed to have political effects *as a form*. In "The Author as Producer," Benjamin points out that the very literary techniques aimed at interrupting existing social relations may in fact end up reproducing them. Thus in the 1930s according to Benjamin "a considerable proportion of so-called left-wing literature possessed no other social function than to wring from the political situation a continuous stream of novel effects for the entertainment of the public" (229). Even social or socialist realism might be used to make "the *struggle against poverty* an object of consumption" (231–32). Only in the 1990s, the struggle against poverty becomes a struggle against trauma, and survivor realism becomes the object of consumption whose social function is to provide "a continuous stream of novel effects." Despite the repetition of these stories of trauma and survival, each one is treated as entirely novel. This way of reading erases the relations of production of the author, as Benjamin points out, as well as of the reader and broader reading and writing publics. It also erases alternative historical approaches to these texts that may cut against the grain of their celebrated realism.

To work against this formalism, this chapter undertakes (perhaps paradoxically) an extended close reading of the novel's figurative and narrative style. Here I treat *Bastard out of Carolina* by returning Allison's style to its deforming aesthetic of truth, one that vests the literary with belief in stories of poverty and abuse without celebrating literature as the primary vehicle for their transformation. Allison's "literary technique" (Benjamin, "The Author as Producer," 223) explores the limits of literary representation as social redemption and insists instead upon the social relations of reading. In my efforts to limn the potential radicalism of the novel, I take up six key elements of its literary technique: first, the public working-class storytelling that resists state law; second, the romantic rewriting of bourgeois patriarchy for the working-class household; third, the figuring of the working-class father's hands in the labor of love; fourth, the narrative fetishism of the white working-class family romance; fifth, the white trash daughter's theft of storytelling labor from the father's hands; and sixth, the unmaking of the incest scene through the stolen labor of the father's self-representation. By tracing these techniques across the text, my reading resists the lure of survivor realism in order to examine the "real" politics of incest as well as the "triumphant authenticity" so often attributed to white trash texts.

Cultures of Realism

Critical arguments over the terrain of realism span several hundred years, but for this chapter the most pressing debates emerged in the late nineteenth and early twentieth centuries. *Bastard out of Carolina* might seem most recognizably situated within the tradition of American literary realism. Certainly critics have suggested as much, insisting that Allison's signature style is part of a longer genealogy of regional realism articulated through the U.S. South but connected to the dominant idioms of national culture. According to Amy Kaplan, American realism has been defined in two ways: formally, through stylistic criteria related to a balance of mimetic and diegetic strategies, and historically, as a genre that emerged between the Civil War and World War II (*The Social Construction of American Realism,* 5).[5] This split has tended to differentiate between social relations outside the text (history) and the narration of those social relations (form). For Kaplan, this resulted in "the treatment of texts as responses to social change [that] implicitly situates literature outside the arena of social history, looking down and commenting upon it" (5). Thus even what Kaplan calls the "antimimetic assumption of poststructuralist theory" tends to "locate the power of realistic texts precisely in their ability to deconstruct their own claims to referentiality" (5). But Kaplan is interested less in what she calls the "history of failure" (6) attributed to American literary realism than in the ways that such representational practices articulated social relations as norms of agency, characterization, and plot. She reads realism in terms of its mode of articulation, forging new social relations through the relations of reading.

Beyond such a textualist approach, Kaplan also suggests that literary realism established the terms of social struggle *over* the forms of representation. In its "competition with other cultural practices, realism also becomes a strategy for defining the social position of the author" (13). Through this account realism becomes a formal and historical tactic, one that makes use of culture and representation to forge new social relations (either affirming or challenging those associated with existing modes of capitalism, nationalism, or familialism). In sum, for Kaplan those who use this tactic are "actively constructing the coherent social world they represent; and they do this not in a vacuum of fictionality but in direct confrontation with the elusive process of social change" (9). This account of a specifically American realism intersects with debates about European formal realism (Watt, *The Rise of the Novel*) and left formalism (Gallagher, "Marxism and the New Historicism"). Ian Watt argues that the rise of the novel coincided with social and philosophical changes in eighteenth-century English society, resulting in "a set of narrative procedures" (33) that are "chronologically consistent" (26) and provide "a more immediate imitation of individual experience set in its temporal and spatial environment" (33). This "formal realism" defined the emerging bourgeois subject of the novel (and the world). In contrast, left writers and critics of the nineteenth and early twentieth centuries laid claim to realism as a tactic of open class struggle. Contesting the alleged bourgeois hegemony of realism, Marxists and leftists argued that the bourgeois individual could be replaced by the representative subject of class struggle, making form itself the vehicle for social struggle (what Gallagher calls left formalism).

Efforts to find the proper form for proletarian struggle preoccupied left activists and critics across the late nineteenth and twentieth centuries, from the socialist realism of the 1934 Soviet Writers' Congress (Denning, *Culture in the Age of Three Worlds,* 53) to Lukàcs's efforts to achieve "typicality" in social realism or critical realism (arguably from *Theory of the Novel* through *Realism in Our Time*). Repudiating, on the one hand, allegedly bourgeois forms of psychological realism and novels of manners and, on the other hand, allegedly bourgeois forms of modernist fragmentation and alienation, these critics insisted that specific literary techniques associated with social realism could capture working-class life and train readers in new forms of class consciousness.[6] These efforts occurred across national borders but often remained national in scope until subsequent decolonization efforts and radical left struggles of the 1950s through 1970s developed what Michael Denning in *Culture in the Age of Three Worlds* calls "The Novelists' International" (51).[7] Denning argues that left novelists of the 1960s and 70s in particular "transmute[d] the earlier proletarian modes of socialist realism into forms of what might be called magical realism" (32), producing a new world novel that circulated in transnational markets with "the Third World as its home, and a vaguely defined magical realism as its aesthetic rubric" (51). Following cold war efforts to reproduce realism and modernism as the binary formations of world superpowers, emergent literary "movements" asserted nonaligned aesthetics as part of a politics of international revolution.

But these diverse literary struggles were never really unified as a single movement, and all too often the literature produced through these struggles was decontextualized when it was read and reviewed in the United States. Novels published and circulated around the world were filtered through what some might call an international division of literary value: the new "world" novel of global literature and novels of U.S. multiculturalism. The problem with this international division of literary value is that it masks a crisis in the meaning and effects of "proletarian" struggle. The transnational racial and sexual formations of the new working and surplus classes, and the potential contradictions they introduce into dominant culture and governance, are hidden by these different valorizations of their literary forms.[8] Novels written by U.S.-based writers of color or from proletarian or minoritized (on the basis of religion, sexuality, or region) backgrounds are often incorporated into the realist aesthetics of multiculturalism. Following what Denning calls the "cultural turn" (3), multiculturalism was positioned to absorb the imminent labor struggles of the new world order into the model forms of U.S. "minority" realism.[9] Instead of locating labor within the social and historical conditions of contemporary modes of production, labor was at times abstracted from the actual conditions of capital and transformed into a rhetorical category, "class." Class could come to represent a "minority" cultural position and identity (rather than a social relation). Class as experience was more easily translatable into American multicultural logics and did not fundamentally challenge multicultural approaches to literature. As a result, so-called minority literatures could be read to recognize the problems of labor exploitation and its impact on "cultural" subjects without actually addressing the transnational political economic conditions that create these cultures of labor.[10]

Within the United States, this multiculturalism has often achieved its domesticating aims by coding new cultural subjects through family romance narratives. These family romances seem to mimic the basic conventions of what was once labeled bourgeois realism—marriage plots, dramas of industry and commerce, gendered conflict (Nancy Armstrong, *Desire and Domestic Fiction*). But they introduce key differences into those conventions, differences frequently interpreted as "culture." Such an interpretation allows readers to value cultural difference by reading family romances whose realist depictions familiarized the unfamiliar without fundamentally changing dominant norms. Survivor realism does a particular kind of work for this multicultural family romance, seeming both to break with and yet to blend two prior forms of literary realism: the bourgeois family romance and proletarian social realism. On one hand, traditional forms of bourgeois family romance enclosed ideological contradictions within the nuclear family. On the other hand, traditional forms of social realism exposed ideological contradictions as the effects of a broader class society. Survivor realism combines these two strategies by representing broader social relations as harmful, but locating the harm inflicted by those social relations primarily within the domain of family. The "survivor" protagonist typically experiences some event or series of events whose harmful effects are localized within the family and focalized through the protagonist's point of view; the protagonist experiences some form of domestic disruption that may be linked to broader systems of social exploitation or degradation, but which is primarily resolved through the protagonist changing his/her family relationships. Representations of incest do a particular kind of work for survivor realism. The revelation of "shocking" family secrets exposes and encloses ideological contradictions as personal trauma, trauma that may be produced by class society but is inevitably realized within the family scene. As a result, the novel's protagonist, and implicitly its author, symbolize survival as the traumatic afterlife of the (multicultural) family romance.

This genealogy of literary realism, variously subnational ("regional"), national ("multicultural"), or global ("world"), does little to explain the literary techniques of *Bastard out of Carolina*. Depending on one's critical approach, the novel might seem to exemplify the regional realism of the U.S. South, the national realism of the multicultural United States, or the magical realism of proletarian world literature. Taken separately, however, each approach estranges class as cultural form from its transnational political economic and social relations. *Bastard out of Carolina* offers one potentially illuminating crossroads between these modes of representation and their social formations. Discussing the way realism has historically produced struggle over national representation, Amy Kaplan points out that "realists contribute to the construction of a cohesive public sphere while they at once resist and participate in the domination of a mass market as the arbiter of America's national idiom" (9), providing "a debate, within the novel form, with competing modes of representation" (13). In Allison's novel, this debate is staged as the juncture of two historical moments, the 1950s of the text's setting and the 1990s of its publication and circulation. And it appears through two specific modes of representation, working-class realism and bourgeois family romance. While survivor realism offers one way to synthesize these moments and modes into new relations of reading, the sections that follow resist this synthesis in order to maintain tensions between modes of representation and their historical referents. In so doing I hope to challenge efforts to nationalize the "minor" family as a cultural formation appropriate to neoliberalism within the United States. Instead, the latent contradiction between these two moments and modes is brought to the fore, sharpening their point of overlap (or pivot) in what by now should be a familiar image: incest. In the narrative modes of *Bastard out of Carolina*, incest "appears" as the image of class antagonism when it is represented through dominant forms of literary realism.

Legal Accidents

As the title no doubt implies, *Bastard out of Carolina* is from its inception a narrative about a family with a vexed relationship to law. In the first place, it is a narrative in which both the family and the story told about it are inaugurated by an "accident"—the complex accident of the protagonist's birth. Early in chapter 1, the protagonist tells the story of how her pregnant mother, while lying in the back of her uncle's truck, "had fallen into her first deep sleep in eight months. She slept so hard, even the accident didn't wake her up" (2). When her uncle's truck strikes another vehicle, sending her mother "through the glass," we are told: "Of course, she didn't wake up for three days, not till after Granny and Aunt Ruth had signed all the papers and picked out my name" (2). This "accident" then results in the mother's absence from the realist scene of the protagonist's birth and her deliverance into a name. As she introduces herself and explains the circumstances of her naming: "I've been called Bone all my life, but my name's Ruth Anne. I was named for and by my oldest aunt—Aunt Ruth. My mama didn't have much to say about it, since strictly speaking, she wasn't there" (1). As a result of the "accident,"

Bone's mother is absent from the scene's "strict speech," unable to have provided the father's name or to "have bluffed her way though it" (3), as she says, and pretend she is married. And, in the mother's narrative absence, her female relatives reveal their confusion at having by law to provide the father's name, resulting in Bone being "certified a bastard by the state of South Carolina" (3).

This story of the accident is used to thematize the parameters of realist reference in the text. The realism of the overall text is, I will argue, tactical; but here in particular realism is thematized within the narrative as a tactic of class resistance. In this first chapter, diegetic realism is forged through working-class resistance to state law. The law is represented as a source of punishment and blame, likely to target the Boatwright men in particular for the "stereotypical" activities attributed to masculine working-class agency—living hard, dying young, drinking, brawling, and sleeping around. In the 1950s of the novel's setting, the law conspired with sociology and the new sciences of social knowledge to increase its "realist" and documentary knowledges of class populations. As Austin Sarat and Jonathan Simon explain this shift, "With the ascendancy of legal realism during the last two-thirds of the twentieth century, both law and social science found themselves engaged in the practical arts of governing to an extent barely imagined in the preceding century. As the state came to reconfigure its approach to governing around problems of the social, both law and social science were invested with new resources and roles" ("Cultural Analysis, Cultural Studies, and the Situation of Legal Scholarship," 6).[11] In this period the tracking of "stereotypical" activities linked social science to state law; the Boatwright men's activities listed above were criminalized and subject to fines and incarceration. The law uses its own version of realism to identify the Boatwrights as a social problem, making their social legibility into legal criminality.

To work against this criminalization, the main characters deploy the "accident" story to defend against the law's power to identify and prosecute them. As Uncle Earle puts it: "The law never done us no good. Might as well get on without it" (5). As the first chapter unfolds, the story of the accident is revealed to be just that, a story, one designed not to refer to what really happened but rather to avert encounters with the law. Thus of the "accident" that sent Bone's mother to the hospital for her unconscious delivery that inaugurated the story's birth, we are told: "My aunt Alma insists to this day that what happened was in no way

Uncle Travis's fault, but I *know* that the first time I ever saw Uncle Travis sober was when I was seventeen and they had just removed half his stomach along with his liver" (2). The story of the accident seeks to protect men's agency from its legal prosecution. Against a system of juridical and disciplinary knowledge that constitutes and comes to know their behavior as social problem, the novel proposes storytelling as a mode of expressly "cultural" resistance. Such storytelling affirms the legitimacy of men's agency as a productive activity even as it repudiates their accountability: "Men could do anything, and everything they did, no matter how violent or mistaken, was viewed with humor and understanding. . . . What men did was just what men did" (23).

Over the course of chapter 1, the Boatwright family uses the accident story to create the illusion of a separate working-class culture with its "own" realism, a tactical mode of episodic storytelling that seeks to define working-class reality in opposition to the realist regimes of law.[12] Cultural agency emerges precisely where social agency is most limited, enabling the working class to avert the reifications of legal realism by slyly deploying fiction to create alternatives to (and within) a limited reality. As the story of the truck "accident" makes clear, however, this working-class storytelling does not serve the Boatwright *women* very well. In its efforts to avert the law's ability to name and document working-class lives as a social problem, storytelling introduces a profound gender difference into the narrative. While the men are protected from law by this working-class storytelling, the women become reified as the instruments of its masculinist resistance. The story of the truck accident renders Bone's mother, Anney, unconscious, a state in which she is unable to tell the story of that other "accident" that brings her to the hospital unwed and pregnant at fifteen. Without storytelling agency of her own, the mother's "accidental" pregnancy can only appear before the law as her fault. Thus Anney gives birth to the reification of her "shame," the word "bastard" on a legal certificate, the child "Bone" whose gendered part in this kinship story will be to realize the consequences of its differential narrative agency. For the Boatwright women, then, the accidental story consigns their agency to a repetition that reproduces their legal stereotype as bodily stigma: "Mama hated to be called trash. . . . The stamp on that birth certificate burned her like the stamp she knew they'd tried to put on her. No-good, lazy, shiftless. She'd work her hands to claws, her back to a shovel shape, her mouth to a bent and awkward smile—anything to deny what Greenville County wanted to name her"

(3). The mother's life work becomes the labor of resisting her shame only to reproduce it as bodily stigma: her hands turned to claws, her back to a shovel.

Thus if the law is vested in penalizing male violence as a source of agency and regulating female sexuality as a locus of shame, the story of the accident only furthers its aims. In *The Limits of Autobiography,* Leigh Gilmore argues that the law links "two related injuries" at the heart of *Bastard out of Carolina*: "illegitimacy and incest" (46). Situating the novel in relation to legal systems establishing paternity in the 1950s, Gilmore argues that the novel critiques the state's false ideal of retributive justice as well as the state law that regulates kinship: "One colludes in obscuring this harm by fetishizing law, by vesting in it all sorts of romantic notions about its ability to reveal the truth" (51). I would like to extend Gilmore's persuasive argument to show that if one colludes in obscuring harm by fetishizing law, one equally colludes in obscuring harm by fetishizing stories, by vesting the story with all sorts of romantic notions about its ability to reveal truth.[13] What is at stake here is the romanticization of storytelling as a specifically masculine working-class resistance to the compulsions of legal realism. This leaves women merely the object lesson and instrument of such stories—they become reified as the body of the law and the moral of the story. For it is the compulsion to remake the world in a realist image of "truth" that compels Anney toward that which ultimately reifies her own stigmatization. This compulsion brings Anney back again and again to the courthouse in an effort to remove the word "bastard" from her legal record. But even when, at the end of the chapter, the courthouse burns down and Bone's birth certificate goes up in flames in what Gilmore calls the "spectacle of a fantasy come true" (55), Anney's narrative labor is not done. While the burning of the court document with the word "bastard" might "free" Anney from her legal shame, the realist constraints of this accidental narrative will live on long after its legal referent has gone.

Bastard Family Romance

It is this afterlife of the opening chapter that poses a problem for many critics attempting to read sexual abuse in relation to the novel's purported working-class realism. The problem here is how to read the novel's depiction of sexual abuse without reproducing the stereotype that such abuse is what happens in poor rural families, a stereotype Allison circulates as a "joke" in her short story "River of Names": *"What's a*

South Carolina virgin? 'At's a ten-year-old can run fast" (*Trash*, 15). In order to avoid conspiring with the law in reproducing stereotypes about poor whites in the South, critics often take the first chapter's masculinist working-class story telling at its word. If the Boatwright accident story is designed to evade exposure to state law, critics seem to conspire with this evasion by reading "working class" as a cultural system of legal reprobations and humiliations that are best expressed in episodic stories, like that of the accident, narrative eddies designed to allow a sympathetic view into the privations and haunting punishments of working-class life. In contrast to the accidental storytelling of working-class culture, the scenes of domestic abuse are then read as the novel's "main plot," a story that moves inexorably forward into what becomes a more "lawful" narration representing the conventional bourgeois family romance.[14] This second movement seems to contradict the first, replacing working-class storytelling with the symbolic union of paternal and legal authority in Daddy Glen.

Many critics implicitly read the second section of the novel as a family romance that conforms to the more familiar literary forms associated with bourgeois kinship and domestic privacy. And they do so by separating Glen from the working-class stories of the first chapter, situating him instead in a nuclear domesticity in which the law sanctions, rather than scrutinizes, his legal standing. Following the first chapter of the novel, this alleged main plot develops into a nuclear family romance that joins Bone, her mother Anney, her half-sister Reese from Anney's first husband Lyle, also killed in a car accident, and Anney's new husband, Glen Waddell. The early chapters of the book track the consolidation of this new family under the paternal head of Daddy Glen: "'Call me Daddy,' Glen explains, "'cause I love your mama, 'cause I love you. I'm gonna treat you right. You'll see. You're mine, all of you, mine'" (36). Their mother, seeking still to remake the legal stigma that attaches itself to her body and her family name, embraces Glen's logic of possessive paternity and celebrates the legal marriage that will produce them as a proper family: "Mama kept telling us that this was a marriage for all of us, that we were taking Glen as our daddy at the same time she was taking him as a husband" (42).

By becoming a legal father, Glen promises to take the family into bourgeois privacy. Critics contrast Glen's assumption of state-sanctioned authority over the nuclear family to the public failures of Boatwright kinship. Whereas the Boatwright's working-class kinship is defined by its public exposure to state law, Glen's marriage encloses Anney, Bone, and

Reese into legal privacy. This reading renders the domestic plot that follows into a normative family romance, one that is contrasted to the accidental stories of working-class culture. In this mode of representation, bourgeois realism is articulated through the scenes of sexual molestation. Bone's sexual abuse at the hands of "Daddy Glen" appears as incest, which establishes Glen as the rightful patriarch of the conventionally middle-class family romance. Glen's ascension to the position of bourgeois father depends upon two, often unstated, propositions: that the incest scene is the new realist expression of patriarchy, and that this patriarchy reveals the social and structural relations between family and state. In the first proposition, the incest scene articulates the representational agency associated with Glen as patriarchal authority. In contrast to the episodic structure of the working-class narration, Glen seems to readers to assume the identity of "Daddy" when he unifies word and deed through the realist incest scene. Here Glen enacts his claims "I love you" and "you're mine" by molesting Bone in the parking lot of the hospital where Anney is giving birth to their child.

This scene unveils Glen as the patriarchal father, critics imply, precisely because it is so formally generic. According to Katie Roiphe and other recent critics, 1990s incest narratives have created a new style of realism, in which "the ancient theme of *Oedipus Rex* is accompanied by the clattering breakfast plates of twentieth-century realism and the tragic, shimmering myth becomes an actual event described in pornographic detail" (65). This realist representation is achieved through one specific (even formulaic) depiction of the incest scene: "We see the act in cinematic detail—the penis, usually described as a 'hard thing,' and the underwear, always described as 'panties.' . . . Then come the obligatory fingers" (Roiphe, "Making the Incest Scene," 70). In *Bastard out of Carolina*, the details and temporality of the first molestation scene are characteristic of this new genre, running from "[he] pulled me up on his lap" through "[he] slid his left hand down between my legs, up against my cotton panties" (46). For Roiphe, it is the peculiar temporality through which these details are presented that constitutes the "realism" of incest, which derives its seeming "liveness" by mimicking other popular forms: "Today's incest scenes have an unmistakably current feel. . . . In the climactic scene of disclosure, the story merges with something we just read in *People* or a scandal we just saw on the local news" (68). The contemporaneity of the incest scene is, in other words, derived from its imbrication with a variety of late twentieth-century media.

166 Surviving the Family Romance?

While Roiphe suggests that readers are mistaking form for reality, Dorothy Hale provides a more complex account of such "social formalism" in her book of the same name. Hale analyzes how particular practices of novel reading contributed to a "novelized conception of social identity" (15); here, however, the "novelization" of social identity takes place through a variety of forms, including *People* magazine and television programs. Novels must compete in the open market of representation, must compel readers to "view" the social in the processes of novel reading by borrowing from and hybridizing other media. In the 1990s, novels have proven more likely to be termed "realist" when they seem to reveal a formerly hidden or secret violation in scenes that incorporate multimedia competition over the "real." Thus it is the nouveau realist detail, as the figure of a contemporaneity condensing newspaper reports and popular media, that constitutes Glen as a bourgeois patriarch: "Of course, the most devastatingly real scenes are those between Bone and 'Daddy Glen,'" Kenan writes. "In fact, the scenes and their aftermath are so brutal one wants not to believe them—though a cursory glance at the newspaper or a local newscast confirms that as much and worse is done to children daily" ("Sorrow's Child," 816).[15] Successful focalization, as Kenan suggests in his summary of the "most real scenes" of *Bastard out of Carolina,* is most often produced through scenes "so brutal one wants not to believe them" (816). In place of older models of ideological contradiction or social antagonism, this mode of realism "reveals" social relations as secret trauma. And incest provides the exemplary "secret" whose multiply mediated "details" seems to promise such realist revelation (Roland Barthes's "reality effect" for 1990s readers).[16]

The second proposition, that this patriarchal scene reveals the structural relations between family and state, in many ways depends upon the first. The novel's first molestation scene both consolidates Glen as a legal father (through the marriage contract) and reveals the patriarchal right entailed in such a role. According to some feminist theorists, the practice of incest is not so much universally prohibited as selectively regulated. This means that sexual use of children in the home is granted as a right to legitimate, state-sanctioned patriarchs. In Nirmal Puwar's interview of Carole Pateman, about her book *The Sexual Contract,* Pateman argues that maintaining sexual access to women is the basis for patriarchal right, a structuring access that constitutes "patriarchy" as a political than a paternal right. The central regulatory aim of the incest taboo, extending Pateman's reading, would be to instrumentalize sexuality for gendered subordination. Thus the incest taboo marks not a putatively neutral state interest in regulating kinship and sexuality, but rather a specific expression of the regulation of gender through sexuality. According to Pateman, "Patriarchy ceased to be paternal long ago. Modern civil society is not structured by kinship and the power of fathers; in the modern world, women are subordinate to men *as men,* or to men as a fraternity" (Puwar, "Interview with Carole Pateman," 3).[17] For Pateman the role of the father in the household is most properly understood in the context of sex right, a political legitimation of patriarchy derived from heteronormative access to women.

Here patriarchy as political right rather than civil or domestic rule dovetails with neoliberal reformulations of family. The equation of legal status and social power presumes a uniform political relation between family and state. All families, according to this logic, are rendered uniform through legal recognition. Extending this logic, all fathers (as men) are granted the same social power when recognized by law. The inclusion of more diverse fathers in the structural account reaffirms the state as the proper locus for familial transformation. Thus precisely as the bourgeois father is deconstructed as the symbol of patriarchal power unifying family and state, the state emerges as the field proper to the regulatory transformation of family forms. Incest provides the pivot or tropological turn for this changing same. The father becomes not just a patriarch, but symbolically "the" patriarch, ascending to the structural position of the "law of the father" linking family and state, what Moira Baker calls the "grid of hetero-patriarchy" ("Dorothy Allison's Topography of Resistance," 24) or what Leigh Gilmore refers to as the "interleaving of the law and the law of the father" (*The Limits of Autobiography,* 53). Glen therefore seems to enact the legal father's phallic authority when his words become his deeds in a realist scene documenting his sovereign agency. Glen, in other words, is taken at his word that he "is" the loving and possessive patriarch of the family romance the moment his domestic sexual agency over the child is rendered "scenic." What is revealed to us through the realist incest scene, in contrast to the accidental working-class stories, is Glen caught in the act of patriarchy, loving and owning the daughter a little more than words typically are permitted to say.

But if fetishizing the law or the story occludes harm, so too does fetishizing the "father" in this way. Such a reading of the first incest scene ultimately pulls Daddy Glen out of the narrative accounts of kinship offered by the novel and locates him instead in a structural one. The problem with such a structural account of the "father," to borrow a line from Rosemary Hennessy, is that it supplements "capitalism's fetishizing of social relations in that it condenses into the nuclear family circle and onto a psychically charged object—the phallus—the more extensive network of historical and social relations the bourgeois family and the father's position within it entail" (*Profit and Pleasure*, 122). Such a structural account not only condenses a more extensive network of social relations into a symbolic "father," however; it also condenses the more extensive network of narrative relations into a realist character, "Daddy Glen." And it is this second condensation, the condensation of narrative relations into realist character, that I would like to argue reproduces and extends the harm of the first. The reading that follows refutes both structural accounts of the law of the father as well as realist accounts of the family romance. Daddy Glen is never revealed as the real structural "father" in the text (or by extension as the social father of its realist referents). Rather, he emerges through a series of narrative relations that interrogate the political aesthetics of both working-class and bourgeois realism. By attending closely to the narrative relations that constitute father and daughter within the text, my remaining reading will ask how the novel stages its own conditions of production in order to return the incest scene to an aesthetics of radical literary distaste.

Laboring Hands

In place of the claim that the father's law is realized in the phrases "I love you" and "you're mine," I would like to suggest that Glen *becomes* the father through the narrative injunction that he uses to connect these phrases: "you'll see." The making of Glen Waddell into "Daddy Glen" occurs not in scenes realized by the performative injunction of structural law, but rather through scenes narrated once again in the episodic mode of the accident. And what we will "see" in these scenes is a very different figure representing the rule of the "father"—not the phallic symbol of a performative legal agency, but the metonym for those condensed relations between kinship, labor, and sexualized violence that will constitute the domestic scene of working-class narration: Daddy Glen's hands.[18] Glen's hands make quite a scene. In the first incest scene in the hospital parking lot, there are no less than eight mentions of Glen's hands in three short paragraphs. The molestation takes place in fact entirely under the rhetorical cover of the hands. We are told, "His hand was hard" (46–47) and "it made me afraid, his big hand" (46). In fact, the sexual referents of the scene emerge entirely through the metonymy of the hands. While we are told that "he was holding himself in his fingers" (47) and "I knew what it was under his hand" (47), these pronouns are only materialized as "a mystery, scary and hard" (47). Thus the mystified referent of the scene is itself what remains "scary" and "hard," a mystification whose object becomes the hands themselves. The hand covers over the referents of sexual agency even as it produces a realist scene of fear and mystery. Glen's sexual agency in the incest scene is actually precluded from realist representation by the hands themselves, which figure a prohibition on the narration of sexual agency akin to the story of the accident.

And once you notice them in the incest scene, Daddy Glen's hands seem to take over the text. Even the narrator takes note of it: "People talked about Glen's temper and his hands" (35). This storytelling makes the hands into a narrative object similar to that of the accident: "'He's quiet, but you make Glen mad and he'll knock you down,' Uncle Earle said good-naturedly. 'Boy uses those hands of his like pickaxes.' If they thought we weren't near enough to hear, Earle and Beau would go on about Daddy Glen's other parts" (61). Glen's agency is not iterative—"he's quiet," after all—but in place of his own speech Glen's hands are remembered and narrated as a silent threat. Glen's "temper" and his "hands" are coupled in stories that equate the potential for violence with the instrumentality of labor. Glen instrumentalizes the hands—"like pickaxes"—even as the story instrumentalizes them, to condense his capacity for violence with his capacity for labor. And, like the story of instrumentality unfolding here, the hands do not disclose "real" relations of power but consolidate instead the promise of realist representation as the premise of social agency (and political power).

My argument here is not to suggest that Glen's hands figure a metonymy that reveals real social relations—quite the contrary. The effort to make hands figure the "real" of white working-class culture has a long tradition in American literature, particularly in populist realism that reproduces the hegemony of whiteness through the allegedly metonymic tropes of labor.[19] The metonym of laboring hands recurs across periods of changing labor migrations, legal regimes of marriage, and relations of private property (including the 1950s of the text's setting and the 1990s of its publication). During such periods of change, the nation's economic and cultural crises are often figured as endangerment to white labor. White labor is figuratively nationalized—although not materially, despite the uneven distributive reforms of social welfare, New Deal, Great Society, and now neoconservative federalisms—such that labor itself figures the "work" of citizenship entitlement as the virile resilience of whiteness. Such figurations enable racist nativisms to seem both explainable because of, but nonetheless extrinsic to, the representative legitimacy of white American labor. The repeated mode of crisis and reconsolidation is perhaps most famously associated with literatures of the emergent twentieth century, when American assimilationism battled xenophobia and anti-immigrant nativisms, and when the American writers produced some of their most powerful valorizations of white labor.

The turn-of-the-twentieth-century crisis in labor and its modes of representation has been repeated across the twentieth century, including in the 1950s of the novel's setting and the 1990s of its production. Starting in the 1950s, Denning suggests, "culture" has been used increasingly to naturalize and negotiate the dynamics of a three-world system, in which struggles between U.S.-defined capitalism and U.S.S.R.-defined communism attempted to absorb literary discourse into the language of "culture" *(Culture in the Age of Three Worlds)*. In the U.S. discourse in particular, culture expressed a necessary commodity-relation of workers to the arts, insisting upon the ameliorative effects of literary culture upon the folk. As cold war discourses absorbed New Deal discourses, culture became a tactic of international self-representation (including U.S. cultures of diversity and the freedom guaranteed by commodities) as well as domestic absorption (promising cultural recognition as the equalizing of past injustices).[20] Between 1945 and 1989, the rise of culture as a critical analytic blended efforts of new progressive social movements and new disciplines of social science (such as communications and, eventually, cultural studies) with these more insidious hegemonic discourses of cultural exceptionalism.

By the 1990s, a radical transformation in international political and economic relations seemed to cause yet another "crisis" in American labor. After the cold war's end, new untrammeled expansions of transnational capitalisms, no longer even nominally national in orientation, transformed the meaning of labor and American citizenship. Just as the three-world system seemed to disappear, a brave new world of globalization emerged in its wake. Capitalism was already in the process of reorganization through post-Fordist production, just-in-time manufacturing, increased reliance on the service sector, and the feminization of labor and labor migration.[21] As Miranda Joseph summarizes this transformation in labor terms, "Within flexible specialization, workers with flexible craft skills use general purpose machines to produce small batches of diverse products; this is contrasted with mass production in which deskilled workers deploy specialized machines to produce long runs of one commodity" (*Against the Romance of Community,* 153).[22] Massive transformations in the racialization of labor and surplus populations led to new forms of national-populism within the United States, as well as new centers of labor organizing. As workers of color increasingly organized in the service sectors, undocumented immigrants became the target of massive popular and legislative campaigns linked with nativisms of earlier periods. These transformations were at least partially refunctioned in the service of national-territorial sovereignty for states of the global North. The global North still benefits from the restructured economies of neoliberalism, and "globalization" serves as a screen for the ongoing political, economic, and cultural inequities of imperialism.

This alleged crisis in national labor led to a resurgence of white populism, linked to the regulatory changes of 1996 laws focused on welfare reform, violence against women, immigration reform, and terrorism.[23] Yet this version of white populism masqueraded as race-neutral, using the cultural logic of family to reorganize labor's legitimacy in relation to the U.S. nation-state. As Miranda Joseph argues in the chapter "Kinship and the Culturalization of Capitalism" in her book *Against the Romance of Community,* the discourse of family played a central role in emerging articulations of national labor. Late twentieth-century changes in capitalism relied on new discourses of family-as-culture, "attend[ing] ever more precisely to place and culture and depend[ing] ever more profoundly on the extra-economic bonds of community and kinship" (147). Capitalism produces new discourses of family as "extra-economic" in order to mask the changing racialization of labor, both in its exploitation as well as in its politicization. As Chandan Reddy explains, new immigration policies used the language of family reunification to mask de facto policies of labor migration and private sponsorship. The United States Immigration Act of 1990 limited visas for "unskilled workers" ("Asian Diasporas, Neo-Liberal Families," 109) even as it raised the numbers of family-sponsored visas. These languages and networks of family unify new labor and migration policies with new representations of authentic American labor. Even as these labor shifts transformed family cultures across the 1990s, residual images of white labor once again dominated popular film and literature, which were focused in particular on earlier migrant laborers and their culturally authentic white ethnic families.

Narrative Fetishism

These changing linkages between whiteness, labor, and family are part of the backdrop of the competing modes of realism staged in *Bastard out of Carolina*. In the 1990s of the novel's publication, Daddy Glen's hands mark a residual realism of white labor "because class images last longer than classes in capitalism" (Denning, *Culture in the Age of Three Worlds*, 229).[24] *Bastard out of Carolina* deliberately casts its representation as nostalgic, a look back to the 1950s of white labor prior to globalization, prior even to the displacements and downsizings of neoliberalism. The narrative contrasts its figure of hands with the "the postmodern concept of culture" defined by the "the generalization of the commodity form" (Denning, 80) to all life realms. Here the text uses hands to break with both neoliberal cultural logics—in which all culture is commodification—and residual cultural logics of the welfare state—in which white-trash culture legitimates its own demise. The hands here represent the promise of cultural representation as a site of contradiction, what David Lloyd and Lisa Lowe in *The Politics of Culture in the Shadow of Capital* describe as the effects of transnational and neocolonial capitalism that "continues to produce sites of contradiction that are effects of its always uneven expansion but that cannot be subsumed by the logic of commodification itself" (1). Thus, following Lloyd and Lowe, I argue that "'culture' obtains a 'political' force when a cultural formation comes into contradiction with economic or political logics that try to refunction it for exploitation or domination" (1).[25] The problem treated in *Bastard out of Carolina* is that economic and political logics try to refunction the images of white labor without transforming the conditions of racialized labor they represent.

Thus Daddy Glen's hands do not represent his authenticity as a working-class patriarch. They figure instead the overdetermination of metonymy to reveal "real" social relations in working-class realism. The hands are figures of storytelling as agency, indeed, but precisely as that agency is reified in and as a specific modes of representation. In other words, the hands are not a structural fetish; they are a narrative one. They appear on page after page, as the object of stories, as the figure of agency, as the admixture of love, violence, and labor that regulates the working-class family romance. Like the story of the accident, the story of Glen's hands acts as a *narrative* prohibition regulating what can and cannot be told. And, like the story of the accident, this prohibition will have strong implications for the gendered difference in narrative agency. As the story goes on: "If they thought we weren't near enough to hear, Earle and Beau would go on about Daddy Glen's other parts" (61). Unlike the pickaxes, Daddy Glen's hands are equated to his "other parts" through substitution, not simile, rendering sexual agency a bodily capital that is the source of a joke: "'He gets crazy when he's angry,' they laughed. 'Use his dick if he can't reach you with his arms and that'll cripple you fast enough.' I was too young to understand what they meant, why they laughed so mean and joked that no woman would ever leave Daddy Glen, or roared and spat comparing the size of his nose to his toes to his fingers" (61–62). Thus Glen's hands figure multiple modes of agency—labor, violence, and sexuality—by collapsing them into a single narrative fetish, an authenticating metonymy that obscures which modes of agency are associated with his domestic rule.

Echoing the narrative relations through which Glen "becomes" working class in the novel—he is born into a middle-class family, descends into the world of working-class labor, and marries into the "criminal underclass" of the Boatwright family—the hands determine the scene of domestic privacy not through characterological volition, but through their own overdetermination by heterodox narrative and social relations. In the domestic scenes, Daddy Glen's hands act as a textual "taboo" resulting in regular aporias of Bone's narration. What Bone can notice and narrate is only the trace of the hands as a substitute for social relations that remain beyond the realist narrative. In the privacy of the domestic scene, without the vehicle of men's storytelling labor, Glen's hands only represent the potentiality of verbs in waiting, but whether for sex, violence, or labor is never clear. With only Bone to narrate, Daddy Glen's hands simply appear as a confusing potentiality: "It wasn't Daddy Glen's sex that made me nervous. It was those hands, the restless way the fingers would flex and curl while he watched me lean close to Mama" (62).

What is striking about Daddy Glen's hands is the way they condense—and mystify—paternal agency as a kind of instrumentality without a story. This is why despite critics' claim that the novel's plot reveals "the ever-increasing violence and sexual advances of [the] stepfather" (Hellman, "Bastard out of Carolina," 260) and "scenes of ever-escalating violence and abuse" (Irving, "Writing It Down So It Would Be Real," 104), there are remarkably few realist scenes of domestic violence in this section of the novel. Instead, what we repeatedly witness are Daddy Glen's hands at and as the scene of a domestic "accident." When Glen squeezes Bone's arm until it leaves a bruise, Anney exclaims: "'Glen, you don't know your own strength!'" to which Glen replies, "But Bone knows I'd never mean to hurt her. Bone knows I love her" (70).

This accidental violence of familial love mimics the episodic narration the Boatwright men have used to avert the law. But in the domestic scene it is the hands, rather than the law, that regulate the familial narrative of evasion. Thus it is the very haunting, autonomous agency of the hands, their condensation of sex and violence, love and possession, labor and kinship, that acts as a paternal prohibition: "'He loves you,' Mama was always saying, and she meant it, but it seemed like Daddy Glen's hands were always reaching for me, trembling on the surface of my skin, as if something pulled him to me and pushed him away at the same time" (105). It is under these hands, "trembling on the surface of my skin," that incest as such disappears almost entirely from the scene and leaves Bone the unconscious victim of an accident: "What did I know?" Bone asks. "What did I believe? I looked at his hands. No, he never meant to hurt me, not really, I told myself, but more and more those hands seemed to move before he could think. His hands were big, impersonal, and fast. I could not avoid them. . . . My dreams were full of long fingers, hands that reached around doorframes and crept over the edge of the mattress" (70).

The instrumentalization of the hands as "story" has one very striking impact in the narrative structure—it produces Bone-the-daughter as the site of failed narration. She comes to represent a representational failure at the heart of "family," the sign "daughter" a dead letter. Yet Glen depends on Bone for her ability to deliver him into legitimate patriarchy, to be the instrument of a domestic self-representation that continues to elude him despite its repeated promise. Through the escalating tension of these chapters, Glen's hands seem as if they are lying in wait for their story, as if sex and violence will at any moment come together with Bone as their narrative instrument. And when that does happen, when Glen's violence does finally erupt into the first full scene of a violent beating, he gratifyingly declares: "'I've waited a long time to do this, too long'" (106). But once he has dragged Bone to the bathroom and begun to strike her with his belt, the scene comes to an abrupt halt: "It hit me and I screamed. Daddy Glen swung his belt again. I screamed at its passage through the air, screamed before it hit me. I screamed for Mama. He was screaming with me, his great hoarse shouts as loud as my high thin squeals, and behind us outside the locked door, Reese was screaming too, and then Mama. All of us were screaming, and no one could help" (106). As the belt is substituted for Daddy Glen's hands, the paternal prohibition seems to be broken. Screaming, one by one, each family member is released from the father's narrative regulation of the family romance. But instead of revealing Daddy Glen's "real" accountability for the violence that has haunted the text, the family joins together as the collective victim of the assault.

A Story Is Being Beaten

In the beating scene that interrupts the family romance, Bone has indeed become the instrument for a different story than that of the domestic accident. But what this story represents is not immediately clear. On the one hand, the story might—but does not—"reveal" the scene exposing Glen's sovereign agency lurking beneath his paternal rule. In this story Glen would emerge narratively as the violent patriarch, reexposed to state law as "white trash" by the dissolution of working-class self-representation. On the other hand, the story might—but does not—"represent" Bone's sudden redemption into realist characterization. In this story Bone would emerge narratively as the surviving daughter, taking up the storytelling agency of the novel's usurped working-class realism. Bone would "survive" as the afterlife of the family romance, a realist storyteller whose "triumphant authenticity" would figure her entry into literary redemption. The first story would document the social problem of working-class violence; the second would resolve that social problem through the narrative survival of the working-class daughter.

Neither happens. After the first realist beating scene in the novel, the family—including Daddy Glen—is unified as the instrument of a "screaming" for which there is no ameliorative witness. The beating scene and its resultant collective scream do not disentangle characters into familial roles, roles through which blame and innocence can be assigned. Instead, the beating scene reveals the working-class family as itself the instrument and object of violence. Joined together in a screaming for which "no one could help," the family takes social form in this scene (rather than in the first molestation scene) precisely because, as Glen had promised, "you'll see." The family members themselves are of course separated by a door, screaming across the interior limit of domestic space. Their inability to see each other, however, is created as a spectacle for the reader, the passive audience for this collective scream. The promise that "you'll see" is realized, but what the reader sees is the failure of realist representation for this domestic scene. For while the spectacle of realist violence collects the family into one articulatory unit, they appear together only as the victim of an assault from nowhere, one that instrumentalizes them to create a spectacle of working-class violence without providing "help." And it is this spectacular failure that bars, once again, Bone's ability to represent *incest*: "I didn't know what to say to her. To say anything would mean trying to tell her everything, to describe those times when he held me tight to his belly and called me sweet names I did not want to hear. I remained silent, stubborn, resentful, and collected my bruises as if they were unavoidable" (111). The documentary demand to "tell everything" means she can't "say anything." Reduced once again to a crisis firmly *within* the domain of family, the realist incest scene would only make more invisible those broader social relations of which the "family" is both symptom and effect.

Instead of either of these two possible narrative resolutions, then, the beating scene induces a major narrative shift, a shift so striking that one critic has commented: "Allison's kitchen sink realism seems to have run amuck" (King, "Hopeful Grief," 123). Just when the novel is poised to represent the hidden conditions of paternal rule and the emergence of the daughter into realism, the plot devolves into scenes that seem increasingly more fantastic than realist. In these middle chapters we suddenly leave the plot as we have known it, and Bone plunges almost exclusively into the magical world of female kin, gospel music, masturbation, biblical salvation, and an extremely strange friendship with the albino child of gospel music agents, Shannon Pearl. And, since Bone has been removed from her domestic scene as the result of increasingly violent beatings and lives off and on with her aunts, Glen suddenly fades from view.

This break with the alleged realism of the novel is reflected in Bone's own assessment of the failed promise of developmental representation: "Growing up was like falling into a hole. The boys would quit school and sooner or later go to jail for something silly. I might not quit school, not while Mama had any say in the matter, but what difference would that make? What was I going to do in five years? Work in the textile mill? Join Mama at the diner? It all looked bleak to me. No wonder people got crazy as they grew up" (178). In earlier chapters, the narrative temporality is foregrounded as a thematic of development: "After that things seemed to move irreversibly forward" (64). In these middle chapters, the theme of developmental time only produces Bone as the site of representational failure: "No part of me was that worshipful, dreamy-eyed storybook girlchild, no part of me was beautiful" (208). Thus for Bone growing up becomes "like sliding down an endless hole, seeing myself at the bottom, dirty, ragged, poor, stupid" (209). "Growing up," the topic of the middle chapters of the book, is in fact represented as "falling into a hole" in terms of the realist temporality of the narrative. Without a future, the middle chapters of the book represent the "present" of realism as itself a narrative impossibility.

These middle chapters have proved perplexing to the novel's critics, since it becomes increasingly difficult to declaim a main incest plot through this section of the novel. In *Between the Body and the Flesh* Lynda Hart has offered the most trenchant reading of these chapters, pointing out that Bone's turn to fantasy should be understood as a central element of the plot. Hart argues that "these fantasies are Bone's own transformations, her own narrative—her 'salvation' if you will. These fantasies seem distinctly theatrical in that they require a spectator and, as such, they inhabit a borderline between fantasy and reality" (179). Throughout the early sections of the book, Bone fantasizes about being burned in a fire: "I would imagine being tied up and put in a haystack while someone set the dry stale straw ablaze. I would picture it perfectly while rocking on my hand. The daydream was about struggling to get free while the fire burned hotter and closer. I am not sure if I came when the fire reached me or after I had imagined escaping it. But I came. I orgasmed on my hand to the dream of fire" (63). After the first beating scene, however, Bone's fantasies change:

> I didn't daydream about fire anymore. Now I imagined people watching while Daddy Glen beat me, though only when it was not happening. When he beat me, I screamed and kicked and cried like the baby I was. But sometimes when I was safe and alone, I would imagine the ones who watched. Someone had to watch—some girl I admired who barely knew I existed, some girl from church or down the street, or one of my cousins, or even somebody I had seen on television. Sometimes a whole group of them would be trapped into watching. They couldn't help or get away. They had to watch. In my imagination I was proud and defiant. (112)

Bone slowly develops this first fantasy into a range of fantasy-scenes in which she is beaten while a crowd looks on, imagines Daddy Glen being caught in the act by witnesses, and suffers the heroic death of a tragic martyr, almost invariably to the narrative end of salvation or redemption. Through these fantasies, Lynda Hart argues, Bone makes herself over into the "heroine" of a story of spectacle, in which the foreclosed scene of incest is translated into the fantasy of a public "beating." The realist scene is transmogrified into a fantasy scene where Bone authors her own salvation. Thus Bone's fantasies seem to remake the foreclosed realist scene into a fantasy of the redemptive spectacle: "Those who watched me, loved me. It was as if I was being beaten for them. I was wonderful in their eyes" (112).

But something besides "fantasies" erupts from the realist beating scene, something that critics have largely overlooked. I would like to suggest that in this section what were previously fantasies take over the narrative, assuming the form of realist scenes. Fantasy becomes, in other words, realism. In order to clarify this point, I read the chapters that follow the realist beating scene as retelling Freud's 1919 essay "A Child Is Being Beaten"—but retelling it in such a way that the "incest taboo" structuring the border between fantasy and reality is dramatically resymbolized. The telos of "A Child Is Being Beaten" has three phases: first, "a child is being beaten" (97) (or "my father is beating the child *whom I hate*" [103]); second, "I am being beaten by my father" (104); and third, a group of boys is being beaten by an adult authority figure ("I am probably looking on" [104]). The third phase is explicitly sexual, frequently accompanied by masturbatory activity. Only the first and third fantasy scenes are conscious, however. The second phase of the fantasy, in which the girl is not spectator but being beaten herself, as Lynda Hart puts it "must remain unconscious because it is an incest fantasy (the beating substituting for the girl's desire for the father's love)" (35).

This summary of the Freudian telos is deceptively simple. The essay itself rests largely on its interpretation of an utterance made by female patients about a beating fantasy. According to Freud, the patient confesses to a fantasy in which "a child is being beaten" (97). This fantasy is later developed into a range of fantasies in which a group of children is being beaten, upon further inquiry it appears by some authority figure. According to Freud, between the first fantasy ("a child is being beaten") and the third ("an indefinite number" [98] of children are being beaten) there must be a foreclosed middle scene that would read: "I am being beaten by my father" (104). Freud argues that the paternal incest taboo is at the heart of the beating fantasy. The conscious fantasies first displace the daughter from the scene (she is a spectator), then displace incest from the scene (beating replaces incestuous desire). Behind the beating, incest. Behind incest, the father as social authority and thereby symbolic law. As Freud explains, "In both cases the beating phantasy has its origins in an incestuous attachment to the father" (117). Erased from this narrative are the literary and social referents of the beating scene, what Freud admits are the source materials for this particular fantasy: realist literature and actual scenes of corporeal punishment. In order to establish: (a) incestuous desire as the agency of the daughter, and (b) the father as the object and prohibition of the daughter's agency, Freud must privilege the father's "unconscious" structural role over and against the "conscious" realism that may or may not establish his authority.

The middle chapters of *Bastard out of Carolina* reverse the order that leads to the father's symbolization in the Freud essay. In both "Family Romances" and "A Child Is Being Beaten," Freud turns to literature to explain the relation between social status, familial role, and psychic representation. Against the presumption that the father's power leads to incestuous desire leads to the beating fantasy, the novel begins with the beating scene as the spectacle that brings the working-class family into realism. If it is true, as Leigh Gilmore suggests in *The Limits of Autobiography*, that telling the story of "a child who is terrorized through routine beatings, frequent molestation, and rape represents a spectacularization of crisis in the mode of family" (59), to what precisely does such "spectacularization" refer? As the novel's realist beating scene reminds us, the father is *not* necessarily revealed as the secret agent of the narrative's violence or desire. Rather, the father is revealed as a kind of narrative "fantasy," a character who emerges in the realist narrative without ever fully establishing his social power or his symbolic authority. His realist characterization depends, on the contrary, on his instrumentalization of the daughter to mediate incest, violence, and domestic legitimacy. When that fails in the first realist beating scene, the novel's realism is interrupted: first by the daughter's fantasies of being beaten in front of spectators, then by the daughter's *realization of her fantasies in realist time*. The scenic presentation of the fantasies as conscious theme disappears; what emerges are realist scenes of which Bone is both participant, spectator, and author.[26]

Unmaking the Incest Scene

At the start of this chapter I suggested that incest appears as the image of class antagonism when it is represented in the dominant forms of literary realism. In particular, two competing modes of representation—working-class episodic stories and bourgeois family romance—are brought together through the pivot of the incest scene. This section attends to the ways incest's "secret" is revealed by the daughter's theft, once again, of the father's self-representation. Here, incest as pivot and secret will be revealed as a ruse of literary realism. When the fantasy of paternal authority and storytelling agency is interrupted by the realist beating scene, the repressed "desire" that emerges in the middle chapters of the novel is the daughter's desire for authorial agency. The "secret" fantasy revealed here is that the daughter can write a better story, can create an audience able to watch the beating scene and hear its collective "screaming" as a call for social justice.[27] Because of the daughter's authorship, the audience would finally be able to witness *incest* as well, be able to hold Glen accountable for his actions without isolating those actions within the family (as caused by a structural Law of the Father) or displacing them outside it (as caused by the aberrance of working-class culture). In so doing, the daughter emerges as the agent of a very different family romance. In her story the pivotal secret of incest will "appear" as the image of the daughter as realist character, who appears to author a scene of her own making.

In *Bastard out of Carolina,* the "unconscious" middle scene is not the one where Bone is being beaten (the unconscious scene of her alleged oedipal desire), but rather the one in which she is a spectator. These middle chapters therefore represent Bone's authorial agency as a desperate attempt to remake the future into her own image, in order to secure characterological self-representation as a defense against "going crazy." Bone narrates her present through a series of domestic doubles, first attempting to find "salvation" in a religious revivalism that is represented as becoming part of an alternative "family" (143). When Bone finds this effort to produce a familial present aimed at salvation fails, an even more startling double emerges in the realist plot: Shannon Pearl. After losing hope that the alternative family or religious revivalism will save her, Bone laments: "It was as if I were mourning the loss of something I had never really had," "something more to hope for," something that "promised vindication" (152). Directly following this lament for the loss of an impossible present that might have given her a better future, a new chapter begins: "I recognized Shannon Pearl immediately on the first Monday of the school year" (153). This "mourning" of her own realist present produces Shannon Pearl, Bone's fantastic narrative double, reteller of horror stories straight out of the newspaper, object of a public, stigmatizing scorn and agent of a private, vengeful rage.

Throughout these chapters, Bone recognizes Shannon as a realist double who promises an alternate representational future: "I watched her face—impassive, self-sufficient, and stubborn; she reminded me of myself, or at least the way that I had come to think of myself" (154). Like and unlike Bone, Shannon represents as spectacle the occluded "reality" of Bone's life: "born too soon," the child of unconditional maternal devotion, "wholly monstrous, a lurching hunched creature shining with sweat and smug satisfaction" (155). Shannon and Bone become the realist doubles for a fantasmatic remaking of the family romance. Shannon acts as Bone's characterological double even as she takes on the characteristics of the author Bone cannot be. Thus Bone reports that Shannon is the author of stories that were "not fantasies like the ones I made up. Shannon's stories had the aura of the real—newspaper headlines and autopsy reports—and she loved best little children who had fallen in the way of large machines" (157). Shannon not only mirrors the promise of Bone's life "made different"; she betokens the ability to narrate that promise as a realism of documentary violence. Shannon becomes a vehicle for Bone to express her confusion that life is not like it is in a book: "I had the idea that because she was so ugly on the outside, it was only reasonable that Shannon would turn out to be saintlike when you got to know her" (157). But Shannon is less like a character in a book than like a vengeful author: "Once she relaxed with me, Shannon invariably told horrible stories, most of which were about the gruesome deaths of innocent children" (157).

Through this doubling, Bone produces *herself* as the missing spectator to the beating scene that defines the bourgeois fantasy of incest as well as its working-class reality. Through her relationship with Shannon, Bone restages her life story as a realist scene. Following from a scene where Bone watches Shannon's humiliation by an adult man who calls her ugly, Bone articulates Shannon's rage as a fire: "I reached for Shannon's hand. She slapped mine away. Her face was blazing. I felt as if a great fire was burning close to me, using up all the oxygen, making me pant to catch my breath. I laced the fingers of my hands together and tilted my head back to look up at the stars. If there was a God, then there would be justice. If there was justice, then Shannon and I would make them all burn" (166). Shannon's face itself becomes the trace of a "great fire" of what has earlier been associated with the fantasy of liberation, retribution, justice. This "burning" is the heat of a present whose referents remain hidden by the regulation of the realist narrative. The "time" of justice is not now, but that impossible "someday" of the future foreclosed by the family romance: "'Someday,' Shannon whispered. 'Yeah,' I whispered back. 'Someday'" (167). The desire for justice takes the form of a burning present, one that will open up the future to alternative modes of realist reference. The "something I never really had," signified by Shannon's materialization in and as the agent and object of "story," is access to the storytelling agency of the realist present. Wanting access to this present becomes a burning desire to burn both legal stigma and its subsequent narrative restrictions, to "make them all burn." This desire to be an agentic part of the present is precisely that which brings Shannon to Bone, that which Shannon mirrors for Bone as domestic double: "All I wanted, I whispered, all I wanted, was a piece, a piece, a little piece of it. Shannon overheard and looked at me sympathetically. She knows, I thought, she knows what it is to want what you are never going to have" (168).

As a result of this staging of the foreclosed "middle scene" of her family romance, Bone is able to reproduce her family romance in the translated form of the realized fantasy. Bone rewrites the accident story by restaging it through the three beating scenes of the Freudian parable, using Shannon as her own instrument through which to "beat" the story of the accident itself. In the first scene, Bone materializes the object of her masturbatory fantasies by stealing a metal hook from her Aunt Raylene. She then masturbates with the hook: "The chain moved under the sheet. I was locked away and safe. What I really was could not be touched. What I really wanted was not yet imagined. Somewhere far away a child was screaming, but right then, it was not me" (193). In this first scene, "a child is being beaten." But in the classic sense of the Freudian scenario, the substitutions of the "I" and the "child" split subjection into its ideational parts. In the "beating" of masturbation, the "I" enacts what has been foreclosed by the beating fantasy—sexual access to the object of desire. But this object is not the father or figure of prohibition, but rather the authority to write fantasy into the present-tense of realism. In the "right then" of the masturbatory scene, the "screaming" continues but is displaced from the agentic "I" of masturbatory fulfillment to "a child." This first displacement makes it possible for Bone to take the place both of the "beaten child," the "no one" who could help in the realist scene of the family beating, and the one who does the beating. The "screaming" becomes the realist trace of this other scene, one that will in its next phase enable Bone to author the scene of her salvation.

In the second scene, that which represents the "third" phase of the Freudian story, Bone is able to take up the multiple positions of the fantasy in this displaced realist present. As Bone's realist double, Shannon spectacularizes Bone's relationship with her own story. Through the vehicle of Shannon, Bone achieves the narrative agency she has thus far been denied, taking up the multiple positions of the fantasy scene to remake accidental realism in her own image. The fantastic realism of these middle chapters returns to the literary origins of Freud's telos itself, revealing the racialized violence at the heart of incest's repressed sexual representation. In "A Child Is Being Beaten" Freud uses *Uncle Tom's Cabin* as a literary source for the beating "fantasy," gesturing to the specifically racialized spectacle of the beating allegedly internalized in the bourgeois family romance (98). In *Bastard out of Carolina,* Shannon and Bone experience a rupture in their friendship when, upon hearing gospel music emanating from a "colored church" (170), they argue over Shannon's use of a racist epithet. Counterposed to the elaborate descriptions of Shannon Pearl as white subject and author of "documentary horrors," the middle chapters represent what Toni Morrison calls the "Africanist presence" (*Playing in the Dark,* 5) in American literature through two additional doubles: the silent faces of black children looking out at Bone from behind windows, and the overheard gospel music emanating from what is implied to be an African American church in the woods.

In the scene at the church, Shannon and Bone's white doubling is broken by an off-scene echo of what is figured as a potentially more "authentic" authorship, an African American gospel music in which they cannot participate (and which produces their disidentification on the grounds of racism).[28] The deployment of black authorship as a trope for "authenticity" serves to sever the white doubles, freeing Bone to take on her own storytelling agency over the accident. It is no "accident," then, that Shannon Pearl—that author of the documentary horror story, that double of the present tense who has given Bone her "reality," that white specter of stolen authenticity—undergoes a death by fire as the third phase of the fantasy. In other words, it is no accident that Bone arrives at Shannon's house just in time to bear witness to Shannon's self-immolation. "I stood still and watched her" (199), Bone begins the story; "Afterward, people kept asking me what happened" (200). Bone's passive spectatorship to her double's death-by-fire remakes the scene of her domestic abuse into a "burning" that takes down not only the legal referent of the novel's beginning, but also the paternal referent of its middle scene. In response to the question of "what happened," Bone tells the story of her own accidental authorship: Shannon's mother "kept screaming '*You!*' over and over like I had done something, but all I had done was watch" (200).

Like the third phase of the fantasy, "several children are being beaten" by an unknown agent. But "being beaten" is made over into its referential pieces—Shannon "burns" the referent of legal stigma that inaugurated working-class storytelling; Bone stands watch as the spectator who will tell the accidental story of that burning reference; and Mrs. Pearl enacts the screaming of accusation that wishes to return "guilt" to the scene. Bone thereby stands witness to her own usurpation of realist agency, taking up the position of the "accidental" storyteller in the scene's wake. Through Mrs. Pearl's "screaming," the beating scene is reproduced. But in this spectacular third-narrative form, it is no longer a child who is being beaten, but a "story." Or, to be more specific, the realist parameters of a "story" inaugurated by an "accident" and propelled by the hands of the working-class family romance. No longer herself the vehicle of the story in which violence interrupts the domestic scene, Bone instead authors a spectacular story of the domestic accident that leaves her watching, blameless, as her own stigmatized white image burns.

The Spectacle of Justice

Echoing the burning of the courthouse as the "spectacle of a fantasy come true," in the transition from the domestic scenes of the novel's center to the public spectacles of the novel's end, it would appear that realism itself is burning. And this time not just as the legal referent of working-class storytelling, but also as the paternal referent of the family romance. "Things come apart so easily when they have been held together with lies" (248), Bone deadpans, and the end of the novel does seem to unravel rather quickly in its spectacular revelations—her relatives discover the welts covering her back after a brutal beating, in response the Boatwright men beat Daddy Glen into the hospital, and Anney leaves Glen yet another time under the pressure of a family bearing witness to their domestic crisis. As Bone remarks: "I kept remembering those last few days like a hurried, confusing dream, not Daddy Glen beating me but the morning Mama told me about Aunt Ruth, not the Woolworth's robbery but talking to Butch, and not the noise and uproar when Benny, Aunt Fay, and Aunt Carr drove off to the hospital with Daddy Glen but those brief horrible moments when Aunt Raylene showed my thighs to Uncle Earle" (249). Undoing the narrative distinctions between public and private, domestic and legal scenes, this series of narrative reversals *purports* to reconstruct a new form of audience who "sees" what was formerly hidden by the episodic narration.

After this series of spectacular revelations, the novel culminates in a rape scene between Glen and Bone whose bloody spectacle can leave no room for accidental doubt. When Glen goes to see Bone where she is staying with her Aunt Alma after the most recent dissolution of the nuclear family, the scene rapidly devolves into a very graphic rape. And this time, it is no accident. We know that because it is all Bone can talk about leading up to and through the scene. When Daddy Glen demands that Bone tell her mother the story of his alibi, to "tell her it's all right" (281), she refuses, instead telling the story of her release from his narrative bar: "I had always been afraid to scream, afraid to fight. I had always felt like it was my fault, but now it didn't matter. I didn't care anymore what might happen. I wouldn't hold still anymore" (282). Bone is ready to scream, but this time in a spectacular cry for the help that had previously been denied her. Every untold story of blame, it seems, has suddenly become a narrative spectacle—"'*You!*' he cursed"; "'*You!*' I told him" (284). Throughout the rape, Bone "screamed" both "inside" and "with all the strength I had"—"'You'll die, you'll die . . . you will rot and stink and cave in on yourself. God will give you to me. Your bones will melt and your blood will catch on fire'" (285). Bone's narrative curse upon him joins her "inside" and public screams in the enactment of her newfound agency to realize her story of vengeance. "Give me something! Give me something!" (285) Bone screams, and, in answer to her realist call of "fire," Anney arrives. As Anney sweeps Bone into her arms and rushes her from the scene, Bone quietly celebrates the irrefutable spectacle that has finally made Glen's sexual violence into a visible story: "Look how hurt I was. There would be a story we could tell. It would be self-defense. It would be justifiable. I grinned to feel the blood trickling down my neck. Look how hurt I was! Thank you, God" (289).

But when the scene is over, the story ends. Anney once again leaves Bone for Glen—despite having witnessed the rape in progress, despite the "realization" of Bone's spectacular fantasy of revelation. And Bone remains behind, remanded to her thoughts, and speaks no more than ten words aloud in the remaining two chapters of the novel.

Critics have struggled with the end of the novel in seeking some form of retribution or redemption. Has Bone's shame been lifted? After all, Anney returns her birth certificate to her with the word "bastard" removed. Has Bone transferred her shame into blame and directed it at the appropriate agents? Laura Patterson suggests that "at the end of the novel, Anney memorializes Bone's escape from patriarchal violence and her own escape from the South when she gives Bone a tangible identity outside the realm of the patriarchy: a birth certificate that bears neither the name of the father nor the stamp 'illegitimate'" ("Ellipsis, Ritual, and 'Real Time,'" 57). Moira Baker argues that "though Bone holds her mother responsible for her choice to stay with Glen, she places responsibility for her sexual abuse squarely on Glen's shoulders," leaving Bone transformed by this "painful but healing insight" ("Dorothy Allison's Topography of Resistance," 26). Through the vehicle of Bone, critics speak of blaming Glen, telling the story of a patriarch textually revealed, exposed to blame if not by plot then by the witnessing reader. At the very least, critics seem to want to insist that the end of the novel offers a lesson in the ethical distribution of guilt, the political value of placing the blame in the right hands. But an equal or more meritocratic distribution of blame is not, *Bastard out of Carolina* suggests, justice. Nor is it the aim of the book. "It's a tragedy," Allison describes her novel in an interview. "The book is essentially a tragedy. I tried to make it big enough and deep enough so it wasn't as easy, wasn't as simple, wasn't predictable" (quoted in Megan, "Moving toward Truth," 77).

By calling her novel a "tragedy," Allison implicitly refuses the conflation of social realism and traumatic redemption so often assigned to her text. In her landmark explanation of the new historicism, Cathy Gallagher has claimed that "under certain historical circumstances, the display of ideological contradictions is completely consonant with the maintenance of oppressive social relations" ("Marxism and the New Historicism," 51). Here I would like to amend her assertion by suggesting that under our present historical circumstances, the display of ideological contradictions has often taken the newly popular form of survivor realism, the celebration of which all too often seems consonant with the social forces that institute "oppression" in the form of "trauma" and seek its redress in the form of "narrative." What I have been calling survivor realism links author and protagonist as the heroes of literary survival, triumphing over the social relations that precede and precipitate the text as itself the vehicle of redemption.

I think it is possible to read *Bastard out of Carolina* as working against these options. *Bastard out of Carolina* uses realism as a tactic and reveals this tactical use by drawing attention to the conditions of its own production. Such tactical realism allows readers to see "competing modes of representation" (Amy Kaplan, *The Social Construction of American Realism,* 13) within the novel form. It also raises questions about the participation of the author in the "mass market as the arbiter of America's national idiom" (13). As Kaplan points out, "If the realists engaged in the construction of a new kind of public sphere, they were also formulating a new public role for the author in the mass market" (13). Allison's novel participates in such construction, specifically as it thematizes the role of the author-survivor in the mass market. Rather than valorize the author-survivor as the ethical mediator of social relations, Allison writes survival as tragedy when it must take shape through dominant modes of representation. Allison's novel is a "tragedy" because it does not offer synthesis of the competing modes of representation I have traced here. The tragedy of Allison's novel then is part of its narrative form, the tragic narration of a range of social relations—political, economic, legal, racial, sexual—that cannot be revealed as the work of a single agent, not even as the condensation of agents into a structural law of the father. And, more important, not in the condensation of social relations into survivor realism, nor even in the consolidation of these two into the figure of the surviving author.

This narrative tragedy allows *Bastard out of Carolina* to offer an alternative imaginary of social justice, one that depends upon a queer and feminist working-class aesthetic to draw attention to the potential limits of authorial production. As Allison states in her volume of short stories *Trash*: "Imagine vengeance. Imagine justice. What is the difference anyway when both are only stories in your head? In the everyday reality you stand still. I stood still. Bent over. Laid down" (38). In the contemporary literary moment, in which narratives of heroic survival are marketed as a consumable spectacle of redemption, to tell a story of survival is not necessarily to interrupt the conditions of its production. And without such interruptions, the transformative potential of this literature can too easily be contained, leading to a romantic heroics of literary survival that fetishizes "everyday reality" while leaving it relatively unchanged. I read *Bastard out of Carolina*'s literary technique as refusing that romantic reality. It is simply a matter of reading its realism awry, allowing those outside its pages to imagine justice as something more than the cultural freedom to stand perfectly, if now collectively, still.

Five

Consensual Relations: The Scattered Generations of Kinship

Should men flash little girls in the park or send dirty messages to kids' chat rooms? No, of course they shouldn't. Should people be punished for molesting children? Absolutely. Anyone who forces sex on any person of any age should be punished. But we have moved beyond appropriate responses to serious offenses to hyperbolic responses to offenses with unproven harms.
—JUDITH LEVINE, "Q and A with Judith Levine"

Critics say that pro-pedophilia activism cannot be dismissed as an irrelevant fringe movement, because it has real-life consequences.
—ROBERT STACY McCAIN, "Promoting Pedophilia"

Does incest fantasy have real-life consequences? I have argued in this book that incest marks a turning point or pivot in relations between family and nation, turning from welfare to neoliberal governance, from modern to postmodern modes of representation. The book's chapters on the federal standardization of harm in childhood disciplines, the popular and legal adjudication of recovered memory, and the experimental and realist novelization of the daughter's agency examined changing uses of fantasy as a mode of articulation. This final chapter asks how the refunctioned incest trope might be used to remake the generational borders of kinship. What happens when this more extensive incest fantasy is reabsorbed into new forms of commodification and regulation? What will remain of kinship if sexuality is "liberated" from the family, and how will incest be articulated in these new formations of intergenerational life? Answers to these questions unfold across three readings of late 1990s texts: the 1998 psychological study by Bruce Rind, Robert Bauserman, and Philip Tromovitch, which explores the possibility that intergenerational sex is not intrinsically harmful for children; Kathryn Harrison's 1997 memoir *The Kiss,* which documents a consensual sexual relationship with her father that began when she was 20; and Sapphire's 1996 novel *Push,* which narrates an adolescent girl's struggle to gain literacy and self-knowledge after bearing two children from her father's sexual abuse. Each text explores a different facet of changing generational kinship and sexuality paradigms. Reading across these texts, this chapter teases out emerging neoliberal hegemonies that threaten to reabsorb more radical incest articulations into its dominant forms.

As the two epigraphs suggest, in the aftermath of the memory wars a different sort of incest debate emerged. This new debate focused on the possibilities of more positive, or at least less harmful, sexual relations between generations—including between kin. Some activists proposed that rights to consent, the legal determinant of legitimate sex, could be extended to those previously disqualified by status (such as children and close kin).[1] Sexual consent restrictions had been justified as protecting subjects from harm. Feminist advocates had pushed to develop laws that would use consent as a standard and recognize sexual harm in situations not involving overt physical force (for example harassment, date rape, incest, and child sexual abuse).[2] According to Judith Levine in a 1998 question-and-answer article about her then-forthcoming book, *Harmful to Minors: The Perils of Protecting Children from Sex,* some of these changes had paradoxically resulted in a more restricted range of permissible sexual activities for some subjects. Sexual conduct became associated with probable harm (rather than possible pleasure), requiring rational risk assessment to predict what acts might inflict harm (and on what actors).[3] Rights to sexual activity could only be granted to those able to predict and avoid harm to themselves and others. This introduced a split between those properly capable of calculating risk and those only capable of experiencing harm, along with a minor industry in academic studies, policy treatises, and aesthetic projects delineating legitimate risk-taking behaviors from harmful ones.

According to Levine and others, these harm standards normalized particular models of risk and responsibility.[4] This had several outcomes: (1) sexual subjects were increasingly brought before the law to adjudicate the meaning of negotiation, compliance, coercion, and consent, thereby strengthening the state's regulation of psychic life; (2) normative modes of conduct were seemingly naturalized in legal interpretations of psychic dispositions; and (3) normative power relations were reproduced between subjects of consent and subjects of harm. These three outcomes were most forcefully realized in the status category of the "child," the vulnerable subject of harm in need of the state's protection from sexual predation and the family's promise of sexual normalization. The child became then a major locus of debate about the aims of sexual liberation and the problematic of consent across liberal sexual rights discourse and more conservative "family values" frameworks. Should the family be maintained as the proper training ground for gender normalcy and healthy, age-appropriate heterosexuality? Or is sexuality increasingly an affair of the public domain, the business of the state and the regulatory apparatuses of school, media, and shopping mall? Should sexuality be governed primarily by consumption and new rationalities of exchange, to be regulated by the state like an emerging market whose traffic must be channeled to best suit the national interest? Or should it be returned to its mid-century moorings, the private property of families in need of more and more protection from the intrusions of commercial public life? These debates tended to split between efforts to liberate sexuality from its moorings in state-sanctioned family life, and efforts to return sexuality to the family as the realm of proper and privatized governance.

In the so-called public sphere, these debates appeared as "sex panics." Following British cultural studies of "moral panic," Philip Jenkins argues that moral panic becomes sex panic (6) when overblown or unrealistic public representations of "successive sex crime crises" (5) lead to changes in cultural consciousness that in turn justify increased policing and criminalization of groups labeled sex offenders. Many critics have located sex panics in historical moments of massive social change, when popular "imaginaries" are mobilized to enable large-scale transformations in policing and property in the public sphere.[5] The sex panics of the 1990s mobilized popular imaginaries of the child to transform cultural norms of policing and property, certainly. But even more important, these panics were part of a change in the ideology and significance of the "public sphere" itself. The twentieth-century category of the child had deliberately blurred the line between what Levine calls "serious offenses" and "offenses with unproven harms." This blurred line (a line that also bars, in Foucault's formulation) could then be drawn and redrawn through childhood sexuality, each time enabling the law and its favored disciplines to remap safety and danger as biopolitical conjuncture on the move. But by the later 1990s the law's ability to marshal the resources of discipline was matched by competing epicenters of knowledge and power. Various domains of popular culture played an equally if not more important role in "manufacturing consent" (as in the book of this title by Chomsky and Herman), challenging the law's exclusive right to draw normative lines in the sand. While some of these popular domains were no doubt supplemental to the law (as I suggested in chapter 2), others strained or outright contested its legitimacy as the "gatekeeper" of legitimacy itself.

This chapter reads three nonchronological flashpoints of hegemonic struggle in the later 1990s—focused, as I noted above, on a psychological study, a memoir, and a novel—to contrast the *appearance* of sex panic with the "disappearing" tactics of minor scandals.[6] Instead of relating these three texts as evidence of a panic about adult-child and close-kin sex, I suggest that each text marks its own minor juncture of family, state, and market as a new line of articulation. What we see across these texts is not a new hegemonic formation, but rather what Inderpal Grewal and Caren Kaplan call "scattered hegemonies." These three different texts show conjuncture once again scattering into new lines of potential articulation. The minor scandal each provoked also suggests new domains of potential enclosure, tactics of disappearance that suture each articulation into a new domain (civil libertarian masculinity, postpatriarchal femininity, and permanent workfare reproductivity). The first text, what has come to be called the Rind study (Rind, Bauserman, and Tromovitch, "A Meta-Analytic Examination of Assumed Properties of Child Sexual Abuse Using College Samples"), contested the inevitable psychological harm of child sexual abuse, going so far as to use its quantitative meta-analysis to suggest that not all childhood sexual experience constituted "abuse" (particularly for boys who consent). The second, Kathryn Harrison's 1997 memoir *The Kiss*, narrates the process through which the author, as a twenty-year-old white middle-class woman, entered a consensual sexual relationship with her father without the threat of physical force or the economic coercion of dependency. The third, Sapphire's 1996 novel *Push*, follows the fictional childhood and adolescence of an economically and educationally impoverished young black woman whose nonconsensual sexual abuse by both her father and mother is printed in excruciatingly explicit detail for public consumption.

Across the minor scandal of these three texts, the lines between family and market are redrawn to articulate a new civil subjectivity modeled on sexual consent. Each text ostensibly treats the harm of incest: the Rind study in relation to boys' and girls' childhood sexual experiences in and outside the home, *The Kiss* in relation to middle-class consensual adult incest, *Push* in relation to child and adolescent sexual abuse in a broader context of family violence and poverty. But each text also offers a risk assessment of the sexuality produced by the family and the market respectively. The Rind study positions the family as a residual context, away from which liberated male child sexuality might develop (via its ability to consent). *The Kiss* positions the family as nostalgic patriarchalism, away from which the daughter's unconscious might work through and supersede its dependence of father-love. *Push* positions the family as governmentalized locus of black "pathology," away from which its departing subjects become a state resource for neoliberal labor. Across these three texts, the "family" as a homogeneous concept disintegrates, revealing three paths of departure from its constraint. Each of the nascent formations of sexuality indicated by these paths is rapidly enclosed in its own marketized domain: deracinated boys enabled to participate as equal civil actors via sexual consent, middle-class white girls able to exit the patriarchal hearth via a contaminated consent that marks their limited ability to calculate risk and harm, and poor or working-class black girls only fit for reproductive workfare as the permanent underclass of the consensual nation. In this chapter I will examine how emerging models of civil subjection reproduce older status hierarchies through the distributive logic of sexual consent. Heading out of the historical crossroads of 1990s neoliberalism, we can discern new generations only just visible on the horizon: the transformed pivot of sex in national culture, and the return of the incest taboo as the remainder of liberalism recoded for neoliberal times.[7]

Minors in the Age of Consent

When the Rind study was first published in the American Psychological Association (APA) professional journal *Psychological Bulletin* in July 1998, nothing much happened. By the end of the 1990s, scientific studies measuring the impact of childhood sexual experience were common enough to be unremarkable. The Rind study questioned the majority psychological opinion that childhood sexual contact is inherently traumatic and leads to long-term psychological harm, but this did not seem immediately likely to gain it public notoriety. Amid its dry technical language and quantitative charts, the Rind study carefully surmises that not all intergenerational sexual contact is inherently traumatic, and that in particular male children may not be as adversely affected by early sexual contact as generally presumed. But despite the careful wording of its findings — "self-reported reactions to and effects from CSA [child sexual abuse] indicated that negative effects were neither pervasive nor typically intense, and that men reacted much less negatively than women" (22)— by May 1999 the Rind study was the center of a public firestorm. Vilified by everyone from the conservative radio host Dr. Laura Schlessinger to the U.S. House of Representatives, the study was widely perceived by both critics and fans to forward a new normative claim about adult-child, and more particularly man-boy, sex.[8] Simply put, intergenerational sex was potentially unharmful and might therefore be legitimated by children's consent. This raised the public question: "Can children actually consent to sex with adults?" (Family Research Council [FRC], "Coalition Calls on APA to Renounce Pedophilia Study in APA Journal," press release, May 12, 1999). The answer was a resounding "No."

Why children could not consent seemed invariably premised on the need for families to oversee childhood development, and supplementally premised on the need for families to protect children from homosexual predation. As Janet Parshall, the FRC's national advocate explains in the press release, "As an organization representing and defending America's families, we believe it is necessary to condemn and reject, in the strongest possible terms, any suggestion that sexual relations between children and adults are anything but abusive, destructive, exploitative, reprehensible, and punishable by law." Citing the positive reaction of the North American Man/Boy Love Association to the study, the FRC additionally linked the threat of pedophilic homosexuality with the (heteronormative) family's right to privacy. News coverage repeatedly emphasized the homosexual-pedophile connection and referenced the authors' former publications on man-boy sex in both the *Journal of Homosexuality* and *Paidika: The Journal of Pedophilia*. As a result of public pressure, in an unprecedented move on July 12, 1999, the United States House of Representatives passed a resolution (voting 355–0) to condemn this scientific study and calling for more careful evaluation of future "questionable" research publications (H. Con. Res. 107, 106th Cong.). The APA retracted its support for the article and printed a public apology, stating that in the future "journal editors will fully consider the social policy implications of articles on controversial topics" (Fowler, public letter).

So did why this obscure study, neither the first of its kind nor even the first of its kind published by these particular authors, became the vehicle for a public reprioritization of morality over policy, popular opinion over science?[9] Why did this purportedly neutral claim about adult-child sex devolve into a furor over the normative role of consent in delineating family authority from sexual perversion? The answer is both too obvious and yet not obvious enough. For some, the public response to the Rind study seemed like classic sex panic. The 1980s had already witnessed a series of sex panics in which child endangerment was used by social conservatives to stigmatize homosexuals and sexual deviants and rally support for various wars against the alleged underbelly of the body politic.[10] Some sex radicals viewed the panicked response to the Rind study as simply another setback in libratory progress, suggesting in contemporary articles such as "Sexual Liberation's Last Frontier" (Erickson) and "Pedophilia and the Culture Wars" (Zuriff) that children's right to sexual consent would be the culminating liberation from the political "repression" of sex. But, as Jonathan Rauch comments in his August 1999 piece "Washington's Other Sex Scandal," such knowing responses to adult-child sex debates are in fact proportionally rare. Summing up the popular response to the Rind study debates, Rauch writes: "Most people who noticed this news probably found it either puzzling or faintly amusing" (2269).[11]

Rauch's article points to a less obvious answer to the Rind study's paradoxical popularity. The sexual politics alluded to in the article's title, "Washington's Other Sex Scandal," had become a national joke in 1999, when the Clinton–Lewinsky affair headlined as the major scandal blurring the lines between sexual and electoral politics.[12] The public defamation of the Rind study resonated with neoliberal ambivalences about the relation between legislative agendas and electoral popularity, social liberalism and fiscal libertarianism, sexual self-determination and family values. The Clinton administration had become famous for its vacillating commitments to sexual minorities and heteronormative majorities, frequently resolving potential contradictions with the panacea of privatization. Children, however, presented an irresolvable contradiction in the terms of neoliberal expansionism.[13] The relation of the market to the family remained unsettled and unsettling, especially since it drew attention to the role of the state in legislating two ostensibly "private" domains. These relations became a flashpoint for domestic neoliberalism. As the Lewinsky–Clinton affair spectacularized, the boundaries between public and private were themselves politicized. Washington's sexual scandals— major and minor—were part of new stratifications in national public consciousness. On one side there were those who wished to see sexual morality returned to state politics; on the other, those who wished to see state politics get out of the business of sexual morality.

At stake in the Rind study debate is the relation between major and minor sexual politics, translated into a struggle over the hegemonic terrain of morality and policy. The most notable quality of this "other" sexual scandal lies in its relation to broader discourses of sexual minority. The Rind study's seeming inconsequence to major affairs of state is linked to its perpetuation of specialized categories for stigmatized sexual practices. Its minor din only amplifies the majority's public disavowal of *children's* sexuality as central to political capital in the United States. Mainstream debates about the political and moral regulation of sexual conduct have rarely touched children's positive capacity for sexual consent. This is because children establish a sure limit to debates about consensuality—children function as the naturalized outside to regulatory constructivism. Everyone knows childhood is socially constructed. That's the point of regulating it, to safeguard construction and route it along the proper channels for citizenship and productive social habits. But such regulation must appear to remain outside the social, must be the natural expression of a modern family-state relationship that needs no justification. This was once the work of the modern incest taboo. In the aftermath of the memory wars—as incest has shifted from taboo, to harm, to fantasy—the legitimacy of regulation itself must find new grounds. Contemporary debates about children's sexual consent, such as that provoked by the Rind study, do more than simply challenge moralistic assessments of children's sexuality, orchestrate homophobic denunciations of extrafamilial pedophilia, or destabilize the sanctity of family authority. Rather, these public debates about children's sexuality expose a broader problematic: the role of sexual consent in neoliberal transformations of national culture.

Sexual consent has historically been the terrain (and training ground) of liberal agency. Sexual historian Pamela Haag points out that "defining consent and violence are profound interpretive acts for liberalism" (xv), acts that have shaped and naturalized the meaning of agency in the United States:

> The opposition of consent to violence . . . underwrites the three dominant social relations of liberal culture: it is relevant to the meaning of sexual freedom; it shapes ideas of citizenship as defined through consent to a "social contract"; and in a market economy driven by ideologies of free contract it contributes centrally to the assumed legitimacy of a labor relation. (xvii–xviii)

Consent delimits the three liberal spheres of subjective agency: political, market (civil), and familial. As the opposite of violence, consent produces the illusion of subjective volition. It legitimates the social contract, or political subjection to state governance, as well as the labor contract, or economic subjection to market distribution. It also legitimates what Carole Pateman calls the "sexual contract," or gendered subjection to familial constraint. Reevaluating Pateman's sexual contract, Wendy Brown suggests that consent operates more subtly in orchestrating gendered differences in liberal agency. Consent establishes what Brown calls "legitimate subordination" by figuring subjective agency as a response to "arrangements and actions that one does not oneself create but to which one submits" (*States of Injury*, 162–63). Consent—specifically sexual consent—creates the ground of liberal subjection against which more active, choice-making and choice-driven agencies appear.

The "child" reveals the representational sleight of hand that binds liberal relations of contract and consent.[14] If consent provides the ground for more articulatory modes of agency—such as economic and marriage contracts—children's sexuality provokes a catachresis in that ground. The internal split between consent and sexual consent hives off sexuality as requiring a special pedagogy of care. Consent (as political legitimation of the social contract) is distinct from sexual consent (as private legitimation of the "sexual contract"). Children are political minors, under the tutelage of parents who owe them a duty of care to train them in the rational orders of civic responsibility, economic industry, and political citizenship. They are also sexual minors. But here their training is different. Whereas children *must* consent to the authority of their parents, they *cannot* consent to sexual activity. As philosopher David Archard explains, "What it is to be a child is to fail, as yet, fully to understand or be able fully to consent to any sexual activity" (*Sexual Consent*, 118). It is through this split in the logic of consent that the majority rights of a liberal population are grounded. Claims that children absolutely *cannot* consent to sexual activity rest on the definition of informed consent, in which knowledge and ability to assess probable outcomes determine entitlement to sexual decision-making. Legal childhood, defined through relational attributes of subordination, dependency, and vulnerability, makes "children" a class particularly susceptible to counternormative seductions (and in need of special state and familial protections).

This alleged inability to rationally negotiate the demands and constraints of liberal life subordinates children to parental authority and legitimates parental authority over sexual intrusion (as I argued in chapter 1). Laws against child sexual abuse have tended to focus not merely on sexual acts, but on erotic dispositions that might interfere with heteronormative sexual development as the path to sexual maturity. Childhood innocence has proven a powerful rationale for policing "perverse" sexual practices. Such a status definition of childhood allows the law to naturalize what Pamela Haag calls "interpretive acts" (*Consent*, xv) determining what psychic and physical relationships violate society's moral norms. Consent hinges on children, heuristically and protectively. Historically, sexual consent upholds relations between family and state more than it recognizes specific forms of sexual agency. Thus despite feminist reform to the Model Penal Code, consent discourse maintains a latent commitment to the marriage contract, the impermissibility of economic inducement for sexual activity, and a particular account of the relations between desire, force, and will. As the 1990s ended, age-of-consent discourse was arguably still concerned to establish legal relations between parental and state authority, using children as a status category to justify a range of regulatory interventions in sexual freedoms. Even under neoliberal transformations, the social relations of authority that subordinate childhood to adult political citizenship structurally negated children's sexual consent.

But it might be more accurate to say that consent produces children as the *case for* political negation. A theory of psychic life that denies children's cognitive decision-making ability even as it depends upon their ability to develop one is simultaneously deployed to negate the political rights of those seen to threaten their development of this ability.[15] Children are used to legitimate the danger of granting consent to adults with perverse sexual practices (they will use this legal protection to induce improper sexual dispositions in children), as well as to represent the constitutive outside of consensual possibility (children have no psychic capacity for rational deliberation). Children provide the rationale for political negation that does not, however, negate subjectivity. Quite the contrary. Children are subjects precisely of negation, subjects produced through a series of competing and conflictual negations that enjoin them to desire, will, and recognize themselves in the social transactions of liberal society. As Archard reiterates, "Non-consensual here means not so much that the child's participation is unwilling, but rather that the child's 'consent' is viewed as not consent proper and is thus discounted" (*Sexual Consent*, 119). The negation of children's capacity for consent holds out the reality of consent proper, the legibility of consent as the mark of real civil and sexual agency granted to proper citizens.

The child has therefore served as a liberal category defined through the negation of adult capacities and entitlements. Citizenship is produced in a cognitive developmental logic, in which children are subjects of "natural" pedagogical vulnerability and necessary legal protection in the form of parental rights. As such, children have historically been used to legitimate the sanctity of heternormativity and the criminalization of sexual minorities. Such political interest in the sexually vulnerable and violable child has been taken by many to be a sign of the fungibility of childhood rather than a reflection of the realities of childhood sexual exploitation. As cultural critic James Kincaid puts it, "'The child' is both a fetish and a flexible construction that is, to a large extent, independent of outside standards like age. Adolescents are stuffed back into childhood when it serves our purposes" (*Erotic Innocence*, 18). Kincaid, Lauren Berlant, and Marilyn Ivy among others have been quick to suggest the ways in which *sexually* suffering children are privileged figures of rightist causes, while those children suffering from nonsexual forms of epistemic violence—such as poverty and neglect—do not raise equivalent emotional and political fervor. Precisely because they symbolize an empty status category, children become figures through which protection from harm is signified as the moral province of the family and the state. The fetishization of children produces a political narrative in which the family appears to be the origin of moral norms rather than an overdetermined site of political regulation.

Thus, while the question "Why did the Rind study provoke such furor?" might seem too obvious to merit extended analysis, I contend that the 1990s saw a shift in the signification of childhood pedagogy and the politics of sexual consent. Here in place of sex panic is sex scandal, an interplay between titillation and taboo, moral outrage and transgressive celebration, that constitutes not a crisis in U.S. sexual norms but rather the public scene of ongoing moral—rather than explicitly political—regulation. Afoot here is a movement from the natural liaison between family and state to a denaturalizing skirmish between science and policy, trafficked in the domain of public moral norms. As Robert Stacy McCain's *Washington Times* article "Promoting Pedophilia" suggests, the "real-life effects" of academic activism are precisely what is at stake. McCain's reported scandal is the threat of academic research determining public policy, in particular "a larger movement within academia to promote 'free sexual expression of children'" (A02) that has gathered steam since 1998. This "larger movement," according to McCain, stems from the Kinsey reports of 1948 and 1952 through recent work by political science professor Harris Mirkin (1999), Johns Hopkins psychology professor John Money, San Francisco State professor Gilbert Herdt, the 2000 Institute for Advanced Study of Human Sexuality article "Sexual Rights of Children" (which states that there is no "inherent harm in sexual expression in childhood" [A02]), and Judith Levine's *Harmful to Minors.* As McCain summarizes the public response to Levine's book: "Researchers and activists say the book is only the most recent in a series of academic arguments for 'consensual' sex involving children" (A02).

Through readings of the Rind study, *The Kiss,* and *Push,* I argue in this chapter that 1990s debates about sexual consent expose a peculiar scandal about family, state, and market relations in neoliberalism. Here children appear at the crossroads of new formations of legitimate and illegitimate sexuality. Unlike early declensions of sexual consent logic, however, children appear both in arguments seeking to extend liberal rights to sexually disenfranchised subjects as well as in critiques of the normative psyche upon which political enfranchisement is based. Across these texts children themselves are speculatively granted sexual consent, but in addition the adult/child axis is challenged through the demarcation of consensual and nonconsensual incest. In the face of these challenges, sex scandals become a primary mode of recontainment. Sex scandals absorb the potentially radical articulation of sexual consent into what Lauren Berlant calls a culture of "public intimacy" coupled with what David Bell and Jon Binnie, in *The Sexual Citizen,* call the regulatory "privatization impulse" (5) of the Clinton era. Here Bell and Binnie pithily figure this response as the marketization of politics made palatable through the marketing of family, figuring all privatization shifts as the return to family values and personal freedoms. The following sections of this chapter ask how precisely sexual consent and its attendant scandals are broken down and recoded into new forms of neoliberal rationality and civic responsibility. How do claims about the capacity for sexual consent uphold—and perhaps even extend—the governing relationship between moral norms and legal authority in these public rationalizations of psychic life? How do university research about childhood extrafamilial consent, a memoir about adult consensual incest, and a novel about incest's compulsion toward workfare create new normalizing scenes of regulation? And what forms of sexual agency will appear as transgression and what as participatory desires in the normal life of the neoliberal citizen?

Liberalizing Fantasy

In many ways, the study by Rind and his colleagues asks precisely these questions about normative policy claims and the real harm of childhood sexual abuse. The Rind study proposes that policy against childhood sexual abuse fails to evaluate whether all sexual activity between adults and children is harmful. Policy simply dictates that such activity is harmful because it *should* be, because it is morally wrong. Children must be protected from harmful sexual contact, and this protection should take the form of increased legislation against sexual information, relations with extrafamilial mentors, and intergenerational sex. According to the study, however, just because the law seeks to uphold a moral norm does not mean it succeeds in doing so. In other words, the study argues that empirical research into the harmfulness of childhood sexual contact can provide evidence that the law fails in its normalizing aims. Rind et al.'s empirical research on the facts of childhood sexual experience suggests that not all sexual contact between adults and children is harmful. Rather, as in the case of adult sexual relations, consent is a logical predictor of positive or negative outcomes for sexual acts (at least nominally, pleasure or harm). In order to demonstrate this claim, the study performs a "quantitative meta-analysis" of fifty-nine preexisting empirical studies of the psychological harm of child sexual abuse (CSA).[16] As the starting point for this inquiry, the study asks: "In the population of persons with a history of CSA, does this experience cause intense psychological harm on a widespread basis for both genders?" (22).

The Rind study suggests that many prior child sexual abuse studies exhibit methodological bias. According to the Rind study, many studies presume a causal relationship between childhood sexual experience and psychological harm, asserting that "posttraumatic stress disorder is a common sequel of CSA in the general population" (22). The Rind study argues that most child sexual abuse studies evaluate harmful impact according to four defining properties: causality, pervasiveness, intensity, and gender equivalence (22). In these studies' findings, these properties recur "irrespective of the population of interest" (22). In 70 percent of the fifty-nine studies analyzed, child sexual abuse includes any experience in which a "sizable age discrepancy existed between the child or adolescent and other person, regardless of the younger person's willingness to participate" (29). In 20 percent CSA included "unwanted sexual experiences only" (29); 73 percent included contact and noncontact; 24 percent contact only; 88 percent provided specific age limits for CSA experience, with 60 percent including "children" up to age sixteen or seventeen and 25 percent at fourteen or younger (29). Under the definitions of many previous studies, sexual relations between a fifteen-year-old and a twenty-five-year-old are rendered formally equivalent to sexual relations between persons aged five and twenty as well as those aged five and ten. The Rind study argues that these definitions of CSA lump together all forms of sexual contact between legal minors and anyone at least five to ten years their senior (29). Citing an earlier study by Rind and Bauserman, the Rind study argues that "appraisals of nonnegative sexual interactions between adults and adolescents described in scientific reports can be biased by the use of negatively loaded terms such as CSA" (22–23).

Such a broad definition of child sexual abuse skews harm findings in the service of upholding statutory definitions protecting children from sexual harm. By combining these disparate cases of childhood sexual contact, such studies make it difficult to determine the true "pathogenicity of CSA" (23). An overly broad definition produces statistical "prevalence" of the experience, a prevalence then more statistically likely to overlap with self-reported negative psychological issues. In other words, the inflated numbers for childhood sexual abuse will appear to correspond to a broader range of psychological negatives. To claim that these phenomena are correlated is to inflate the relationship between childhood sexual contact and psychological negatives without actually demonstrating more than the statistical preponderance of both in a random population sample. The Rind study's meta-analysis suggests that earlier studies conflate self-reported negative outcomes (depression, anxiety, mood disorder) with a reported childhood incident of sexual contact with an older person.[17] Self-reported negatives statistically correlated to childhood sexual contact (broadly defined) are then reported as evidence of causation. Such overly broad definitions confound a number of variables that might, according to the Rind study, better measure pathogenicity. Gender differences, levels of consent (or wanted and unwanted experiences), and family environment in particular would need to be measured in order to clarify whether the negative psychological effects correlate with CSA or other factors currently confounded with it.[18]

Much of the Rind study focuses on the difference between such assumed formal properties of CSA (causality, pervasiveness, intensity, and gender equivalence) and "empirical and phenomenological" (45) data tracked through meta-analysis. In the introduction and discussion of their findings, Rind et al. contrast "legal and moral" (45) assertions of wrong with empirically measurable demonstrations of harm, complaining that "researchers have often failed to distinguish between 'abuse' as harm done to a child or adolescent and 'abuse' as a violation of social norms" (22). The study focuses on the need to differentiate between "empirically" measurable harm and "socio-legal" (43) wrong or, to put it more simply, between phenomenological persons and moralistic laws. As the study explains, we must differentiate between "the repeated rape of a 5-year-old girl by her father and the willing sexual involvement of a mature 15-year-old adolescent boy with an unrelated adult. Although the former case represents a clear violation of the person with implications for serious harm, the latter may represent only a violation of social norms with no implications for serious harm" (23). Following detailed explanation of the meta-analytic process and its findings, the closing "Discussion" section puts forward new empirical claims about CSA, its typically confounding factors, and personal harm. While the study did find some correlation between "poorer psychological adjustment" (42) and CSA, it ultimately suggested that confounding factors such as family environment, degree of willingness, degree of force, age at experience, and gender ultimately seemed more closely correlated to negative adjustment outcomes (42). The study ultimately surmises that "CSA does not produce pervasive and intensely negative effects regardless of gender" (42) and that "the negative potential of CSA for most individuals who have experienced it has been overstated"(42).[19]

While critics of the study have attacked its scientific accuracy—alleging outdated sources, biases inherent in college sampling, improper quantitative methodology, and so on—here I will sidestep the claim about adequate scientificity and focus instead on the kinds of political narratives produced by and about the Rind study.[20] In particular, I am interested in the political narratives attributed *to* the Rind study, or interpretations of hidden meanings in the Rind study's own scientific language. While the study was, as Janice Haaken and Sharon Lamb point out in "The Politics of Child Sexual Abuse Research," "framed as a dispute between science and public morality," it "stirs deeper uncertainties over the place of child sexual abuse in politics" (7). The Rind study itself states directly that "the findings of the current review should not be construed to imply that CSA never causes intense harm for men or women—clinical research has well documented that in specific cases it can" (42) and that in particular cases of forced and/or incestuous sex are likely to cause harm (45). Yet the study has been read by diverse critics as intrinsically political; its seemingly neutral scientific language is read as a complex semiotic code, one that denotes the "empirical" even as it sets moral and political signifiers adrift in an emergent account of psychological truth. Haaken and Lamb suggest that to some degree the political hermeneutics of science is at the heart of the study: "Like the Bible, the scientific literature is vast enough to support a wide range of opinions and viewpoints" (8). Like the Bible, this literature can be taken as depicting unmediated factuality or requiring heuristic sensitivity, depending on its readers.

Commentators on the Rind study have differed widely in their understanding of its claims. Carol Tavris points out in "The Uproar over 'Sexual Abuse' and Its Findings" that long-lasting harm is not the only rationale for criminalization, therefore the study should not be interpreted as making political claims—"a criminal act is still a criminal act, even if the victim eventually recovers" (16). Conversely, Haaken and Lamb read political claims in the studies findings and offer a very sanguine interpretation, construing the findings as antipoverty ("The effects of poverty and other broad indicators of family well-being outweighed sexual abuse as a factor associated with mental health problems in adulthood" [8-9]), anti–sex panic (avoiding "the heat of sexual hysteria" [8]), and tacitly feminist (showing how "the boundary between the normative sexuality and abuse for girls is a murky one"[12] and providing a critique of "the socialization of gender roles" [12]). And in "Sexual Liberation's Last Frontier" Julia A. Erickson says that the study analyzes "the facts about the effects of sexual activity between children and adults as separate from culture in which these children and adults exist" (23), raising important questions that "cannot be understood in the absence of an awareness of the culture in which it exists" (25). Erickson finds the study's assertion that it has no political agenda "a hollow reassurance" (23), and says that the study clearly has "a liberationist agenda" (23) whether it admits it or not.

So does the Rind study offer a critique of normative gender roles, or does it uphold them? How does it articulate a political "agenda" through the language of empirical fact? Much of the study's controversy focuses on its effort to evaluate willingness in child and youth sexual encounters. As Lynn M. Phillips, in her essay "Recasting Consent," explains the problem of willingness: "Legally, willingness and consent have been distinguished from one another. . . . Indeed, the concept of statutory rape is based on the notion that the ability to consent to sexual relations is a function of age, rather than of willingness or desire" (84). The law distinguishes between "informed consent" on the part of adults and "simple consent" or willingness on the part of children and youth. The Rind study uses "level of consent" (33) as a moderating variable, implicitly suggesting that willingness should be understood as a mode of consent rather than as its constitutive, and cognitive, precursor. This suggests that children have the capacity for willingness toward sexual relations, even if they do not have what the law decrees as the appropriate rational capacities for informed consent. Despite the stated focus on willingness, however, gender serves as the primary modifier for harm outcomes (in relation to age, force, degree of willingness, and family relationship). In general, girls experienced more negative outcomes than boys, regardless of other "moderator variables" (27) such as degree of willingness. Only "boys" reported more positive effects when willing sexual experiences were added to the statistics, "implying that willingness was associated with no impairment to psychological adjustment" (45). "Girls," however, seemed to maintain an overall lower level of positive self-reporting and a higher level of negative effects, even when willing encounters were taken into consideration (43).

One of the main questions raised by the study then is how to interpret such "empirical" measures of gender identity as the grounds for meaningful willingness and the rationale for psychological harm. Willingness only mitigated harmfulness in boys' sexual experiences; girls reported harm regardless of their willingness. Rind et al. offer two speculations on the cause of this phenomenon. First, the study quotes other studies' speculations on biological or social factors explaining gendered differences in sexual experience. These quotes are offered neutrally, and the Rind study takes no position on their claims. For example, "Schultz and Jones (1983) noted that men tended to see these sexual experiences as an adventure and curiosity-satisfying, whereas most women saw it as an invasion of their body or a moral wrong" (43). The Rind study explains that these findings are "consistent with more general gender differences in response to sex among young persons" (43), citing Sorenson (*Adolescent Sexuality in Contemporary America*) that in response to initial sexual experience "girls report[ed] negative reactions such as feeling afraid, guilty, or used, and boys predominantly report[ed] positive reactions such as feeling excited, happy, and mature" (43). The study cites Kinsey et al. (*Sexual Behavior in the Human Male*) and Sorenson (*Adolescent Sexuality in Contemporary America*) that "boys are more sexually active than girls, masturbate more frequently, and require less physical stimulation for arousal" (43), and Fischer and Lazerson (*Human Development*) that such experiences "are likely due to an interaction between biologically based gender differences and social learning of traditional sex roles" (43).The seeming neutrality of these descriptive claims is then conjoined with the second approach, in which family environment is used to explain the failure of willingness to mitigate harm for girls. This explanation speculates that gender discrepancy is the result of specific empirical experiences. Echoing the findings of Baker and Duncan ("Child Sexual Abuse" 1985), the Rind meta-analysis found that girls reported experiencing sexual contact at lower ages, with more force, less willingness, and more often in the context of family relations, thereby mitigating the measurable effect of positive variables (43). Coercive conditions such as these minimize the likelihood that even willingness will result in pleasure or positive effects. Or, in other words, the contexts in which girls make sexual choices nullify the relevance of their willingness, even for themselves.

Are these two speculations contradictory? One sociobiological, one sociopolitical? Are we to understand, following Haaken and Lamb, that this is an implicit critique of gender normalization and its hierarchical arrangement within and through the family? Or does gender come first, a biophysiological cause routed through the family, subject to its punishments but ultimately ungoverned by them? The Rind study itself refuses to answer these questions, but the authors' account of family environment within its findings as well as in a separate article points in the latter direction. The study isolates six variables in family environment that are frequently confounded with child sexual abuse outcomes: nonsexual abuse and neglect, adaptability, conflict and pathology, family structure, support and bonding, and traditionalism (38). The study found that family environment confounded with child sexual abuse explained "nine times more adjustment variance" than child sexual abuse alone, which "is consistent with the possibility that the CSA-adjustment relation may not reflect genuine effects of CSA" (43). Ultimately, the study finds that "nonsexual negative childhood experiences" (44) are more important in the assessment of harm outcomes, affirming the findings of Higgins and McCabe ("The Relationship of Child Sexual Abuse and Family Violence to Adult Adjustment") and Palotta ("Intrafamilial and Extrafamilial Sexual Abuse Vulnerability Factors") of "the role of family violence, rather than CSA, in explaining current adjustment problems" (44). Such "family dysfunction" (43) includes physical abuse, physical neglect, and verbal abuse; also cited as potentially relevant are Burnam et al. ("Sexual Assault and Mental Disorders in a Community Population") who suggest that "family or community environment" (43) plays a key role, and Pope and Hudson ("Does Childhood Sexual Abuse Cause Adult Psychiatric Disorders?") who posit "genetic factors" (43) that "predispose" (43) familial subjects to harm.

Once again, statistical overlap has been confused with correlation, and thus causation. When child sexual abuse and family problems appear in the same case, the Rind study cites Ageton ("Vulnerability to Sexual Assault") that there is evidence that "family problems preceded, rather than followed, CSA" (43). The only time child sexual abuse appears to "cause" (43) family problems is in the case of incest, but then again it is the familial nature of the sexual activity that causes a problem, not the sexual activity itself (citing Briere and Elliott, "Sexual Abuse, Family Environment, and Psychological Symptoms"). To put it in my own words, the Rind study's careful navigation of citational sources suggests that although girls more often experience sex in the context of force or dysfunctional families, in those cases there is no empirically solid evidence that the *sexual* experience and not the force and dysfunction cause harm. The family emerges as the culprit, but only to the degree that it is radically divorced from conditions of sexual activity, desire, or willingness. As a result, the family is returned once again to its biopolitical function, the home of genetic predisposition coupled with "community" problems (typically code for racialized or minority groups). Sexuality in contrast becomes conduct. Sexuality is liberated from the family, a specifically gendered conduct released from its once constraining context. Willingness in this account produces the boy as a protoliberal individual, the subject of desire who negotiates sexuality *externally,* both psychologically and socially prepared to exit the family domain. Girls lack this external and extensive capacity of willingness. Their sexuality is negotiated *internally,* in the psychological and social failure of willingness to separate girls from their family environment (due to greater levels of coercion and force). Girls' potential sexuality is determined (once again) by the family and enclosed within its circuits as gender identity. And, when sexual abuse appears within the family, it may be the result of genetic inheritance and community dysfunction. Thus even as the family appears to be the only empirically verifiable source of harmful child sexual abuse, the harm of that experience is unintelligible as anything other than dysfunctional sociobiological gender identity (not sexual experience).

This is admittedly a strong reading of the study, which itself claims only that "empirical evidence . . . suggests a more cautious opinion" (46) about CSA harm outcomes. But in a defense of their study ("Condemnation of a Scientific Article"), the authors state their own political position about these facts far more clearly. Within the study, Rind et al. contrast the "true nature" of CSA effects with the "conflation of morality and science" that "created iatrogenic victims" (45). In the authors' reply to the condemnation of their scientific article, Rind et al. make this account far more explicit. It is the feminist "anti-incest campaign" (4) whose undue influence on science and policy has induced "secondary victimization stemming from overreaction" (5) and "profound iatrogenesis in the 1980s and 1990s" (6). Within the study itself, we are told that incest is the only form of child sexual experience that is likely to have harmful outcomes. But we are also warned that it is still unclear whether sexual experience or a dysfunctional family (in which incest occurs) is the cause of harm. But in their own interpretation of the study, Rind et al. suggest that incestuous trauma is most likely a false positive, a form of "secondary victimization" and "iatrogenesis" fostered by feminist antisex moralism. If girls think that sexual abuse caused harm, it is sex panic.

The Rind study served as a flashpoint in the shifting sexual politics of the late 1990s. "This has been a period of shifting cultural borders," Haaken and Lamb explain, "the borders of gender, sexuality, and normative conceptions of family life" (11). The relationship of the family to the state, and of both to issues of sexual protectionism and sexual liberation, was very much in play. It was not clear if the family would remain the "safe haven" of liberalism or would be explicitly opened to the public domain under neoliberalism. The marketization of family and what Berlant calls public intimacy were already under way; the political evisceration of familial privacy and parental rights, however, remained a key debate between neoliberals, neoconservatives, traditional liberals, leftists, feminists, and sex radicals. The very ambiguity of the Rind study is key to its role in these debates; as I argued in chapter 1, disciplinary knowledge provides a key resource for shifting articulations of governance and the spatial relations of family and state. This ambiguous account seems to contrast intrusive private moralism with public sexual freedom, reversing even as it updates the tactics of conventional liberalism. The gender of girls is in fact shaped by iatrogenic moralism against sex, again that which appears from *outside the family* to reconstitute its normal social relations as structurally violative. Sexual agency is constituted over and against the confines of family, certainly, but family is not the confining condition of gendered violence. Rather, it is sociolegal and feminist moralism that instrumentalizes the concept of "family" to do violence to sexual freedom. The real agent of sexual harm is, in effect, the moralization of sexual politics (whether neoconservative or feminist).

From Phallus to Kiss

This reaction against a so-called feminist sexual politics was relatively widespread. Pro-sex feminism and pro-sex liberationist activism were unevenly related, with the family an ever-widening abyss between them. Even as the Rind study is attributed with participating in what G. E. Zuriff, in "Pedophilia and the Culture Wars," calls "the assault on the primacy of the traditional nuclear family over the past quarter century" (31), including changes in norms of "heterosexuality, the necessity for two parents, marriage, gendered division of labor, hierarchy of power, and biological relatedness" (35), the study was interpreted by some as extending arguments about childhood sexuality to incorporate familial sexual relations as proper to it. As Zuriff summarizes the implications of this shift, "In arguing that adult-child sexual relations are usually not harmful to the child, these scholars appeared to stand at the next frontier for deconstructing the family, the prohibition against sex within the family. Can a psychologically healthy and therefore societally sanctioned family consist of a child and a stable, emotionally supportive pedophile?" (35–36). In arguing that sexual harm is divorced from family environment, Zuriff notes that the Rind study opens the doors to rationalize family sexual relations. After all, "if father-child sex is not as harmful as had been thought, the traditional family is not as dangerous as thought" (38).

Perhaps then there is no such thing as child sexual abuse. There are positive or neutral sexual experiences (for boys) and panicked negatives based on sex moralism (for girls). What seemed to be a critique of the family—as the context correlated to harm outcomes, the place of increased force and nonconsensual intergenerational sexual contact as well as the hostile gendering of girls—suddenly turns into a defense of it. The family as such is not problematic until feminist moralism intrudes upon it and insists upon localizing harm within its borders. Masquerading as science, feminist moralism installs incest fantasies in the field of empirical truth. Rind et al. seek to restore incest fantasy to its rightful place, on the side of irrationality, and liberate more empirically minded boyhood sexuality from its familial clutches. Haaken and Lamb resist this finale, warning against efforts to redraw the borders of gender and generations so cleanly in the tracks left by prior modes of liberalism. Ultimately, they say "statistical analysis of competing data sets do not do justice to what is at stake in the battle over the status of child sexual abuse as a cause of adult suffering, and particularly women's suffering. We need an alternative means of entering into the psychological and social meaning of these accounts. . . . Likewise, we need an alternative means of entering into an understanding of children's agency and sexuality" (14).

Kathryn Harrison's memoir *The Kiss* seems almost cued to enter the discussion at this juncture. *The Kiss* explicitly investigates the fantasy-driven politics of morality, lingering in the realm of the fantastic and the imaginary to show how family exists far, far outside its empirical domestic context. Harrison's memoir is interested in the reach of fantasy, both as the effect of domestic familialism and its normative confines as well as the instrument for realizing a release otherwise unavailable. The memoir is written as fairy tale, a parable about a family triangle in which "the kiss" puts the daughter into a deep sleep.[21] Written in a minimalist style with lyrical and poetic resonances, *The Kiss* was considered scandalous because it told an autobiographical story of consensual, white middle-class incest from the point of view of an adult daughter. The narrator, Harrison's younger persona, reconnected with her long-estranged father when she was a college student of twenty and ultimately became involved in a sexual relationship with him. This section explores how fantasy and morality are shaped by this narrative, looking in particular at its scandalously gendered account of sexual consent. By writing incest as a fairy-tale return to the scene of Oedipus, *The Kiss* rearticulates fantasies of incestuous consent in order to mobilize the daughter's agency away from the "context" of the nuclear family.

The memoir opens: "We meet at airports. We meet in cities where we've never been before. We meet where no one will recognize us" (3). The collective pronoun, coupled with the intimate verb, changes the meaning of the predicate in all three sentences. "Airports," "cities where we've never been before," and "where no one will recognize us" are joined as the mythical location of narration. A new form of intimacy is concocted through this narrative opening, in which the couple-pronoun is articulated through late modern transit, geographic novelty, and an unrecognizing audience: "One of us flies, the other brings a car, and in it we set out for some destination. Increasingly, the places we go are unreal places: the Petrified Forest, Monument Valley, the Grand Canyon—places as stark and beautiful and deadly as those revealed in satellite photographs of distant planets. Airless, burning, inhuman" (3). By the third paragraph, the reader discovers that "we" are father and daughter, involved in a sexual relationship that mimics but exceeds the physical geography of familial intimacy: "Against such backdrops, my father takes my face in his hands. He tips it up and kisses my closed eyes, my throat" (3). Through these opening paragraphs familial desire is uprooted. The geography of household and of paternity are set in motion, as the two travel across the country ("The road always stretches endlessly ahead and behind us" [3]) and across the prohibited geography of each other's bodies. A touch establishing the median ground of parental intimacy (face in hands, kissing closed eyes) becomes the terrain of passion ("I feel his fingers in the hair at the nape of my neck. I feel his hot breath on my eyelids" [3]).

This new geography becomes the narrative form of the book: "Separated from family and from the flow of time, from work and from school . . . these nowheres and notimes are the only home we have" (4). A parable of travel, the narrative eschews causation and follows instead an itinerant path in and out of the family home. After this first chapter, the narrative moves back and forth in time, from the episodes of the affair to the moments of childhood memory, from their first adult meeting to her isolated listening to his audio letters on cassette tapes in the car. Here we learn that the narrator's father left her mother and her during her very early childhood, and that she was raised by her maternal grandparents in their house. The narrator has lamented his loss from this time, grieving and building up her defense against grief in the image of the lost father. "My father is an absence," she tells us, "a hole like one of those my grandmother cuts out of family photographs" (5). The characters of childhood are presented in the style of fairy tale, her grandmother's screams like "the long howl of the werewolf" (7) and her somnambulant mother a refusal of her existence: "As long as my mother refuses consciousness, she refuses consciousness of me: I do not exist" (8). Through the fairy-tale style we are given an empty, fantasmatic oedipal triangle, the mother who remains "romantically fixated, albeit from a distance, on my father" (9), the lost father the image of a hole and a ghost in the home (literally at times), the daughter with only spectral figures through which to forge her identity.[22] When she starts college, a reunion between herself, her father, and her mother sparks a new relationship between father and daughter that will spiral into an affair. After a passionate good-bye kiss in the airport this first time, the narrator will receive letters, phone calls, tape recordings, and entreaties to become closer and commit more deeply to the father-daughter bond.[23]

The Kiss might be read as an autobiographical meditation on the different contexts of fantasy and consent. Her father works through seduction, persuading the narrator to have sex with him by becoming the arbiter of her value. He offers recognition, love, witness, seemingly exploiting her desire for a father and unfamiliarity with the conventions of such desire. On one tape the narrator reports, "*Girl*, he calls me. *Oh, girl. My girl*" (28). The explicit articulation of what the Rind study claims, "girl" here becomes the term through which the narrator is made into daughter as a status category. Her ambivalence only deepens the effect: "I play the tape over and over, pushing the rewind button so that I can hear as often as I like the sound of my father telling me he wants me" (28). She will say of his visits that her father begins to "*see* me into being" (63). This combination of look and words will become his way of articulating her as daughter, of fashioning her into his "girl." His fashioning explicitly focuses on her whiteness, her portrayal as a thin white girl with very long blond hair, framed over and over in backdrops against which her unchanging image appears atemporal. Her father takes many pictures, with the explanation that "he thinks only in words, a text unrelieved by any sensual memory" (87), what she imagines as "an endless march of articulation" (87–88). If he "sees her into being," she provides the visual register through which he can think her into being. He must record her image, to be able to think her into seeing. This is the meaning of articulation in this text; later she will say, "He knows exactly what language to use, what noose of words to cast around my neck" (109).

At one point before she has agreed to have sex with him, he provides a lesson in familialism simultaneously disturbing and familiar. Taking out a pen she describes as "among the phallic possessions that he most esteems" (132), her father draws concentric circles representing their two beings overlapped almost entirely. This conventional scene seems at first to present his desire for her as an insistence on primordial possession: two beings intertwined from the beginning, with no middle and no end. But his insistence on "possessing" her through sex is marked by a difference from childhood incest. The narrator remarks, "He must possess me physically, for only that will reassure him of my commitment to him" (135). The threat that she is mobile, that she is not tied to his domestic authority or pedagogical power haunts his logic of possession throughout the memoir. His need for "commitment" is expressed as the drama of their postdomestic union. She is not yet another phallic possession, and thus the circles attempt to provide a belated lesson in the pedagogics of paternal possession discussed in the last chapter. As members of the white middle class, father and daughter here have missed their original inscription into displaced desire. Now his desire for possession, as well as her desire for patriarchal love, is represented as a search for origins that must be located and secured outside the domain of the domestic family.

The contexts of fantasy and consent raise similar questions to those asked in the Rind study: Is there harm in nonnormative sexual conduct? Or is it only the moral prohibition on that conduct that inflicts harm? The moral prohibition on incest is at the center of the narrator's decision-making process in response to her father's articulation of her as daughter. Her father is a "man of God" (11) who explains that his desire to "make love" (107) to her is divinely sanctioned: "'God gave you to me,' he says" (108).[24] Disturbed by his recourse to absolute morality to sanction their potential affair, the narrator states, "I am beginning to learn what it means: *unspeakable*" (117). "Unspeakable" here captures the dual legacies of incest as an unspeakable desire (the sine qua non of speech) and unspeakable act (incest is not taboo, merely speaking about it is). The memoir tells the story of oedipalization in reverse order, tracking back from adulthood to a scene of fundamental childhood pedagogy writ large. Thus their sexual relationship is described as a process of rendering her unconscious. When they finally do have sex, she becomes unconscious, with only a "composite, generic memory" (136) of the event. She feels asleep, she reports, as she does when she hears his voice on the phone, receives his letters and tape-recorded messages of love. "I sleep not because of the shock of my father's lust—at least not shock in the sense of something sudden and surprising" (138), she explains, but rather become of the moral awakening it requires of her: "I want to avoid contemplating the enormity of what we're doing—an act that defines me, that explains who I am, because in it is all the hurt and anger and hunger of my past, and in it, too, is the future" (138–39). The narrator's metaphorical and at times literal sleep is avoidance, but not precisely of the sexual act itself. Rather, she needs to avoid incest's signification. The shock of her father's turn from desire to "lust" is the shock of recognition, a shock she will avoid in "consenting" to an affair that ultimately renders her unconscious.

The narrator is put to sleep by the shock of recognizing the significance of the oedipal crisis. But this is where *The Kiss* departs from conventional fairy tale. A passionate kiss from her father, in the airport after their first adult meeting following his absence for many years, sends her into sleep, a long sleep through which she will seemingly fall into a somnambulist affair with her father. The entire memoir is told then as fantasy, in the Freudian sense of the term, an exploration of the fantastic nature of consensual father-daughter incest. Her processes of consent are represented as tacit submission, with tears and emotional struggle, a relinquishment of volition rather than an enactment of it. In one struggle over the exchange of sex for love, the narrator thinks, "Please don't make this the price, I beg silently" (107). Sleep is the dominant motif for entry into this logic of exchange, a falling asleep that makes agency into surrender. Her agency becomes defined by its passivity, its inscribability. Here whiteness is depicted as the resource for *value,* her long blond hair a repeated incitement to desire and visual reproduction, her father taking photo after photo of what she describes as a blank white girl whose hair makes her seem juxtaposed against the changing scenery. Her value is produced through the processes of her surrender, her unconsciousness, her becoming template to the modes of paternal production.

This is the key to the narrative movement, from airport/unknown city/unrecognizing audience through the father into the daughter's self-definition. In their postdomestic reenactment, the father articulates the daughter but also gives her freedom from the nuclear household. When she returns to college she lives in a shared household where she feels invisible: "It's a surpassingly pleasant and leafy neighborhood in which we live, the house itself an emblem of middle-American comfort and normalcy, and this is undoubtedly why I can't take my place in it" (132). Sex with her father provides a paradoxical liberation from the nuclear household. In the end, this liberation also requires her to leave him behind: "Once he was unknown in his absence, and now that I have known him, and he me, the rest of my life depends on our exile from each other" (202). She describes this process as "returning him—all evidence of the man—to his original relationship to me: the lost father" (28). As the memoir ends the narrator will slowly extricate from her father through the deaths of her grandfather and then her mother. By the end of the memoir, the narrator has come to realize that it is her mother both she and her father seek through each other. Thus the memoir ends with a father lost, found, and lost again, but a mother finally lifted from reality into a dream: "In this dream, I feel that at last she knows me, and I her. I feel us stop hoping for a different daughter and a different mother" (207).

In her article "Postpatriarchal Endings in Recent U.S. Fiction," Ellen G. Friedman suggests that there is "weakening of the oedipal stronghold" in recent fiction, and that "the plot endings of some recent US fiction delineate a pattern that can best be described as postpatriarchal" (696). In these recent texts the "father or his substitute" (697) do not make a symbolic impact on the narrative. Rather the father is "drawn as life-sized and survived without recourse to nomadism or another extracultural alternative" (697). Friedman remarks that in these texts the "life-sized" father is "embodied, exposed, and vulnerable" (693). *The Kiss* seems to match this description: "In every photograph, he is a tiny figure in a suit and glasses; the only person in the frame, still, he is never in the center or its foregrounds, he seems as incidental as a bystander" (6). As part of this diminution of the patriarch, Friedman also suggests that "postpatriarchal fiction pitches narrative in the direction of the present and future rather than the past" (697). *The Kiss* offers an odd twist on this claim. By the end of the narrative, incest has seemingly liberated the adult narrator from the confines of a highly gendered, feminized, white middle-class existence. She is harmed by her father's sexual exploitation of her willingness, but this harm is part of what will shape her as a more agentic, and self-representing, adult. Late in the narrative we are told that her sister from her father's second marriage has contacted her through her publisher (171). The narrator—Harrison herself, the reader is reminded— is a successful author. Her literary achievement comes in the aftermath of this experience: whether it is causal or correlative remains subject to critical interpretation, much like the empirical findings of the Rind study.

The literary establishment, much like the policy establishment in response to the Rind study, found *The Kiss*'s publication a scandal. In her analysis of the memoir's popular reviews, Laura Frost notes repeated accusations of Harrison's "profiteering" from her experience with incest ("After Lot's Daughters," 217). This complaint had been leveled about the boom of incest-themed novels and memoirs in general. As Janice Doane and Devon Hodges commented in 2001, "Just thirty years ago, a good local library might have been able to provide its patrons with two or three books on the topic of incest. Today . . . it may even seem that incest is now talked about too much" (*Telling Incest,* 1). Critics concerned that incest is "talked about too much" are worried primarily about the collapsed relationship between market drives and sexual storytelling.

As Doane and Hodges observe, critics are concerned, in other words, that "women's testimonies about incest have become formulaic, marketable products" (1). For Katie Roiphe, writing in "Making the Incest Scene," this explains the popularity of those lesser literary talents, mainly women, who produce predictable stories of childhood incest for a titillated audience eager to consume incest stories as a cheap thrill of private secrets revealed, what Roiphe calls a "bargain basement epiphany" (68) predicated on the market logic that "sex sells" (71). But *The Kiss* seemed to provoke particular scandal among its reviews: "In the mid- to late 1990s publishing climate, where nothing seemed to be too extreme to confess, Harrison's memoir makes evident what 'going too far' means" (Frost, "After Lot's Daughters," 227). The commercial success of the memoir, its publication and promotion as a reputable literary text, was the source of scandal: "Telling this story of adult incest in a fictional guise was almost acceptable; telling and actively promoting it as an autobiography was taboo" (218).

What interests me about *The Kiss*'s reception is its excitation of moral disapproval as an incitement to buy the book. According to Laura Frost, "The coy titles of such reviews—'Daddy's Girl Cashes In,' 'Sex with Daddy,' 'Pants on Fire!'—demonstrate the moral valence coloring most of the criticism as well as the difficulty in discussing adult father-daughter incest in any terms other than puns, parody, or indictment" (213–14). Frost insists that "puns" and "parody" are linked to indictment, as if an indirect repetition of the incest is the only way to "discuss" adult incest. *The Kiss* was at fault for failing to represent incest at an adequate linguistic distance. As memoir, as consensual, as complex, the story of incest told by the daughter appeared too literal. Curiously, the critical insistence on puns exacerbates the pornographic referents of a memoir with few detailed sex scenes. In this critical trajectory of misappropriated body parts and low-level literalism—of puns taken for penises—the reviews produce a "parody" of moral censure. But here it is not the memoir that titillates, but the discourse of morality generated around it. If *The Kiss* fails to pun, its reviewers will not. The frisson of transgression is reintroduced, making the book into a marketable object for pleasurable consumption. The aim is the arousal of the audience whose "punning" pleasure is then perceived to be at a remove from the violation so described, so that "the author seemed to be feigning a victim status in order to capitalize on a publishing trend that was, in turn, presented as the moral high road of expiation" (Frost, 216). The figuration of the incest pun is, Frost implies, female agency in the context of market-driven sexuality. The female autobiographer will be liberated by the father from the family not through sexual agency represented within the book, but rather through the market agency that receives her self-representation as evidence of the distance she has come from the patriarchal family romance.

The Poverty of Scandal

Frost suggests that *The Kiss* refuses to represent explicit sex scenes in order to enable more complex representation of female agency. The evasion of explicit sex scenes allows this memoir to figure the daughter's agency as determined by innocence as well as knowledge, desire as well as passivity. Since Frost claims "sex scenes would necessarily raise questions about the narrator's agency and complicity" (225), "the evasion of sexual scenes in *The Kiss* may be an attempt to forestall voyeurism" (228). But this alleged strategy does not seem to get the desired effect, since critical reviews of the book reconstitute the incest scene as the commercial and moral subject of the book. Sapphire's *Push* has been accused of making the opposite mistake. *Push* includes explicit sex scenes as well as sexually graphic language throughout, a level of detail accused of revealing, as Katie Roiphe notes once again in "Making the Incest Scene," "the selling principle at work. Sex sells and perverse sex sells more—a sentiment confirmed during the fierce bidding war for Sapphire's *Push*" (71).[25] For Roiphe, the $500,000 advance Knopf paid for the unfinished manuscript put a price tag on "the commercial potential of this particular form of suffering" (71). Implicitly and explicitly denigrating the literary merit of *Push* throughout her review, Roiphe returns again and again to the incestuous content of the novel as the key to its value. The fact that "one of the most talked about bidding wars in the publishing world this year was not over a new thriller by Michael Crichton or John Grisham but over a half-written first novel by an unknown female poet who calls herself Sapphire" (68) is for Roiphe a sure sign that publishers valued explicit (and perverse) sex over other forms of literary thrill. For Roiphe, the "non-standard" English of the novel's main text is part of its sensationalism. Here according to Roiphe "Sapphire's novel itself is aptly named. The idea behind the larger literary trend toward sensationalism seems to be to push one step further, to push for the purest rage, the most lurid crime, the most innocent victim. The idea, finally, is to shock the virtually unshockable modern reader" (71).[26]

Roiphe's snide denigration of the literary value of *Push* is central to the issues I am raising. For Roiphe the literary value of *Push* is defined completely through its marketability, its ability to shock. To indicate that the bidding war was unmerited, Roiphe cites the opening line of the novel: "I was left back when I was twelve because I had a baby for my fahver" (3). Roiphe allows this sentence to signal for her own readers the implicit shock of the text, a shock she implies is no longer achievable merely through incestuous content but which also requires the shock of poverty— the economic poverty of the main characters, and also the alleged "poverty" of the literary style. Here the nonstandard written English marks the shock value of the text for Roiphe, allowing her not to say directly what she implies: that this writing is itself impoverished, the mark of an effort to shock. According to Roiphe, it is this shock of poverty that makes *Push* a valued commodity on the literary market. The obverse of the punning dismissals of the consensual white incest of *The Kiss,* here critical parataxis does the work of undermining the linguistic power of the text. Roiphe's citation collapses incestuous reproduction and educational alienation as the shock value of the text. If *The Kiss* won't yield the incest scene, marked by the punning insistence on that secret revelation by the critics, *Push* yields the scene again and again, in language that takes language itself as an obstacle to incest's representation. As an extended meditation on literacy and the racialized power relations of English language use, *Push* interrupts some of the presumptions about language in debates about literary incest.

This book opened with Roiphe's citation of *Push* to make her point about the denigration of American family romance: "We is a nation of raped children" (*Push,* 68–69). Here I would like to end where I began: with the linguistic scandal of *Push.* Roiphe implies that poverty is the scandal of *Push*'s literary value. I would suggest instead that the poverty of scandal is a literary device guiding the stylistics of the text, which provide a critique of the alignment of very particular language practices with social mobility, economic entitlements, and social visibility. *Push* comprises the journal entries of Claireece Precious Jones, an African American adolescent who has given birth twice before the age of eighteen, both times following incestuous assaults by her father. The entries are directed at an unspecified audience, one of the techniques deployed by the text to enfold its literary audience with the pedagogical audience within the plot itself. Precious begins writing journal entries during her literacy classes at an alternative school, learning to read and write in English as part of her preparation for a G.E.D. class. The journal entries were assigned by her teacher, Blue Rain, who assists Precious and the other students to find their voice in the process of finding skills in written English. Over the pedagogy of the story, English-language use becomes the key to self-knowledge and self-narration. Precious comes to write her story (presumably the entries that make up the text) over the course of this class, telling the reader/her teacher about her father and mother's sexual abuse and neglect as well as the neglect and denigration she experienced in the public education system up until this point. Her inability to read and write is linked to the context of sexual abuse in her family, but it rapidly becomes part of a broader critique of the role of state and economic forces in creating the conditions of her life's poverty.[27] After finding out that she is HIV-positive, Precious develops her critical voice even further, leading her to "push" onward toward her goals of a high school diploma and a future in college.

To return this passage to its context within the novel, "We is a nation of raped children" is a statement originally made by Precious's teacher, Ms. Rain, translated into Precious's own words for her journal. It marks a crucial moment in the pedagogy of personality traced by the narrative itself. Before this moment, Precious has written very much as an individual. Her own story is isolated from the start: "My name is Claireece Precious Jones. I don't know why I'm telling you that. Guess 'cause I don't know how far I'm gonna go with this story, or whether it's even a story or why I'm talkin'; whether I'm gonna start from the beginning or right from here or two weeks from now" (3). Her story is entwined with its presentation as a story—she focuses throughout on the materialism of writing, how access to print culture is part of broader cultural materialism that has rendered her valueless and inaudible. Throughout the text the presentation of words on the page is rendered pedagogical. One series plays with the presentation of the alphabet and self-sense making, how the alphabet is transformed into a vehicle for self-representation: "ABCDEFGHIJKLMNOPABCDEFGHIJKLMNOPQRS. There are 26 letters in our alphabet. Each letter has a sound. A Day at the Beach Shore ABCDE-FGHIJKLMNOPABCDEFGHIJKLMNOPQRS" (58). Interspersed with her own entries are excerpted entries from her earlier journal exchanges with Ms. Rain. These entries trace a progressive editorial transformation, in which language use is corrected, modified, and moved toward more standardized practice. Her first entry, "li Mg o mi m" translates "*Little Mongo on my mind*" (61).[28] Later the text includes its first "correction" within its

print presentation, "say lat no evn a dog (*say later not even a dog*)" (71).
"Evn" is circled on the page. A dated journal entry included in the subsequent text includes self-corrections for spelling: "she say u notice yr
spelin change wen yu hav feelins not tal bout in book" (100).

Here, learning how to write is linked to literacies of the self. Spelling
is a process of imitation. But without models, the words on the page
"change," unable to articulate feelings not already talked about in books.
And this is where the real complexity of the novel emerges: is self-literacy
an intrinsically normalizing process? Or can it be radicalizing? Is the trajectory of the novel merely a cliché, a narrative of self-empowerment
through education? Or is there more to its textualization of the self as a
practice of social literacy? In the classroom the students read *The Color
Purple* as guide (81), a model Precious is given for her own life as well as
for a more tolerant relation to difference (of homosexuality, for example). *The Color Purple* teaches her to accept Ms. Rain as "a butch" (95),
and she begins questioning the heterosexist masculinism of her former
hero, Farrakhan. The images on her walls are slowly modified, with
Alice Walker and Harriet Tubman added to the poster of Farrakhan. Her
learning in this process is both linguistic and social, a process of translation signaled by the word "push." When she is giving birth to her first
child, a Puerto Rican ambulance attendant coaches Precious through her
labor pains: "I want you to push, you hear me momi, when that shit hit
you again, go with it and push, Preshecita. *Push*" (10). This phrasing is
repeated by Ms. Rain in scenes of literacy training: "I want you to try,
push yourself Precious, go for it" (54); "Precious, you gotta push" (97).
In each of these instances, a model for articulation is provided, and
Precious replies: "And I do" (10, 97). Being asked to push connected
the scenes of reproductive and intellectual labor, a model and imitation
through which Precious comes to articulate her agency as a crossing over
that is simultaneously a forging of connections.

This process of articulation focuses on the textualization of meaning,
the syntax through which feelings gain social meaning. Self-expression
is linked with finding a translatable syntax of the self, commented on at
one point as the discovery of capitalization: "Sick with a capital S (capital letter is how you start off sentence or say something with deep shit
meaning like Fuck with capital F you mad or some shit like that!)" (82).
Proper capitalization is linked with proper value, with determining her
own value in the eyes of the world. After winning a literacy award in
1988, her own language within the text changes. Her syntax becomes

less direct, experimenting with more figurative connections. If in the early pages her similes move one or two words along ("like on TV" [5] or "like the polices" [6]), later she writes "song caught on me like how plastic bags on tree branches" (87), and "it's a movie, splashing like swimming pool at Y, in my head" (87). Language itself becomes tropological, revealed in its constituting differences. If literacy forces her into so-called proper syntax, it also provides her access to the deforming aspects of language. The classroom pedagogy moves into the connotative rather than allegedly denotative function of language (a ruse the text itself has belied from the beginning). As they learn to read literature, Ms. Rain tells them that "the author has a message and the reader's job is to decode that message as thoroughly as possible. A good reader is like a detective, she say, looking for clues in the text" (108). This period also marks the beginning of Precious's written movement into public space, her linkage of her own mobility with the writing process. After discovering she is HIV-positive, Precious explains: "I gotta learn more than ABCs now. I got to learn more than read write, this big BIG" (93). Writing becomes the practice of articulation as translation, as survival. As Ms. Rain tells Precious, "If you just sit there the river gonna rise up drown you! Writing could be the boat carry you to the other side" (97).

It does indeed sound like a classic tale of uplift, in which literacy and knowledge lead to self-empowerment. But I would suggest that the novel reveals a slightly different understanding of "pedagogy" in its articulation of competing learning contexts. In *Push,* the growing language skills of the narrator are linked to her growing critical and narrative skills. This allows her to begin telling an alternative story of her family life, not only the violence of incest but also of the educational, labor, and political system that produced the family as "context." Precious writes, "The tesses paint a picture of me wif no brain. The tesses paint a picture of me an' my muver—my whole family, we more than dumb, we invisible" (30). *Push* becomes an articulation of value as the problem of incest's representation: "Miz Rain say value. Values determine how we live much as money do. I say Miz Rain stupid there. All I can think is she don't know how to have NOTHIN'" (64). Here the play on value is key—perhaps the first pun of the book, one that draws attention to the extensive capacity of language to draw distinctions between social and economic values that undermine the daughter's agency. Precious creates her own dialectic on value and language, one that reconstitutes the economic conditions of language use: "My name mean somethin' valuable—Precious" (67). She goes from wanting to be Janet Jackson, "a sexy girl don't no one get to fuck. A girl for value" (112) to a slow valuing of her own skills. She moves from "if I have a fantasy it be how I look" (114) to a fantasy of herself as a poet, a writer, and a student. In the face of broader social and educational devaluation, she comes to insist on her capacities as a student and a critical thinker.

The successful pedagogy of school clarifies the role of the state in shaping family as context. Thus after the sentence "I think I was rape" (68) comes a series of statements putting this one in a broader and broader context. "I think what my fahver do is what Farrakhan said the white man did to the black woman" (68), Precious goes on to explain, and then, "My baby is pretty baby. I don't not love him. He is a rapist's baby. But that's OK, Miz Rain say we is a nation of raped children, that the black man in America today is the product of rape" (68–69). Finally we return to the context of Roiphe's emblematic quote. But here that passage signifies quite differently. The double negative of "I don't not love him" follows on the positive valuation of her baby's beauty and precedes the baby's genealogy out of rape. Her own ability to bestow value, to assert love, is captured between an objective grammatical structure and the genealogy of rape. This genealogy is then attributed to the national history of U.S. racial formations, in which "Miz Rain" has sanctioned the baby's love by saying that the nation itself is founded in such acts. The very system of value in which her baby arrives is part of a longer system of interracial rape. What is added, here, is the problematic of intraracial incest. Precious must find a syntax to name and value her own baby when there are no models from which to do so. Her model, therefore, becomes the scene of the classroom. Her citation of Ms. Rain is an effort to produce a new syntax, the syntax of a young mother whose own literary value must interrupt these competing systems that erase her.

Resituating the emblematic quote "We is a nation of raped children" raises issues of amanuensis, how Precious comes to write her own story. Here Precious seems to cite Ms. Rain but in fact translates her, putting the teacher's soothing words into her own syntax. I asked earlier if this pedagogy was libratory or normalizing. It seems to me that it is rather about the politics of intertextuality, in a context where textual literacy is itself a primary obstacle to active participation in systems of value. "What is a normal life?" (114), Precious asks. It depends on how the context of the classroom is mobilized to reshape broader interinstitutional forms of power. In therapy with a white social worker mandated to her during this time, Precious talks about the past, about the now, and thinks about the future (115). The therapist encourages her to write memories of her family in a notebook, but Precious is skeptical of the agenda behind this writing. After stealing her file from the social worker, Precious and her friends use their new reading skills to decode the file, which explains that "the client" (118) aspires to college but is recommended instead for job skills training: "In keeping with the new initiative on welfare reform I feel Precious would benefit from any of the various workfare programs in existence" (119).[29] In the 1990s of the novel's setting, Precious's education is limited to her entrance into low-paid labor mandated by the state. But now Precious brings this text back to the classroom for collective analysis, where they evaluate the broader apparatus that shapes the "impoverished" family from welfare (68) to workfare (119). Their discussion focuses on how the state uses incest and other family violence to feed its need for inexpensive labor, "slave labor" (122) that replaces low-income workers with workfare labor. By the end of the novel, Precious has joined an incest survivors group and closes the novel reading to her son, "In his beauty I see my own. He pulling on my earring, want me to stop daydreaming and read him a story before nap time. I do" (140).

The middle section of the book focuses on the creation of an alternate collectivity, the collectivity of the classroom. What it performs is akin to the collective "we" opening *The Kiss*. Here a collective narrative is created, once again, after the narrator has left home. But here the world is not the open, destinationless stage of liberation through which consensual incest may be explored. Rather, the world is the classroom. The "we" is the collective of students and teacher, a pedagogy somewhat different from that offered to the narrator by her father in *The Kiss*. The narrator of *The Kiss* dropped out of college in order to explore her involvement with her father, who tells her, "Everyone will have to understand that for now I am your school. I am what you have to learn" (81). In *Push*, however, the school is the substitute for family, a training in self-knowledge as self-writing. As Precious explains, "What I gonna be, queen of babies? No, I gonna be queen of those ABCs—readin' 'n writin'" (75). As a result of her departure from family for school, Precious creates a memoir from literacy:

I am Precious ABCDEFGHIJKLMNOPQRSTUVWXYZ
My baby is born
My baby is black
I am girl

I am black
I want house to live. (76)

In *Push,* pedagogy is both complicit with the state, training future laborers for workfare, as well as resistant, focused on the critical thinking and
writing skills of independence. *Push* uses the memoir form but distorts it,
comments on it as seamless self-writing, breaks down the literacy of learning to write in English, then standardized English, and then the conventions of writing the "self." Precious debates her teacher about whether
The Color Purple provides a "fairy tale ending" or "realism" (83). Writing of the Langston Hughes halfway house where she lives, Previous says,
"1/2way between the life you had and the life you want to have. Ain't that
nice. You should read that book if you have a chance" (84). Being halfway
between the past and the future defines the literacy training of the present.
Whether that training is for "self-empowerment" in neoliberalism, training into workfare, or critical radicalism, the text leaves undetermined.

Ellen Friedman's arguments about postpatriarchal narratives would
seem to include *Push* as well as *The Kiss.* Friedman insists that these
narratives are overtly multicultural, marking a departure from "the old
narrative tied to Oedipus" which "is associated with racism, sexism,
abandonment, and a paralyzing nostalgia for the oedipal father" (699)
and a movement toward a genre that crosses "ethnic, race, and gender
lines" (706). In *Push,* the father does once again seem absent. Apart from
descriptions of the scenes of rape, he is not present, living elsewhere,
secondary to the role of Precious's mother or teacher. But rather than
serving as a powerful figure of fantasy, he is almost incidental to the plot,
there in literalized flashbacks of verbal and sexual denigration, not ele-
vated to the absent symbol of patriarchy. Here the daughter does not
depart through the fantasy of the father, turning him real and then leaving his reality behind. Instead, the reality of the father delimits Precious's
fantasy of her future.[30] This reality is the precondition for her "consent"
to workfare exploitation, to becoming part of the inexpensive workforce
of the state. It seems true then that so-called postpatriarchal narratives
use the agency of the daughter for national self-extension, that these
daughters, as Friedman suggests, "seem to extend representational possibility in their depiction of post-oedipal survival" (707). But these narratives might also extend new social relations within and through the
logic of family. The problem with the postpatriarchal account is that it is
not a liberation from social power relations. Rather, it marks the emergent formations of power as they are being articulated. This particular

movement toward the future breaks the residual oedipal narrative into its component parts: empirically minimal harm (liberalized fantasy), desired/ consented adult (kiss), and scandal of other issues (poverty).

Thus "postpatriarchal fiction" does move into the "unnamed beyond" (Friedman, 699), allowing "the nation, perhaps one instance at a time, to let go of its oedipal romance to allow for a more pluralistic understanding of what it is" (708). In what seems to constitute "postoedipal survival" different articulations create new formations of fantasy and reality. In the Rind study, this means boys (universal) will be liberated from the family to explore intergenerational and nonheteronormative sexual agency. In *The Kiss,* white middle-class girls will be liberated from the tyranny of niceness and passivity attributed to them by oedipal domesticity. In *Push,* black poor girls will be liberated from the poverty of family in order to participate in new regimes of state-mandated labor. Thus *The Kiss* and *Push* take their main characters in two different directions. The one, a middle-class white woman with long flowing blond hair, departs from the family to consent to sex with her father outside the home, as an adult. The second, a poor black adolescent girl debased by racist attitudes toward skin color and body image, departs from the family to consent to labor exploitation by the state. In both these literary texts, the daughter's consent is explored between the poles of politics and family. *The Kiss* shows the daughter's consent as a migration away from domestic space, paradoxically realized in her sexual relationship with her father. *Push* shows the daughter's consent as a similar migration, but here it is from the nonconsensual sexual abuse in the home to consent to pedagogical reconstruction. Precious Jones "consents" to her own remaking in textual form, learning to practice written and cultural literacy as the making of fairy tales out of one's own life.

Neoliberal Incest Taboo? or, The Valorization of Value

What ties these texts together, then, is the question of consent, or rather consent and its limits. According to Vijay Prashad, "Consent, under neoliberalism, is bred through the promotion of cruel forms of cultural nationalism" (*Keeping Up with the Dow Joneses,* xx). This chapter suggests that *some* elements of neoliberal "cultural nationalisms" turn on the changing referents of incest. As older social relations administered by the welfare state are disassembled, new cultural relations emerge to suture "civil society" to economic and political governmentality. What is required is to manufacture popular consent within new cultural constraints.

Cultural nationalisms have required new formations of family, more flexible ties between domesticity and descent, marriage and markets. For critics of the family such as Ann Anagnost, this transformation raises the question of value: "The phantom-like nature of value—what could be a more compelling topic in the wake of the bursting of the 1990s economic bubble, when the value of the new economy seemed suddenly to dissipate overnight? Where did value go? And how can it be that, in the midst of a global restructuring of capitalism, certain things that formerly seemed to have so much value are now deemed to be what society (or something called that) can no longer afford?" ("The Corporeal Politics of Quality [Suzhi]," 189).[31] For Anagnost and others, the value(s) being negotiated within and as family are transforming the political and economic relations of sexuality and civil subjectivity.

In the three discourses of value discussed here—from phallus as absolute standard, to kiss as transaction, to poverty as push—the family as context for state management and regulation has changed. In "Asian Diasporas, Neo-Liberal Families," Chandan Reddy argues that "the redistributive functions traditionally associated with the welfare state are indistinguishable from the social reproduction and growth of capital. Put otherwise, we can say that while the welfare state is organized to reproduce labor power and simultaneously regulate/capture labor, the current 'postwelfare state' governmentality is organized to produce wealth through the extension and production of new domains and modes of valorization" (104). These new domains dearticulate family from sexuality in some arenas, only to relocalize it in other ways. Reddy looks at the "different functionings of family in the current elaboration of racial and neoliberal capitalism" to explore "how the deployment of sexuality subtends and is anchored by the contemporary capitalist mode of production" (108). In different contexts, such as family reunification, gay asylum, and transnational adoption, the valorization of value has been slowly detached from its modern arrangements of property and labor. This results in new formations of value, articulated in complex ways through consumption, mobility, and affect. As Anagnost argues in her essay "Scenes of Misrecognition," which looks at transnational adoptions, "Parenting has become a newly intensified domain for the production of middle-class subjectivity for the adult. How is it that parents imbue this privatized domain of practice as a locus for determining their social value as 'good parents' and for the production of an intensified aura of sentiment surrounding family life?" (391).[32]

For my study, incest narratives in particular "confront daunting problems in charting a new path beyond patriarchal rule" (to use the words of Janice Haaken, *Pillar of Salt,* 7). Scandal produces a new market value for family problems, making the problem family a resource for new relations of production and consumption. The problem that incest families present resolves itself not into a postpatriarchal world, but into a future where gender and capital are entering new co-constitutions. As Rosemary Hennessey points out, "'Lifestyle' consumer culture promotes a way of thinking about identity as malleable because open to more and more consumer choices rather than shaped by moral codes or rules. In this way 'lifestyle' identities can seem to endorse the breakup of old hierarchies in favor of the rights of individuals to enjoy new pleasures without moral censure" ("Queer Visibility in Commodity Culture," 166). Such a "stylization of life" (166) promises to "dissolve fixed status groups" (166), subordinating the family as the unit of political normalization and turning toward the market to render an amoralized identity legible. According to Pamela Haag, such an "ironic convergence of radical and liberal views of sexual relations" (*Consent,* 88) enables the (figurative) marketization of sexuality to uphold the legitimacy of market relations and extend the promise of liberal politics in neoliberal ways. The "promotion of sex commodification *as* a renegade freedom" (88) might be meant to overturn conventional moralism, but it does so by counterposing the privatizing gender of the family with the publicizing sexuality of the market. What Wendy Brown, in *States of Injury,* calls "the masculinism of the civil subject cut loose from the family" (139) becomes the new frontier of neoliberal politics.

Incest has played a particularly powerful role in these reformulations of family and sexuality, precisely because of its historical articulation as the taboo differentiating fantasy from reality. As Reddy points out, "Neoliberalism has most powerfully affected the imagined relation between the state and civil society, disorganizing the fantasy structure if not the actual operation of the so-called closed welfare economies hegemonic during the period of neoliberalism's emergence" ("Asian Diasporas, Neo-Liberal Families," 103). This "disorganized" fantasy structure precipitates the "scattered hegemonies" of incest without its singular taboo.[33] The incest taboo once drew a line through "sexuality," barring certain acts and producing desires that take the form of fantasy. In the absence of this singular bar or taboo, the relationship between fantasy and reality is no longer clearly demarcated by the family/state conjuncture. Near century's end, sexual consent emerged as the new figure delineating fantasy from reality. As Pat Califia observes in her early writings on sex radicalism, "Legally, a free society must distinguish between the fantasy or thought of committing a crime and the actual crime" (*Public Sex*, 174). In a neoliberal society, "freedom" remains linked to the regulation of psychic and social life. In particular, the pedagogical normalization of childhood remains tied to the regulation of fantasy, the law's ability to "distinguish between the fantasy . . . and the actual crime" of incest.

But now "the law" and its marshal forces—incest taboo, rule of rules, interdiction, father's law—are not the central mechanism governing right from wrong, fantasy from actual crimes, or (as Levine stated it) hyperbolic from actual harms. As each text has demonstrated, the governance formations tying civil society to state increasingly take the form of fantasy. Across psychological studies, scandalous memoirs, and populist fictions of resistance, the fantasy of incest comes to replace its taboo as a governing trope of neoliberal kinship. This is the "neoliberal incest taboo": a civil rule delineating actual crime from fantasy according to market principles, which in turn scatter incest fantasy into newly hegemonic formations of labor and property, privacy and public action. Through new logics of consent, sexual liberation is articulated through diversified norms regulating the entitlements of psychic life. New orders of reason and fantasy seem to mark the "end" of the patriarchal family romance. But they also mark a new beginning. As we turn from the twentieth century into the twenty-first, incest continues to haunt the ideologies of U.S. nationalism and its practices of enfranchisement and dispossession. Only now incest's ghosts are being absorbed into neoliberalism as fantasy, a form of fantasy articulated *within* the American grain of civil governance. In emergent forms of civil agency modeled on the market, the status relations that once inhered in the "natural," prepolitical unit of the family appear to dissolve, only to reproduce those status relations through the formal "equality" of civil actors. The "public sphere" is deliberately (and deliberatively) reconstituted through incest fantasy's multiple lines of articulation. What Prashad calls "cruel forms of cultural nationalism" produce civil and sexual freedoms for some, economic and political subordination for others. And through the valorization of these scattered hegemonies as the vanguard freedom of the nation, incest reappears at the crossroads of sexual liberation, simultaneously a moral atavism and a biopolitical force for twenty-first-century life.

Conclusion

Beyond the Incest Taboo

Should Incest be in the criminal statutes at all? And if Incest is
appropriately included within crimes, how should the offense be defined
and titled? . . . Is it an offense against the person, a crime against
morality, a family offense, or all of the above? What is the gravamen or
essence of the offense? How do we perceive the harm?

— LEIGH BIENEN, "Symposium: Defining Incest"

Incest poses a peculiar problem in the conceptualization of justice. If incest
is an offense, it is difficult to discern precisely what has been offended by
acts of incest. If the offense is to be discerned from the infliction of harm,
it is equally unclear how that harm should be defined and measured. This
book has argued that incest served as a principle of articulation (both
pivot and secret) across welfare and neoliberal governmentality, crossing
over and forging connections between changing formations of culture,
law, and literature. Throughout, I have sought to address how these formations become fixed forms within cultures of neoliberalism. In trying
to resist this cultural formalism, my readings of incest have drawn on legislation, court opinions, popular journalism, novels, and memoirs. The
aim has been to show the possibility of determination otherwise within
and across various domains, despite the efforts of dominant culture to
reduce the politics of incest to mere culturalism. The final question is how
to use these readings to conceptualize alternative forms of justice for incest. In related work outside the academy, I have been part of a collective
that formulates alternative justice responses to incest and child sexual
abuse. The result has been slow, locally based efforts to develop community organizing and alternative justice mechanisms aimed at prevention
and transformative response within the contexts of neoliberalism. These
efforts, still incomplete, are a major resource for this book, an archive of

collective thought and practice that guides my explorations here. The specific work of this text, however, has been to examine the uses of literature and popular culture about incest within the dominant cultures of neoliberalism. Its concluding question then is how literature and popular culture articulate justice through the trope of incest.

Justice is often theorized in its difference from law. In *Residues of Justice,* Wai Chee Dimock argues that "the search for justice . . . is very much an abstraction, and perhaps an exercise in reduction as well, stripping away apparent differences to reveal an underlying order, an order intelligible, in the long run, perhaps only in quantitative terms" (2). The search for justice is a search for representational equivalence. Justice comes to depend upon both abstraction—of the ideal of justice—and reduction—the establishment of objective correlatives for ontological truth. Dimock suggests justice is "a language whose charge is to disentangle the world, to resolve its conflicts into a commensurate order—is a language that abstracts as much as it translates and omits as much as it abstracts" (5). The aim of the commensurate, which must fail, establishes justice as an ideal language through which law operates to its limited ends. For Dimock the incommensurability of justice introduces a diversity of linguistic forms into the domain of rationality: "The concept of justice . . . has never been without a zone of problematic residuum, a zone marked above all by the nontransparent relation between the various descriptive languages enlisted on its behalf" (8). Law becomes the formal category through which such "various descriptive languages" appear coherent, rational. The concept of law covers over the "problematic residuum" of justice, the residue through which its dream of adequation can never be realized.

In the case of incest, the law allegedly represents justice by adequating such diverse descriptive languages to the legal measurement of harm and risk. How incest is to be "defined and titled," as the epigraph from Bienen suggests, is intrinsically linked to translating the diverse languages comprising justice into the representation of rational law. Both Bienen and Kathleen Daly point out that incest has no normative definition. The law appears to rationalize disparate social languages of incest, to produce an order of commensurability from normative chaos. In fact, this lack of social consensus legitimates law. Without law, there would be no order of commensurability through which to seek justice for this "harm." But incest law also produces a crisis in the language of justice. If the law rationalizes incest through the homology of sovereign state and sovereign father, this homology renders state intervention into proper patriarchal householding "unjust." As Daly points out, in her essay "Sexual Assault and Restorative Justice," "We are trying to solve a justice problem that cannot ultimately be solved" (62). The law's underlying order of commensurability is premised on restoring equity in quantitative, and equivalent, terms. In incest cases, this abstracts the nature of harm into property relations, normative sexual violability, and interests in harmonious families. Incest law rationalizes normative harm but cannot find an order of commensurability through which these norms "adequate" to the daughter's alleged justice. Heteroglossia returns as the residue of justice; in particular, languages of domestic sexual power and its gendered effects become the residue of justice articulated in the domain of law.

If the legitimacy of law is predicated on the commensurate distribution of justice, how do we measure the commensurate in societies organized through radical incommensurabilities, or societies "structured in dominance" (to use a term from Stuart Hall, "Race, Articulation, and Societies Structured in Dominance")? As Daly asks, "How do we treat harms as 'serious' without engaging in harsh forms of punishment or hyper-criminalisation? How do we 'do justice' in an unequal society?" (62). All too frequently, the law reproduces inequity as the logic of commensurability. If the law is not adequate to the task of doing justice, how do we figure limits to the exercise of power? According to Dimock, literary language provides an "alternative language" (8) to the "two primary languages of justice, law and philosophy" (8). Dimock proposes that literature can reveal the underlying order of commensurability as a system of false equivalences, displaying the residual inequities of the false ideal of adequation (for some this is aligned with ethics over politics). For Dimock the language of literature "dispenses justice almost as a generic requisite and brings to that dispensation almost a generic question mark" (8), revealing the necessary residue of justice as part of its referential order. Literature represents justice *as a language.* And, in so doing, it reveals its own representational logic as a form of violence, allowing the incommensurate residue of justice to appear as itself "representation." Dimock writes, "We might think of literature, then, as the textualization of justice, the transposition of its clean abstractions into the messiness of representation. . . . Literature, in this sense, might be said to be the very domain of the incommensurate" (10).

But contemporary literature does not provide an alternative language of justice. Instead, it is part of new normative languages of justice that are no longer tethered to the distributive functions of state law. Dimock predicates the false ideal of commensurability on the "nontransparent relation" (8) between its "various descriptive languages" (8). Here literature has become another descriptive language enlisted on behalf of this commensurate ideal. This book has explored the "nontransparent relation" between various descriptive languages—law, psychology, popular culture, and literature—as well as the mode through which some transparency has been reified—harm, risk, property, labor, and consent. Unfortunately, none of these languages is automatically outside or antagonistic to neoliberal ideals of commensurate justice. Incest representations across domains have in fact become an explicit part of neoliberal justice, often establishing extralegal arenas that supplement (and at times replace) the law as the vehicle for cultural recognition and redress. While this transformation can promote radical articulations as well, all too often this work is enclosed in critical and popular receptions that emphasize the formalism (if not formality) of justice over and against more materialist social change. Incest literature has become a primary domain of the commensurate, not far afield at times from the empirical and quantitative measurements of incest in law proper.

Incest must be situated in relation to the changes of neoliberalism, precisely because it has been used to forge new connections between modes of representation and modes of governmentality. The overarching problem lies in neoliberalism's absorption of the imaginary as a zone of regulation, achieved precisely in the attempt to do it justice. New formations of the social and its alleged "imaginaries," including popular and juridical discourses, suture the rational and figurative orders of law and literature. The effort to "do justice" on incest has paradoxically produced new ways of regulating intangible properties of psychic and social life. "Representation" is increasingly a mode of governmentality, controlled by media monopolies and highly regulated forms of print culture. In this context the law's mediation of harm and literature's modes of revelation work together to incorporate increasingly specific affective and corporeal dimensions of sexual harm. These harms then extend beyond physical and mental injury to what Lydia Lee, in her note on the Child Pornography Prevention Act of 1996, calls virtual injury, a harm to normative reference in certain ways. Lee explores the impact of the 1996 act on normative reference, arguing that the law has new aims in regulating the symbolic harm of representation itself.[1] New statutes against virtual child pornography attempted to change the rationale of harm protection in justice findings. If traditional child pornography law was "justified on rationales that assumed the involvement of actual minors in the production of child pornography" ("Note," 648), the new law could be justified on market rationales of harm. Pondering the rationale for the new law, the Maine district court in *U.S. v. Hilton* expressed concern that, indeed, "pornography featuring images that appear to be of children will stimulate the market for child pornography in the same way as pornography featuring actual children" (647).[2]

Neoliberal governmentality has shown a keen interest in the relations of figuration, and the incest trope has played an important role in legitimating its transformations. Yet this study has focused entirely on the domestic effects of new cultural nationalisms within the United States. How might these readings of incest intersect with transnational accounts of neoliberalism within and against "a U.S. frame" (to use Cherniavsky's phrase, from her "Subaltern Studies in a U.S. Frame")? One option is to read incestuous trauma and the memory wars as an explicitly neoliberal form of cultural imperialism. In his book *Rewriting the Soul* Ian Hacking makes this argument about multiple personality, which he links to the recovered memory phenomena and to etiologies of childhood incest. According to Hacking, multiple personality is a symptom of North American cultural reach across the globe. Replicating older versions of American exceptionalism, Hacking asks: "How can it be everywhere in North America and nonexistent in the rest of the world until it is carried there by missionaries, by clinicians who seem determined to establish beachheads of multiple personality in Europe and Australia?" (14). Erica Burman makes a similar argument, suggesting that "it could be argued that FMS [false memory syndrome] is a peculiarly U.S. issue—the North American TV drama with its obligatory courtroom scene writ large. Yet False Memory Societies now exist all over Europe, Australia, and New Zealand" ("Reframing Current Controversies around Memory," 22). The context of "social breakdown" (26) and the "feminization of therapy" (27) are perceived to be exemplary of U.S. culture, which then articulate cross-nationally in other white-settler colonial nations around the globe.

A second option is to situate the rise of incest as child sexual abuse as the outgrowth of longer genealogies of colonialism. This involves a broader consideration of the transnational conditions through which "children" have been unevenly produced as a status category, from earlier colonial laws on marriage, family arrangements, age of consent, and sexual conduct to more recent international child labor laws, emergent laws on child trafficking, international debates about proper age of consent limits (as well as differences between economic and sexual domains of consent), connections between secularism and state legitimacy, modes of domesticity and patriarchalism, and access to health and economic resources. In "Shifting Contexts, Shaping Experiences" Marie Lovrod situates child sexual abuse within broader categories of "educating for empire," arguing that "the category of 'child' as 'educable subject' becomes a highly contested term as the nation mobilizes its various technologies for creating social hierarchies through models of education that mirror and ground differential international development policies, all in efforts that stabilize some economic positions at the expense of others" (35). Along with M. Jacqui Alexander, Larry EchoHawk, Lisa Eronson Fontes, Gioconda Batres Mendez, Emma Perez, the Queer Press Collective, and Melba Wilson, Lovrod explores how survivor narratives intersect with and at times intervene in the production of the category "child" in these complex systems of empire. Arguing that "the category 'child' is one of the most important and malleable sites where differential development mobilizes violence against subaltern social positions (including targeting specific child populations for sexual and other forms of exploitation)," Lovrod points out that "education" into specific literacies of print culture can be part of this broader process of child sexual abuse as "educating for empire" (36).

These two positions stake out two histories of childhood in relation to processes of imperialism and transnationalism. The first positions the United States as cultural imperialist as well as national exception to broader processes of childhood vulnerability to sexual violence. Incest is articulated in a U.S. frame, but as a falsehood. This process of national/ exceptionalist articulation and subsequent repudiation then extends across the globe, particularly to societies with similar geohistories of colonial settlement and national racialization. The second view positions the United States as one location among many in a transnational economy structured through differential access to safety, health care, economic well-being, and political security. Child sexual abuse (rather than incest per se) occurs across social and national contexts, but how it is articulated will be highly mediated by international divisions of labor and humanity (see Alexander, "Erotic Autonomy as a Politics of Decolonization"). In this second position, child sexual abuse and exploitation are products of complex, transnational and translocal systems of intimacy, neglect, and exposure (Stoler, *Carnal Knowledge and Imperial Power*). How abuse and exploitation are articulated varies considerably, both in practice as well as in processes of empirical documentation, legal intervention, social interpretation, and cultural dissemination. Certainly debates about childhood, sexual choice, and sexual victimization have emerged quite widely and in divergent territorial and imagined communities. Sexual violence in colonial practices, the targeting of children and young adults in particular, the infantilizing of cultural others, the erotic logic of dependency, the decimation of generational transmission through boarding schools and other interventions in indigenous practices, and the ongoing subjection of colonized youth to sexual violence and exploitation (often linked to economic and political deprivation) make it impossible to take seriously the exceptionalism of the U.S. case.

What is "exceptional," however, is the rhetorical force of "American" incest, the ideology of representation at work when female U.S. citizens "said incest." If incest serves as pivot and secret across formations of governmentality and culture, then incest is one overdetermined figure hiding the necessity for "subaltern studies in [or of] a U.S. frame" (to paraphrase Cherniavksy's title). Or, in other words, American incest *nationalizes* what have always been transnational conditions of labor, racialization, exploitation, and domination. It is the "U.S. frame" that makes the nexus of gendered subordination, racial exploitation, and sexual domination "appear" *as incest*. Those transnational conditions of childhood that emerge as limits of biopower—massively exploitative labor conditions, the decimation of diverse kinship practices, the normalization of sexual intimacies that create childhood as a "crisis" to be managed by emergent (neoliberal) governmentalities—appear when enclosed within the United States through images of incest. These images, as this book has argued, lend themselves to processes of governmentalization and localized discipline as much as abstractions of state sovereignty and national security.

This conclusion therefore resituates Louise Armstrong's "women" as U.S. citizens. Across the 1980s, incest survivors provided a universal particular for new forms of national popular culture. The memory wars that ensued delegitimated women from positions of articulation, using them instead as instruments of larger neoliberal cultural transformations in the meaning of justice. Yet this articulation of incest within a national popular frame lived on, especially after women had been disbarred from participation in its meaning. Ann Levett calls this the broader spectrum of "problems of cultural imperialism in the study of child sexual abuse," in an article of this title, looking not only at the cultural imperialism of U.S. approaches in other contexts (South Africa in her case) but at the forms of cultural imperialism within the United States as well. Rather than taking the United States as the exceptional location in which incest has been articulated, her argument suggests different approaches to the interarticulation of child sexual abuse across conditions and contexts. On the one hand, Levett argues that "in this time, Western patriarchal social systems are easily able to take up and accommodate some liberal and feminist demands while giving minimal attention to the workings of power which led to the identification of social phenomena of concern in the first place" (52). On the other, these reduced analytics are then circulated transnationally as part of research projects that replicate the cultural reductions of a dominant Western framework. As a result Levett points out that there is little "'cross-cultural' study" (57), and what does exist tends to import "naively positivist empiricism" (58).

The articulation of incest within a U.S. frame has depended upon the pressures of neoliberalism and the so-called cultural transformations of globalization. The seeming "nationalization" of incest in the 1990s reproduced a national "imaginary" even as it restructured that imaginary to serve new, somewhat more flexible ends. It is certainly not the end of nationalism, as Vijay Prashad argues in *Keeping Up with the Dow Joneses* and as has become increasingly clear in the opening decade of the twenty-first century (Puar, *Terrorist Assemblages*). But it is a moment where the constructions of cultural nationalisms are in flux, and where the coordinates of modern family and welfare state are being recoded for a more securitized, bureaucratized, and marketized society of the future. The seeming ascendancy of culture over the social or the national was part of the transformations of this period, allowing new formations of cultural nationalism even as the ideologies of genealogy, natality, and futurity of citizenship were recrafted. To some extent, the work of this transformation was achieved by dominant tropes of incest. What happened when "women said incest" is that they were remade into the image of U.S. citizens, precisely at a moment when citizenship was being reorganized. Much of the nascent radicalism of various approaches to childhood and sexuality were transformed into bureaucratic entities with only partial relations to feminism (of any definition). Some transnational alliances were formed in this period, but all too often they articulated this struggle within the dominant across national borders. This approach did not adequately diagnose and intervene in the transnational systems of governance, economy, and social struggle that shape childhood sexual vulnerability. And when this occurs, the cultural politics of the global North can too easily become cultural imperialism, failing to consider difference not only in political and cultural economy but in the differential production of state power across national borders.

But once again, this is not the only way to tell this story. This book's aim has been to look for radical possibilities within incest articulations in the United States in the 1990s. Literature has been the primary site for excavating these alternatives, a choice guided primarily by my disciplinary training (English) as well as by my own proclivities of imagination and desire. My choice here was to focus on incest as a dominant, and to explore the role of print culture in securing and challenging the dominant in this period. Even within that choice, I focused on dominant forms of print culture, published novels and memoirs that received at least some popular and critical attention. This creates space for readings of aesthetically intriguing texts, which are primarily intended to open imaginative space and gesture toward latent tendencies in broader cultural paradigms. But it omits space for more radical alternatives to dominant culture and print media. Within academic study, anthropology and performance studies (to name just two disciplines) might provide nuanced readings of social practice through which to study the articulation of childhood sexuality. Outside of the academy, some of the most exciting work is taking place in emergent forms of social justice organizing, in which prevention and response to child sexual abuse is articulated outside of dominant modes of governmentality and rubrics of citizenship. Performance art, smaller networks of publication, and even discourse communities have been producing potentially more radical strains of articulation as well.

This book explored the making and unmaking of incest as a contemporary object of study within the U.S. academy, from my own limited vantage point in a department of English. This trains my focus on the domains of dominant print culture that articulate what Dimock in *Residues of Justice* calls "the dream of objective adequation." As Dimock explains, "It is this dream of objective adequation which makes the concept of justice intelligible in the first place: intelligible not only in retributive justice, where we yearn for a punishment equal to the crime, and not only in compensatory justice, where we yearn for a redress equal to the injury, but also, I might add, in distributive justice, where we yearn for a benefit equal to the desert" (6). This book asked how everybody's family romance produced a "dream of objective adequation" through which incest would enable the U.S. nation-form to become more "just." The dream was articulated in the hybrid forms of the welfare state and its neoliberal transformations, in which incest provides a trope to turn harm to risk across the territories of family and nation. But this dream was taken up and rearticulated as a nightmare in the texts explored across chapters 3 and 4, in which the languages of law and literature were interrogated for their objectification of daughters as part of this dream.

Yet somewhere between the dream of objective adequation and the nightmare of instrumental representation, the daughter forges a dialectic through which a different possibility of justice becomes visible. As the narrator of *The Kiss* explains the self-negation performed by the dream of objective adequation: "Someday a sentence will come to me, a magic sentence that will undo all that is wrong and make everything right. But until that sentence comes, I say nothing" (31). In *Thereafter Johnnie* Cynthia Jane (Janie) similarly longs to put "a name to this age," a dream in which "I made the words to describe it, day and night a dream of articulation, a knowledge in me that whatever is can be spoken exactly and there is a word for everything" (200). In the failures of this dream— of articulation as objective adequation—justice will remain repudiation, a mark of what is yet to come, as Patricia explains in a journal entry: "I am unloved. And the purpose of this journal is to probe out of the innocent paper, a response, an answer, a secret language to interpret and own and finally recognize as a handful of blood smeared and dried irregularly on the paper. The blood is an event I remember, dipped from the warm bowl of the heart" (33). In these pages that possibility is not yet realized. But perhaps that realization is happening "somewhere and somewhen" beyond the page, "*when* and *if*," as Johnnie would say, "*while*."

Acknowledgments

A book is, in reality, a very queer thing, abounding in metaphysical subtleties and theological niceties. An academic monograph doubly so. Richard Morrison made publishing the pleasure it should be, and I was fortunate to receive the expert assistance of Adam Brunner, Laura Westlund, and the entire production team at the University of Minnesota Press. My thanks go also to Lisa Duggan and Vikki Bell, the Press's reviewers, whose insightful comments gave this book its final shape. I am grateful for permission to reprint material from *Discourse: Journal for Theoretical Studies in Media and Culture* and the *Southern Literary Journal,* as well as permission to include images by Matt Mahurin (from *Time,* 1993) and Chris Buck (from *Newsweek,* 2006). This project has received generous support from multiple sources: I thank Wellesley College for a Horton-Hollowell Dissertation Fellowship; the University of California at Berkeley for a Mellon Dissertation Fellowship and a Center for the Study of Sexual Culture Dissertation Fellowship; and the University of Washington for two Junior Faculty Development Awards in the College of Arts and Sciences, a Society of Scholars Research Fellowship from the Walter Chapin Simpson Center for the Humanities, and a Royalty Research Fund Fellowship.

This book traces its academic origins to Wellesley College. There I was fortunate to take a women's studies class with Leigh Gilmore, whose initial support for a thesis on incest encouraged me to apply to graduate school. At the University of California at Berkeley, graduate colleagues Hershini Bhana, Glenda Carpio, Dale Carrico, Amy Huber, Homay King, Jasbir Puar, Masha Raskolnikov, Matt Richardson, James Salazar, Gayle Salomon, Karen Tongson, and Catherine Zimmer shaped my thinking and shared my time. Activist work with Staci Haines and Sara Kershnar, cofounders of Generation Five, pushed my ideas in new directions. Dorothy Hale provided welcome guidance during early research, while Saidiya Hartman's ability to translate my nervous explanations into crystallized points helped shaped the first draft of this book. Judith Butler proved a remarkably generous interlocutor whose capacity to predict my arguments kept me racing forward. And Caren Kaplan's unflagging guidance helped me to situate my analysis in a transnational frame. Finally, Chris Nealon honed my research questions and steadied my resolve during final revisions.

New colleagues at the University of Washington moved the project into its current form. Luther Adams, Carolyn Allen, Miriam Bartha, Bruce Burgett, Jessica Burstein, Zahid Chaudhary, Kate Cummings, Tom Foster, Gary Handwerk, Tara Javidi, Sydney Kaplan, Eng-Beng Lim, Tom Lockwood, Ted Mack, Joycelyn Moody, Naomi Murakawa, Brian Reed, Priti Ramamurthy, Henry Staten, Vinay Swamy, and Kathy Woodward each involved themselves with my work in different ways. I owe an abiding debt to cross-institutional colleagues Kate Bedford, Eva Cherniavsky, Laura Chrisman, Habiba Ibrahim, Amy Kapczynski, David Kazanjian, Jodi Melamed, Chandan Reddy, Sonnet Retman, James Salazar, Caroline Simpson, and Nikhil Singh, each of whom read draft portions of this book (some multiple times). Alys Weinbaum deserves more thanks than I can give for acting as both interlocutor and cheerleader at every stage. Graduate students in trauma and testimony, law and literature, family romance, novel theory, and psychoanalysis courses contributed vitally to my thinking, with thanks in particular to Julie Kae, Anoop Mirpuri, and Marissa Solomon (of Fordham Law School) for research assistance. The lecture and conference audiences who have listened patiently over the years, including repeat commentators Lauren Berlant and Robyn Wiegman, also have my gratitude. And I could not have written this book without the WORD writing group, and Scott Swaner in particular; I miss his company every time I face the screen.

My final thanks go to those personal networks that have sustained me across the years. My mother, Maureen Wall, and sister, Blake Howard, remain the touchstones for this work; I thank them for their unremitting sharpness and idiosyncratic sense of humor. I have already named many close friends among the colleagues who gave so much of their time and support to this project, so I will merely repeat my deep gratitude for their compassion and criticism (in well-timed oscillations). I add thanks to Shira Bezalel, Stany Harkins, Sharon Kerr, Jocelyn Saidenberg, Jenny Terry, Todd Shepard, Tim Wall, and John Zaia, each of whom helped sustain me through the past decade. And for Shelley Halstead, my thanks for giving me a space to garden. Beyond these groups, many others have helped me to arrive here, and my warmest gratitude extends to those names and faces unspecified in these pages.

Notes

Preface

1. For a case chronology see Jesse Friedman's Web site, www.freejesse.net/Addendum.html. See also the comments by the director of *Capturing the Friedmans* in Jarecki, "Secrets and Lies."

2. These statistics are cited in Bass and Davis, *The Courage to Heal*, 20.

3. On the McMartin preschool case and the Kelly Michaels case, see Eberle and Eberle, *Abuse of Innocence*; Nathan and Snedecker, *Satan's Silence*.

4. Neoliberalism describes the movement from Keynesianism to monetarism associated with Friedrich Hayek and the Austrian school of economics and Milton Friedman and the Chicago school of economics. See Harvey, *Brief History of Neoliberalism*.

5. These policies have been identified with neoliberalism, although Williamson himself disputes this conflation ("What Should the World Bank Think").

6. On "America" as neoliberal signifier, see Grewal, *Transnational America*, 2.

7. See Catherine Gallagher, *Nobody's Story*.

Introduction

1. On incest in emergent English language literature, see Archibald, *Incest and the Medieval Imagination*; Carmichael, *Law, Legend, and Incest in the Bible*; and Freccerro, "Queer Nation, Female Nation." On early modern incest studies, see Boehrer, *Monarchy and Incest in Renaissance England*; Ford, *Patriarchy and Incest from Shakespeare to Joyce*; McCabe, *Incest, Drama and Nature's Law*; Shell, *The End of Kinship*. The epigraph to this Introduction is taken from Laura Miller's article on Slate.com, May 28, 2002, www.salon.com/weekly/incest960610.html.

2. Roiphe's genealogy begins with English sibling incest novels such as Daniel Defoe's *Moll Flanders*, transmuted by the "gothic imaginations" ("Making the Incest Scene," 68)

of southern U.S. writers such as William Faulkner and Erskine Caldwell, literalized as "graphic sexual abuse"(68) by black women writers in the 1970s and popularized by mainstream white authors in the 1990s.

3. On the incest boom, see Kincaid, *Erotic Innocence.* On overstated "boom" claims and for a list of incest titles, see Doane and Hodges, *Telling Incest.* On media cooptation of incest, see Alcoff and Gray, "Survivor Discourse."

4. For a feminist critique of race and reproduction in Anderson and Balibar, see Weinbaum, *Wayward Reproductions.*

5. On romantic and early novelistic incest, see Battestin, "Henry Fielding"; Hudson, *Sibling Love*; T. G. A. Nelson, "Incest in the Early Novel"; Nickel, "'Ingenious Torment'"; Thorslev, "Incest as Romantic Symbol"; and in particular Pollak, *Incest and the English Novel.*

6. Fukuyama's essay, written in 1989, became the book *End of History and the Last Man* (1992).

7. See, for example, Friedman, *The Lexus and the Olive Tree*; Huntington, *The Clash of Civilizations.*

8. For examples from this vast scholarship, see Chase, *Spaces of Neoliberalism*; Comaroff and Comaroff, *Millennial Capitalism*; DeMartino, *Global Economy*; Duggan, *Twilight of Equality?*; Dunkley, *Free Trade Adventure*; Enloe, *Morning After*; Escobar, *Encountering Development*; Frank, *One Market under God*; Gibson-Graham, *End of Capitalism*; Hall, Held, and McGrew, *Modernity and Its Futures*; Harvey, *Brief History* and *Condition of Postmodernity*; Robbins, *Feeling Global*; Soja, *Postmodern Geographies*; Vlachou, *Contemporary Economic Theory.*

9. This kind of historical exceptionalism has been contested by Thomas Bender, *Rethinking American History*; Chakrabarty, *Provincializing Europe*; Lindebaugh and Rediker, *The Many-Headed Hydra*; Mehta, *Liberalism and Empire*; O'Rourke and Williamson, *Globalization and History.* I cite this exceptionalist account as a key discourse of the period, not as its analytic resolution.

10. Selected titles in trauma and memory include Antze and Lambek, *Tense Past*; Bal, Crewe, and Spitzer, *Acts of Memory*; Belau and Ramadanovic, *Topologies of Trauma*; Bracken, *Trauma, Culture and Philosophy*; Farrell, *Post-Traumatic Culture*; Miller and Tougaw, *Extremities*; Santner, *Stranded Objects*; James E. Young, *Texture of Memory.*

11. On medicalized suffering in neoliberalism, see Bracken and Petty, *Rethinking*; Edmondson, "Marketing Trauma"; Feldman, "Memory Theaters"; Kleinman and Kleinman, "Appeal of Experience"; Yaeger, "Consuming Trauma."

12. On culture, see Lloyd and Lowe, *Politics of Culture*; Lloyd and Thomas, *Culture and the State.* On multiculturalism, see Denning, *Culture in the Age of Three Worlds*; Dillard, *Guess Who's Coming to Dinner Now?*; Ferguson, *Aberrations in Black*; Gordon and Newfield, *Mapping Multiculturalism*; Melamed, "Spirit of Neoliberalism"; San Juan, *Racism and Cultural Studies*; Yudice, *The Expediency of Culture.*

13. In *The Political Unconscious,* Jameson defines the "ideology of form" as "the symbolic messages transmitted to us by the coexistence of various sign systems which are themselves traces or anticipations of modes of production" (76). Novels of this period transmitted seemingly contradictory sign systems linked to competing modes of production, which were often too quickly synthesized into a semiotics of familial trauma. For an exemplary critique of this ideology of form, see Lisa Lowe, *Immigrant Acts.* On familial nostalgia, see Coontz, *The Way We Never Were* and *The Way We Really Are*; Stacey, *Brave New Families* and *In the Name of the Family.*

14. The *Oxford English Dictionary* traces "trope" from its origins in Ancient Greek *(tropos)* as a turn (as in "the 'turning' of the sun at the tropic") to its current rhetorical

meaning as "a figure of speech which consists in the use of a word or phrase in a sense other than that which is proper to it; also, in casual use, a figure of speech; figurative language." In its turn from the proper, the trope transforms not only the "proper use" of a word but also its "casual" appearance as figurative language. See Butler, *Excitable Speech*; White, *Tropics of Discourse*.

15. On determination otherwise, see Spivak, "Rani of Sirmur" (258).

16. This essay was written in 1908 and first published in Rank, *Der Mythus von der Gerburt des Helden* (1909). See also Rank, *Incest Theme in Literature* (1912). Citations from Freud, "Family Romances."

17. See Judith Daniels, *Subverting the Family Romance*; Greenfield, *Mothering Daughters*; van Boheemen, *Novel as Family Romance*.

18. On the nuclear family's emergence in Europe, see Aries, *Centuries of Childhood*; Donzelot, *Policing of Families*; Engels, *Origin of the Family*; Flandrin, *Families in Former Times*; Foucault, *History of Sexuality*; Scott and Tilly, *Women, Work and Family*; Zaretsky, *Capitalism*. In the United States, see Freedman and D'Emilio, *Intimate Matters*; Hawes and Nybakken, *Family and Society*.

19. See Nancy Armstrong, *Desire*; Flanders, *Structures of Experience*; Flint, *Family Fictions*; Haggerty, *Unnatural Affections*; Macfarlane, *Marriage and Love*; McCrea, *Impotent Fathers*; Trumbach, *Rise of the Egalitarian Family*; Watt, *Rise of the Novel*.

20. For feminist critiques of familial nationalism, see Grewal and Kaplan, *Scattered Hegemonies*; Kaplan, Alarcon, and Mooallem, *Between Woman and Nation*; McClintock, Mufti, and Shohat, *Dangerous Liaisons*; Mohanty and Alexander, *Feminist Genealogies*; Mohanty, Russo, and Torres, *Third World Women*; Yuval-Davis and Anthias, *Women-Nation-State*; Yuval-Davis and Werbner, *Women, Citizenship and Difference*.

21. Numerous poststructuralist critics have joined Marx and Freud, each negotiating the dramas of primary repression/alienation in different ways. Across their work, Judith Butler, Kaja Silverman, Hortense Spillers, and Slavoj Žižek have insisted upon the social determinations of oedipalization, situating it squarely within Marxian and Foucauldian frameworks linked to changing modes of production. See in particular Silverman's treatment of Althusser in "The Dominant Fiction," in her *Male Subjectivity at the Margins* (15–51), and Hortense Spillers's call for a "psychoanalytics" that refuses the primacy of white bourgeois oedipality and singular primary repression in "All the Things You Could Be."

22. Kazanjian's "figure of the graft" (*Colonizing Trick*, 21) captures the "actively forced articulation" (22) of late seventeenth- and eighteenth-century internationalisms in dominance. Edwards argues that whenever the "African diaspora is articulated," its acts of "translation" produce "a constitutive *décalage* in the very weave of the culture" (*Practice of Diaspora*, 13).

23. On psychoanalytic fantasy, see Laplanche, *Life and Death in Psychoanalysis*; Laplanche and Pontalis, *Language of Psycho-Analysis*. On political fantasy, see Berlant, *Anatomy of National Fantasy*; Burgin, Donald, and Kaplan, *Formations of Fantasy*; Jacqueline Rose, *States of Fantasy*; Žižek, *Sublime Object*.

24. The *Oxford English Dictionary* defines fantasy and phantasy together, beginning with definitions from "scholastic psychology": "a. Mental apprehension of an object of perception; the faculty by which this is performed. b. The image impressed on the mind by an object of sense." This dual sense, of mental apprehension as both object and instrument, echoes across later definitions focused on the veridical failures of fantasy to represent facts. Thus "a spectral apparition, phantom; an illusory appearance" becomes "delusive imagination, hallucination; the fact or habit of deluding oneself by imaginary perceptions or reminiscences." Later psychoanalytically influenced definitions of "a day-dream arising from conscious or unconscious wishes or attitudes" (1926) transform "a mental image, a

product of imagination, fiction, figment" to "a supposition resting on no solid rounds; a whimsical or visionary notion or speculation."

25. On African American family romances, see DuCille, *Coupling Convention*; Claudia Tate, *Domestic Allegories* and *Psychoanalysis*. On anticolonial family romances, see Backus, *Gothic Family Romance*; Verges, *Monsters and Revolutionaries*.

26. On related logics of land expropriation and racialized personhood, see Mary Pat Brady, *Extinct Lands*.

27. See Castronovo, *Fathering the Nation*; Cherniavsky, *That Pale Mother Rising*; Davidson, *Revolution and the Word*; Fliegelman, *Prodigals and Pilgrims*; Amy Kaplan, *Anarchy of Empire*; Dana Nelson, *National Manhood*; Warner, *Letters of the Republic*. On colonial and settler family romances more generally, see Chrisman, *Rereading the Imperial Romance*; McClintock, *Imperial Leather*; Debra J. Rosenthal, *Race Mixture*; Sharpe, *Allegories of Empire*; Sommer, *Foundational Fictions*.

28. On pre-1970s U.S. incest literature, see Barnes, *Incest and the Literary Imagination*; Boose and Flowers, *Daughters and Fathers*; Dalke, "Original Vice"; Sanchez-Eppler, "Temperance in the Bed of a Child"; Stewart, "Exogamous Relations"; Elizabeth Wilson, "Not in This House"; Zender, "Faulkner."

29. Books and anthologies treating Freudian fantasy's racial formations include Abel, Christian, and Moglen, *Female Subjects*; Cheng, *The Melancholy of Race*; Eng, *Racial Castration*; Khanna, *Dark Continents*; Lane, *Psychoanalysis of Race*; Hortense Spillers, *Black, White, and in Color*; Viego, *Dead Subjects*; Walton, *Fair Sex*.

30. On transnationalism and family, see Anagnost, "Scenes of Misrecognition"; Eng, "Transnational Adoption"; Ong, *Flexible Citizenship*; Parrenas, *Servants of Globalization*; Reddy, "Asian Diasporas."

1. Laying Down the Law

1. On hysteria, see Bland and Doan, *Sexology in Culture*. On race and empire, see McClintock, *Imperial Leather*; Stoler, *Carnal Knowledge and Imperial Power* and *Race and the Education of Desire*. On law, see Burdett, "The Hidden Romance of Sexual Science"; Gilman, "Sibling Incest, Madness, and the Jews"; Von Braun, "Blutschande"; Weinbaum, *Wayward Reproductions*. On ethnology, see Asad, *Anthropology and the Colonial Encounter*; Carsten, *After Kinship*; Farber, *Conceptions of Kinship*; Faubion, *The Ethics of Kinship*; Franklin and McKinnon, *Relative Values*; Parkin and Stone, *Kinship and Family*; Schneider, *A Critique of the Study of Kinship*; Yanagisako and Delaney, *Naturalizing Power*. On capitalism, see Engels, *Origin of the Family, Private Property, and the State*; Foucault, *History of Sexuality*.

2. Charcot's experiments at the Salpêtrière drew together gynecological studies of the wandering womb and neurological studies of shock. Janet departed from this neurological viewpoint of genealogical inheritance. See Leys, *Trauma*.

3. Following an 1881 degree in physiology and neurology, Freud worked from 1885 to 1886 with Charcot and began his correspondence with the nose-and-throat specialist Wilhelm Fliess in 1887. In 1895, Freud and Josef Breuer published *Studies on Hysteria*. See Hacking, *Rewriting the Soul*; Leys, *Trauma*.

4. On the seduction debate see Laplanche, "Sexuality and the Vital Order," in *Life and Death in Psychoanalysis*, 25–47; Masson, *The Assault on Truth*; Bennet Simon, "Fact and Fantasy in the History of Freud's Views on Incest and Seduction"; Triplett, "The Misnomer of Freud's 'Seduction Theory.'"

5. Freud offers no consistent theory of the incest taboo; see *Three Essays* for one dominant schema. For critique of this schema see Judith Butler, *Antigone's Claim, Bodies That Matter*, and *Gender Trouble*; Gayle Rubin, "The Traffic in Women."

6. For different accounts of this conjunction, see Gilman, *The Case of Sigmund Freud*; Hacking, *Rewriting the Soul*; Pellegrini, *Performance Anxieties*; Weinbaum, *Wayward Reproductions*.

7. *Totem and Taboo* was first published in *Imago* as a series of four articles (1912–13), turned into the book *Totem und Tabu* in 1913, and translated into English as *Totem and Taboo* in 1918. For a reading of homosexuality in *Totem*, see Eng, *Racial Castration*.

8. Freud dismisses "eugenics" (*Totem and Taboo*, 154) and protection of "progeny" as explanations. On temporal versus biological racism, see Lloyd, "Race under Representation." On Freud's civilizational discourse, see Khanna, *Dark Continents*.

9. Lacan's approach led to splits from the Société Parisienne de Psychanalyse to form the Société Française de Psychanalyse, then again to form the Ecole Freudienne de Paris. On Lacan and American ego psychology, see Viego, *Dead Subjects*.

10. Lacan avoids a too strict synthesis of these processes and constantly insists, as here in *The Seminar of Jacques Lacan, Book VII*, that "the phallus is nothing more than a signifier" (314) and that "in our theory the sole function of the father is to be a myth, to be always only the Name-of-the-Father, or in other words nothing more than a dead father, as Freud explains in *Totem and Taboo*" (309). But Lacan also makes consistent recourse to the "law of the prohibition of incest" (67) to figure "the fundamental laws of the signifying chain" (62), allowing him to use incest paradoxically to signify "the relation to the signifier and to the law of discourse" (6).

11. In *Male Subjectivity at the Margins,* Kaja Silverman argues that the "dominant fiction" produced through particular symbolic orders and modes of production can be disentangled from Lacan's fundamental structures of kinship and language. If kinship only retroactively posits signifiers for the lost real, this account opens alternative significations. See also Gallop, *Reading Lacan*; Silverman, "The Lacanian Phallus."

12. See Judith Butler, "The Lesbian Phallus" and *Bodies That Matter*; Butler and Rubin, "Sexual Traffic."

13. Published in French in 1976 (*Histoire de la Sexualité*), the volume was translated into English in 1977. See also Deleuze and Guattari, *Anti-Oedipus*.

14. As Foucault reminds us, the Freudian incest taboo "assumes an adversary position with respect to the theory of degenerescence" even as it serves as a "mechanism for attaching sexuality to the system of alliance" and "functions as a differentiating factor in the general technology of sex" (*History of Sexuality*, 130).

15. French citations from *Il Faut Défendre la Société* (1997).

16. Orthogonal articulation is modeled by nineteenth-century working-class housing estates, in which the "grid pattern . . . articulated, in a sort of perpendicular way, the disciplinary mechanisms that controlled the body, or bodies, by localizing families (one to a house) and individuals (one to a room)" (Foucault, *Society Must Be Defended*, 251). Regulatory mechanisms are present in this grid, creating "pressures that the very organization of the town brings to bear on sexuality and therefore procreation" (251) such as incentives to save for housing, insurance, and so on.

17. Foucault explains that "theoretical paradox" has "as its corollary a sort of practical disequilibrium" (*Society Must Be Defended*, 240).

18. See Archibald, *Incest and the Medieval Imagination*, 9–52. See also shifts from ecclesiastical to statutory law in *State v. Marvin K. Kaiser* 663 P.2d 839 (Wash. App. 1983), discussed in Eskridge and Hunter, *Sexuality, Gender, and the Law* (274–80), and Myers et al., "Prosecution of Child Sexual Abuse in the United States."

19. On early sex law for subjects "white by law" (Lopez, *White by Law*), see Franke, "Becoming a Citizen"; Haag, *Consent*; Schulhofer, *Unwanted Sex*; Stanley, *From Bondage to Contract*. On the legal state of exception applied to black women, see Saidiya Hartman, *Scenes of Subjection*.

20. For readings of incest in Leviticus, see Carmichael, *Law, Legend, and Incest in the Bible.*

21. This case, *State v. Chamley* 568 N.W.2d 607 (S.D. 1997), heard an appeal of conviction on several counts of sexual contact with a minor (against three girls aged eight through ten). The decision was reversed and remanded on appeal.

22. See also Brown and Brown, *The Hanging of Ephraim Wheeler.* Incest appears fleetingly in sexual conduct and morality prosecutions. See also Shah, "Between 'Oriental Depravity' and 'Natural Degenerates'"; Stavig, "'Living in Offense of Our Lord'"; Peter Wallenstein, "Polygamy, Incest, Fornication, Cohabitation"; Daniel Williams, "The Gratification of That Corrupt and Lawless Passion." In Canadian contexts, see Chunn, "Secrets and Lies." On incest and sterilization cases, see Wray, *Not Quite White.*

23. On these justifications, see Arens, *The Original Sin*; Vikki Bell, *Interrogating Incest*; Fox, *The Red Lamp of Incest*; Meiselman, *Incest*; Twitchell, *Forbidden Partners.*

24. This has been repeated more recently in *Muth v. Frank* 412 F.3d 808 (7th Cir. 2005). In this case siblings Allen and Patricia Muth appealed their imprisonment for adult marital incest (they were raised separately until the age of eighteen). The U.S. Court of Appeals for the Seventh Circuit held that *Lawrence v. Texas* 539 U.S. 558 (2003), which found laws barring consensual homosexual sodomy unconstitutional, did not apply to consensual adult incest. For a recent review of U.S. incest law see Harvard Law Review, "Note: Inbred Obscurity."

25. "Governmentality" is the transcript of a lecture delivered at the Collège de France in February 1978, translated into English by Colin Gordon in 1981. See Burchell, Gordon, and Miller, *The Foucault Effect*; Mitchell, "Society, Economy, and the State Effect."

26. On Foucault's history of childhood, see Aries, *Centuries of Childhood*; Flandrin, *Families in Former Times*; and Hughes, "Thinking about Children."

27. For general overviews of child welfare policy, see Ashenden, *Governing Child Sexual Abuse*; Eekelaar and Nhlapo, *The Changing Family*; McLaren, Menzies, and Chunn, *Regulating Lives*; Barbara J. Nelson, *Making an Issue of Child Abuse*; Pelton, *The Social Context of Child Abuse and Neglect*; Piven and Cloward, *Regulating the Poor*; Pleck, *Domestic Tyranny*; Prout and James, *Constructing and Reconstructing Childhood*; Scarre, *Children, Parents, and Politics*; Sommerville, *The Rise and Fall of Childhood*; Theodore J. Stein, *Child Welfare and the Law*; Stephens, *Children and the Politics of Culture*; Wollons, *Children at Risk in America*; Zimmerman, *Family Policy.*

28. Child protection statutes have existed since 1825, but prosecution was rare. By the 1870s, private agencies began targeting urban poor whose child-rearing strategies differed from white middle-class norms. In 1874, the New York Society for the Prevention of Cruelty to Children was founded and developed rationales for legal intervention into families on child welfare grounds. By 1875, New York laws allowed incorporation of societies to prevent cruelty to children, which often worked closely with law enforcement agencies. See Levine and Levine, *Helping Children,* 208–12.

29. The societies for the prevention of cruelty to children were replaced by formal laws governing the rights of parents in relation to the duty of the state to protect children, resulting in the body of parental rights and *parens patriae* doctrine across *Meyer v. Nebraska* 262 U.S. 390, 402 (1923), *Pierce v. Society of Sisters* 268 U.S. 510 (1925), *Prince v. Massachusetts* 321 U.S. 158 (1944), and *In re Gault* 387 U.S. 1 (1967). On child law, see Ramsey and Abrams, *Children and the Law in a Nutshell.* On parental rights, see Archard, *Children, Rights and Childhood*; Clark, *The Law of Domestic Relations in the U.S.*; Sanford N. Katz, "Parental Rights and Social Responsibility in American Child Protection Law"; Olsen, "The Family and the Market"; Soifer, "Moral Ambition, Formalism, and the 'Free World'"; Woodhouse, "Constitutional Interpretation and the Re-constitution of the Family in the United States and South Africa" and "'Who Owns the Child?'"

30. See Costin, Karger, and Stoesz, *The Politics of Child Abuse in America.*

31. Federalization followed the 1909 White House Conference on Child Dependency; the Children's Bureau was established within the Department of Commerce and Labor in 1912 and granted federal jurisdiction over child protection (focused on reducing infant mortality and improving maternal health). In 1916, the Keating–Owen Act introduced child labor law subsequently ruled unconstitutional in 1918. This became part of *parens patriae* as the balance between local and federal regulation; see Rosenthal and Louis, "The Law's Evolving Role."

32. While the Social Security Act of 1935 required centralized welfare services, uniform services throughout a state, and the combination of child welfare and child protection in agencies supported with public money, no specific child protective service was mandated in public welfare agencies; see Levine and Levine, *Helping Children.*

33. The 1960 White House Conference recommended that states allow the "community" to designate an agency for child protection. The 1961 legislation of aid for foster care remanded decisions to courts in order to balance what had been perceived as biased agency intervention. But no procedures were established to formalize new decision-making standards for intervention; see Rosenthal and Louis, "The Law's Evolving Role."

34. By 1967, all states had passed mandatory reporting laws for professionals (Levine and Levine, *Helping Children,* 187). Early legislation directed reports to agencies that would begin criminal prosecutions; the perceived reluctance to report transformed laws and redirected cases to child protection authorities. See Antler, "The Rediscovery of Child Abuse"; Morgan, "A Child of the Sixties."

35. On the welfare–warfare state, see Abramsky, *Hard Time Blues*; Wendy Brown, *States of Injury;* Ruth Wilson Gilmore, *Golden Gulag*; Parenti, *Lockdown America*; Prashad, *Keeping Up with the Dow Joneses.*

36. Shaped to pass President Nixon, the Federal Child Abuse Prevention and Treatment Act (CAPTA) of 1974 emphasized state responsibility in *parens patriae* to protect children from physical abuse rather than to ensure their overall welfare and economic security.

37. Leroy Pelton points out that the "the myth of classlessness" allows child abuse to be represented as both "psychodynamic problems" and an "epidemic" ("Child Abuse and Neglect," 31).

38. Federal law requiring due process protections to protect children's best interest have tended to rely on psychological experts to define and interpret harm (Rosenthal and Louis, "The Law's Evolving Role," 69).

39. See also Weiss et al., "A Study of Girl Sex Victims"; and Brunhold, "Observations after Sexual Trauma Suffered in Childhood."

40. Devlin points out that Weinburg's statistic is for incest prosecution, not occurrence. Her own research on incest trials of the period suggests that the state was more likely to find in favor of the daughter than were psychoanalytic clinicians ("'Acting Out the Oedipal Wish'"). See also Devlin, *Relative Intimacy;* Gordon, *Heroes of Their Own Lives;* Sacco, "Sanitized for Your Protection"; Satter, "The Sexual Abuse Paradigm in Historical Perspective."

41. See also Finkelhor, *Sexually Victimized Children;* Rush, "The Sexual Abuse of Children"; Russell, *Behind Closed Doors in White South Africa* and "The Incidence and Prevalence of Intra-familial and Extra-familial Sexual Abuse of Female Children"; Walters, *Physical and Sexual Abuse of Children.*

42. Foucault's disregard of gender has led to accusations that he misreads gendered sexual domination. For Foucault's views on age of consent, see "Sexual Morality and the Law"; on feminist analyses of Foucault's position, see Vikki Bell, *Interrogating Incest.*

43. The 1962 Model Penal Code reformulated sexual assault law; 1960s state legislatures incorporated some recommendations; 1970s feminist reforms sought to expand the
range of misconduct covered by sexual assault law, repeal the marital exemption and the
resistance rule (in some states), and modify evidentiary standards. See Berger, Searles, and
Neuman, "Rape Law Reform"; Estrich, "Is It Rape?"; Rachel Hall, "'It Can Happen to
You'"; Odem and Clay-Warner, *Confronting Rape and Sexual Assault*; Phipps, "Children,
Adults, Sex and the Criminal Law"; Schulhofer, *Unwanted Sex*; Searles and Berger, *Rape
and Society*.

44. Some claim the horror of incest was used to criminalize sex. See Angelides, "Feminism, Child Sexual Abuse, and the Erasure of Child Sexuality"; Hacking, *Rewriting the
Soul* (62).

45. Summit claims the 1975–80 collaboration led to "the real explosion" in child sexual abuse awareness (in Corwin, "An Interview with Roland Summit," 8). He developed
the theory of child sexual abuse accommodation syndrome during this period. On CSA
governmentality, see Reavey and Warner, *New Feminist Stories of Child Sexual Abuse*;
Robertson, *Crimes against Children*.

46. On legal analogy, see also Halley, "'Like-Race' Arguments"; Reddy, "Time for
Rights?"; Somerville, "Queer *Loving*."

47. See Schulhofer, *Unwanted Sex,* on force standards, 25–33; on incest cases, 44–45.
U.S. sexual consent ages range from fourteen to eighteen, with an average age of sixteen (and
some exceptions for those close in age). On juvenile legal status, see Levesque, *Adolescents,
Sex, and the Law*. On sexual education in the United States, see Judith Levine, *Harmful to
Minors*; internationally, see Waites, *The Age of Consent*. On childhood sexuality and chil-
dren's rights, see Freeman, *The Moral Status of Children*; Heinze, *Of Innocence and
Autonomy*; Purdy, *In Their Best Interest?* For a philosophical overview, see Archard, *Sexual Consent*.

48. *People v. Martinez* 903 P.2d 1037, 1042 (Cal. 1995). Cited in Phipps, "Children,
Adults, Sex, and the Criminal Law" 40. Phipps offers an overview of national trends with
some state-specific analysis. Here he examines interpretations of California Penal Code,
section 288, prohibiting "lewd and lascivious acts" with a child under fourteen.

49. *Commonwealth v. Lavigne* 676 N.E.2d 1170 (Mass. App. Ct. 1997). Cited in
Phipps, "Children, Adults, Sex and the Criminal Law," 47. This court found that "touching the inner thigh of a fully clothed boy within three inches of his genitals was an indecent touching."

50. Bienen points out that state appellate courts have demonstrated confusion about
prosecutions of sexual abuse between members of the same family, muddling issues of consent and corroboration for victims under the age of consent. See also Kathleen Daly, "Sexual Assault and Restorative Justice"; Garst, "Survey of Developments in North Carolina
Law, 1987"; Leonore Simon, "Symposium"; Tempkin, "Do We Need the Crime of Incest?"
On varied effects, see Feiner, "The Whole Truth"; Floyd, "Note"; Ross, Warren, and
McGough, "Special Theme"; Wood, "Refined Raw."

2. Legal Fantasies

1. On these acts, see Jacqueline Bhabha, "Inconsistent State Intervention and Sepa-
rated Child Asylum-Seekers" and "The 'Mere Fortuity' of Birth?"; Bhattacharjee, "Private
Fists and Public Force" and "The Public/Private Mirage"; Bhattacharjee and Silliman,
Policing the National Body; Goldman, "The Violence Against Women Act"; Katzenstein,
The Culture of National Security; Mink, *Whose Welfare?*; Prashad, *Keeping Up with the
Dow Joneses*; Anna Marie Smith, "The Sexual Regulations Dimension of Contemporary
Welfare Law"; Volpp, " (Mis)Identifying Culture."

2. Here Adler with Underwood ("Freud in Our Midst") summarizes an interview with Jonathan Lear, psychiatrist and professor of philosophy at the University of Chicago.

3. On "recovered memory," see Freyd, *Betrayal Trauma*; Herman, *Trauma and Recovery*; Terr, *Unchained Memories*; van der Kolk, *Psychological Trauma*; Williams and Banyard, *Trauma and Memory*. On "false memory," see Crews, *The Memory Wars*; Loftus and Ketcham, *The Myth of Repressed Memory*; Ofsche and Watters, *Making Monsters*; Pendergrast, *Victims of Memory*; Wakefield and Underwager, *Return of the Furies*.

4. VAWA 1994 was part of the Violent Crime Control and Law Enforcement Act of 1994 (PL-103-332), introducing new penalties for gender-based and sexual assault along with new grants for law enforcement and prosecution (STOP grants). The Welfare Reform Act included stipulations and "incentives" for heterosexual marriage and mandated reporting of paternity, alongside a lifetime ban on benefits for those with a drug conviction. The 1996 Immigration Reform Act reauthorized family reunification policies of 1986, privatizing economic support and duties of care for new migrants (Reddy, "Asian Diasporas, Neo-Liberal Families").

5. On uneven national and cross-national origins and lack of consolidated "movement," see Louise Armstrong, *Rocking the Cradle of Sexual Politics*.

6. On this conference, see Louise Armstrong, *Rocking the Cradle of Sexual Politics*, 74. On "victim" to "survivor," see Lamb, "Constructing the Victim."

7. See, in order, Bass and Thornton, *I Never Told Anyone*; McNaron and Morgan, *Voices in the Night*; Vera Gallagher, *Speaking Out, Fighting Back*; Adams and Fay, *No More Secrets*. See also Mirikatani, *Watch Out!*

8. Raymond Williams defines structure of feeling "methodologically" as a "cultural hypothesis, actually derived from attempts to understand such elements and their connections in a generation or period" (*Marxism and Literature*, 132–33). Structures of feeling often show up outside the social, in "the personal or the private, or as the natural or even the metaphysical" (125).

9. On 1980s multiculturalism, see Benhabib, *The Claims of Culture*; Dillard, *Guess Who's Coming to Dinner Now?*; Ferguson, *Aberrations in Black*; Gordon and Newfield, *Mapping Multiculturalism*; Hesse, *Un/settled Multiculturalisms*; San Juan, *Racism and Cultural Studies*.

10. On television coverage of incest before and through this period, see Janet Walker, *The Traumatic Paradox*.

11. Thesis 13 from Guy Debord, *The Society of the Spectacle*, in the Black and Red edition (1977). All further citations will reference the thesis number from this unpaginated text.

12. Following the Economic Opportunity Act of 1964, new social science knowledges were developed to study the roles of self-esteem and empowerment in alleviating social and economic inequities (Cruikshank, *The Will to Empower*). See also Barry, Osborne, and Rose, *Foucault and Political Reason*; Bratich, Packer, and McCarthy, *Foucault, Cultural Studies, and Governmentality*; Richard Harvey Brown, *The Politics of Selfhood*; Lang, "The NGO-ization of Feminism."

13. The war on drugs included the 1984 Sentencing Reform Act introducing mandatory sentencing and the 1986–88 Anti-Drug Abuse Act specifying stricter sentencing for crack cocaine. On the 1980s conservative agenda, see Edsall and Edsall, *Chain Reaction*; Ruth Wilson Gilmore, *Golden Gulag*; Lipsitz, *The Possessive Investment in Whiteness*; Lo and Schwartz, *Social Policy and the Conservative Agenda*.

14. See Bogle, "Brixton Black Women's Centre"; Jane Cousins Mills, "'Putting Ideas into Their Heads.'" On culturally specific approaches to incest, see Chandler, "Identifying Your Own Healing Path"; Fontes, *Sexual Abuse in Nine North American Cultures*; Perez, "Sexuality and Discourse."

15. Here Bogle is explicitly addressing the exploitation of survivor-based organizations as service providers, a practice linked to the exploitation of black survivors by statutory bodies as a statistical resource for legislative agendas.

16. In addition to the works cited in note 9 of my Introduction, see Douglass and Vogler, *Witness and Memory*; Geoffrey Hartman, *The Longest Shadow*; Joshua Hirsch, *Afterimage*; Marianne Hirsch, *Family Frames*; Kaplan and Wang, *Trauma and Cinema*; LaCapra, *Representing the Holocaust*; Felman and Laub, Testimony; Rothberg, *Traumatic Realism*; Saltzman and Rosenberg, *Trauma and Visuality in Modernity*.

17. For alternatives to the trauma concept, see Feldman, *Formations of Violence*; Fujitani, White, and Yoneyama, *Perilous Memories*; Kleinman, Das, and Lock, *Social Suffering*; Scarry, *The Body in Pain*; Yoneyama, *Hiroshima Traces*.

18. See Caruth's influential *Unclaimed Experience*.

19. The British physician John Erichsen studied the physiology of shock (from railway accidents) in the 1860s; German neurologist Paul Oppenheim defined the disease "traumatic neurosis" as hidden changes in the brain; Americans George W. Crile and Walter B. Cannon and Russian Ivan Pavlov conducted related experiments between 1860 and 1920. See Leys, *Trauma*; Hacking, *Rewriting the Soul*.

20. On the "cathartic method," see Breuer and Freud, *Studies on Hysteria*. On Freud's later theory of external trauma, see *Beyond the Pleasure Principle*. For a revision of oedipal trauma, see Ferenczi, "Confusion of Tongues between Adult and Child"; Van Haute and Geyskens, *Confusion of Tongues*.

21. Abram Kardiner explored trauma syndrome from war, later developed by William Sargant, Roy Grinker, and John Spiegel on World War II combat fatigue; see Leys, *Trauma*.

22. On the reduction of "history" to subjective trauma, see Caruth, *Unclaimed Experience*; Huyssen, *Twilight Memories*.

23. Following the Breuer collaboration *(Studies on Hysteria),* Freud posited sexual etiologies for hysterical symptoms in "The Aetiology of Hysteria," "Further Remarks on the Neuro-psychoses of Defence," and "Heredity and the Aetiology of the Neuroses." Across these 1896 papers the alleged sexual perpetrators changed, as did the number of cases. Hall Triplett suggests that Freud masked his lack of real statistics with various claims about siblings, servants, and parents, only retroactively naming the father as culprit when he translated these "findings" into the Oedipus complex; see "The Misnomer of Freud's 'Seduction Theory.'"

24. Ernst Kris first used the term "seduction theory" in the introduction to the first volume of Fliess/Freud correspondence (1950) (Triplett, "The Misnomer of Freud's 'Seduction Theory'"). See also Masson, *The Assault on Truth*; Alice Miller, *For Your Own Good*; Bennet Simon, "Fact and Fantasy in the History of Freud's Views on Incest and Seduction."

25. In 2006 Adler writes: "Resistance came early from a bourgeoisie appalled by one of Freud's central tenets, that young children have a sexual fantasy life—a theory that American adults rejected by a margin of 76 to 13 in a *Newsweek* Poll" ("Freud in Our Midst," 44).

26. In "An Autobiographical Study" Freud uses the language of mistake to describe this period, reporting on the "error into which I fell for a while" (20) before "I was able to draw the right conclusion from my discovery" (21). While Freud names his right conclusion "*Oedipus complex*" (21), in this case of mistaken identity one might also conclude he discovered the mistake as mode of identification (or articulation). As Lacan explains in his "Rome Discourse," "The ambiguity of the hysterical revelation of the past is due not so much to the vacillation of its content between the imaginary and the real, for it is situated in both. Nor is it because it is made up of lies. The reason is that it presents us with

the birth of truth in speech, and thereby brings us up against the reality of what is neither true nor false" ("Function and Field of Speech," 47). This is also how Jean Laplanche, in *Life and Death in Psychoanalysis,* glosses Freud's account of the *"proton pseudos"* (47) or first lie revealed by hysteria (which Laplanche tacitly connects to "the point of articulation between instinct and drive" [13]). Here I question whether the mistake can be used to wrench what Spillers calls "psychoanalytics" from the truth and lies of its oedipal birth.

27. Critics argue that too many behaviors are given a single traumatic etiology and that trauma is somatized (Lamb, "Constructing the Victim," 113). See also Laura Brown, "Not Outside the Range"; Ann Scott, "Feminism and the Seductiveness of the 'Real Event'"; O'Dell, "The 'Harm' Story in Childhood Sexual Abuse." On alternative somatics, see Haines, *The Survivor's Guide to Sex.*

28. Eli Zaretsky argues that using Salem witch hunts to explain the Clinton impeachment evacuates history of any content ("The Culture Wars of the 1960s and the Assault on the Presidency").

29. Pamela Freyd published her version of events under the pseudonym "Jane Doe" ("How Could This Happen"), also circulated to Jennifer Freyd's colleagues in the Psychology Department at the University of Oregon. Jennifer Freyd later delivered a paper on these events ("Theoretical and Personal Perspectives on the Delayed Memory Debate"). See also Freyd, *Betrayal Trauma.*

30. On FMS and the media, see Kitzinger, "The Gender Politics of News Production" and *Framing Abuse.*

31. On psychic mimeticism, see Borch-Jacobsen, *Freudian Subject, Remembering Anna O.,* and "Self-Seduced" (on false memory); Leys, *Trauma.* For a countermodel, see Ngai, "Jealous Schoolgirls, Single White Females, and Other Bad Examples."

32. For different disciplinary approaches to these debates, see Antze and Lambek, *Tense Past*; Brown, Scheflin, and Hammond, *Memory, Trauma Treatment, and the Law*; Burman, "Reframing Current Controversies around Memory"; Margaret A. Hagen, "Damaged Goods?"; Hamilton, "False Memory Syndrome and the Authority of Personal Memory-Claims"; Kowalski, "Applying the 'Two Schools of Thought' Doctrine to the Repressed Memory Controversy"; Kenny, "The Proof Is in the Passion"; S. Lowe, "Culturally Interpreted Symptoms of Culture-Bound Syndromes"; Pezdek and Banks, *The Recovered Memory/False Memory Debate*; Potter, "Loopholes, Gaps, and What Is Held Fast"; Scheflin, "Ground Lost"; Showalter, *Hystories*; Robin, "Social Construction of Child Abuse and False Allegations"; Schacter and Scarry, *Memory, Brain, and Belief*; Tavris, "The Uproar over Sexual Abuse Research and Its Finding"; Weinstein, "Repressed Memory Revisted: Popular Culture's Impact on the Law-Psychotherapy Debate"; van der Kolk and van der Hart, "The Intrusive Past."

33. Consuming popular materials was often linked to false memory: "If such recovered memories are indeed false, where do they originate? From two sources, critics say: the popular culture and misguided or inept therapy" (Jaroff, "Lies of the Mind," 56).

34. A ProjectMuse news search between 1990 and 1999 turns up 343 articles on "false memory syndrome" spanning a range of high- and middle-brow publications in the United States, Great Britain, and Canada. See the influential work by Watters, "Doors of Memory"; Wright, "Remembering Satan"; and the report "Divided Memories," *Frontline,* produced by Ofra Bikel (Public Broadcasting Service, 1995).

35. Mahurin is an illustrator and video director; he also created the controversial 1994 *Time* "mug shot" cover of O. J. Simpson.

36. The photos portray a possibly multiracial group in a shopping mall, an apparently upper-middle-class white nuclear family playing catch, a male/female black couple in a bourgeois bedroom, a group of white male students in school uniform facing a female

teacher, and four twenty-something seemingly white men and women purchasing tickets at a mall movie theater.

37. *Tyson v. Tyson* 107 Wn. 2d 72 (1986). In this first appellate decision on repressed memory, twenty-six-year-old Nancy Louise Tyson filed a complaint on August 26, 1983, against her father, Dwight Robert Tyson, for sexual abuse perpetrated against her between the ages of three and eleven (1960–69). She had recalled the incidents one year before she filed suit at age twenty-six (requiring that the statute of limitations be tolled).

38. On child sexual abuse civil cases see Margaret J. Allen, "Comment"; Bulkley, "Introduction"; Ernsdorff and Loftus, "Let Sleeping Memories Lie?"; Brian D. Gallagher, "Note, Damages, Duress, and the Discovery Rule"; Ann M. Hagen, "Note"; Handler, "Note"; Lamm, "Note"; McConnell, "Incest as Conundrum"; Salten, "Note."

39. 18 U.S.C. &3283 (1994).

40. Early civil cases are difficult to track. In *Olsen v. Hooley* (865 P.2d 1345 [Utah 1993]) the Utah Supreme Court determined that the accuracy of recovered memory as evidence must be taken up by triers of fact. In 1990, the *Franklin* case (*Franklin v. Stevenson and Kiniry* 987 P.2d 22 [Utah 1999]) produced a guilty verdict in a criminal trial on the basis of recovered memories, subsequently repealed in 1998. See Kliger, "The Making and Unmaking of a Modern Memory."

41. The FMSF built on earlier legal work by Victims of Child Abuse Laws (VOCAL) and "parental alienation syndrome," "divorce-related malicious mother syndrome," and "false accusation syndrome."

42. *Daubert v. Merrell Dow Pharmaceutical* 509 U.S. 579 (1993). *Daubert* ruled on a case originally brought by the parents of a minor child against a company producing Benedectin. The case focused on the scientific debate over evidence of a connection between Benedectin and birth defects.

43. *Frye v. United States* 54 App. D.C. 46 (1923).

44. On insurance imaginaries, see Patel, "Risky Subjects."

45. *State v. Hungerford* (Hillsborough County Superior Court Decree [N.H. 5-23-1995], 142 N.H. 110; 697 A.2d 916 [1997]) and *State v. Quattrocchi* (681 A.2d 879 [R.I. 1996], C.A. No. P92-3759 Superior Court of Rhode Island [1999]).

46. The defendant in *Quattrochi* was first convicted in 1994 of two counts of first-degree sexual assault in *State v. Quattrocchi* P1/92-3759A Providence County Superior Court (1994), in Rhode Island, the first criminal case involving recovered memory. The original State case presented evidence from two additional girls who reported sexual assaults by Quattrocchi, which were later barred as prejudicial on appeal (*State v. Quattrocchi* 681 A.2d 879 [R.I. 1996]).

47. These two cases combined a charge of incestuous abuse by a father and sexual abuse by a former teacher on the basis of recovered memories; both the accusers were women in their twenties. These cases were combined to determine admissibility in pretrial evidentiary hearing in 1995.

48. This admissibility hearing took two weeks and included the two complainants and seven psychological professionals: Dr. Daniel Brown, Dr. Bessel A. van der Kolk, Dr. Jon Robert Conte, Dr. Elizabeth Loftus, Dr. Paul McHugh, Ms. Susan Jones, and Dr. James Hudson.

49. This is similar to arguments reported in *Franklin v. Stevenson and Kiniry* 987 P.2d 22 (Utah 1999), which summarized a prior ruling of judgment notwithstanding the verdict (j.n.o.v.) that "drew on a parallel between hypnotic suggestion and communicating with one's metaphorical inner child and concluded that these therapeutic techniques were 'hypnosis-like' in nature" (2). For a longer discussion of "hypnosis-like" therapy, see Kanovitz, "Hypnotic Memories and Civil Sexual Abuse Trials." On *Daubert* and CSA cases,

see Spadaro, "An Elusive Search for the Truth"; Wakefield and Underwager, *Return of the Furies,* 338–40.

50. Writing for the court, Justice Clifton stated that "we recognize that treating the testimony of a percipient witness to a crime as scientific evidence is novel in our law, and that it does not fit precisely within the confines of Rule 702" (*State v. Hungerford* 142 N.H. 110, 119–20). But the court concluded that since "a recovered memory that previously had been completely absent from a witness's conscious recollection . . . cannot be separated from the process, if any, that facilitated the recovery" (120), the testimony of a percipient witness required scientific expertise to determine its reliability. See Bandes, "Empathy, Narrative, and Victim Impact Statements"; Conte, "Memory, Research, and the Law"; Olio, "Are 25 Percent of Clinicians Using Potentially Risky Therapeutic Practices?"; Pope, "Memory, Abuse, and Science" and "What Psychologists Better Know about Recovered Memories"; and Richardson, "Notes and Comments."

51. Regarding the first four criteria, the court found that there was substantial publication, but not general acceptance on the concept of recovered memory. And recovered memory failed the empirical research test, since it is unethical to conduct research on highly traumatic events in a laboratory setting. This means that the rate of falsehood is impossible to determine.

52. This admissibility hearing lasted fourteen days and included testimony from nine witnesses, seven of whom testified as experts: Gina, Dr. Daniel Brown, Patricia Gavin-Reposa, Dr. Barry Wall, Dr. Paul Appelbaum, Dr. Paul McHugh, Dr. Richard Ofshe, Dr. William Grove, and Dr. Elizabeth Loftus. These hearings are recorded in *State of Rhode Island's Daubert Hearing Brief* (corrected version, July 13, 1998).

53. See Linda Meyer Williams's longitudinal survey, "Recall of Childhood Trauma," in which female children brought to a hospital for child sexual assault later failed to recall those incidents and controls in laboratory settings. On recovered memory verification, see Ross E. Cheit, www.brown.edu/Departments/Taubman_Center/Recovmem/.

54. *Ramona v. Ramona* No. 645970 Cal. Super. Ct. Orange County (filed Dec. 31, 1990). Cynthia Grant Bowman and Elizabeth Mertz reconstruct these facts from media coverage since no official trial transcript exists: In 1989, a nineteen-year-old University of California, Irvine, student, Holly Ramona, entered therapy with Marche Isabella MFCC for bulimia and depression. Four months into therapy, Holly Ramona experienced "flashbacks" about child sexual abuse perpetrated by her father, Gary Ramona. Following a sodium amytal interview with Dr. Richard Rose, chief of psychiatry at Western Medical Center, Holly was briefly hospitalized. Holly Ramona filed suit against her father, although Isabella, Rose, and her mother advised against it; she later refiled in Napa County (*Ramona v. Ramona* No. 62124 Cal. Super. Ct. Napa County [filed Apr. 2, 1991]). See also Johnston, *Spectral Evidence;* Kliger, "The Making and Unmaking of a Modern Memory."

55. *Ramona v. Isabella* No. 61898 Cal. Super. Ct. (filed Oct. 7, 1991).

56. *Dillon v. Legg* 68 Cal. 2d 728 (1968) and *Molien v. Kaiser Foundation Hospitals* 27 Cal. 3d 916 (1980). In *Dillon v. Legg,* the court recommended case-by-case adjudication. On third-party liability, see Diamond, "*Dillon v. Legg* Revisited"; Hampton, "Note"; Perlin, "*Tarasoff* and the Dilemma of the Dangerous Patient"; Schachner, "'False Memory' Risk Surfaces"; Steven R. Smith, "Mental Health Malpractice in the 1990s."

57. Bowman and Mertz cite the "difficulty of showing causation of injuries" ("A Dangerous Direction," 575) since often "results are not tangible or quantifiable" (575). For a later case determining new ruling in this arena, see *Tarasoff v. Regents of the Univ. of Cal.* 551 P.2d 334 (Cal. 1976). The *Tarasoff* case "emphasized forseeability as the most important factor in determining duty" (Bowman and Metzer, "A Dangerous Direction," 578).

58. *Sullivan v. Cheshier* 846 F. Supp. 654, 659 (N.D. Ill. 1994).

59. The 1994 *Sullivan* Court allowed the loss of consortium and malpractice claims, stating "from these facts, a jury could infer that the memories were false and intentionally or recklessly implanted by Dr. Cheshier. . . . It would be hard to doubt that the family relationship would be seriously and negatively affected in this situation. A trier of fact could reasonably lay it at Dr. Cheshier's door," *Sullivan v. Cheshier* 846 F. Supp. 654, 663 (N.D. Ill. 1994).

60. See Hacking on "Memoro-Politics" in *Rewriting the Soul*; Flannery, *Post-Traumatic Stress Disorder*; Krystal, "Integration and Self-Healing in Post-Traumatic States."

61. See Vikki Bell, "The Vigilant(e) Parent and the Paedophile," 112–17; Rachel Hall, "'It Can Happen to You'"; Nikolas Rose, *Powers of Freedom*.

62. The California "Three Strikes" bill (1994), linked to the 1993 murder of Polly Klaas, set mandatory sentences of twenty-five years to life after a third offense; the 1996 federal Megan's Law (for Megan Kanka) mandated community notification about convicted sex offenders; the 1997 Amber Alert (for Amber Hagerman) legislated public notification of child abductions; Jennifer's Law, or the Child Abuse Protection and Enforcement Act of 2000 (unlike the former Child Abuse Protection and *Treatment* Act), was attached to the Crime Identification Technology Act of 1998 to increase monies for enforcement and policing in order to protect children from sexual predators. On sex offenders and justice, see Van Duyn, "Note"; Yantzi, *Sexual Offending and Restoration*.

63. See *Stogner v. California* (01-1757) 539 U.S. 607 (2003) and *Smith v. Doe* (01-729) 538 U.S. 84 (2003). The *Stogner* ruling explicitly addresses the danger of retroactive criminalization in times of alleged terrorism, and might best be situated "horizontally" in relation to the era's legal struggles over torture and terrorism (see Puar, *Terrorist Assemblages*).

64. See Ruth Wilson Gilmore in *Golden Gulag* on surplus state power.

3. Seduction by Literature

1. See Britt, "The Author, the Relative, and a Question of Incest"; David Mills, "Can You Believe It?" and "Three Therapists' Opinions." One piece featured three therapists evaluating the credibility of her autobiographical work in progress.

2. Herron reports entering therapy in 1989 and beginning to have flashbacks of sexual abuse from age two approximately six months later. See also Doten, "An Odyssey into the Abyss."

3. See Doane and Hodges, *Telling Incest*; Sielke, *Reading Rape*; Tal, *Worlds of Hurt*.

4. See Champagne, *The Politics of Survivorship*; DeSalvo, *Virginia Woolf*; Hamer, *Incest*; McLennan, *Nature's Ban*.

5. Tal clarifies that she defines "self-conscious sexual assault narratives" as ones "in which authors have taken as their primary subject the specific incident(s) of sexual assault that traumatized them" (273).

6. Criticism includes Breau, "Incest and Intertextuality in Carolivia Herron's *Thereafter Johnnie*," on intertextuality; Champagne, *The Politics of Survivorship*, on Lacan; Christian, "Epic Achievement," on black feminist tradition; Brenda Daly, "Whose Daughter Is Johnnie?" on myth; Keizer, "The Geography of the Apocalypse," on space.

7. See, in contrast, Bakhtin's account of dialogism as conjunction between centralization and heteroglossia, *The Dialogic Imagination*; see also Gates, *The Signifying Monkey*; Henderson, "Speaking in Tongues."

8. See Lisa Lowe, *Immigrant Acts*.

9. The historical demand for African American autobiography and treatment of all African American literature as autobiographical is countered by efforts to recognize African American novel writing and challenge the racial formations of fiction subtending this literary history. See DuCille, "Where in the World Is William Wells Brown?"

10. On black women writers and critical family romances, see Candice Jenkins, *Private Lives, Proper Relations*; Keizer, "The Geography of the Apocalypse" and *Black Subjects*; McDowell, "Reading Family Matters"; Rody, *The Daughter's Return*; Rushdy, *Remembering Generations*; Sharpe, *Ghosts of Slavery*.

11. Here Yukins works off the arguments of Marianne Hirsch, *Family Frames*.

12. See Diotima of Mantinea in Plato's *Symposium*.

13. See Jakobsen and Pelligrini, "World Secularisms at the Millennium."

14. Benjamin's "Theses on the Philosophy of History" marks the juncture between classical Marxist accounts of dialectical materialism and more messianic or mystical interpretations of historical dialectics. Intertexts include Robinson, *Black Marxism*, on racial capitalism; Feldman, *Formations of Violence,* on the eschatology of violence; Klein, "On the Emergence of Memory in Historical Discourse," on memory's historical mystifications.

15. Property signifies "a bundle of rights, including the right to use, the right to transfer, and the right to exclude, as well as rights of transmissibility and security" (Woodhouse, "'Who Owns the Child?'" 1045).

16. See Best, *The Fugitive's Properties*; Stanley, *From Bondage to Contract*; Franke "Becoming a Citizen"; Horwitz, *The Transformation of American Law*. Related literary studies include Gillian Brown, *Domestic Individualism*; Daniels and Kennedy, *Over the Threshold*; Fliegelman, *Prodigals and Pilgrims*; Greven, *Spare the Child*; Sanchez-Eppler, *Dependent States*; Thomas, *American Literary Realism and the Failed Promise of Contract*.

17. Liberalism encloses more complex formations of seduction and subordination (including discourses of BDSM) within this grammar of sexuality. See Wendy Brown, *States of Injury*; Califia, *Public Sex*.

18. On commodities and status see Patel, "Ghostly Appearances." *Thereafter Johnnie*'s 1970s American status system focuses on textiles; Patel explores technology in India during the 2000s.

19. See also Archard, *Children, Rights and Childhood*; Brewer, *By Birth or Consent*; Bridgeman, Monk, et al., *Feminist Perspectives on Child Law*; Katz, "Parental Rights and Social Responsibility in American Child Protection Law"; McGillivray, *Governing Childhood*. On nineteenth-century property, see Post, "Rereading Warren and Brandeis"; Vandevelde, "The New Property of the Nineteenth Century"; Warren and Brandeis, "The Right to Privacy."

20. On fugitivity and property, see Best, *The Fugitive's Properties*. On whiteness and property, see Harris, "Whiteness as Property"; Wiegman, "Intimate Publics." On an "authorial parent" model, see Chan, "The Authorial Parent."

21. The vagrant threatens to throw John Christopher into the ocean, exclaiming, "You ain't nothin' but a little black boy, maybe you ought to die!" (82). In place of this immediate punishment, the curse instead seizes John Christopher through his liberal telos, to be enacted when "you're grown up and you think you're happy" (82).

22. In "The Last Time," the "infant girl-child's" experience of incest is represented as a rising sea, while the father's hand remains an "onlyness" (16).

23. In his study of the "shriek" attributed to the enslaved aunt in Frederick Douglass's autobiography, Moten suggests that "the speaking commodity thus cuts Marx; but the shrieking commodity cuts Saussure, thereby cutting Marx doubly: this by way of an irruption of phonic substance that cuts and augments meaning with a phonographic, rematerializing inscription" (*In the Break*, 13–14).

24. See also Hammonds, "Black (W)holes and the Geometry of Black Female Sexuality" and "Toward a Genealogy of Black Female Sexuality"; Melba Wilson, *Crossing the Boundary*.

25. William Wells Brown's *Clotel* is one of this novel's main intertexts. Brown's 1853 edition of *Clotel, or The President's Daughter* told the eponymous story of the daughter of a United States president who was sold as a slave, a fate replicated for the daughters of the following generation(s). First published in England, three subsequent editions published in the United States between 1860 and 1867 erased the presidential reference in the title, as well as the historical reference to Thomas Jefferson's sexual relationship with Sally Hemings, a woman enslaved by Jefferson. Hemings was the half-sister of Jefferson's wife, Martha Wayles Skelton; she was fifteen when the sexual relationship with Jefferson began. See DuCille, "Where in the World Is William Wells Brown?"

26. On domination and legitimation in incest discourse, see Vikki Bell, *Interrogating Incest*.

27. From Eva: "They mingled so much with each other, it was hard to tell who was the possessor and who was the possessed" (206).

28. See Spillers, "Mama's Baby, Papa's Maybe."

29. See Marcus, "Fighting Bodies, Fighting Words"; Mardrossian, "Toward a New Feminist Theory of Rape."

4. Surviving the Family Romance?

1. Allison's publications after 1992 include the essay collection *Skin* (1994), a performance piece and memoir, *Two or Three Things I Know for Sure* (1995), and a novel, *Cavedweller* (1999).

2. See Amireh and Majaj, *Going Global*; Ferguson, *Aberrations in Black*; Melamed, "The Spirit of Neoliberalism"; Gordon and Newfield, *Mapping Multiculturalism*; San Juan, *Racism and Cultural Studies*.

3. See Moira P. Baker, "Dorothy Allison's Topography of Resistance"; Curry, "I Ain't No Friggin' Little Wimp"; Donlon, "'Born on the Wrong Side of the Porch.'" See Cvetkovitch on queer survival (*An Archive of Feelings*, 83–117). Additional criticism includes Boyd, "Crossover Blues"; Fine, "Gender Conflicts and Their 'Dark' Projections in Coming of Age White Female Southern Novels"; Horvitz, *Literary Trauma*; Sylvia Rubin, "Allison Makes Art of Trauma"; Linda Tate, *A Southern Weave of Women*.

4. As Allison herself explains her choice to write a novel after so much autobiography, "What I really needed was to know that my life was a proper subject for fiction" (Boyd, "Crossover Blues," 20), an evaluation she jokingly links in another interview to a literary marketplace that fetishizes the authentic author: "My trick was to get a book contract" (Megan, "Moving toward Truth," 72).

5. On focalization as the balance of mimetic and diegetic strategies, see Genette, *Narrative Discourse*.

6. Genre studies have argued the novel is either fundamentally disciplinary (D. A. Miller, *The Novel and the Police*) or fundamentally heterogeneous and heteroglossic (Bakhtin, *The Dialogic Imagination*). See also McKeon, *Theory of the Novel*. For feminist revisions see Nancy Armstrong, *Desire and Domestic Fiction*; Radway, *Reading the Romance*; Tompkins, *Sensational Designs*.

7. Forms that resulted from these experiments include: neorealism, testimonial literature, historical romance, and magical or marvelous realism (Denning, *Culture in the Age of Three Worlds*). See also Chrisman, *Rereading the Imperial Romance*.

8. On transnational capitalism, racial formation, and literature by U.S. women of color, see Grace Hong, *The Ruptures of American Capital*.

9. On class and the cultural turn, see Rouse, "Thinking through Transnationalism"; Yudice, *The Expediency of Culture.*

10. On efforts to retheorize "class" in the specific conditions of its emergence across world-historical contexts, see Chakrabarty, *Provincializing Europe*; Mehta, *Liberalism and Empire.*

11. See also Horwitz, *The Transformation of American Law*; Kahn, *The Cultural Study of Law*; Sarat and Kearns, *Law in the Domains of Culture.*

12. On the cultural turn in legal studies, see Binder and Weisberg, *Literary Criticisms of Law*; Sarat and Simon, "Cultural Analysis, Cultural Studies, and the Situation of Legal Scholarship."

13. Allison links romanticized storytelling with gendered harm in her interview with Rowe.

14. As Kenan explains, "This far more bitter than sweet *Bildungsroman*'s real subject is not 'Trash' . . . but the explosive and often difficult to understand world of child abuse" ("Sorrow's Child," 815). And Irving: "Abusive domestic circumstances fuels the narrative momentum" ("'Writing It Down So That It Would Be Real,'" 104).

15. On the authenticity of "unbelievable" survivor stories, see Ronai, "In the Line of Sight at *Public Eye.*"

16. See, for example, Curry, "I Ain't No Friggin' Little Wimp," on the girl-child's pained focalization of domestic violence and class oppression; Patterson, "Ellipsis, Ritual, and 'Real Time,'" on the "real time" of the rape experience as a new chronotope of narration.

17. See in contrast Wendy Brown, *States of Injury*; Hennessey, "Queer Visibility in Commodity Culture."

18. On metonymy, U.S. legal structures, and the fetishism of labor, see Best, *The Fugitive's Properties*; Dimock, *Residues of Justice.*

19. See Sherwood Anderson, "Hands," on sexuality, labor, and storytelling: "The story of Wing Biddlebaum is a story of hands" (10); "The slender expressive fingers, forever active, forever striving to conceal themselves in his pockets or behind his back, came forth and became the piston rods of his machinery of expression" (10), "Perhaps our talking of them will arouse the poet who will tell the hidden wonder story of the influence for which the hands were but fluttering pennants of promise" (11).

20. On the cultural turn in state formation, see Steinmetz, *State/Culture.*

21. This account is contested in Gibson-Graham, *The End of Capitalism*; Sassen, *Globalization and Its Discontents.*

22. For one overview, see John Allen, "Post-Industrialism/Post-Fordism."

23. See Lipsitz, *The Possessive Investment in Whiteness*; Lott, *Love and Theft*; Roediger, *Toward the Abolition of Whiteness* and *Wages of Whiteness*; George J. Sanchez, "Reading Reginald Denny"; Wiegman, "Whiteness Studies and the Paradox of Particularity." On the 1990s, see Bhattacharjee and Silliman, *Policing the National Body*; Cherniavksy, *Incorporations*; Prashad, *Keeping Up with the Dow Joneses*; Reddy, "Asian Diasporas, Neo-Liberal Families."

24. On this image repertoire, see Delgado and Stephanic, *Critical White Studies*; Newitz and Wray, *White Trash*; Wray, *Not Quite White.*

25. Lloyd and Lowe, *The Politics of Culture in the Shadow of Capital,* discuss colonial sites where extraction of surplus requires different social relations of reproduction to production. In the U.S. context, immigration and impoverishment produce related effects; see Goode and Maskovsky, "Neoliberalism and Poverty"; Luibheid, *Entry Denied.*

26. For alternative readings of writing-as-beating, see Sedgwick, "A Poem Is Being Written" and Barbara Claire Freeman, "Moments of Beating."

27. Bone acts out all her fantasies in realist time: breaking into the Woolworth's where she was once publicly shamed for stealing, pilfering a metal hook from Aunt Raylene to incorporate into her masturbation, and developing the game "Mean Sisters" featuring girls acting out retaliatory violence against storybook male kin.

28. It is unclear if the text upholds or critiques this figuring of black authenticity through the overheard gospel song; see Morrison, *Playing in the Dark*. On religion in the novel, see Cobb, "Uncivil Wrongs."

5. Consensual Relations

1. See O'Carroll, *Paedophilia*; Tsang, *The Age Taboo*; Wolff, *The Age of Consent*.

2. See Ann J. Cahill, *Rethinking Rape*; Dripps, "Beyond Rape"; McSherry, "No! (Means No?)"; Naffine, "Possession"; Schulhofer, *Unwanted Sex*.

3. *Harmful to Minors* page, Web site of University of Minnesota Press, April 2002, www.upress.umn.edu/HarmfultoMinorsQandA.html.

4. On feminist harm standards, see MacKinnon, *Only Words* and *Sexual Harassment of Working Women*. On feminist critiques of harm standards, see Califia, *Public Sex*; Evans, *Sexual Citizenship*; Franke, "Theorizing Yes"; Halley, "Sexuality Harassment"; Gayle Rubin, "Thinking Sex"; Schultz, "Reconceptualizing Sexual Harassment."

5. On child sex panic and sexual psychopath laws across the twentieth century, see Philip Jenkins, *Moral Panic*. Jenkins points out that between 1988 and 1990, the number of sex offenders in prison had increased by 47 percent (from 58,000 to 85,000). See more generally, Burgett, "On the Mormon Question"; Hall and Jacques, *New Times*; Neil Miller, *Sex-Crime Panic*; Shah, *Contagious Divides*.

6. On scandal as part of the "routine self-maintenance" (xii) of modern societies, see D. A. Miller *The Novel and the Police*.

7. On sexual formations in the 1990s, see Enloe, *The Morning After*; Manalansan and Cruz-Malavé, *Queer Globalizations*; Warner, *The Trouble with Normal*. In the new millennium, see Puar, *Terrorist Assemblages*.

8. Critics concerned about policy claims included Dr. Laura Schlessinger, the Christian Coalition, the National Association on Research and Therapy of Homosexuality (NARTH), ChildHelp USA, the National Law Center for Children and Families, and OneVoice/ACAA.

9. See Rind and Tromovitch, "A Meta-Analytic Review of Findings from National Samples"; Rind, "Biased Use of Cross-Cultural and Historical Perspectives on Male Homosexuality in Human Sexuality Textbooks."

10. For classic sex panic arguments on the late 1970s "kiddie porn panic" and the 1980s homosexual-pedophile panics led by Anita Bryant, see Califia, *Public Sex*; Gayle Rubin, "Thinking Sex."

11. See also Duin, "Critics Assail Study Affirming Pedophilia"; Erica Goode, "Study on Child Sex Abuse Provokes a Political Furor."

12. See Berlant and Duggan, *Our Monica, Ourselves*.

13. Clinton administration policy included the National Child Protection Act of 1993, the Child Abuse Accountability Act of 1994, and the Child Pornography Prevention Act (CPPA) of 1996. On childhood in this period, see Postman, *The Disappearance of Childhood*; Strickland, *Growing Up Postmodern*; Zelizer, *Pricing the Priceless Child*. Queer accounts include Bruhm and Hurley, *Curiouser*; Edelman, *No Future*.

14. Here "child" will mark the limit of variegated juvenile statutes. See Levesque, *Adolescents, Sex, and the Law*; Levine, *Harmful to Minors*; Phillips, "Recasting Consent."

15. See Berlant, *The Queen of America Goes to Washington City*; Ivy, "Have You

Seen Me?"; Kincaid, *Erotic Innocence*; Kitzinger, "Defending Innocence"; McCreery, "Innocent Pleasures?"

16. Spiegel describes meta-analysis as a "review technique" that "compares different studies statistically by weighting them, taking into account the 'effect size,' the magnitude of the effect observed, and also the number of subjects involved" ("Suffer the Children," 18). Meta-analysis is designed to control for differences in sample size across studies, weighting larger samples more heavily.

17. The study lists eighteen adjustment problems as "psychological correlates of CSA" (28): alcohol problems, anxiety, depression, dissociation, eating disorders, hostility, interpersonal sensitivity, locus of control, obsessive-compulsive symptoms, paranoia, phobia, psychotic symptoms, self-esteem, sexual adjustment, social adjustment, somatization, suicidal ideation, wide adjustment (28).

18. This problem is particularly marked in qualitative studies, which Rind et al. accuse of intrinsic subjectivism and reliance on narrative (24). But the few existing quantitative studies are limited by statistical samplings confounding factors of gender difference, levels of consent, and family environment (25–26). Rind et al. defend their use of "negative reactions and self-reported effects" (35) in college samples as (a) less biased than clinical or legal samples, and (b) more attuned to the subject's own interpretation and incurring less researcher bias (26–27).

19. Proposed "moderator variables" (27) for CSA—force, penetration, duration, frequency, incest (34)—were selectively correlated. "Penetration, duration, and frequency did not moderate outcomes" (45), while force measured medium magnitude. Using its findings, the study proposes a more specific terminology be developed, including adult-child sex, child sexual abuse, adult-adolescent sex, and adolescent sexual abuse (46).

20. Spiegel argues that (1) the more heavily weighted studies involved lower levels of trauma and higher age groups; (2) the study evaluates each symptom separately, minimizing patterns of symptoms by evaluating cause-outcome relations one symptom at a time; and (3) such patterns are only considered when they enter "family dysfunction as a variable" to demonstrate other sequelae for negative outcome ("The Price of Abusing Children and Numbers"). For additional critiques, see "Consequences of Child Sexual Abuse," special issue of *Sexuality and Culture*.

21. On the memoir as intertextual critique of incest fairy tales, see Marshall, "The Daughter's Disenchantment." See also Douglas, "'Blurbing' Biographical"; Eakin, "Breaking Rules"; Frost, "After Lot's Daughters"; Parker, "Counter-Transference in Reading Autobiography"; Powers, "Doing Daddy Down"; Thomas R. Smith, "How Our Lives Become Stories"; Spinner, "When 'Macaroni and Cheese Is Good' Enough"; Yoshikawa, "The New Face of Incest?"

22. Early sections in Harrison, *The Kiss* treat her genealogy: her mother's family were European-identified Jewish converts to Catholicism (she lives with her maternal grandmother); her father's family is Protestant and working class (she is later groped by her paternal grandfather, and her father's initial sexual contact is initiated at her maternal grandmother's house). She later describes the period of incest as one of "exile."

23. She discloses the kiss to her boyfriend, whose strong reaction elicits retraction, and becomes isolated from others: "I realize I'm in a kind of shock" (75), "I ask myself if I haven't perhaps made the whole thing up, an overwrought fantasy inspired by wanting too much to be admired and loved" (86).

24. The narrator takes a journey to Europe, returns to college, and eventually moves to New York. Her father sends letters that blend discourses of seduction and exploitation: "*I gave you my flesh and blood, my spirit. It is my heart that beats within you. I have as much right to you as any one, as much as you have to yourself*" (156). She later moves

in with him to write for a year, a period in which she says, "My father's possessing me physically seems increasingly to be just that: Each time, he takes a little more of my life; each time, there is less of me left" (165).

25. Criticism includes Clarke, "An Identity of One's Own"; Brenda Daly, "Seeds of Shame or Seeds of Change?"; Donaldson, "'Handing Back Shame'"; Liddell, "Agents of Pain and Redemption in Sapphire's *Push*"; Romaine, "On Writing in Tongues"; Rountree, "Overcoming Violence." On the novel's relation to medical discourses, see Bhuvaneswar and Shafer, "Survivor of That Time, That Place"; Stanford, "It Tried to Take My Tongue."

26. Explicit language includes: "pussy and dick" (12); "Daddy put his pee-pee smelling thing in my mouth, my pussy, but never hold me. I see me, first grade, pink dress dirty sperm stuffs on it" (18); "He is intercoursing me. Say I can take it. Look you don't even bleed, virgin girls bleed. You not virgin. I'm seven" (39). "The white shit drip off his dick. Lick it lick it" (57); "I tell counselor I can't talk about Daddy now. My clit swell up I think Daddy. Daddy sick me, disgust me, but still he sex me up" (111).

27. Education is a primary theme; the text is dedicated "for children everywhere" and has two epigraphs from William Wordsworth and the Talmud on pedagogy.

28. The relation between written literacy and cultural literacy is dramatized in her school exercises:

A is fr Afrc
(for Africa)
B is for u bae
(you baby)
C is cl w bk
(colored we black). (65)

29. The counselor also writes: "The client seems to view the social service system and its proponents as her enemies, and yet while she mentions independent living, seems to envision social services, AFDC, as taking care of her forever" (120). In contrast to this, the class discusses the politics of workfare: "Ms Rain say it's a big country. Say bombs cost more than welfare" (76).

30. When "Ms Rain say write our fantasy of ourselves" (113), she develops her fantasy of being a writer.

31. See also Spivak, "Scattered Speculations on the Question of Value."

32. See also Eng, "Transnational Adoption and Queer Diasporas." Franke focuses on "natalist" responses to globalization but concurs with Anagnost in saying that "parenting is described as productive social activity while, in many regards, parenting has become as much or more about consumption than production" ("Theorizing Yes," 193).

33. Lloyd and Lowe examine "'discoordinated' structures of civil society" (*The Politics of Culture in the Shadow of Capital,* 14) in colonial and postcolonial sites. Neoliberalism produces discoordination within the United States and/or reveals the modes of discoordination concealed by prior ideologies, now celebrated as liberalization and even, in the sexual domain, liberation (Puar, *Terrorist Assemblages*; Reddy, "Asian Diasporas, Neo-Liberal Families").

Conclusion

1. The Child Pornography Prevention Act (CPPA) added four new categories of criminal liability to the category of child pornography. Lee argues that two of the new categories, barring material depicting an actual minor or appearing to depict an "identifiable" minor, can be justified by previous U.S. Supreme Court decisions in *New York v. Feber* 458 U.S. 747 (1982) and *Osborne v. Ohio* 495 U.S. 103 (1990), while another

category barring material promoted as depicting a minor is likely supported by tort law ("Note," 640). Her article focuses on the First Amendment issues raised by the final category, barring material appearing to depict a minor (which might include computer-generated material), and reviews contradictory lower court rulings that may lead to Supreme Court ruling.

2. *U.S. v. Hilton* 999 F. Supp. 131 (D. Me. 1998) at 134–35, which held that while virtual child pornography might have constitutional protection, CPPA was both content-neutral and narrowly tailored since it did not suppress speech but targeted "harmful secondary effects" of protected speech (345). *U.S. v. Hilton* also struck down part of this statute on vagueness grounds (Lee, "Note," 647), citing concerns about the difficulties of determining age for depictions of "post-pubescent individuals" (137). This contrasts with *Free Speech Coalition v. Reno* 1997 WL 487758 (N.D. Cal. Aug. 12, 1997), which upheld CPPA. The California case was appealed through the U.S. Supreme Court, where *Ashcroft v. Free Speech* 535 U.S. 234 (2002) struck down as overbroad the categories barring material promoted as depicting a minor or appearing to depict a minor (so-called virtual child pornography).

Bibliography

Abel, Elizabeth, Barbara Christian, and Helene Moglen, eds. *Female Subjects in Black and White: Race, Psychoanalysis, Feminism.* Berkeley: University of California Press, 1997.

Abraham, K. "The Experiencing of Sexual Traumas as a Form of Sexual Activity." In *Selected Papers,* edited by K. Abraham. London: Hogarth, 1927. 47–62.

Abramsky, Sasha. *Hard Time Blues: How Politics Built a Prison Nation.* New York: St. Martin's Press, 2002.

Adams, Caren, and Jennifer Fay. *No More Secrets: Protecting Your Child from Sexual Assault.* San Luis Obispo, Calif.: Impact Publishers, 1981.

Adams, Lorraine. "Almost Famous: The Rise of the 'Nobody' Memoir." *Washington Monthly* 34.4 (April 2002): 42–48.

Adler, Jerry, with Anne Underwood. "Freud in Our Midst." *Newsweek,* March 27, 2006, 43–49.

Ageton, Suzanne S. "Vulnerability to Sexual Assault." In *Rape and Sexual Assault II,* edited by Ann Wolbert Burgess. New York: Garland, 1988. 221–43.

Alcoff, Linda, and Laura Gray. "Survivor Discourse: Transgression or Recuperation?" *Signs* 18 (1993): 260–90.

Alexander, M. Jacqui. "Erotic Autonomy as a Politics of Decolonization: An Anatomy of Feminist and State Practices in the Bahamas Tourist Economy." In *Feminist Genealogies, Colonial Legacies, Democratic Futures,* edited by M. Jacqui Alexander and Chandra Talpade Mohanty. New York: Routledge, 1997. 63–100.

Allen, Charlotte Vale. *Daddy's Girl: A Memoir.* New York: Wyndham Books, 1980.

Allen, John. "Post-Industrialism/Post-Fordism." In *Modernity and Its Futures: Understanding Modern Societies,* edited by Stuart Hall, David Held, and Tony McGrew. Cambridge: Polity Press, 1993. 169–220.

Allen, Margaret J. "Comment: Tort Remedies for Incestuous Abuse." *Golden Gate University of Law Review* 13 (1983): 617–28.

Allison, Dorothy. *Bastard out of Carolina.* New York: Plume, 1992.

——. "Believing in Literature." In *Trash*. Ithaca, N.Y.: Firebrand, 1994. 165–82.

——. *Cavedweller*. New York: Dutton, 1998.

——. *Skin: Talking about Sex, Class and Literature*. Ithaca, N.Y.: Firebrand, 1994.

——. *Trash*. Ithaca, N.Y.: Firebrand, 1988.

——. *Two or Three Things I Know for Sure*. New York: Dutton, 1995.

——. *The Women Who Hate Me: Poetry 1980–1990*. Ithaca, N.Y.: Firebrand, 1991.

Althusser, Louis. "Ideology and Ideological State Apparatuses." In *Lenin and Philosophy and Other Essays*, translated by Ben Brewster. New York: Monthly Review Press, 1972. 127–86.

American Association for Health, Physical Education and Recreation. *Children in Focus: Their Health and Activity*. Washington, D.C.: Department of the National Education Association, 1954.

Amireh, Amal, and Lisa Suhair Majaj, eds. *Going Global: The Transnational Reception of Third World Women Writers*. New York: Garland Publishing, 2000.

Anagnost, Ann. "The Corporeal Politics of Quality (*Suzhi*)." *Public Culture* 16.2 (Spring 2004): 189–208.

——. "Scenes of Misrecognition: Maternal Citizenship in the Age of Transnational Adoption." *positions: east asia cultures critique* 8.2 (2000): 389–421.

Anderson, Benedict. *Imagined Communities: Reflections on the Origin and Spread of Nationalism*. London: Verso, 1991.

Anderson, Sherwood. "Hands." In *Winesburg, Ohio*. New York: W. W. Norton, 1996.

Angelides, Steven. "Feminism, Child Sexual Abuse, and the Erasure of Child Sexuality." *GLQ: A Journal of Lesbian and Gay Studies* 10.2 (2004): 141–77.

Angelou, Maya. *I Know Why the Caged Bird Sings*. New York: Random House, 1970.

Antler, Stephen. "The Rediscovery of Child Abuse." 1976. Reprinted in *The Social Context of Child Abuse and Neglect*, edited by Leroy H. Pelton. New York: Human Sciences Press, 1981. 39–54.

Antze, Paul, and Michael Lambek, eds. *Tense Past: Cultural Essays in Trauma and Memory*. London: Routledge, 1996.

Archard, David. *Children, Rights and Childhood*. New York: Routledge, 1993.

——. *Sexual Consent*. Oxford: Westview Press, 1998.

Archibald, Elizabeth. *Incest and the Medieval Imagination*. Oxford: Clarendon Press, 2001.

Arens, W. *The Original Sin: Incest and Its Meaning*. New York: Oxford University Press, 1986.

Aries, Philippe. *Centuries of Childhood: A Social History of Family Life*. Translated by Robert Baldick. New York: Knopf, 1962.

Armstrong, Louise. *Kiss Daddy Goodnight: A Speak Out on Incest*. New York: Hawthorne Books, 1978.

——. *Rocking the Cradle of Sexual Politics: What Happened When Women Said Incest*. New York: Addison-Wesley, 1994.

Armstrong, Nancy. *Desire and Domestic Fiction: A Political History of the Novel*. New York: Oxford University Press, 1988.

Asad, Talal, ed. *Anthropology and the Colonial Encounter*. Atlantic Highlands, N.J.: Humanities Press, 1973.

Ashenden, Sam. *Governing Child Sexual Abuse*. London: Routledge, 2003.

Backus, Margot Gayle. *The Gothic Family Romance: Heterosexuality, Child Sacrifice, and the Anglo-Irish Colonial Order*. Durham, N.C.: Duke University Press, 1999.

Baker, Anthony W., and Sylvia P. Duncan. "Child Sexual Abuse: A Study of Prevalence in Great Britain." *Child Abuse and Neglect* 9.4 (1985): 457–67.

Baker, Houston A., Jr. "Critical Memory and the Black Public Sphere." *Public Culture* 7 (1994): 3–33.

Baker, Moira P. "Dorothy Allison's Topography of Resistance." *Harvard Gay and Lesbian Review* (Summer 1998): 23–26.

Bakhtin, Mikhail. *The Dialogic Imagination: Four Essays*. Edited by Michael Holquist and Vadim Liapunov, translated by Vadim Liapunov and Kenneth Brostrom. Austin: University of Texas Press, 1982.

Bal, Mieke, Jonathan Crewe, and Leo Spitzer, eds. *Acts of Memory: Cultural Recall in the Present*. Hanover, N.H.: University Press of New England, 1999.

Baldwin, James. "Everybody's Protest Novel." In *Notes of a Native Son*. New York: Dial Press, 1955. 13–23.

Balibar, Etienne. "The Nation Form: History and Ideology." In *Race, Nation, Class: Ambiguous Identities*, by Etienne Balibar and Immanuel Wallerstein. London: Verso, 1991. 86–106.

Bamyeh, Mohammed A. "The New Imperialism: Six Theses." *Social Text 62* 18.1 (Spring 2000): 1–29.

Bandes, Susan. "Empathy, Narrative, and Victim Impact Statements." *University of Chicago Law Review* 63.2 (Spring 1996): 361–412.

Barnes, Elizabeth L., ed. *Incest and the Literary Imagination*. Gainsville: Florida University Press, 2002.

Barnett, Louise. *Ungentlemanly Acts: The Army's Notorious Incest Trial*. New York: Hill and Wang, 2001.

Barry, Andrew, Thomas Osborne, and Nikolas Rose, eds. *Foucault and Political Reason: Liberalism, Neoliberalism and Rationalities of Government*. Chicago: University of Chicago Press, 1996.

Barthes, Roland. "The Reality Effect." Translated by Richard Howard. Reprinted in *The Novel: An Anthology of Criticism and Theory, 1900–2000*, edited by Dorothy J. Hale. Oxford: Blackwell, 2006. 229–34.

Bass, Ellen, and Laura Davis. *The Courage to Heal: A Guide for Women Survivors of Child Sexual Abuse*. New York: HarperCollins, 1988.

Bass, Ellen, and Louise Thornton, eds. *I Never Told Anyone: Writings by Women Survivors of Child Sexual Abuse*. New York: HarperCollins, 1991.

Battestin, Martin C. "Henry Fielding, Sarah Fielding, and 'the Dreadful Sin of Incest.'" *Novel* 13 (1979). 6–18.

Belau, Linda, and Petar Ramadanovic, eds. *Topologies of Trauma: Essays on the Limit of Knowledge and Memory*. New York: Other Press, 2002.

Bell, David, and Jon Binnie. *The Sexual Citizen: Queer Politics and Beyond*. Cambridge: Polity Press, 2000.

Bell, Vikki. *Interrogating Incest: Foucault, Feminism and the Law*. London: Routledge, 1993.

———. "The Vigilant(e) Parent and the Paedophile: The News of the World Campaign 2000 and the Contemporary Governmentality of Child Sexual Abuse." In *New Feminist Stories of Child Sexual Abuse: Sexual Scripts and Dangerous Dialogues*, edited by Paula Reavey and Sam Warner. New York: Routledge, 2003. 108–28.

Bender, L., and A. Blau. "The Reactions of Children to Sexual Relations with Adults." *American Journal of Orthopsychiatry* 7 (1937): 500–518.

Bender, L., and A. E. Grugett. "A Follow-up Report on Children Who Had Atypical Sexual Experience." *American Journal of Orthopsychiatry* 22 (1952): 825–37.

Bender, Thomas, ed. *Rethinking American History in a Global Age*. Berkeley: University of California Press, 2002.

Benhabib, Seyla. *The Claims of Culture: Equality and Diversity in the Global Era*. Princeton, N.J.: Princeton University Press, 2002.

Benjamin, Walter. "The Author as Producer." In *Reflections: Essays, Aphorisms, Autobiographical Writings*, edited by Peter Demetz, translated by Edmund Jephcott. Schocken Books, 1978. 220–38.

———. "A Berlin Chronicle." In *Reflections: Essays, Aphorisms, Autobiographical Writings*, edited by Peter Demetz, translated by Edmund Jephcott. New York: Schocken Books, 1978. 3–60.

———. "Paris, Capital of the Nineteenth Century." In *Reflections: Essays, Aphorisms, Autobiographical Writings*, edited by Peter Demetz, translated by Edmund Jephcott. New York: Schocken Books, 1978. 146–62.

———. "Theses on the Philosophy of History." In *Illuminations: Essays and Reflections*, edited by Hannah Arendt, translated by Harry Zohn. New York: Schocken Books, 1968. 253–64.

Berger, Ronald J., Patricia Searles, and W. Lawrence Neuman. "Rape-Law Reform: Its Nature, Origins, and Impact." In *Rape and Society: Readings in the Problem of Sexual Assault*, edited by Ronald J. Berger and Patricia Searles. Boulder, Colo.: Westview Press, 1995. 223–32.

Berlant, Lauren. *The Anatomy of National Fantasy: Hawthorne, Utopia, and Everyday Life*. Chicago, Ill.: University of Chicago Press, 1991.

———. *The Queen of America Goes to Washington City: Essays on Sex and Citizenship*. Durham, N.C.: Duke University Press, 1997.

———. "The Subject of True Feeling: Pain, Privacy, and Politics." In *Feminist Consequences: Theory for the New Century*, edited by Elisabeth Bronfen and Misha Kavka. New York: Columbia University Press, 2001. 126–60.

Berlant, Lauren, and Lisa Duggan, eds. *Our Monica, Ourselves: The Clinton Affair and the National Interest*. New York: New York University Press, 2001.

Berns, Roberta M. *Child, Family, School, Community: Socialization and Support*. Orlando, Fl.: Harcourt, 2001.

Best, Stephen. *The Fugitive's Properties: Law and the Poetics of Possession*. Chicago, Ill.: University of Chicago Press, 2004.

Bhabha, Jacqueline. "Inconsistent State Intervention and Separated Child Asylum-Seekers." *European Journal of Migration and Law* 3.3–4 (July 2001): 283–314.

———. "The 'Mere Fortuity' of Birth? Are Children Citizens?" *Differences: A Journal of Feminist Cultural Studies* 15.2 (Summer 2004): 91–117.

Bhattacharjee, Annanya. "Private Fists and Public Force: Race, Gender, and Surveillance." In *Policing the National Body: Race, Gender and Criminalization in the United States*, edited by Annanya Bhattacharjee and Jael Silliman. Boston, Mass.: South End Press, 2002.

———. "The Public/Private Mirage: Mapping Homes and Undomesticating Violence Work in the South Asian Immigrant Community." In *Feminist Genealogies, Colonial Legacies, Democratic Futures*, edited by M. Jacqui Alexander and Chandra Talpade Mohanty. New York: Routledge, 1997. 308–29.

Bhattacharjee, Annanya, and Jael Silliman, eds. *Policing the National Body: Race, Gender and Criminalization in the United States*. Boston, Mass.: South End Press, 2002.

Bhuvaneswar, Chaya, and Audrey Shafer. "Survivor of That Time, That Place: Clinical Uses of Violence Survivors' Narratives." *Journal of Medical Humanities* 25.2 (Summer 2004): 109–27.

Bienen, Leigh B. "Symposium: Defining Incest." *Northwestern University Law Review* 92.4 (Summer 1998): 1501–1640.

Binder, Guyora, and Robert Weisberg. *Literary Criticisms of Law.* Princeton, N.J.: Princeton University Press, 2000.

Bland, Lucy, and Laura Doan, eds. *Sexology in Culture: Labeling Bodies and Desires.* London: Polity Press, 1998.

Blume, E. Sue. *Secret Survivors: Uncovering Incest and Its Aftereffects in Women.* New York: Ballantine Books, 1990.

Boehrer, Bruce Thomas. *Monarchy and Incest in Renaissance England: Literature, Culture, Kinship and Kingship.* Philadelphia: University of Pennsylvania Press, 1992.

Bogle, Marlene T. "Brixton Black Women's Centre: Organizing on Child Sexual Abuse." *Feminist Review* 28 (January 1988): 132–35.

Boose, Lynda E., and Berry S. Flowers, eds. *Daughters and Fathers.* Baltimore, Md.: Johns Hopkins University Press, 1989.

Borch-Jacobsen, Mikkel. *The Freudian Subject.* Translated by Catherine Porter. Stanford, Conn.: Stanford University Press, 1991.

———. *Remembering Anna O.: A Century of Mystification.* New York: Routledge, 1996.

———. "Self-Seduced." In *Unauthorized Freud: Doubters Confront a Legend,* edited by Frederick Crews. New York: Viking, 1998. 45–53.

Bowman, Cynthia Grant, and Elizabeth Mertz. "A Dangerous Direction: Legal Intervention in Sexual Abuse Survivor Therapy." *Harvard Law Review* 109.3 (January 1996): 549–639.

Boyd, Blanche McCrary. "Crossover Blues." Interview with Dorothy Allison. *Nation* 257.1 (July 5, 1993): 20–22.

Bracken, Patrick. *Trauma, Culture and Philosophy in the Postmodern Age.* London: Whurr Publishers, 2002.

Bracken, Patrick J., and Celia Petty, eds. *Rethinking the Trauma of War.* London: Free Association Books, 1998.

Brady, Katherine. *Father's Days: A True Story of Incest.* New York: Dell, 1985.

Brady, Mary Pat. *Extinct Lands, Temporal Geographies: Chicana Literature and the Urgency of Space.* Durham, N.C.: Duke University Press, 2002.

Bratich, Jack Z., Jeremy Packer, and Cameron McCarthy, eds. *Foucault, Cultural Studies, and Governmentality.* Albany: State University of New York Press, 2003.

Breau, Elizabeth. "Incest and Intertextuality in Carolivia Herron's *Thereafter Johnnie.*" *African American Review* 31.1 (Spring 1997): 91–103.

Breuer, Josef, and Sigmund Freud. *Studies on Hysteria.* Translated by James Strachey, edited by James Strachey in collaboration with Anna Freud, assisted by Alix Strachey and Alan Tyson. New York: Basic Books, 1957.

Brewer, Holly. *By Birth or Consent: Children, Law, and the Anglo-American Revolution in Authority.* Chapel Hill: University of North Carolina Press, 2005.

Bridgeman, Jo, and Daniel Monk, eds. *Feminist Perspectives on Child Law.* London: Cavendish Publishers, 2000.

Briere, John, and Diana M. Elliott. "Sexual Abuse, Family Environment, and Psychological Symptoms: On the Validity of Statistical Control." *Journal of Consulting and Clinical Psychology* 61.2 (1993): 284–88.

Britt, Donna. "The Author, the Relative, and a Question of Incest: Carolivia Herron's Disputed Tale of Childhood Horror." *Washington Post,* June 25, 1991, D1.

Brown, Charles Brockden. *Wieland, or The Transformation.* Amherst, N.Y.: Prometheus Books, 1997.

Brown, Daniel, Alan W. Scheflin, and D. Corydon Hammond. *Memory, Trauma Treatment, and the Law.* New York: W. W. Norton: 1998.

Brown, Gillian. *The Consent of the Governed: The Lockean Legacy in Early American Culture.* Cambridge, Mass.: Harvard University Press, 2001.

———. *Domestic Individualism: Imagining Self in Nineteenth-Century America.* Berkeley: University of California Press, 1990.

Brown, Irene Quenzler, and Richard D. Brown. *The Hanging of Ephraim Wheeler: A Story of Rape, Incest, and Justice in Early America.* Cambridge, Mass.: Belknap, 2003.

Brown, Laura. "Not Outside the Range: One Feminist Perspective on Psychic Trauma." In *Trauma: Explorations in Memory and History,* edited by Cathy Caruth. Baltimore, Md.: Johns Hopkins University Press, 1995. 100–112.

Brown, Richard Harvey, ed. *The Politics of Selfhood: Bodies and Identities in Global Capitalism.* Minneapolis: University of Minnesota Press, 2003.

Brown, Wendy. "Neo-Liberalism and the End of Liberal Democracy." In *Edgework: Critical Essays on Knowledge and Politics.* Princeton, N.J.: Princeton University Press, 2005. 37–59.

———. *States of Injury: Power and Freedom in Late Modernity.* Princeton, N.J.: Princeton University Press, 1995.

Brown, William Wells. *Clotel, or The President's Daughter.* New York: Modern Library, 2000.

Bruhm, Steven, and Natasha Hurley, eds. *Curiouser: On the Queerness of Children.* Minneapolis: University of Minnesota Press, 2004.

Brunhold, H. "Observations after Sexual Trauma Suffered in Childhood." *Excerpta Criminologica* 11 (1964): 5–8.

Bulkley, Josephine. "Introduction: Background and Review of Child Sexual Abuse: Law Reforms in the Mid-1980s." *University of Miami Law Review* 40 (1985): 5–18.

Burchell, Graham, Colin Gordon, and Peter Miller, eds. *The Foucault Effect: Studies in Governmentality.* Chicago, Ill.: University of of Chicago Press, 1991.

Burdett, Carolyn. "The Hidden Romance of Sexual Science: Eugenics, the Nation, and the Making of Modern Feminism." In *Sexology in Culture: Labelling Bodies and Desires,* edited by Lucy Bland and Laura Doan. London: Polity Press, 1998. 44–59.

Burgett, Bruce. "On the Mormon Question: Race, Sex, and Polygamy in the 1850s and the 1990s." *American Quarterly* 57.1 (2005): 75–102.

Burgin, Victor, James Donald, and Cora Kaplan, eds. *Formations of Fantasy.* New York: Methuen, 1986.

Burman, Erica. "Reframing Current Controversies around Memory." *Philosophy, Psychiatry and Psychology* 8.1 (2001): 21–32.

Burnam, M. Audrey, Judith A. Stein, Jaqueline M. Golding, Judith M. Siegel, Susan B. Sorenson, Alan B. Forsythe, and Cynthia A. Telles. "Sexual Assault and Mental Disorders in a Community Population." *Journal of Consulting and Clinical Psychology* 56.6 (1988): 843–50.

Butler, Judith. *Antigone's Claim.* Stanford: Stanford University Press, 2000.

———. *Bodies That Matter: On the Discursive Limits of "Sex."* New York: Routledge, 1993.

———. *Excitable Speech: A Politics of the Performative.* New York: Routledge, 1997.

———. *Gender Trouble: Feminism and the Subversion of Identity.* New York: Routledge, 1990.

Butler, Judith, and Gayle Rubin. "Sexual Traffic: An Interview with Gayle Rubin." *differences* 6.2–3 (Summer–Fall 1994): 62–99.

Butler, Sandra. *Conspiracy of Silence: The Trauma of Incest.* San Francisco, Calif.: Volcano Press, 1978.

Cahill, Ann J. *Rethinking Rape.* Ithaca, N.Y.: Cornell University Press, 2001.

Cahill, Courtney Megan. "'What Is Our Bane, That Alone We Have in Common': Incest, Intimacy, and the Crisis of Naming." *Studies in Law, Politics and Society* 21 (2000): 3–63.

Califia, Pat. *Public Sex: The Culture of Radical Sex.* 1994. San Francisco, Calif.: Cleis Press, 2000.

Carmichael, Calum M. *Law, Legend, and Incest in the Bible: Leviticus 18–20.* Ithaca, N.Y.: Cornell University Press, 1997.

Carsten, Janet. *After Kinship.* New York: Cambridge University Press, 2004.

Caruth, Cathy, ed. *Trauma: Explorations in Memory.* Baltimore, Md.: Johns Hopkins University Press, 1995.

———. "Trauma and Experience: Introduction." In *Trauma: Explorations in Memory,* edited by Cathy Caruth. Baltimore, Md.: Johns Hopkins University Press, 1995. 3–12.

———. *Unclaimed Experience: Trauma, Narrative, History.* Baltimore, Md.: Johns Hopkins University Press, 1996.

Castronovo, Russ. *Fathering the Nation: American Genealogies of Slavery and Freedom.* Berkeley: University of California Press, 1995.

Chakrabarty, Dipesh. *Provincializing Europe: Postcolonial Thought and Historical Difference.* Princeton, N.J.: Princeton University Press, 2000.

Champagne, Rosario. *The Politics of Survivorship: Incest, Women's Literature, and Feminist Theory.* New York: New York University Press, 1996.

Chan, Merry Jean. "The Authorial Parent: An Intellectual Property Model of Parental Rights." *New York University Law Review* 78 (2003): 1186–1226.

Chandler, Clarissa. "Identifying Your Own Healing Path." In *Loving in Fear: An Anthology of Lesbian and Gay Survivors of Child Sexual Abuse,* edited by Queer Press Collective. Toronto, Canada: Queer Press, 1991. 144–52.

Charcot, Jean-Martin. *Lectures on the Diseases of the Nervous System: Delivered at La Salpêtrière.* Birmingham, Ala.: Classics of Neurology and Neurosurgery Library, 1985.

Chase, Jaquelyn, ed. *The Spaces of Neoliberalism: Land, Place and Family in Latin America.* Bloomfield, Conn.: Kumarian Press, 2002.

Cheng, Anne. *The Melancholy of Race: Psychoanalysis, Assimilation, and Hidden Grief.* New York: Oxford University Press, 2001.

Cherniavsky, Eva. *Incorporations: Race, Nation, and the Body Politics of Capital.* Minneapolis: University of Minnesota Press, 2006.

———. "Subaltern Studies in a U.S. Frame." *boundary 2* 23.2 (1996): 85–110.

———. *That Pale Mother Rising: Sentimental Discourses and the Imitation of Motherhood in 19th-Century America.* Bloomington: Indiana University Press, 1995.

Chomsky, Noam, and Edward S. Herman. *Manufacturing Consent: The Political Economy of the Mass Media.* New York: Pantheon, 2002.

Chrisman, Laura. *Rereading the Imperial Romance: British Imperialism and South African Resistance in Haggard, Schreiner, and Plaatje.* Oxford: Oxford University Press, 2000.

Christian, Barbara. "Epic Achievement." *Women's Review of Books* 9.1 (October 1991): 6–7.

Chuh, Candice. *Imagine Otherwise: On Asian Americanist Critique.* Durham, N.C.: Duke University Press, 2003.

Chunn, Dorothy E. "Secrets and Lies: The Criminalization of Incest and the (Re)Formation of the 'Private' in British Columbia, 1890–1940." In *Regulating Lives: Historical Essays on the State, Society, the Individual, and the Law,* edited by John McLaren, Robert Menzies, and Dorothy E. Chunn. Toronto, Canada: University of British Columbia Press, 2002. 120–44.

Clark, Homer H., Jr. *The Law of Domestic Relations in the U.S.* 2nd ed. St. Paul, Minn.: West Publishing, 1988.

Clarke, Cheryl. "An Identity of One's Own: A Review of *Push*, by Sapphire." In *The Best of the Harvard Gay and Lesbian Review*, edited by Richard Schneider Jr. Philadelphia, Pa.: Temple University Press, 1997. 246–50.

Cobb, Michael. "Uncivil Wrongs: Race, Religion, Hate, and Incest in Queer Politics." *Social Text* 23.3–4 (2005): 251–74.

Cohen, Neil A. "Child Welfare History in the United States." In *Child Welfare: A Multicultural Focus*, edited by Neil A. Cohen. Boston, Mass.: Allyn and Bacon, 1992. 14–38.

Comaroff, Jean, and John L. Comaroff, eds. *Millennial Capitalism and the Culture of Neoliberalism.* Durham, N.C.: Duke University Press, 2001.

"Consequences of Child Sexual Abuse." Special Issue, *Sexuality and Culture* 4.2 (Spring 2000).

Conte, Jon R. "Memory, Research, and the Law: Future Directions." In *Trauma and Memory*, edited by Linda Meyer Williams and Victoria L. Banyard. Thousand Oaks, Calif.: Sage Publications, 1998.

Coontz, Stephanie. *The Way We Never Were: American Families and the Nostalgia Trap.* New York: HarperCollins, 1992.

———. *The Way We Really Are: Coming to Terms with America's Changing Families.* New York: BasicBooks, 1997.

Corwin, David L. "An Interview with Roland Summit." In *Critical Issues in Child Sexual Abuse: Historical, Legal, and Psychological Perspectives*, edited by Jon R. Conte. Thousand Oaks, Calif.: Sage Publications, 2002. 1–26.

Costin, L., H. J. Karger, and D. Stoesz. *The Politics of Child Abuse in America.* New York: Oxford University Press, 1996.

Cravens, Hamilton. "Child Saving in Modern America, 1870s–1990s." In *Children at Risk in America: History, Concepts, and Public Policy*, edited by Roberta Wollons. New York: State University of New York Press, 1993. 3–31.

Crenshaw, Kimberle Williams. "Mapping the Margins: Intersectionality, Identity Politics, and Violence against Women of Color." In *Critical Race Theory: The Key Writings That Formed the Movement*, edited by Kimberle Crenshaw, Neil Gotanda, Gary Peller, and Kendall Thomas. New York: New Press, 1995. 357–83.

Crews, Frederick. *The Memory Wars: Freud's Legacy in Dispute.* New York: New York Review of Books, 1995.

Cruikshank, Barbara. *The Will to Empower: Democratic Citizens and Other Subjects.* Ithaca, N.Y.: Cornell University Press, 1999.

Curry, Renee R. "I Ain't No Friggin' Little Wimp: The Girl 'I' Narrator in Contemporary Fiction." In *The Girl: Constructions of the Girl in Contemporary Fiction by Women*, edited by Ruth O. Saxton. New York: St. Martin's Press, 1998. 95–105.

Cvetkovich, Ann. *An Archive of Feelings: Trauma, Sexuality, and Lesbian Public Cultures.* Durham, N.C.: Duke University Press, 2003.

Dalke, Anne. "Original Vice: The Political Implications of Incest in the Early American Novel." *Early American Literature* 23 (1988): 188–201.

Daly, Brenda. "Seeds of Shame or Seeds of Change? When Daughters Give Birth to Their Fathers' Children." In *This Giving Birth: Pregnancy and Childbirth in American Women's Writing*, edited by Julie Tharp and Susan MacCallum-Whitcomb. Bowling Green, Ohio: Popular Press, 2000. 103–23.

———. "Whose Daughter Is Johnnie? Revisionary Myth-Making in Carolivia Herron's *Thereafter Johnnie*." *Callaloo* 18.2 (1995): 472–91.

Daly, Kathleen. "Sexual Assault and Restorative Justice." In *Restorative Justice and Family Violence*, edited by Heather Strang and John Braithwaite, 62–88. New York: Cambridge University Press, 2002.

Daniels, Christine, and Michael V. Kennedy, eds. *Over the Threshold: Intimate Violence in Early America*. New York: Routledge, 1999.

Daniels, Judith. *Subverting the Family Romance: Women Writers, Kinship Structures, and the Early French Novel*. Lewisburg, Pa.: Bucknell University Press, 2000.

Davidson, Cathy. *Revolution and the Word: The Rise of the Novel in America*. New York: Oxford University Press, 1992.

Debord, Guy. *The Society of the Spectacle*. Translated by Fredy Perlman and Jon Supak. Detroit, Mich.: Black and Red, 1977.

DeFoe, Daniel. *Moll Flanders*. New York: Oxford University Press, 1961.

Deleuze, Gilles, and Felix Guattari. *Anti-Oedipus: Capitalism and Schizophrenia*. Translated by Robert Hurley, Mark Seem, and Helen R. Lane. Minneapolis: University of Minnesota Press, 1983.

Delgado, Richard, and Jean Stephanic, eds. *Critical White Studies: Looking behind the Mirror*. Philadelphia, Pa.: Temple University Press, 1997.

DeMartino, George F. *Global Economy, Global Justice: Theoretical Objections and Policy Alternatives to Neoliberalism*. New York: Routledge, 2000.

Denning, Michael. *Culture in the Age of Three Worlds*. London: Verso, 2004.

DeSalvo, Louise. *Virginia Woolf: The Impact of Childhood Sexual Abuse on Her Life and Work*. New York: Ballantine, 1989.

Devlin, Rachel. "'Acting Out the Oedipal Wish': Father-Daughter Incest and the Sexuality of Adolescent Girls in the United States, 1941–1965." *Journal of Social History* 38.3 (Spring 2005): 609–33.

———. *Relative Intimacy: Fathers, Adolescent Daughters, and Postwar American Culture*. Chapel Hill: University of North Carolina Press, 2005.

Diamond, John L. "Dillon v. Legg Revisited: Toward a Unified Theory of Compensating Bystanders and Relatives for Intangible Injuries." *Hastings Law Journal* 35 (1984): 477–504.

Dillard, Angela. *Who's Coming to Dinner Now? Multicultural Conservatism in America*. New York: New York University Press, 2001.

Dimock, Wai Chee. *Residues of Justice: Literature, Law, Philosophy*. Berkeley: University of California Press, 1996.

Doane, Janice, and Devon Hodges. *Telling Incest: Narratives of Dangerous Remembering from Stein to Sapphire*. Ann Arbor: University of Michigan Press, 2001.

Doe, Jane. "How Could This Happen? Coping with a False Accusation of Incest and Rape." *Issues in Child Abuse Accusations* 3.3 (1991): 154–65.

Donaldson, Elizabeth. "'Handing Back Shame': Incest and Sexual Confession in Sapphire's *Push*." In *Transgression and Taboo: Critical Essays*, edited by Vartan P. Messier and Nandita Batra. Mayagüez, Puerto Rico: College English Association–Caribbean Chapter (CEA–CC), 2005. 51–59.

Donlon, Jocelyn Hazelwood. "'Born on the Wrong Side of the Porch': Violating Traditions in *Bastard out of Carolina*." *Southern Folklore* 55.2 (1998): 133–44.

Donzelot, Jacques. *The Policing of Families*. Translated by Robert Hurley. New York: Pantheon Books, 1979.

Doten, Patti. "An Odyssey into the Abyss: Writing and Therapy Help Her Unlock Long-Buried Memories of Sexual Abuse." *Boston Globe*, July 15, 1991, 30.

Douglas, Kate. "'Blurbing' Biographical: Authorship and Autobiography." *Biography* 24.4 (Fall 2001): 806–26.

Douglass, Ana, and Thomas A. Vogler, eds. *Witness and Memory: The Discourse of Trauma.* New York: Routledge, 2003.

Dripps, Donald A. "Beyond Rape: An Essay on the Difference between the Presence of Force and the Absence of Consent." *Columbia Law Review* 92 (November 1992): 1780–1809.

DuCille, Ann. *The Coupling Convention: Sex, Text, and Tradition in Black Women's Fiction.* New York: Oxford University Press, 1993.

———. "Where in the World Is William Wells Brown? Thomas Jefferson, Sally Hemings, and the DNA of African-American Literary History." *American Literary History* 12.3 (2000): 443–62.

Duggan, Lisa. *The Twilight of Equality? Neo-Liberalism, Cultural Politics, and the Attack on Democracy.* Boston, Mass.: Beacon Press, 2003.

Duin, Julia. "Critics Assail Study Affirming Pedophilia." *Washington Times,* March 23, 1999, A1.

Dunkley, Graham. *The Free Trade Adventure: The WTO, the Uruguay Round and Globalism—A Critique.* London: Zed Books, 1997.

Eakin, Paul John. "Breaking Rules: The Consequences of Self-Narration." *Biography* 24.1 (Winter 2001): 113–27.

Eberle, Paul, and Shirley Eberle. *The Abuse of Innocence: The McMartin Preschool Trial.* Amherst, N.Y.: Prometheus Books, 2003.

EchoHawk, Larry. "Child Sexual Abuse in Indian Country: Is the Guardian Keeping in Mind the Seventh Generation?" *New York University Journal of Legislation and Public Policy* 5 (2001–2002): 83–128.

Edelman, Lee. *No Future: Queer Theory and the Death Drive.* Durham, N.C.: Duke University Press, 2004.

Edmondson, Laura. "Marketing Trauma and the Theatre of War in Northern Uganda." *Theatre Journal* 57.3 (2005): 451–74.

Edsall, Thomas Byrne, and Mary D. Edsall, eds. *Chain Reaction: The Impact of Race, Rights and Taxes on American Politics.* New York: W. W. Norton, 1991.

Edwards, Brent Hayes. *The Practice of Diaspora: Literature, Translation, and the Rise of Black Internationalism.* Cambridge, Mass.: Harvard University Press, 2003.

Eekelaar, John, and Thandabantu Nhlapo, eds. *The Changing Family: Family Forms and Family Law.* Oxford: Hart Publishing, 1998.

Elliott, J. F. *The "New" Police.* Springfield, Ill.: Charles C. Thomas Publisher, 1973.

Ellison, Ralph. *Invisible Man.* New York: Random House, 1952.

Eng, David. *Racial Castration: Managing Masculinity in Asian America.* Durham, N.C.: Duke University Press, 2001.

———. "Transnational Adoption and Queer Diasporas." *Social Text* 76 21.3 (Fall 2003): 1–37.

Engels, Friedrich. *The Origin of the Family, Private Property, and the State, in the Light of the Researches of Lewis H. Morgan.* New York: International Publishers, 1942.

Enloe, Cynthia. *The Morning After: Sexual Politics at the End of the Cold War.* Berkeley: University of California Press, 1993.

Erickson, Julia A. "Sexual Liberation's Last Frontier." *Society* 37.4 (May–June 2000): 21–25.

Ernsdorff, Gary M., and Elizabeth F. Loftus. "Let Sleeping Memories Lie? Words of Caution about Tolling the Statute of Limitations in Cases of Memory Repression." *Journal of Criminal Law and Criminology* 84.1 (Spring 1993): 129–174.

Escobar, Arturo. *Encountering Development: The Making and Unmaking of the Third World.* Princeton, N.J.: Princeton University Press, 1995.

Eskridge, William N., Jr. "Essay: The Many Faces of Sexual Consent." *William and Mary Law Review* 37 (Fall 1995): 47–67.

Eskridge, William N., Jr., and Nan D. Hunter. *Sexuality, Gender, and the Law.* Foundation Press, 1997.

Estrich, Susan. "Is It Rape?" In *Rape and Society: Readings in the Problem of Sexual Assault,* edited by Ronald J. Searles and Patricia Searles. Boulder, Colo.: Westview Press, 1995. 183–93.

Evans, David T. *Sexual Citizenship: The Material Construction of Sexualities.* New York: Routledge, 1993.

Farber, Bernard. *Conceptions of Kinship.* New York: Elsevier North Holland, 1981.

Farrell, Kirby. *Post-Traumatic Culture: Injury and Interpretation in the Nineties.* Baltimore, Md.: Johns Hopkins University Press, 1998.

Faubion, James, ed. *The Ethics of Kinship: Ethnographic Inquiries.* Lanham, Md.: Rowman and Littlefield, 2001.

Faulkner, William. *The Sound and the Fury.* Edited by David Minter. New York: W. W. Norton, 1994.

Feiner, Leslie. "The Whole Truth: Restoring Reality to Children's Narrative in Long-Term Incest Cases." *Journal of Criminal Law and Criminology* 87.4 (Summer 1997): 1385–1429.

Feldman, Allen. *Formations of Violence: The Narrative of the Body and Political Terror in Northern Ireland.* Chicago, Ill.: University of Chicago Press, 1991.

———. "Memory Theaters, Virtual Witnessing, and the Trauma-Aesthetic." *Biography* 27.1 (2004): 163–202.

Felman, Shoshana. *Jacques Lacan and the Adventure of Insight: Psychoanalysis in Contemporary Culture.* Cambridge, Mass.: Harvard University Press, 2004.

Felman, Shoshana, and Dori Laub. *Testimony: Crises in Witnessing in Literature, Psychoanalysis, and History.* New York: Routledge, 1992.

Ferenczi, Sandor. "Confusion of Tongues between Adult and Child." *International Journal of Psychoanalysis* 30 (1949): 225–30.

Ferguson, Roderick A. *Aberrations in Black: Toward a Queer of Color Critique.* Minneapolis: University of Minnesota Press, 2004.

Fine, Laura. "Gender Conflicts and Their 'Dark' Projections in Coming of Age White Female Southern Novels." *Southern Quarterly* 36.4 (Summer 1998): 121–29.

Finkelhor, David. *Sexually Victimized Children.* New York: Free Press, 1979.

Fischer, Kurt W., and Arlyne Lazerson. *Human Development: From Conception through Adolescence.* New York: W. H. Freeman, 1984.

Flammang, C. J. *The Police and the Underprotected Child.* Springfield, Ill.: Charles C. Thomas Publisher, 1970.

Flanders, W. Austin. *Structures of Experience: History, Society and Personal Life in the Eighteenth-Century British Novel.* Columbia: University of South Carolina Press, 1984.

Flandrin, Jean-Louis. *Families in Former Times: Kinship, Household, and Sexuality.* Translated by Richard Southern. New York: Cambridge University Press, 1979.

Flannery, Raymond B. *Post-Traumatic Stress Disorder: The Victim's Guide to Healing and Recovery.* New York: Crossroad Publishing, 1992.

Fliegelman, Jay. *Prodigals and Pilgrims: The American Revolution against Patriarchal Authority, 1750–1800.* New York: Cambridge University Press, 1982.

Flint, Christopher. *Family Fictions: Narrative and Domestic Relations in Britain, 1688–1798.* Stanford, Conn.: Stanford University Press, 1998.

Floyd, Christie I. "Note: Admissibility of Prior Acts Evidence in Sexual Assault and Child

Molestation Cases in Kentucky: A Proposed Solution that Recognizes Cultural Context." *Brandeis Law Journal* 38 (Fall 1999–Fall 2000): 133–58.

Fontes, Lisa Aronson, ed. *Sexual Abuse in Nine North American Cultures: Treatment and Prevention.* Thousand Oaks, Calif.: Sage Publications, 1995.

Ford, Jane M. *Patriarchy and Incest from Shakespeare to Joyce.* Gainesville: University Press of Florida, 1998.

Foreman, Gabrielle P. "'Reading Aright': White Slavery, Black Referents, and the Strategy of Histotextuality in *Iola Leroy.*" *Yale Journal of Criticism* 10.2 (Fall 1997): 327–54.

Foucault, Michel. "Governmentality." In *The Foucault Effect: Studies in Governmentality,* edited by Graham Burchell, Colin Gordon, and Peter Miller. Chicago, Ill.: University of Chicago Press, 1991. 87–104.

——. *Histoire de la Sexualité: La Volonté de Savoir.* Paris: Gallimard, 1976.

——. *The History of Sexuality, Volume 1: An Introduction.* Translated by Robert Hurley. New York: Vintage, 1978.

——. *Il Faut Défendre la Société: Cours au Collège de France (1975–1976).* Paris: Seuil/Gallimard, 1997.

——. "Politics and the Study of Discourse." In *The Foucault Effect: Studies in Governmentality,* edited by Graham Burchell, Colin Gordon, and Peter Miller. Chicago, Ill.: University of Chicago Press, 1991. 53–72.

——. "Questions of Method." In *The Foucault Effect: Studies in Governmentality,* edited by Graham Burchell, Colin Gordon, and Peter Miller. Chicago, Ill.: University of Chicago Press, 1991. 73–86.

——. "Sexual Morality and the Law." Translated by Alan Sheridan. In *Politics, Philosophy, Culture: Interviews and Other Writings, 1977–1984,* edited by Lawrence D. Kritzman. New York: Routledge, 1988. 271–85.

——. *Society Must Be Defended: Lectures at the College de France, 1975–76.* Edited by Mauro Bertani and Alessandro Fontana, translated by David Macey. New York: Picador, 2003.

Fox, Robin. *The Red Lamp of Incest.* New York: Dutton, 1980.

Frank, Thomas. *One Market under God: Extreme Capitalism, Market Populism, and the End of Economic Democracy.* New York: Random House, 2000.

Franke, Katherine M. "Becoming a Citizen: Reconstruction Era Regulation of African American Marriages." *Yale Journal of Law and the Humanities* 11 (Summer 1999): 251–309.

——. "Theorizing Yes: An Essay on Law, Feminism, and Desire." *Columbia Law Review* 101.1 (2001): 181–208.

Franklin, Sarah, and Susan McKinnon, eds. *Relative Values: Reconfiguring Kinship Studies.* Durham, N.C.: Duke University Press, 2001.

Freccero, Carla. "Queer Nation, Female Nation: Marguerite de Navarre, Incest, and the State in Early Modern France." *MLQ: Modern Language Quarterly* 65.1 (March 2004): 29–47.

Freedman, Estelle B., and John D'Emilio. *Intimate Matters: A History of Sexuality in America.* Harper and Row, 1992.

Freeman, Barbara Claire. "Moments of Beating: Addiction and Inscription in Virginia Woolf's 'A Sketch of the Past.'" *diacritics* 27.3 (Fall 1997): 65–76.

Freeman, Michael. *The Moral Status of Children: Essays on the Rights of the Child.* Cambridge, Mass.: Kluwer Law International, 1997.

Freud, Sigmund. "The Aetiology of Hysteria." In *The Standard Edition of the Complete Psychological Works of Sigmund Freud,* vol. 3, edited by James Strachey. London: Hogarth Press and the Institute of Pscho-Analysis, 1962. 207–8.

——. "An Autobiographical Study." In *The Freud Reader*, edited by Peter Gay, translated by James Strachey. New York: W. W. Norton, 1989. 3–41.

——. *Beyond the Pleasure Principle*. Edited and translated by James Strachey. New York: W. W. Norton, 1961.

——. "A Child Is Being Beaten: A Contribution to the Origin of Sexual Perversions." In *Sexuality and the Psychology of Love*, edited by Philip Reif, translated by Alix and James Strachey. New York: Collier Books, 1963. 107–32.

——. "Creative Writers and Day-Dreaming." In *The Freud Reader*, edited by Peter Gay, translated by James Strachey. New York: W. W. Norton, 1989. 436–43.

——. "Family Romances." *The Freud Reader*, edited by Peter Gay, translated by James Strachey. New York: W. W. Norton, 1989. 297–300.

——. "Further Remarks on the Neuro-psychoses of Defence." In *The Standard Edition of the Complete Psychological Works of Sigmund Freud*, vol. 3, edited by James Strachey. London: Hogarth Press and the Institute of Psycho-Analysis, 1962. 163–85.

——. "Heredity and the Aetiology of the Neuroses." *The Standard Edition of the Complete Psychological Works of Sigmund Freud*, vol. 3, edited by James Strachey. London: Hogarth Press and the Institute of Pscho-Analysis, 1962. 143–56.

——. *Three Essays on the Theory of Sexuality*. Edited and translated by James Strachey. New York: Basic Books, 1962.

——. *Totem and Taboo: Some Points of Agreement between the Mental Lives of Savages and Neurotics*. Edited and translated by James Strachey. New York: W. W. Norton, 1950.

Freyd, Jennifer J. *Betrayal Trauma: The Logic of Forgetting in Childhood Abuse*. Cambridge, Mass.: Harvard University Press, 1996.

——. "Theoretical and Personal Perspectives on the Delayed Memory Debate." In *Proceedings of the Center for Mental Health at Foote Hospital's Continuing Education Conference*. Ann Arbor, Mich.: Foote Hospital, 1993. 69–108.

Friedman, Ellen G. "Postpatriarchal Endings in Recent U.S. Fiction." *MFS: Modern Fiction Studies* 48.3 (2002): 693–712.

Friedman, Thomas L. *The Lexus and the Olive Tree: Understanding Globalization*. New York: Farrar Straus Giroux, 1999.

Fromm, Erich. *The Sane Society*. New York: Holt, Rinehart, and Winston, 1955.

Frost, Laura. "After Lot's Daughters: Kathryn Harrison and the Making of Memory." In *Extremities: Trauma, Testimony, and Community*, edited by Nancy K. Miller and Jason Tougaw. Urbana: University of Illinois Press, 2002. 213–29.

Fujitani, Tak, Geoffrey M. White, and Lisa Yoneyama, eds. *Perilous Memories: The Asia-Pacific War(s)*. Durham, N.C.: Duke University Press, 2001.

Fukuyama, Francis. *The End of History and the Last Man*. New York: Free Press, 1992.

Gallagher, Brian D. "Note: Damages, Duress, and the Discovery Rule: The Statutory Right of Recovery for Victims of Childhood Sexual Abuse." *Seton Hall Legislative Journal* 17 (1993): 505–40.

Gallagher, Catherine. "Marxism and the New Historicism." In *The New Historicism*, edited by H. Aram Veeser. London: Routledge, 1989. 37–48.

——. *Nobody's Story: The Vanishing Acts of Women Writers in the Marketplace, 1670–1820*. Berkeley: University of California Press, 1994.

Gallagher, Vera, ed. *Speaking Out, Fighting Back: Personal Experiences of Women Who Survived Child Sexual Abuse in the Home*. Seattle, Wash.: Madrona Publishers, 1985.

Gallop, Jane. *Reading Lacan*. Ithaca, N.Y.: Cornell University Press, 1985.

Garst, Serina Montgomery. "The General Fear Theory and Intrafamilial Sexual Assault." *North Carolina Law Review* 66 (September 1988): 1177–1190.

Gates, Henry Louis, Jr., ed. *The Signifying Monkey: A Theory of African American Literary Criticism.* New York: Oxford University Press, 1989.

Genette, Girard. *Narrative Discourse: An Essay in Method.* Translated by Jane E. Lewin. Ithaca, N.Y.: Cornell University Press, 1983.

Gibson-Graham, J. K. *The End of Capitalism (As We Knew It): A Feminist Critique of Political Economy.* Oxford: Blackwell, 1996.

Gilman, Sander L. *The Case of Sigmund Freud: Medicine and Identity at the Fin de Siècle.* Baltimore, Md.: Johns Hopkins University Press, 1994.

——. "Sibling Incest, Madness, and the Jews." In *Love + Marriage = Death: And Other Essays on Representing Difference.* Stanford, Conn.: Stanford University Press, 1998.

Gilmore, Leigh. *The Limits of Autobiography: Trauma, Testimony, Theory.* Ithaca, N.Y.: Cornell University Press, 2000.

Gilmore, Ruth Wilson. *Golden Gulag: Prisons, Surplus, Crisis and Opposition in Globalizing California.* Berkeley: University of California Press, 2007.

Gilroy, Paul. *The Black Atlantic: Modernity and Double Consciousness.* Cambridge, Mass.: Harvard University Press, 1993.

Goldman, Maurice. "The Violence Against Women Act: Meeting Its Goals in Protecting Battered Immigrant Women?" *Family and Conciliation Courts Review* 37.3 (July 1999): 375–92.

Goode, Erica. "Study on Child Sex Abuse Provokes a Political Furor." *New York Times,* June 13, 1999, 33.

Goode, Judith, and Jeff Maskovsky, eds. *The New Poverty Studies: The Ethnography of Power, Politics, and Impoverished People in the United States.* New York: New York University Press, 2001.

Gordon, Avery, and Chris Newfield, eds. *Mapping Multiculturalism.* Minneapolis: University of Minnesota Press, 1996.

Gordon, Linda. *Heroes of Their Own Lives: The Politics and History of Family Violence, Boston, 1880–1960.* New York: Penguin, 1988.

Gottesman, Roberta. *The Child and the Law.* St. Paul, Minn.: West Publishing, 1981.

Gray, Paul. "The Assault on Freud." *Time,* November 29, 1993, 47–51.

Greenfield, Susan C. *Mothering Daughters: Novels and the Politics of Family Romance, Frances Burney to Jane Austen.* Detroit, Mich.: Wayne State University Press, 2002.

Greven, Philip. *Spare the Child: The Religious Roots of Punishment and the Psychological Impact of Physical Abuse.* New York: Alfred A. Knopf, 1991.

Grewal, Inderpal. *Transnational America: Feminisms, Diasporas, Neoliberalisms.* Durham, N.C.: Duke University Press, 2005.

Grewal, Inderpal, and Caren Kaplan, eds. *Scattered Hegemonies: Postmodernity and Transnational Feminist Practices.* Minneapolis: University of Minnesota Press, 1994.

Haag, Pamela. *Consent: Sexual Rights and the Transformation of American Liberalism.* Ithaca, N.Y.: Cornell University Press, 1999.

Haaken, Janice. *Pillar of Salt: Gender, Memory, and the Perils of Looking Back.* New Brunswick, N.J.: Rutgers University Press, 1998.

Haaken, Janice, and Sharon Lamb. "The Politics of Child Sexual Abuse Research." In *Society* 37.4 (May 2000): 7–14.

Hacking, Ian. "The Making and Molding of Child Abuse." *Critical Inquiry* 4 (Winter 1991): 253–88.

——. *Rewriting the Soul: Multiple Personality and the Sciences of Memory.* Princeton, N.J.: Princeton University Press, 1995.

Hagen, Ann M. "Note: Tolling the Statute of Limitations for Adult Survivors of Childhood Sexual Abuse." *Iowa Law Review* 76 (1991): 355–82.

Hagen, Margaret A. "Damaged Goods? What, If Anything, Does Science Tell Us about the Long-Term Effects of Childhood Sexual Abuse?" *Skeptical Inquirer* 25.1 (January–February 2001): 54–56.

Haggerty, George E. *Unnatural Affections: Women and Fiction in the Later Eighteenth Century.* Bloomington: Indiana University Press, 1998.

Hale, Dorothy J. *Social Formalism: The Novel in Theory from Henry James to the Present.* Stanford, Conn.: Stanford University Press, 1998.

Hale, Matthew. *The History of the Pleas of the Crown.* 1736. Edited by C. M. Gray. Chicago, Ill.: Chicago University Press, 1971.

Hall, Rachel. "'It Can Happen to You': Rape Prevention in the Era of Risk Management." *Hypatia* 19.3 (Summer 2004): 1–19.

Hall, Stuart. "Race, Articulation and Societies Structured in Dominance." In *Sociological Theories: Race and Colonialism.* Paris: UNESCO, 1980. 305–45.

Hall, Stuart, and Martin Jacques, eds. *New Times: The Changing Face of Politics in the 1990s.* New York: Verso, 1990.

Hall, Stuart, David Held, and Tony McGrew, eds. *Modernity and Its Futures: Understanding Modern Societies.* Cambridge: Polity Press, 1993.

Halley, Janet. "'Like-Race' Arguments." In *What's Left of Theory? New Work on the Politics of Literary Theory,* edited by Judith Butler, John Guillory, and Kendall Thomas. New York: Routledge, 2000. 40–74.

———. "Sexuality Harassment." In *Left Legalism/Left Critique,* edited by Wendy Brown and Janet Halley. Durham, N.C.: Duke University Press, 2002. 80–104.

Hamer, Mary. *Incest: A New Perspective.* Cambridge: Polity Press, 2002.

Hamilton, Andy. "False Memory Syndrome and the Authority of Personal Memory-Claims: A Philosophical Perspective." *Philosophy, Psychiatry, and Psychology* 5.4 (1998): 283–97.

Hammonds, Evelyn M. "Black (W)holes and the Geometry of Black Female Sexuality." In *Feminism and Race,* edited by Kum-Kum Bhavnani. New York: Oxford University Press, 2001. 379–93.

———. "Toward a Genealogy of Black Female Sexuality: The Problematic of Silence." In *Feminist Genealogies, Colonial Legacies, Democratic Futures,* edited by M. Jacqui Alexander and Chandra Talpade Mohanty. New York: Routledge, 1997. 170–82.

Hampton, Lawrence P. "Note: Malpractice in Psychotherapy: Is There a Relevant Standard of Care?" *Case Western Reserve Law Review* 35 (1984): 251–81.

Handler, Carolyn B. "Note: Civil Claims of Adults Molested as Children: Maturation of Harm and the Statute of Limitations Hurdle." *Fordham Urban Law Journal* 15 (1987): 709–42.

Hardt, Michael, and Antonio Negri. *Empire.* Cambridge, Mass.: Harvard University Press, 2000.

Harris, Cheryl. "Whiteness as Property." In *Critical Race Theory: The Key Writings That Formed the Movement,* edited by Kimberle Crenshaw, Neil Gotanda, Gary Peller, and Kendall Thomas. New York: New Press, 1995.

Harrison, Kathryn. *The Kiss: A Memoir.* New York: Avon Books, 1997.

Hart, Lynda. *Between the Body and the Flesh: Performing Sadomasochism.* New York: Columbia University Press, 1998.

Hartman, Geoffrey. *The Longest Shadow: In the Aftermath of the Holocaust.* Bloomington: Indiana University Press, 1996.

Hartman, Saidiya. *Scenes of Subjection: Terror, Slavery, and Self-Making in Nineteenth-Century America.* New York: Oxford University Press, 1997.

Harvard Law Review. "Note: Inbred Obscurity: Improving Incest Laws in the Shadow of the 'Sexual Family.'" *Harvard Law Review* 119.8 (June 2006): 2464–2485.

Harvey, David. *A Brief History of Neoliberalism.* New York: Oxford University Press, 2007.

——. *The Condition of Postmodernity: An Enquiry into the Conditions of Cultural Change.* Cambridge: Blackwell, 1990.

Hawes, Joseph M., and Elizabeth I. Nybakken, eds. *Family and Society in American History.* Urbana: University of Illinois Press, 2001.

Heinze, Eric, ed. *Of Innocence and Autonomy: Children, Sex, and Human Rights.* London, England: Ashgate Publishing, 2000.

Hellman, David. "Bastard out of Carolina." *Library Journal* 126.10 (June 1, 2001): 260.

Henderson, Mae Gwendolyn. "Speaking in Tongues: Dialectics, Dialogics, and the Black Woman Writer's Literary Tradition." In *Changing Our Own Words,* edited by Cheryl Wall. New Brunswick, N.J.: Rutgers University Press, 1989. 16–37.

Henke, Suzette A. *Shattered Subjects: Trauma and Testimony in Women's Life-Writing.* New York: St. Martins Press, 1998.

Hennessy, Rosemary. *Profit and Pleasure: Sexual Identities in Late Capitalism.* New York: Routledge, 2000.

——. "Queer Visibility in Commodity Culture." In *Social Postmodernism: Beyond Identity Politics,* edited by Linda Nicholson and Steven Seidman. Cambridge: Cambridge University Press, 1995. 142–83.

Herman, Judith Lewis. *Trauma and Recovery.* New York: BasicBooks, 1992.

Herman, Judith Lewis, with Lisa Hirschman. *Father-Daughter Incest.* Cambridge, Mass.: Harvard University Press, 1981.

Herron, Carolivia. *Thereafter Johnnie.* New York: Random House, 1991.

Hesse, Barnor, ed. *Un/settled Multiculturalisms: Diasporas, Entanglements, Transruptions.* London: Zed Books, 2000.

Higgins, Daryl J., and Marita P. McCabe. "The Relationship of Child Sexual Abuse and Family Violence to Adult Adjustment: Toward an Integrated Risk-Sequelae Model." *Journal of Sex Research* 31.4 (1994): 255–66.

Hirsch, Joshua. *Afterimage: Film, Trauma, and the Holocaust.* Philadelphia, Pa.: Temple University Press, 2004.

Hirsch, Marianne. *Family Frames: Photography, Narrative, and Postmemory.* Cambridge, Mass.: Harvard University Press, 1997.

Hong, Grace Kyungwon. *The Ruptures of American Capital: Women of Color Feminism and the Culture of Immigrant Labor.* Minneapolis: University of Minnesota Press, 2006.

Hopkins, Pauline. *Of One Blood, or The Hidden Self.* New York: Washington Square Press, 2004.

Horvitz, Deborah M. *Literary Trauma: Sadism, Memory and Sexual Violence in American Women's Fiction.* Albany: State University of New York Press, 2000.

Horwitz, Morton. *The Transformation of American Law, 1870–1960.* New York: Oxford University Press, 1992.

Hudson, Glenda A. *Sibling Love and Incest in Jane Austen's Fiction.* London: MacMillan, 1992.

Hunt, Lynn. *The Family Romance of the French Revolutions.* Berkeley: University of California Press, 1992.

Huntington, Samuel. *The Clash of Civilizations and the Remaking of the World Order.* New York: Simon and Schuster, 1996.

Hutcheon, Linda. *A Poetics of Postmodernism: History, Theory, Fiction.* New York: Routledge, 1988.

Huyssen, Andreas. *Twilight Memories: Marking Time in a Culture of Amnesia.* New York: Routledge, 1995.

Irving, Katrina. "'Writing It Down So That It Would Be Real': Narrative Strategies in Dorothy Allison's *Bastard out of Carolina.*" *College Literature* (Spring 1998): 94–107.

Ivy, Marilyn. "Have You Seen Me? Recovering the Inner Child in Late Twentieth Century America." *Social Text* 37 (1993): 227–52.

Jakobsen, Janet K., with Ann Pellegrini. "World Secularisms at the Millenium." *Social Text* 18.3 (Fall 2000): 2–16.

Jameson, Fredric. *The Political Unconscious: Narrative as a Socially Symbolic Act.* Ithaca, N.Y.: Cornell University Press, 1981.

———. *Postmodernism, or The Cultural Logic of Late Capitalism.* Durham, N.C.: Duke University Press, 1991.

Janet, Pierre. *The Major Symptoms of Hysteria: Fifteen Lectures Given in the Medical School of Harvard University by Pierre Janet.* New York: Macmillan, 1907.

Jarecki, Andrew. "Secrets and Lies." *Guardian,* March 19, 2004.

Jaroff, Leon. "Lies of the Mind." *Time,* November 29, 1993, 52–59.

Jenkins, Candice M. *Private Lives, Proper Relations: Regulating Black Intimacy.* Minneapolis: University of Minnesota Press, 2007.

Jenkins, Philip. *Moral Panic: Changing Concepts of the Child Molester in Modern America.* New Haven, Conn.: Yale University Press, 1998.

Johnston, Moira. *Spectral Evidence: The Ramona Case: Incest, Memory, and Truth on Trial in Napa Valley.* Boulder, Colo.: Westview Press, 1997.

Jones, Gayl. *Corregidora.* Boston, Mass.: Beacon Press, 1986.

Joseph, Miranda. *Against the Romance of Community.* Minneapolis: University of Minnesota Press, 2002.

Kahn, Paul W. *The Cultural Study of Law: Reconstructing Legal Scholarship.* Chicago, Ill.: University of Chicago Press, 2000.

Kanovitz, Jacqueline. "Hypnotic Memories and Civil Sexual Abuse Trials." *Vanderbilt Law Review* 45 (1992): 1185–1262.

Kaplan, Amy. *The Anarchy of Empire in the Making of U.S. Culture.* Cambridge, Mass.: Harvard University Press, 2002.

———. *The Social Construction of American Realism.* Chicago, Ill.: University of Chicago Press, 1988.

Kaplan, Ann E. *Trauma Culture: The Politics of Terror and Loss in Media and Literature.* New Brunswick, N.J.: Rutgers University Press, 2005.

Kaplan, Caren, Norma Alarcon, and Minoo Mooallem, eds. *Between Woman and Nation: Nationalisms, Transnational Feminisms, and the State.* Durham, N.C.: Duke University Press, 1999.

Kaplan, E. Ann, and Ban Wang, eds. *Trauma and Cinema: Cross-Cultural Explorations.* Hong Kong: Hong Kong University Press, 2003.

Katz, Sanford N. "Parental Rights and Social Responsibility in American Child Protection Law." In *The Changing Family: Family Forms and Family Law,* edited by John Eekelaar and Thandabantu Nhlapo. Oxford: Hart Publishing, 1998. 433–52.

Katzenstein, Peter J., ed. *The Culture of National Security.* New York: Columbia University Press, 1996.

Kazanjian, David. *The Colonizing Trick: National Culture and Imperial Citizenship in Early America.* Minnesota: University of Minnesota Press, 2003.

Keizer, Arlene R. *Black Subjects: Identity Formation in the Contemporary Narrative of Slavery.* Ithaca, N.Y.: Cornell University Press, 2004.

———. "The Geography of the Apocalypse: Incest, Mythology, and the Fall of Washington City in Carolivia Herron's *Thereafter Johnnie.*" *American Literature* 72.2 (June 2000): 387–416.

Kempe, Henry, et al. "The Battered Child Syndrome." 181 *Journal of the American Medical Association* 181.17 (1962): 17–24.

Kenan, Randall. "Sorrow's Child: *Bastard out of Carolina* by Dorothy Allison." *Nation* 255.22 (December 28, 1992): 815–16.

Kenny, Michael. "The Proof Is in the Passion: Emotion as an Index of Veridical Memory." In *Believed-In Imaginings: The Narrative Construction of Reality*, edited by Joseph De Rivera and Theodore R. Sabin. Washington, D.C.: American Psychological Association, 1998. 269–94.

Khanna, Ranjanna. *Dark Continents: Psychoanalysis and Colonialism*. Durham, N.C.: Duke University Press, 2003.

Kincaid, James R. *Child-Loving: The Erotic Child and Victorian Culture*. New York: Routledge, 1992.

———. *Erotic Innocence: The Culture of Child-Molesting*. Durham, N.C.: Duke University Press, 1998.

King, Vincent. "Hopeful Grief: The Prospect of a Postmodernist Feminism in Allison's *Bastard out of Carolina*." *Southern Literary Journal* 33.1 (Fall 2000): 122–40.

Kinsey, Alfred C., Wardell Baxter Pomeroy, and Clyde E. Martin. *Sexual Behavior in the Human Male*. Philadelphia, Pa.: Saunders, 1948.

Kitzinger, Jenny. "Defending Innocence: Ideologies of Childhood." *Feminist Review* 28 (1988): 77–87.

———. *Framing Abuse: Media Influence and Public Understanding of Sexual Violence against Children*. London: Pluto Press, 2004.

———. "The Gender Politics of News Production: Silenced Voices and Fake Memories." In *News, Gender, and Power*, edited by Cynthia Carter et al. London: Routledge, 1998. 186–203.

Klein, Kerwin Lee. "On the Emergence of Memory in Historical Discourse." *Representations* 69 (Winter 2000): 127–50.

Kleinman, Arthur, and Joan Kleinman. "The Appeal of Experience, the Dismay of Images: Cultural Appropriations of Suffering in Our Times." In *Social Suffering*, edited by Arthur Kleinman, Veena Das, and Madelaine Lock. Berkeley: University of California Press, 1997. 1–23.

Kleinman, Arthur, Veena Das, and Madelaine Lock, eds. *Social Suffering*. Berkeley: University of California Press, 1997.

Kliger, Robyn Aileen. "The Making and Unmaking of a Modern Memory: An Anthropological Account of the Repressed Memory Controversy." Ph.D. disertation. University of California, Berkeley, with the University of California, San Francisco, 2000.

Knapp, Stephen. "Collective Memory and the Actual Past." *Representations* 26 (Spring 1989): 123–49.

Kowalski, M. "Applying the 'Two Schools of Thought' Doctrine to the Repressed Memory Controversy." *Journal of Legal Medicine* 19.4 (1998): 503–47.

Krystal, Henry. "Integration and Self-Healing in Post-Traumatic States: A Ten-Year Retrospective." *American Imago* 48.1 (1991): 93–118.

Lacan, Jacques. "The Function and Field of Speech and Language in Psychoanalysis." In *Écrits: A Selection*, translated by Alan Sheridan. New York: W. W. Norton, 1982. 30–113.

———. *The Seminar of Jacques Lacan, Book VII: The Ethics of Psychoanalysis (1959–1960)*. Edited by Jacques-Alain Miller, translated by Dennis Porter. New York: W. W. Norton, 1992.

LaCapra, Dominick. *Representing the Holocaust: History, Theory, Trauma*. Ithaca, N.Y.: Cornell University Press, 1994.

Lamb, Sharon. "Constructing the Victim: Popular Images and Lasting Labels." In *New Versions of Victims: Feminists Struggle with the Concept,* edited by Sharon Lamb. New York: New York University Press, 1999. 108–38.

——, ed. *New Versions of Victims: Feminists Struggle with the Concept.* New York: New York University Press, 1999.

Lamm, Jocelyn B. "Note: Easing Access to the Courts for Incest Victims: Toward an Equitable Application of the Delayed Discovery Rule." *Yale Law Journal* 100 (1991): 2189–2208.

Lane, Christopher, ed. *The Psychoanalysis of Race.* New York: Columbia University Press, 1998.

Lang, Sabine. "The NGO-ization of Feminism: Institutionalization and Institution Building within the German Women's Movements." In *Global Feminisms since 1945,* edited by Bonnie G. Smith. London: Routledge, 2000. 290–304.

Laplanche, Jean. *Life and Death in Psychoanalysis.* Translated by Jeffrey Mehlman. Baltimore, Md.: Johns Hopkins University Press, 1976.

Laplanche, Jean, and Jean-Bertrand Pontalis. *The Language of Psycho-Analysis.* Translated by Donald Nicholson-Smith. New York: W. W. Norton, 1974.

Lee, Lydia W. "Note: Child Pornography Prevention Act of 1996: Confronting the Challenges of Virtual Reality." *Southern California Interdisciplinary Law Journal* 8 (Spring 1999): 639–81.

Levesque, Roger J. R. *Adolescents, Sex, and the Law: Preparing Adolescents for Responsible Citizenship.* Washington, D.C.: American Psychological Association, 2000.

Levett, Ann. "Problems of Cultural Imperialism in the Study of Child Sexual Abuse." In *New Feminist Stories of Child Sexual Abuse: Sexual Scripts and Dangerous Dialogues,* edited by Paula Reavey and Sam Warner. New York: Routledge, 2003. 52–76.

Levine, Judith. *Harmful to Minors.* Minneapolis: University of Minnesota Press, 2002.

Levine, Murray, and Adeline Levine. *Helping Children: A Social History.* New York: Oxford University Press, 1992.

Lévi-Strauss, Claude. *The Elementary Structures of Kinship.* Edited by Rodney Needham, translated by James Harle Bell, John Richard von Sturmer, and Rodney Needham. Boston, Mass.: Beacon Press, 1969.

Leys, Ruth. *Trauma: A Genealogy.* Chicago, Ill.: University of Chicago Press, 2000.

Liddell, Janice Lee. "Agents of Pain and Redemption in Sapphire's *Push.*" In *Arms Akimbo: Africana Women in Contemporary Literature,* edited by Janice Lee Liddell, Yakini Belinda Kemp, and Beverly Guy-Sheftall. Gainesville, Fl.: University Press of Florida, 1999. 135–46.

Lindebaugh, Peter, and Marcus Rediker. *The Many-Headed Hydra: Sailors, Slaves, Commoners, and the Hidden History of the Revolutionary Atlantic.* Boston, Mass.: Beacon Press, 2000.

Lipsitz, George. *The Possessive Investment in Whiteness: How White People Profit from Identity Politics.* Philadelphia, Pa.: Temple University Press, 1998.

Lloyd, David. "Race under Representation." *Oxford Literary Review* 13 (Spring 1991): 62–94.

Lloyd, David, and Lisa Lowe, eds. *The Politics of Culture in the Shadow of Capital.* Durham, N.C.: Duke University Press, 1997.

Lloyd, David, and Paul Thomas. *Culture and the State.* New York: Routledge, 1997.

Lo, Clarence, and Michael Schwartz, eds. *Social Policy and the Conservative Agenda.* Malden, Mass.: Blackwell Publishers, 1998.

Loftus, Elizabeth, and Katherine Ketcham. *The Myth of Repressed Memory: False Memories and Allegations of Sexual Abuse.* New York: St. Martin's Press, 1994.

Lopez, Ian F. Haney. *White by Law: The Legal Construction of Race.* New York: New York University Press, 1996.

Lott, Eric. *Love and Theft: Blackface Minstrelsy and the American Working Class.* New York: Oxford University Press, 1995.

Lovrod, Marie. "Shifting Contexts, Shaping Experiences: Child Abuse Survivor Narratives and Educating for Empire." *Meridians: Feminism, Race, Transnationalism* 5.2 (2005): 30–56.

Lowe, Lisa. *Immigrant Acts: On Asian American Cultural Politics.* Durham, N.C.: Duke University Press, 1996.

Lowe, S. "Culturally Interpreted Symptoms of Culture-Bound Syndromes." *Social Science and Medicine* 21 (1985): 187–97.

Luce, Henry. "The American Century." *Life,* February 17, 1941. Reprinted in *Diplomatic History* 23.2 (Spring 1999): 159–71.

Luibhéid, Eithne. *Entry Denied: A History of U.S. Immigration Control.* Minneapolis: University of Minnesota Press, 2002.

Lukács, Georg. *Realism in Our Time: Literature and the Class Struggle.* Translated by John and Necke Mander. New York: Harper, 1964.

———. *The Theory of the Novel.* Translated by Anna Bostok. Cambridge, Mass.: MIT Press, 1974.

Lye, Colleen. *America's Asia: Racial Form and American Literature, 1893–1945.* Princeton, N.J.: Princeton University Press, 2004.

Lynch, Deidre, and William B. Warner, eds. *Cultural Institutions of the Novel.* Durham, N.C.: Duke University Press, 1996.

Macfarlane, Alan. *Marriage and Love in England: Modes of Reproduction, 1300–1840.* New York: B. Blackwell, 1986.

Manalansan, Martin, and Arnaldo Cruz-Malavé, eds. *Queer Globalizations: Citizenship and the Afterlife of Colonialism.* New York: New York University Press, 2002.

Maraecek, Jeanne. "Trauma Talk in Feminist Clinical Practice." In *New Versions of Victims: Feminists Struggle with the Concept,* edited by Sharon Lamb. New York: New York University Press, 1999. 158–82.

Marcus, Sharon. "Fighting Bodies, Fighting Words: A Theory and Politics of Rape Prevention." In *Feminists Theorize the Political,* edited by Judith Butler and Joan Scott. New York: Routledge, 1992. 385–403.

Mardrossian, Carine. "Toward a New Feminist Theory of Rape." *Signs* 27.3 (Spring 2002): 743–75.

Marshall, Elizabeth. "The Daughter's Disenchantment: Incest as Pedagogy in Fairy Tales and Kathryn Harrison's *The Kiss.*" *College English* 66.4 (2004): 403–26.

Marx, Karl. *Capital: A Critique of Political Economy.* Translated by Ben Fowkes. New York: Vintage Books, 1977.

Masson, Jeffrey Moussaieff. *The Assault on Truth: Freud's Suppression of the Seduction Theory.* New York: Pocket Books, 1984.

———, ed. and trans. *The Complete Letters of Sigmund Freud to Wilhelm Fliess, 1887–1904.* Cambridge, Mass.: Harvard University Press, 1985.

McCabe, Richard. *Incest, Drama and Nature's Law, 1550–1700.* New York: Cambridge University Press, 1993.

McCain, Robert Stacy. "Promoting Pedophilia." *Washington Times,* April 19, 2002, A02.

McCall, Cheryl. "The Cruelest Crime, Sexual Abuse of Children." *Life* (December 1984): 35–42.

McClintock, Anne. *Imperial Leather: Race, Gender and Sexuality in the Colonial Contest.* New York: Routledge, 1995.

———. "'No Longer in a Future Heaven': Gender, Race, and Nationalism." In *Dangerous Liaisons: Gender, Nation, and Postcolonial Perspectives,* ed. Anne McClintock, Aamir Mufti, and Ella Shohat. Minneapolis: University of Minnesota Press, 1997. 89–112.

McClintock, Anne, Aamir Mufti, and Ella Shohat, eds. *Dangerous Liaisons: Gender, Nation, and Postcolonial Perspectives.* Minneapolis: University of Minnesota Press, 1997.

McConnell, Joyce. "Incest as Conundrum: Judicial Discourse on Private Wrong and Public Harm." *Texas Journal of Women and the Law* 1 (1992): 143–72.

McCrea, Brian. *Impotent Fathers: Patriarchy and Demographic Crisis in the Eighteenth-Century Novel.* Newark: University of Delaware Press, 1998.

McCreery, Patrick. "Innocent Pleasures? Children and Sexual Politics." *GLQ: Journal of Lesbian and Gay Studies* 10.4 (2004): 617–30.

McDowell, Deborah E. "Reading Family Matters." In *Changing Our Own Words,* edited by Cheryl A. Wall. New Brunswick, N.J.: Rutgers University Press, 1989. 75–97.

McDowell, Jeanne. "It Came from Outer Space." *Time,* November 29, 1993, 56.

McGillivray, Anne, ed. *Governing Childhood.* Hanover, N.H.: Dartmouth Publishing, 1997.

McIntosh, Mary. "Introduction to an Issue: Family Secrets as Public Drama." *Feminist Review* 28 (January 1988): 6–15.

McKeon, Michael, ed. *Theory of the Novel: A Historical Approach.* Baltimore, Md.: Johns Hopkins University Press, 2000.

McKinnon, Catherine. *Only Words.* Cambridge, Mass.: Harvard University Press, 1993.

———. *Sexual Harassment of Working Women.* New Haven, Conn.: Yale University Press, 1979.

McLaren, John, Robert Menzies, and Dorothy E. Chunn, eds. *Regulating Lives: Historical Essays on the State, Society, the Individual, and the Law.* Toronto: UBC Press, 2002.

McLennan, Karen Jacobsen, ed. *Nature's Ban: Women's Incest Literature.* Boston, Mass.: Northeastern University Press, 1996.

McNally, Richard J. *Remembering Trauma.* Cambridge, Mass.: Belknap Press, 2005.

McNaron, Toni A. H., and Yarrow Morgan, eds. *Voices in the Night: Women Speaking about Incest.* San Francisco, Calif.: Cleis Press, 1982.

McSherry, Bernadette. "No! (Means No?)." *Alternative Law Journal* 18 (1993): 27–30.

Megan, Carolyn E. "Moving toward Truth: An Interview with Dorothy Allison." *Kenyon Review* 16.4 (Fall 1994): 71–83.

Mehta, Uday Singh. *Liberalism and Empire: A Study in Nineteenth-Century British Liberal Thought.* Chicago, Ill.: University of Chicago Press, 1999.

Meiselman, Karin C. *Incest: A Psychological Study of Causes and Effects with Treatment Recommendations.* San Francisco, Calif.: Jossey-Bass Publishers, 1978.

Melamed, Jodi. "The Spirit of Neoliberalism: From Racial Liberalism to Neoliberal Multiculturalism." *Social Text* 24.4 (Winter 2006): 1–24.

Melville, Herman. *Pierre, or The Ambiguities.* New York: Kessinger Publishing, 2004.

Mendez, Gioconda Batres. "Father-Daughter Incest: Case Studies in Costa Rica." In *The Costa Rican Women's Movement: A Reader,* edited and translated by Ilse Abshagen Leitinger. Pittsburgh, Pa.: University of Pittsburgh Press, 1997. 170–79.

Miller, Alice. *For Your Own Good: Hidden Cruelty in Childhood and the Roots of Violence.* Translated by Hildegarde Hannum and Hunter Hannum. New York: Noonday Press, 1990.

Miller, D. A. *The Novel and the Police.* Berkeley: University of California Press, 1988.

Miller, Nancy K., and Jason Tougaw, eds. *Extremities: Trauma, Testimony, and Community.* Champaign-Urbana: Illinois University Press, 2002.

Miller, Neil. *Sex-Crime Panic: A Journey to the Paranoid Heart of the 1950s.* Los Angeles, Calif.: Alyson Press, 2002.

Mills, David. "Can You Believe It?" *Washington Post,* June 25, 1991, D2.

———. "Three Therapists' Opinions." *Washington Post,* June 25, 1991, D3.

Mills, Jane Cousins. "'Putting Ideas into Their Heads': Advising the Young." *Feminist Review* 28 (January 1988): 163–75.

Mink, Gwendolyn, ed. *Whose Welfare?* Ithaca, N.Y.: Cornell University Press, 1999.

Mirikatani, Janice, ed. *Watch Out! We're Talking: Speaking Out about Incest and Abuse.* San Francisco, Calif.: Glide World Press, 1993.

Mirkin, Harris. "Sex, Science, and Sin: The Rind Report, Sexual Politics, and American Scholarship." *Sexuality and Culture* 4.2 (Spring 2000): 82–100.

Mitchell, Timothy. "Society, Economy, and the State Effect." In *State/Culture: State-Formation after the Cultural Turn,* edited by George Steinmetz. Ithaca, N.Y.: Cornell University Press, 1999. 6–97.

Mohanty, Chandra Talpade, and Jacqui Alexander, eds. *Feminist Genealogies, Colonial Legacies, Democratic Futures.* New York: Routledge, 1997.

Mohanty, Chandra Talpade, Ann Russo, and Lourdes Torres, eds. *Third World Women and the Politics of Feminism.* Bloomington: Indiana University Press, 1991.

Moon, Daniel. "'Unnatural Fathers and Vixen Daughters': A Case of Incest, San Diego, California, 1894." *Journal of the West* 39.4 (Fall 2000): 8–16.

Morgan, Kimberly. "A Child of the Sixties: The Great Society, the New Right, and the Politics of Federal Child Care." *Journal of Policy History* 13.2 (2001): 215–50.

Morris, Michelle. *If I Should Die before I Wake.* New York: Dell, 1984.

Morrison, Toni. *Beloved.* New York: Plume, 1988.

———. *The Bluest Eye.* Philadelphia, Pa.: Chelsea House, 1999.

———. *Playing in the Dark: Whiteness and the Literary Imagination.* New York: Vintage, 1993.

Moten, Fred. *In the Break: The Aesthetics of the Black Radical Tradition.* Minneapolis: University of Minnesota Press, 2003.

Mullahy, Patrick. *Oedipus: Myth and Complex (A Review of Psychoanalytic Theory).* New York: Hermitage Press, 1948.

Murray, Julie M. Kosmond. "Repression, Memory, Suggestibility: A Call for Limitations on the Admissibility of Repressed Memory Testimony in Sexual Abuse Trials." *University of Colorado Law Review* 66 (1995): 477–522.

Myers, John E. B., Susan E. Diedrich, Devon Lee, Kelly Fincher, and Rachel M. Stern. "Prosecution of Child Sexual Abuse in the United States." In *Critical Issues in Child Sexual Abuse: Historical, Legal, and Psychological Perspectives,* edited by Jon R. Conte. Thousand Oaks, Calif.: Sage Publications, 2002. 27–70.

Nabokov, Vladimir. *Lolita.* New York: Putnam, 1958.

Naffine, Ngaire. "Possession: Erotic Love in the Law of Rape." *Modern Law Review* 57 (1994): 10–37.

Nathan, Debbie, and Michael Snedecker. *Satan's Silence: Ritual Abuse and the Making of a Modern American Witchhunt.* Lincoln, Neb.: Author's Choice Press, 2001.

Nelson, Barbara J. *Making an Issue of Child Abuse: Political Agenda Setting for Social Problems.* Chicago: University of Chicago Press, 1984.

Nelson, Dana. *National Manhood: Capitalist Citizenship and the Imagined Fraternity of White Men.* Durham, N.C.: Duke University Press, 1998.

Nelson, T. G. A. "Incest in the Early Novel and Related Genres." *Eighteenth-Century Life* 16.1 (1992): 127–62.

Newitz, Annalee, and Matt Wray, eds. *White Trash: Race and Class in America.* New York: Routledge, 2006.

Ngai, Sianne. "Jealous Schoolgirls, Single White Females, and Other Bad Examples: Rethinking Gender and Envy." *Camera Obscura* 16.2 (2001): 177–228.

Nickel, Terri. "'Ingenious Torment': Incest, Family and the Structure of Community in the Work of Sarah Fielding." *The Eighteenth Century* 36.3 (1995).

Nora, Pierre. "Between Memory and History: *Les Lieux de Memoire.*" *Representations* 26 (Spring 1989): 7–24.

O'Carroll, Tom. *Paedophilia: The Radical Case.* London: Peter Owen, 1980.

O'Dell, Lindsay. "The 'Harm' Story in Childhood Sexual Abuse: Contested Understandings, Disputed Knowledges." In *New Feminist Stories of Child Sexual Abuse: Sexual Scripts and Dangerous Dialogues,* edited by Paula Reavey and Sam Warner. New York: Routledge, 2003. 131–47.

O'Rourke, Kevin H., and Jeffrey G. Williamson. *Globalization and History: The Evolution of a Nineteenth-Century Atlantic Economy.* Cambridge, Mass.: MIT Press, 1999.

Odem, Mary E., and Jody Clay-Warner, eds. *Confronting Rape and Sexual Assault.* Wilmington, Del.: Scholarly Resources, 1998.

Oellerich, Thomas D. "Rind, Tromovitch, and Bauserman: Politically Incorrect — Scientifically Correct." *Sexuality and Culture* 4.2 (Spring 2000): 67–81.

Ofsche, Richard, and Ethan Watters. *Making Monsters: False Memories, Psychotherapy, and Sexual Hysteria.* New York: Scribner's, 1994.

Olio, Karen A. "Are 25% of Clinicians Using Potentially Risky Therapeutic Practices? A Review of the Logic and Methodology of the Poole, Lindsay et al. Study." *Journal of Psychiatry and Law* (Summer 1996): 277–98.

Olsen, Frances E. "The Family and the Market: A Study of Ideology and Legal Reform." *Harvard Law Review* 96 (May 1983): 1497–1578.

Ong, Aihwa. *Flexible Citizenship: The Cultural Logics of Transnationality.* Durham, N.C.: Duke University Press, 1999.

Pallotta, Gina M. "Intrafamilial and Extrafamilial Sexual Abuse Vulnerability Factors and Long-Term Psychological Adjustment in a College Population." Ph.D. dissertation, West Virginia University, 1991.

Parenti, Christian. *Lockdown America: Police and Prisons in the Age of Crisis.* New York: Verso, 1999.

Parker, David. "Counter-Transference in Reading Autobiography: The Case of Kathryn Harrison's *The Kiss.*" *Biography* 25.3 (2002): 493–504.

Parkin, Robert, and Linda Stone, eds. *Kinship and Family: An Anthropological Reader.* Oxford: Blackwell, 2004.

Parreñas, Rhacel Salazar. *Servants of Globalization: Women, Migration, and Domestic Work.* Stanford, Conn.: Stanford University Press, 2001.

Patel, Geeta. "Ghostly Appearances: Time Tales Tallied Up." *Social Text* 18.3 (Fall 2000): 47–66.

———. "Risky Subjects: Insurance, Sexuality, and Capital." *Social Text* 24.4 (Winter 2006): 25–65.

Pateman, Carole. "The Patriarchal Welfare State." In *Democracy and the Welfare State,* edited by A. Gutman. Princeton, N.J.: Princeton University Press, 1988. 194–233.

———. *The Sexual Contract.* Stanford, Conn.: Stanford University Press, 1988.

Patterson, Laura S. "Ellipsis, Ritual, and 'Real Time': Rethinking the Rape Complex in Southern Novels." *Mississippi Quarterly* 54.1 (Winter 2000–2002): 37–58.

Pellegrini, Ann. *Performance Anxieties.* New York: Routledge, 1996.

Pelton, Leroy H. "Child Abuse and Neglect: The Myth of Classlessness." In *The Social Context of Child Abuse and Neglect,* edited by Leroy H. Pelton. New York: Human Sciences Press, 1981. 23–38.

——, ed. *The Social Context of Child Abuse and Neglect.* New York: Human Sciences Press, 1981.

Pendergrast, Mark. *Victims of Memory: Sex Abuse Accusations and Shattered Lives.* Hinesburg, Vt.: Upper Access Press, 1995.

Perez, Emma. "Sexuality and Discourse: Notes from a Chicana Survivor." In *Chicana Critical Issues,* edited by Norma Alarcon, Rafaela Castro, Emma Perez, Beatriz Pesquera, Adaljiza Sosa Riddell, and Patricia Zavella. Berkeley, Calif.: Third Woman Press, 1993. 42–71.

Perlin, Michael L. "Tarasoff and the Dilemma of the Dangerous Patient: New Directions for the 1990's." *Law and Psychology Review* 16 (1992): 29–64.

Pezdek, Kathy, and William P. Banks. *The Recovered Memory/False Memory Debate.* San Diego, Calif.: Academic Press, 1996.

Phillips, Lynn M. "Recasting Consent: Agency and Victimization in Adult-Teen Relationships." In *New Versions of Victims: Feminists Struggle with the Concept,* edited by Sharon Lamb. New York: New York University Press, 1999. 82–107.

Phipps, Charles A. "Children, Adults, Sex and the Criminal Law: In Search of Reason." *Seton Hall Legislative Journal* 22 (1997): 1–141.

Piven, Frances Fox, and Richard A. Cloward. *Regulating the Poor: The Functions of Public Welfare.* New York: Vintage Books, 1993.

Pleck, Elizabeth. *Domestic Tyranny: The Making of Social Policy against Family Violence from Colonial Times to the Present.* New York: Oxford University Press, 1987.

Pollak, Ellen. *Incest and the English Novel, 1684–1814.* Baltimore, Md.: Johns Hopkins University Press, 2003.

Pope, Harrison G., and James I. Hudson. "Does Childhood Sexual Abuse Cause Adult Psychiatric Disorders? Essentials of Methodology." *Journal of Psychiatry and Law* (Fall 1995): 363–81.

Pope, Kenneth. "Memory, Abuse, and Science: Questioning Claims about the False Memory Syndrome Epidemic." *American Psychologist* 51.9 (September 1996): 957–74.

——. "What Psychologists Better Know about Recovered Memories, Research, Lawsuits, and the Pivotal Experiment." *Clinical Psychology: Science and Practice* 2.3 (September 1995): 304–15.

Post, Robert C. "Rereading Warren and Brandeis: Privacy, Property, and Appropriation." *Case Western Reserve Law Review* 41 (1991): 647–80.

Postman, Neil. *The Disappearance of Childhood.* New York: Vintage: 1994.

Potter, Nancy. "Loopholes, Gaps, and What Is Held Fast: Democratic Epistemology and Claims to Recovered Memories." *Philosophy, Psychiatry, and Psychology* 3.4 (1996): 237–54.

Povinelli, Elizabeth. "Notes on Gridlock: Genealogy, Intimacy, Sexuality." *Public Culture* 14.1 (2002): 215–38.

Powers, Elizabeth. "Doing Daddy Down." *Commentary* 103.6 (June 1997): 38–41.

Prashad, Vijay. *Keeping Up with the Dow Joneses: Debt, Prison, Workfare.* Cambridge, Mass.: South End Press, 2003.

Proulx, E. Annie. *The Shipping News.* New York: Simon and Schuster, 1994.

Prout, Alan, and Allison James, ed. *Constructing and Reconstructing Childhood: Contemporary Issues in the Sociological Study of Childhood.* Washington, D.C.: Falmer Press, 1997.

Puar, Jasbir. *Terrorist Assemblages: Homonationalism in Queer Times*. Durham, N.C.: Duke University Press, 2007.

Purdy, Laura M. *In Their Best Interest? The Case against Equal Rights for Children*. Ithaca, N.Y.: Cornell University Press, 1992.

Puwar, Nirmal. "Interview with Carole Pateman: The Sexual Contract, Women in Politics, Globalization and Citizenship." *Feminist Review* 70 (2002): 123–33.

Queer Press Collective, eds. *Loving in Fear: An Anthology of Lesbian and Gay Survivors of Childhood Sexual Abuse*. Toronto: Queer Press, 1991.

Radway, Janice. *Reading the Romance: Women, Patriarchy, and Popular Literature*. Chapel Hill: University of North Carolina Press, 1991.

Ramsey, Sarah H., and Douglas E. Abrams. *Children and the Law in a Nutshell*. 2nd ed. St. Paul, Minn.: West Group, 2003.

Rank, Otto. *The Incest Theme in Literature and Legend: Fundamentals of a Psychology of Literary Creation*. Translated by Gregory C. Richter. Baltimore, Md.: Johns Hopkins University Press, 1992.

———. *Der Mythus von der Geburt des Helden*. Leipzig: Deuticke, 1909.

Rauch, Jonathan. "Washington's Other Sex Scandal." *National Journal* 31.32 (August 7, 1999): 2269–2270.

Reavey, Paula, and Sam Warner, eds. *New Feminist Stories of Child Sexual Abuse: Sexual Scripts and Dangerous Dialogues*. New York: Routledge, 2003.

Reddy, Chandan. "Asian Diasporas, Neo-Liberal Families: Re-Viewing the Case for Homosexual Asylum in the Context of 'Family Rights.'" *Social Text* 84.85 (Fall–Winter 2005): 101–20.

———. "Time for Rights? *Loving*, Gay Marriage, and the Limits of Legal Justice." *Fordham Law Review* 76.6 (2008): 2849–2872.

Richardson, Lonnie Brian. "Notes and Comments: Missing Pieces of Memory: A Rejection of 'Type' Classifications and a Demand for a More Subjective Approach Regarding Adult Survivors of Child Sexual Abuse." *St. Thomas Law Review* 11 (Spring 1999): 515–544.

Richmond, Douglas R. "Bad Science: Repressed and Recovered Memories of Childhood Sexual Abuse." *University of Kansas Law Review* 44 (1996): 517–66.

Rind, Bruce. "Biased Use of Cross-Cultural and Historical Perspectives on Male Homosexuality in Human Sexuality Textbooks." *Journal of Sex Research* 35.4 (1998): 387–407.

Rind, Bruce, Robert Bauserman, and Philip Tromovitch. "Condemnation of a Scientific Article: A Chronology and Refutation of the Attacks and a Discussion of Threats to the Integrity of Science." *Sexuality and Culture* 4.2 (Spring 2000): 1–62.

———. "Debunking the False Allegation of 'Statistical Abuse': A Reply to Spiegel." *Sexuality and Culture* 4.2 (Spring 2000): 101–11.

———. "A Meta-Analytic Examination of Assumed Properties of Child Sexual Abuse Using College Samples." *Psychological Bulletin* 124.1 (1998): 22–53.

Rind, Bruce, and Philip Tromovitch. "A Meta-Analytic Review of Findings from National Samples on Psychological Correlates of Child Sexual Abuse." *Journal of Sex Research* 34.3 (1997): 237–55.

Robbins, Bruce. *Feeling Global: Internationalism in Distress*. New York: New York University Press, 1999.

Roberts, Dorothy. *Killing the Black Body: Race, Reproduction, and the Meaning of Liberty*. New York: Pantheon Books, 1997.

Robertson, Stephen. *Crimes against Children: Sexual Violence and Legal Culture in New York City, 1880–1960*. Chapel Hill : University of North Carolina Press, 2005.

Robin, Michael. "Social Construction of Child Abuse and False Allegations." *Child and Youth Services* 15.2 (1991): 1–34.

Robinson, Cedric. *Black Marxism: The Making of the Black Radical Tradition.* Chapel Hill: University of North Carolina Press, 2000.

Rody, Caroline. *The Daughter's Return: African-American and Caribbean Women's Fictions of History.* New York: Oxford University Press, 2001.

Roediger, David R. *Toward the Abolition of Whiteness: Essays on Race, Politics, and Working Class History.* New York: Verso, 1994.

———. *Wages of Whiteness: Race and the Making of the American Working Class.* New York: Verso, 1999.

Roiphe, Katie. "Making the Incest Scene: In Novel after Novel, Writers Grope for Dark Secrets." *Harper's Magazine* (November 1995): 65–71.

Romaine, Barbara. "On Writing in Tongues: An Experiment in Simulated Literary Translation." *Translation Review* 65 (2003): 16–22.

Ronai, Carol Rambo. "In the Line of Sight at *Public Eye: In Search of a Victim.*" In *New Versions of Victims: Feminists Struggle with the Concept,* edited by Sharon Lamb. New York: New York University Press, 1999. 139–57.

Rose, Jacqueline. *States of Fantasy.* Oxford: Clarendon Press, 1996.

Rose, Nikolas. *Powers of Freedom: Reframing Political Thought.* Cambridge: Cambridge University Press, 1999.

Rosenthal, Debra J. *Race Mixture in Nineteenth-Century U.S. and Spanish American Fictions: Gender, Culture, and Nation Building.* Chapel Hill: University of North Carolina Press, 2004.

Rosenthal, Marguerite, and James A. Louis. "The Law's Evolving Role in Child Abuse and Neglect." In *The Social Context of Child Abuse and Neglect,* edited by Leroy H. Pelton. New York: Human Sciences Press, 1981. 55–89.

Ross, David F., Amye R. Warren, and Lucy S. McGough, eds. "Special Theme: Hearsay Testimony in Trials Involving Child Witnesses." *Psychology, Public Policy, and Law* 5.2 (June 1999).

Rothberg, Michael. *Traumatic Realism: The Demands of Holocaust Representation.* Minneapolis: University of Minnesota Press, 2000.

Rountree, Wendy A. "Overcoming Violence: Blues Expression in Sapphire's *Push.*" *Atenea* 24.1 (June 2004): 133–43.

Rouse, Roger. "Thinking Through Transnationalism: Notes on the Cultural Politics of Class Relations in the Contemporary United States." *Public Culture* 7.2: 353–402.

Rowe, Michael. "'We're As American As You Can Get.'" *Harvard Gay and Lesbian Review* (Winter 1995): 5–10.

Rubin, Gayle. "Thinking Sex: Notes for a Radical Theory of the Politics of Sexuality." In *Pleasure and Danger: Exploring Female Sexuality,* edited by Carole S. Vance. 1984. 267–319.

———. "The Traffic in Women: Notes on the 'Political Economy' of Sex." In *Toward an Anthropology of Women,* edited by R. Reiter. New York: Reiter, 1975. 157–210.

Rubin, Sylvia. "Allison Makes Art of Trauma." *San Francisco Chronicle,* August 16, 1995, E3.

Rush, Florence. *The Best Kept Secret: Sexual Abuse of Children.* Englewood Cliffs, N.J.: Prentice-Hall, 1980.

———. "The Sexual Abuse of Children: A Feminist Point of View." In *Rape: The First Sourcebook for Women,* edited by Noreen Connell and Cassandra Wilson. New York, 1974. 64–75.

Rushdy, Ashraf, H. A. *Remembering Generations: Face and Family in Contemporary African American Fiction.* Chapel Hill: University of North Carolina Press, 2001.

Russell, Diana, E. H. *Behind Closed Doors in White South Africa: Incest Survivors Tell Their Stories.* New York: St. Martin's Press, 1997.

——. "The Incidence and Prevalence of Intra-familial and Extra-familial Sexual Abuse of Female Children." *Child Abuse and Neglect* 7 (1983): 133–46.

——. *The Secret Trauma: Incest in the Lives of Girls and Women.* New York: Basic Books, 1986.

Sacco, Lynn. "Sanitized for Your Protection: Medical Discourse and the Denial of Incest in the United States, 1890–1940." *Journal of Women's History* 14 (Fall 2002): 80–104.

Salten, Melissa G. "Note: Statutes of Limitations in Civil Incest Suits: Preserving the Victim's Remedy." *Harvard Women's Law Journal.* 7 (1984): 189–220.

Saltzman, Lisa, and Eric Rosenberg, eds. *Trauma and Visuality in Modernity.* Hanover, N.H.: University Press of New England, 2006.

San Juan, E., Jr. *Racism and Cultural Studies: Critiques of Multiculturalist Ideology and the Politics of Difference.* Durham, N.C.: Duke University Press, 2002.

Sanchez, George J. "Reading Reginald Denny: The Politics of Whiteness in the Late Twentieth Century." *American Quarterly* 47.3 (September 1995): 388–94.

Sanchez-Eppler, Karen. *Dependent States: The Child's Part in the Nineteenth-Century American Culture.* Chicago, Ill.: University of Chicago Press, 2005.

——. "Temperance in the Bed of a Child: Incest and Social Order in Nineteenth-Century America." *American Quarterly* 47.1 (March 1995): 1–33.

Santner, Eric L. *Stranded Objects: Mourning, Memory, and Film in Postwar Germany.* Ithaca, N.Y.: Cornell University Press, 1990.

Sapphire. *Push.* New York: Vintage Books, 1996.

Sarat, Austin, and Jonathan Simon. "Cultural Analysis, Cultural Studies, and the Situation of Legal Scholarship." In *Cultural Analysis, Cultural Studies, and the Law: Moving Beyond Legal Realism,* edited by Austin Sarat and Jonathan Simon. Durham, N.C.: Duke University Press, 2003. 1–34.

Sarat, Austin, and Thomas R. Kearns, eds. *Law in the Domains of Culture.* Ann Arbor: University of Michigan Press, 1998.

Sassen, Saskia. *Globalization and Its Discontents: Essays on the New Mobility of People and Money.* New York: New Press, 1998.

Satter, Beryl. "The Sexual Abuse Paradigm in Historical Perspective: Passivity and Emotion in Mid-Twentieth-Century America." *Journal of the History of Sexuality* 12.3 (2003): 424–64.

Scarre, George, ed. *Children, Parents, and Politics.* New York: Cambridge University Press, 1989.

Scarry, Elaine. *The Body in Pain: The Making and Unmaking of the World.* New York: Oxford University Press, 1985.

Schachner, Michael. "'False Memory' Risk Surfaces: Providing Mental Health Benefits Could Lead to Lawsuits." *Business Insurance* 28.26 (June 27, 1994): 14–15.

Schacter, Daniel L., and Elaine Scarry, eds. *Memory, Brain, and Belief.* Cambridge, Mass.: Harvard University Press, 2000.

Scheflin, Alan W. "Ground Lost: The False Memory/Recovered Memory Therapy Debate." *Psychiatric Times* 16.11 (November 1999). Available at www.psychiatrictimes.com.

Schneider, David. *A Critique of the Study of Kinship.* Ann Arbor: University of Michigan Press, 1984.

Schulhofer, Stephen J. *Unwanted Sex: The Culture of Intimidation and the Failure of Law.* Cambridge, Mass.: Harvard University Press, 1998.

Schultz, Leroy, and Preston Jones. "Sexual Abuse of Children: Issues for Social Service and Health Professionals." *Child Welfare* 62.2 (1983): 99–108.

Schultz, Vicki. "Reconceptualizing Sexual Harassment." *Yale Law Journal* 107.6 (April 1998): 1683–1805.

Scott, Ann. "Feminism and the Seductiveness of the 'Real Event.'" *Feminist Review* 28 (January 1988): 88–102.

Scott, Joan, and Louise Tilly. *Women, Work and Family.* New York: Methuen, 1987.

Searles, Patricia, and Ronald J. Berger, eds. *Rape and Society: Readings in the Problem of Sexual Assault.* Boulder, Colo.: Westview Press, 1995.

Sedgwick, Eve Kosofsky. *Epistemology of the Closet.* Berkeley: University of California Press, 1990.

———. "A Poem Is Being Written." In *Tendencies.* Durham, N.C.: Duke University Press, 1993. 177–214.

Seltzer, Mark. *Serial Killers: Death and Life in America's Wound Culture.* New York: Routledge, 1998.

Shah, Nayan. "Between 'Oriental Depravity' and 'Natural Degenerates': Spatial Borderlands and the Making of Ordinary Americans." *American Quarterly* 57.3 (2005): 703–25.

———. *Contagious Divides: Epidemics and Race in San Francisco's Chinatown.* Berkeley: University of California Press, 2001.

Sharpe, Jenny. *Allegories of Empire: The Figure of Woman in the Colonial Text.* Minneapolis: University of Minnesota Press, 1993.

———. *Ghosts of Slavery: A Literary Archaeology of Black Women's Lives.* Minneapolis: University of Minnesota Press, 2003.

Shell, Marc. *The End of Kinship: 'Measure for Measure,' Incest, and the Ideal of Universal Siblinghood.* Stanford, Conn.: Stanford University Press, 1988.

Showalter, Elaine. *Hystories: Hysterical Epidemics and Modern Culture.* New York: Columbia University Press, 1997.

Sielke, Sabine. *Reading Rape: The Rhetoric of Sexual Violence in American Literature and Culture, 1790 – 1990.* Princeton, N.J.: Princeton University Press, 2002.

Silverman, Kaja. "The Lacanian Phallus." *differences* 4.1 (1992): 84–115.

———. *Male Subjectivity at the Margins.* New York: Routledge, 1992.

Simon, Bennet. "Fact and Fantasy in the History of Freud's Views on Incest and Seduction." *History of Psychiatry* 17.3 (September 1994): 571–81.

Simon, Leonore. "Symposium: Therapeutic Jurisprudence: Sex Offender Legislation and the Antitherapeutic Effects on Victims." *Arizona Law Review* 41 (Summer 1999): 485–533.

Smiley, Jane. *A Thousand Acres.* New York: Random House, 1991.

Smith, Anna Marie. "The Sexual Regulations Dimension of Contemporary Welfare Law: A Fifty State Overview." *Michigan Journal of Gender and Law* 8.2 (2002): 121–218.

Smith, Steven R. "Mental Health Malpractice in the 1990s." *Houston Law Review* 28 (1991): 209–84.

Smith, Thomas R. "How Our Lives Become Stories: Making Selves (review)." *Biography* 23.3 (Summer 2000): 534–38.

Soifer, Aviam. "Moral Ambition, Formalism, and the 'Free World' of DeShaney." *George Washington Law Review* 57 (1989): 1513–1532.

Soja, Edward W. *Postmodern Geographies: The Reassertion of Space in Critical Social Theory.* London: Verso, 1989.

Somerville, Siobhan. "Queer *Loving*." *GLQ: A Journal of Lesbian and Gay Studies* 11.3 (2005): 335–70.

Sommer, Doris. *Foundational Fictions: The National Romances of Latin America.* Berkeley: University of California Press, 1991.

Sommerville, C. John. *The Rise and Fall of Childhood.* Beverly Hills: Sage Publications, 1982.

Sophocles. *Oedipus the King.* Translated by Bernard Knox. New York: Pocket Books, 2005.

Sorensen, Robert C. *Adolescent Sexuality in Contemporary America (The Sorensen Report).* New York: World Publishing, 1973.

Spadaro, Joseph A. "An Elusive Search for the Truth: The Admissibility of Repressed and Recovered Memories in Light of Daubert v. Merrell Dow Pharmaceuticals, Inc." *Connecticut Law Review* 30 (1998): 1147–1198.

Spiegel, David. "The Price of Abusing Children and Numbers." *Sexuality and Culture* 4.2 (Spring 2000): 63–66.

———. "Suffer the Children: Long-Term Effects of Sexual Abuse." *Society* 37.4 (May–June 2000): 18–20.

Spillers, Hortense. "'All the Things You Could Be If Sigmund Freud's Wife Was Your Mother': Psychoanalysis and Race." In *Black, White, and in Color: Essays on American Literature and Culture.* Chicago, Ill.: University of Chicago Press, 2003. 376–427.

———. "Mama's Baby, Papa's Maybe: An American Grammar Book." *Diacritics* (Summer 1987): 65–81.

———. "'The Permanent Obliquity of an In[pha]llibly Straight': In the Time of the Daughters and Fathers." In *Daughters and Fathers,* edited by Lynda E. Boose and Betty S. Flowers. Baltimore, Md.: Johns Hopkins University Press, 1989. 157–80.

Spinner, Jenny. "When 'Macaroni and Cheese Is Good' Enough: Revelation in Creative Nonfiction." *Pedagogy* 4.2 (Spring 2004): 316–22.

Spivak, Gayatri Chakravorty. "The Rani of Sirmur: An Essay in Reading the Archives." *History and Theory* 24.3 (October 1985): 247–72.

———. "Scattered Speculations on the Question of Value." 1985. Reprinted in *The Spivak Reader: Selected Works of Gayatri Chakravorty Spivak,* edited by Donna Landry and Gerald MacLean. New York: Routledge, 1996. 107–40.

Stacey, Judith. *Brave New Families: Stories of Domestic Upheaval in Late Twentieth-Century America.* New York: Basic Books, 1990.

———. *In the Name of the Family: Rethinking Family Values in the Postmodern Age.* Boston, Mass.: Beacon Press, 1996.

Stanford, Ann Folwell. "It Tried to Take My Tongue: Domestic Violence, Healing, and Voice in Sandra Cisneros's 'Woman Hollering Creek,' Bebe Moore Campbell's *Your Blues Ain't Like Mine,* and Sapphire's *Push.*" In *Bodies in a Broken World: Women Novelists of Color and the Politics of Medicine.* Chapel Hill, N.C.: University of North Carolina Press, 2003. 109–36.

Stanley, Amy Dru. *From Bondage to Contract: Wage Labor, Marriage, and the Market in the Age of Slave Emancipation.* Cambridge: Cambridge University Press, 1998.

Stavig, Ward. "'Living in Offense of Our Lord': Indigenous Sexual Values and Marital Life in the Colonial Crucible." *Hispanic American Historical Review* 75.4 (1995): 597–622.

Stein, Gertrude. *Everybody's Autobiography.* Cambridge, Mass.: Exact Change, 1993.

Stein, Theodore J. *Child Welfare and the Law.* Washington, D.C.: CWLA Press, 1998.

Steinberg, Sybil. "*Cavedweller.*" *Publishers Weekly* 245.18 (May 4, 1998): 35.

Steinmetz, George, ed. *State/Culture: State-Formation after the Cultural Turn.* Ithaca, N.Y.: Cornell University Press, 1999.

Stephens, Sharon, ed. *Children and the Politics of Culture.* Princeton, N.J.: Princeton University Press, 1995.

Stewart, Susan. "Exogamous Relations: Travel Writing, the Incest Prohibition, and Hawthorne's *Transformation.*" In *Culture/Contexture: Explorations in Anthropology and Literary Studies,* edited by E. Valerie Daniel and Jeffrey M. Peck. Berkeley: University of California Press. 132–55.

Stoler, Ann Laura. *Carnal Knowledge and Imperial Power: Race and the Intimate in Colonial Rule.* Berkeley: University of California Press, 2002.

——. *Race and the Education of Desire: Foucault's History of Sexuality and the Colonial Order of Things.* Durham, N.C.: Duke University Press, 1995.

Strickland, Ronald, ed. *Growing Up Postmodern: Neoliberalism and the War on the Young.* Lanham, Md.: Rowman and Littlefield, 2002.

Summit, Roland C. "The Child Sexual Abuse Accommodation Syndrome." *Child Abuse and Neglect* 7 (1983): 177–93.

Survivors of Child Sexual Abuse. "Noticeboard." *Feminist Review* 28 (January 1988): 3.

Tal, Kali. *Worlds of Hurt: Reading the Literatures of Trauma.* New York: Cambridge University Press, 1996.

Tate, Claudia. *Domestic Allegories of Political Desire: The Black Heroine's Text at the Turn of the Century.* New York: Oxford University Press, 1992.

——. *Psychoanalysis and Black Novels: Desire and the Protocols of Race.* New York: Oxford University Press, 1998.

Tate, Linda. *A Southern Weave of Women: Fiction of the Contemporary South.* Athens: University of Georgia Press.

Tavris, Carol. "The Uproar over Sexual Abuse Research and Its Finding." *Society* 37.4 (May–June 2000): 15–17.

Temkin, Jennifer. "Do We Need the Crime of Incest?" *Current Legal Problems* 44 (1991): 185–216.

Terdiman, Richard. *Present Past: Modernity and the Memory Crisis.* Ithaca, N.Y.: Cornell University Press, 1993.

Terr, Lenore. *Unchained Memories: True Stories of Traumatic Memories, Lost and Found.* New York: Basic Books, 1994.

Thomas, Brook. *American Literary Realism and the Failed Promise of Contract.* Berkeley: University of California Press, 1997.

Thorslev, Peter. "Incest as Romantic Symbol." *Comparative Literature Studies* 2 (1965): 41–58.

Tompkins, Jane. *Sensational Designs: The Cultural Work of American Fiction, 1790–1860.* New York: Oxford University Press, 1985.

Triplett, Hall. "The Misnomer of Freud's 'Seduction Theory.'" *Journal of the History of Ideas* 65.4 (2004): 647–65.

Trumbach, Randolph. *The Rise of the Egalitarian Family: Aristocratic Kinship and Domestic Relations in Eighteenth-Century England.* New York: Academic Press, 1978.

Tsang, Daniel, ed. *The Age Taboo: Gay Male Sexuality, Power, and Consent.* London: Gay Men's Press, 1981.

Twitchell, James. *Forbidden Partners: The Incest Taboo in Modern Culture.* New York: Columbia University Press, 1987.

van Boheemen, Christine. *The Novel as Family Romance: Language, Gender, and Authority from Fielding to Joyce.* Ithaca, N.Y.: Cornell University Press, 1987.

van der Kolk, Bessel, ed. *Psychological Trauma.* Washington, D.C.: American Psychiatric Press, 1987.

van der Kolk, Bessel A., and Onno van der Hart. "The Intrusive Past: The Flexibility of Memory and the Engraving of Trauma." In *Trauma: Explorations in Memory,* edited by Cathy Caruth. Baltimore, Md.: Johns Hopkins University Press, 1995. 158–82.

Van Duyn, Amy L. "Note: The Scarlet Letter Branding: A Constitutional Analysis of Community Notification Provisions in Sex Offender Statutes." *Drake Law Review* 47 (1999): 635–59.

Van Haute, Philippe, and Tomas Geyskens, eds. *Confusion of Tongues: The Primacy of Sexuality in Freud, Ferenczi, and Laplanche.* New York: The Other Press, 2004.

Vandevelde, Kenneth J. "The New Property of the Nineteenth Century: The Development of the Modern Concept of Property." *Buffalo Law Review* 29.2 (Spring 1980): 325–70.

Vergès, Françoise. *Monsters and Revolutionaries: Colonial Romance and Métissage.* Durham, N.C.: Duke University Press, 1999.

Vickroy, Laura. *Trauma and Survival in Contemporary Fiction.* Charlottesville: University of Virginia Press, 2002.

Viego, Antonio. *Dead Subjects: Toward a Politics of Loss in Latino Studies.* Durham, N.C.: Duke University Press, 2007.

Vlachou, Andiana, ed. *Contemporary Economic Theory: Radical Critiques of Neoliberalism.* New York: St Martin's Press, 1999.

Vogel, Paula. *How I Learned to Drive.* New York: Dramatists Play Service Inc., 1997.

Volpp, Leti. "(Mis)Identifying Culture: Asian Women and the 'Cultural Defense.'" *Harvard Women's Law Journal* 17 (1994): 57–102.

Von Braun, Christina. "*Blutschande*: From the Incest Taboo to the Nuremberg Racial Laws." In *Encountering the Other(s): Studies in Literature, History and Culture,* edited by Gisela Brinker-Gabler. Albany: State University of New York Press, 1995. 127–48.

von Krafft-Ebing, Richard. *Psychopathia Sexualis.* Translated by Franklin S. Klaf. New York: Arcade, 1965.

Waites, Matthew. *The Age of Consent: Young People, Sexuality, and Citizenship.* London: Palgrave, 2005.

Wakefield, Hollida, and Ralph Underwager. *Return of the Furies: An Investigation into Recovered Memory Therapy.* Chicago, Ill.: Open Court Publishing, 1994.

Walker, Alice. *The Color Purple.* Orlando, Fl.: Harcourt, 1982.

Walker, Janet. *Trauma Cinema: Documenting Incest and the Holocaust.* Berkeley: University of California Press, 2005.

Wallenstein, Peter. "Interlude: Polygamy, Incest, Fornication, Cohabitation—And Interracial Marriage." In *Tell the Court I Love My Wife: Race, Marriage, and Law—An American History.* New York: Palgrave Macmillan, 2002. 123–32.

Wallerstein, Immanuel. *After Liberalism.* New York: New Press, 1995.

Walters, David R. *Physical and Sexual Abuse of Children: Causes and Treatment.* Bloomington: Indiana University Press, 1975.

Walton, Jean. *Fair Sex, Savage Dreams: Race, Psychoanalysis, Sexual Difference.* Durham, N.C.: Duke University Press, 2001.

Ward, Elizabeth. *Father-Daughter Rape.* London: Women's Press, 1984.

Warner, Michael. *The Letters of the Republic: Publication and the Public Sphere in Eighteenth-Century America.* Cambridge, Mass.: Harvard University Press, 1990.

———. *The Trouble with Normal: Sex, Politics, and the Ethics of Queer Life.* New York: Free Press, 1999.

Warren, Samuel, and Louis Brandeis. "The Right to Privacy." *Harvard Law Review* 4.5 (1890): 193–220.

Watson, R. "Sexual Abuse: The Growing Outcry Over Child Molesting." *Newsweek,* May 14, 1984: 30–36.

Watt, Ian. *The Rise of the Novel: Studies in Defoe, Richardson, Fielding.* Berkeley: University of California Press, 1957.

Watters, Ethan. "Doors of Memory." *Mother Jones* (January–February 1993): 24–29, 76–77.

Weinbaum, Alys Eve. *Wayward Reproductions: Genealogies of Race and Nation in Transatlantic Modern Thought.* Durham, N.C.: Duke University Press, 2004.

Weinberg, S. Kirson. *Incest Behavior.* New York: Citadel Press, 1955.

Weinstein, Stuart. "Repressed Memory Revisted: Popular Culture's Impact on the Law-Psychotherapy Debate." *Law and Popular Culture: Current Legal Issues,* Vol. 7. Edited by Michael Freeman. New York: Oxford University Press, 2004.

Weiss, J., et al. "A Study of Girl Sex Victims." *Psychiatric Quarterly Supplement* 29 (1955): 1–28.

White, Hayden. *Tropics of Discourse: Essays in Cultural Criticism.* Baltimore, Md.: Johns Hopkins University Press, 1978.

Wiegman, Robyn. "Intimate Publics: Race, Property, and Personhood." *American Literature* 74.4 (December 2002): 859–85.

———. "Whiteness Studies and the Paradox of Particularity." *Boundary 2* 26.3 (1999): 115–50.

Williams, Daniel. "The Gratification of That Corrupt and Lawless Passion: Character Types and Themes in Early New England Rape Narratives." In *A Mixed Race: Ethnicity in Early America,* edited by Frank Shuffelton. New York: Oxford University Press, 1993. 194–221.

Williams, Linda Meyer. "Recall of Childhood Trauma: A Prospective Study of Women's Memories of Child Sexual Abuse." *Journal of Consulting and Clinical Psychology* 62.2 (1994): 1167–1176.

Williams, Linda Meyer, and Victoria L. Banyard, eds. *Trauma and Memory.* Thousand Oaks, Calif.: Sage Publications, 1998.

Williams, Patricia. *The Alchemy of Race and Rights.* Cambridge, Mass.: Harvard University Press, 1991.

Williams, Raymond. *Marxism and Literature.* Oxford: Oxford University Press, 1977.

Williamson, John. "What Should the World Bank Think about the Washington Consensus?" *World Bank Research Observer,* 15.2 (August 2000): 251–64.

Wilson, Elizabeth. "Not in This House: Incest, Denial, and Doubt in the White Middle-Class Family." *Yale Journal of Criticism* 8.1 (1995): 35–57.

Wilson, Melba. *Crossing the Boundary: Black Women Survive Incest.* London: Seal Press, 1993.

Wolff, Geoffrey. *The Age of Consent.* New York: Knopf, 1995.

Wollons, Roberta, ed. *Children at Risk in America: History, Concepts, and Public Policy.* New York: State University of New York Press, 1993.

Wood, Jennifer K. "Refined Raw: The Symbolic Violence of Victims' Rights Reforms." *College Literature* 26.1 (Winter 1999): 150–69.

Woodhouse, Barbara Bennett. "Constitutional Interpretation and the Re-constitution of the Family in the United States and South Africa." In *The Changing Family: Family Forms and Family Law,* edited by John Eekelaar and Thandabantu Nhlapo. Oxford: Hart Publishing, 1998. 463–82.

———. "'Who Owns the Child?': Meyer and Pierce and the Child as Property." *William and Mary Law Review* 33 (1992): 995–1122.

Woodward, Kathy. "Statistical Panic." *differences* 11.2 (1999): 177–203.

Wray, Matt. *Not Quite White: White Trash and the Boundaries of Whiteness.* Durham, N.C.: Duke University Press, 2006.

Wright, Lawrence. "Remembering Satan." *New Yorker:* part 1, May 17, 1993, 60–81; part 2, May 24, 1993, 54–76.

Yaeger, Patricia. "Consuming Trauma; or, The Pleasures of Merely Circulating." In *Extremities: Trauma, Testimony, and Community,* edited by Nancy K. Miller and Jason Tougaw. Urbana: University of Illinois Press, 2002. 25–51.

———, ed. *Refiguring the Father: New Feminist Readings of Patriarchy.* Carbondale: Southern Illinois University Press, 1989.

Yanagisako, Sylvia, and Carol Delaney, eds. *Naturalizing Power: Essays in Feminist Cultural Analysis.* New York: Routledge, 1995.

Yantzi, Mark. *Sexual Offending and Restoration.* Scottdale, Pa.: Herald Press, 1998.

Yardley, Jonathan. "Blab, Memory." *Washington Post,* February 14, 2000, C02.

Yoneyama, Lisa. *Hiroshima Traces: Time, Space, and the Dialectics of Memory.* Berkeley: University of California Press, 1999.

Yoshikawa, Mako. "The New Face of Incest? Race, Class, and the Controversy over Kathryn Harrison's *The Kiss.*" In *Incest and the Literary Imagination,* edited by Elizabeth Barnes. Gainesville: University Press of Florida, 2002. 358–76.

Young, Allan. *The Harmony of Illusions: Inventing Post-Traumatic Stress Disorder.* Princeton, N.J.: Princeton University Press, 1997.

Young, Elizabeth. "Southern Cross." *Village Voice* 43.11 (March 17 1998): 124.

Young, James E. *The Texture of Memory: Holocaust Memorials and Meaning.* New Haven, Conn.: Yale University Press, 1993.

Yúdice, George. *The Expediency of Culture: Uses of Culture in the Global Era.* Durham, N.C.: Duke University Press, 2003.

Yukins, Elizabeth. "Bastard Daughters and the Possession of History in *Corregidora* and *Paradise.*" *Signs* 28.1 (Autumn 2002): 221–47.

Zaretsky, Eli. *Capitalism, the Family, and Personal Life.* New York: Harper and Row, 1976.

———. "The Culture Wars of the 1960s and the Assault on the Presidency: The Meaning of the Clinton Impeachment." In *Our Monica, Ourselves,* edited by Lauren Berlant and Lisa Duggan. New York: New York University Press, 2001. 9–33.

Zelizer, Viviana A. *Pricing the Priceless Child: The Changing Social Value of Children.* New York: Basic Books, 1985.

Zender, Karl F. "Faulkner and the Politics of Incest." *American Literature* 70.4 (1998): 739–65.

Zimmerman, Shirley L. *Family Policy: Constructed Solutions to Family Problems.* Thousand Oaks, Calif.: Sage Publications, 2001.

Žižek, Slavoj. *The Sublime Object of Ideology.* New York: Verso, 1989.

Zuriff, G. E. "Pedophilia and the Culture Wars." *Public Interest* 138 (Winter 2000): 29–39.

Index

Abraham, K., 55
"Acting Out the Oedipal Wish" (Devlin), 56
activism, 60, 67, 72–73, 75
Acts of Parliament, Statute of Westminster I (1275), 43
Adler, Jerry, 70, 71, 95, 251n2, 252n25
adolescents, 65, 198, 260n14
Adolescent Sexuality in Contemporary America (Sorenson), 204
"Aetiology of Hysteria, The" (Freud), 83
"After Lot's Daughters" (Frost), 214, 215
agency, 36, 66, 132; accident story and, 162; authorial/representational, 148–49, 151, 180; childhood, 84; civil, 197, 227; cultural, 162; daughter's, 148, 188; fantasy as, 13; female, 216; legal, 62, 65–66, 168; market, 126; social, 162, 169; working-class, 161. *See also* sexual agency
Alchemy of Race and Rights, The (Williams), 123
Alcoff, Linda, 73
Alexander, M. Jacqui, 233
Allen, Charlotte Vale, 74
alliance, deployment of, 35, 36, 40, 41

Allison, Dorothy, 10, 152, 154, 258n1, 258n4, 259n13; as author-survivor, 187; on *Bastard,* 186; family violence and, 23; literary technique and, 155; mainstream literary taste and, 152; realist style of, 154; tragedy and, 187; Young on, 153–54
"Almost Famous: The Rise of 'Nobody' Memoir" (Adams), 3
Amber Alert, 112, 256n62
American Medical Association, 86
American Psychiatric Association, 81
American Psychological Association (APA), 85–86, 192, 193
Anagnost, Ann, 225, 262n32
Anderson, Benedict, 4, 14
Angelou, Maya, 10, 74, 115
Anney, 163, 164; Bone and, 162, 165, 185; Daddy Glen and, 184, 185; Glen's hands and, 173–74
anthropology, 26, 27, 29, 30
Anti-Drug Abuse Act (1986–88), 251n13
Antler, Stephen, 50
Appelbaum, Paul, 255n52
Archard, David, 136, 196, 197
Archibald, Elizabeth, 42
Archive of Feelings, An (Cvetkovich), 80

Armstrong, Louise, 21, 67, 75, 234;
on incest industry, 78; *Kiss Daddy
Goodnight* and, 74, 115; on
sexual use of children, 58–59
Armstrong, Nancy, 159
articulation, 13, 19, 63, 76, 191, 211,
220; fantasy as, 15–18, 20, 22, 85,
188; incest, 68, 189, 234, 235, 236;
Marxist discourse of, 15; national/
exceptionalist, 233; point of, 253n26;
principle/process/point of, 15, 219,
228, 253n26; race and, 41, 79, 189;
radical, 231, 236; social, 107. *See also*
orthogonal articulation
Ashcroft v. Free Speech (2002), 263n2
"Asian Diasporas, Neo-Liberal Families"
(Reddy), 225
"Assault on Freud, The" (Gray), 70, 91
Assault on Truth, The (Masson), 83
"Author as Producer, The" (Benjamin),
155
"Autobiographical Study, An" (Freud),
252n26

Baker, Houston A., 148
Baker, Moira, 167, 186, 205
Baldwin, James, 10
Balibar, Etienne, 4, 14, 20
Bamyeh, Mohammed A., 112
Barnes, Djuna, 116
Barnett, Louise, 44
Barr, Roseanne, 2
Barthes, Roland, 166
Bass, Ellen, xiv–xv, 75
"Bastard Daughters and the Possession of
History" (Yukins), 122
Bastard out of Carolina (Allison), 2, 23,
187; literary technique of, 159, 187;
praise for, 154; publication of, 152,
153; social realism/family romance and,
24; as survivor story, 154
battered child syndrome, 51
Baudelaire, Charles, 98
Bauserman, Robert, 188, 191, 201
beating scene, 174–79
"Believing in Literature" (Allison), 152
Bell, David, 199
Bell, Vikki, xv, 12, 42, 44
Beloved (Morrison), 147
Bender, L., 55

Bender, Thomas, 119
Benjamin, Walter, 22, 69, 72, 112, 138,
150, 257n14; on allegory, 98, 129; on
memory, 11, 123; social realism and,
155
Berlant, Lauren, 8, 110, 198; exploited
child and, 80; public intimacy and, 199,
207; trauma/recovery and, 79–80
"Berlin Chronicle, A" (Benjamin), 11, 69,
123
Berns, Roberta M., 67
Best, Stephen, 19, 62, 65–66
Best Kept Secret, The (Rush), 2
Between the Body and the Flesh (Hart),
177
Bienen, Leigh, 60, 228, 229; incest laws
and, 42, 44; on legal reforms, 63; on
sexual abuse prosecutions, 250n50
Binnie, Jon, 199
biopolitics, 38, 39, 41, 54, 139, 190,
206
biopower, 37–38, 41, 67; limits of, 39, 40,
42, 59, 234; meaning value of, 44;
orthogonal articulation of, 42, 67;
trauma and, 81
"Blab, Memory" (Yardley), 3
Black Atlantic, The (Gilroy), 120
black middle class: rise of, 10, 134
black women: agency of, 151; antiracist
articulations of, 79; novels/
autobiographies of, 115–16; sexual
abuse and, 116, 118
Blau, A., 55
Bluest Eye, The (Morrison), 74, 115
Blume, E. Sue, 86
Boatwright men: accidental violence and,
173–74; beating by, 184; as social
problem, 161
Bogle, Marlene T., 78–79, 252n15
Bone: Anney and, 162, 165, 185; beating
scene and, 175; Daddy Glen and, 166,
173–74, 177, 185, 186; fantasy and,
177–78, 179, 181, 182–83, 185;
kinship story and, 162; naming of,
160–61; narrative agency and, 174,
180, 183; patriarchal violence and,
185–86; rape scene and, 185;
representational failure and, 176;
sexual abuse of, 165, 185; Shannon
and, 176, 180–83

Bowman, Cynthia Grant, 108, 109, 255n54, 255n57
Boyd, Blanche McCrary, 154
Brady, Katherine, 74
Breau, Elizabeth, 128, 145–46
Breuer, Josef, 81, 90, 246n3
Breuer-Freud cathartic method, 81
Britt, Donna, 114
"Brixton Black Women's Centre" (Bogle), 78
Brown, Charles Brockden, 1
Brown, Daniel, 254n48, 255n52
Brown, Wendy, xvii, 133, 135, 196, 226
Brown, William, 81
Brown, William Wells, 258n25
Bryant, Anita, 260n10
Buck, Chris, 95; photo by, 97
Burman, Erica, 232
"But Enough about Us" (Miller), 1
Butler, Judith, 245n21, 246n5, 247n12
Butler, Sandra, 56, 57–58

Cahill, Courtney Megan, 42, 44–45, 46, 53
Caldwell, Erskine, 244n2
Califa, Pat, 227
California Penal Code, 250n48
California Task Force to Promote Self-Esteem and Personal and Social Responsibility, 76–77
Cannon, Walter B., 252n19
capitalism, 12, 20, 22, 23, 71, 133, 138, 157, 171; global/transnational, 170, 225, 258n8; kinship and, 129, 171; racial, 19, 129
Capturing the Friedmans (documentary), ix, x, xi, xiv, 243n1
Carnal Knowledge and Imperial Power (Stoler), 234
Caruth, Cathy, 6, 118, 119
Cavedweller (Allison), 153, 258n1
Centers for Disease Control (CDC), 9
Charcot, Jean-Martin, 29, 81, 246n2, 246n3
Cherniavsky, Eva, 21, 232, 234
Cheshier, William Lesley, 109, 256n59
child abuse, 49, 50, 57, 77, 259n14; analogy of, 60; child sexual abuse and, 61; definitions of, 53; discovery of, 51;

disease model of, 52; laws, 53, 63; protection from, 52, 53; sex crime and, 62
Child Abuse Accountability Act (1994), 260n13
Child Abuse Prevention and Treatment Act (CAPTA) (1934), 249n36
Child Abuse Protection and Enforcement Act (2000), 256n62
Child, Family, School, Community (Berns), 67
childhood: adolescents and, 198; legal, 196; scholarship on, 25; sexual expression in, 199; status definition of, 197
"Child Is Being Beaten, A" (Freud), 24, 178, 179, 183
child labor law, 50, 233, 249n31
child neglect, 51, 52, 57, 205
child pornography, ix, x, 231–32, 262n1, 263n2
Child Pornography Prevention Act (CPPA) (1996), 231, 260n13, 262n1, 263n2
child protection, 22, 27, 47, 50, 51, 52, 57, 60, 61, 67, 249n32; federal jurisdiction over, 249n31; implementation of, 53–54
child protective services, 46, 47, 48, 50, 53, 58, 59, 61, 62
Child Protective Services (CPS), 9
"Children, Adults, Sex and the Criminal Law" (Phipps), 64
Children in Focus (American Association for Health, Physical Education and Recreation), 66
"Child Saving in Modern America" (Cravens), 49
child sexual abuse, ix, xiii, 9, 21, 59, 65, 67, 82–83, 84, 99, 115, 189, 192–93, 201, 205, 209; debates about, xi–xii; defining, 61, 64, 201; empirical claims about, 202; formal properties of, 201–2; gendered experience of, 87; impact of, xv, 200, 202, 205; laws, 63–64; medical terminology for, 60; myths of, 78; prosecution of, xiii, 62, 100; reality of, xv, 90, 92; response to, 61; social validity of, 101; stories of, 73, 91; studies of, 25, 200

"Child Sexual Abuse" (Baker and
Duncan), 205
"Child Sexual Abuse Accommodation
Syndrome, The" (Summit), 62
child welfare, xvi, 46–48, 49, 50, 62,
249n32; disciplinary institutions of,
60; services, 51, 52; socioeconomic
contexts of, 51; transformation of,
52
"Child Welfare History in the United
States" (Cohen), 52
Chomsky, Noam, 191
Christian Coalition, 260n8
Chuh, Candice, 121
citizenship, 170, 197, 198, 235, 236;
capitalist, 112; infantile, 8, 10;
racialized, 20
civilization, 30, 31, 32
civil society, 126, 135, 227, 262n33
civil suits, 100, 101, 110
class, 15, 157, 259n10; as experience,
158; race and, 41
Clinton-Lewinsky affair, 194
Clotel (Brown), 258n25
Cohen, Neil, 52
"Collective Memory and the Actual Past"
(Knapp), 117
Color Purple, The (Walker), 74, 219,
223
commodity, 18, 19, 134
Commonwealth v. Lavigne (1997), 64
*Complete Letters of Sigmund Freud to
Wilhelm Fliess, The* (Masson), 83
consciousness-raising groups, xv, 9, 73
consent, 43, 64, 133, 141, 191, 215, 224,
231; age of, 63, 192–99, 232, 233,
249n32; context of, 211, 212; contract
and, 134, 196; level of, 201, 204;
limitations of, 189, 195–96;
manufacturing, 190; politics of, 97,
198
Conspiracy of Silence (Butler), 56
Conte, Jon Robert, 254n48
contract: consent and, 134, 196
Corregidora (Jones), 115
countersuggestion, 90, 93, 99, 105, 107
Courage to Heal, The (Bass and Davis),
xiv–xv, 74, 75
CPPA. *See* Child Pornography Prevention
Act

Cravens, Hamilton, 49
"Creative Writers and Day Dreaming"
(Freud), 16–17
Crenshaw, Kimberle, 78
Crews, Frederick, x, 71, 88, 89, 90
Crichton, Michael, 216
Crile, George W., 252n19
Crime Identification Technology Act
(1998), 256n62
criminal justice, 9, 54, 57, 59, 62, 100
"Crossover Blues" (Boyd), 154
"Cruelest Crime, Sexual Abuse of
Children, The" (McCall), 75
Cruickshank, Barbara, 47, 48, 54, 77
cultural imperialism, 25, 232, 235,
236
cultural logics, xvii, xviii, 7, 8, 172
culture, 3, 9, 10, 57, 80, 170, 235; as
difference, 7, 153, 159; national, 127,
195; postmodern concept of, 172;
white trash, 172; working-class, 164,
165. *See also* popular culture
Culture in the Age of Three Worlds
(Denning), 157, 170
Curry, Renee, 154
Cvetkovich, Ann, 80

Daddy Glen. *See* Waddell, Glen
Daddy's Girl (Allen), 74
Daly, Kathleen, 229, 230
"Dangerous Direction, A" (Bowman and
Mertz), 108
Darwin, Charles, 30, 31, 71
Daubert rule, 104, 105, 106
Daubert v. Merrell Dow Pharmaceutical
(1993), 102, 103, 254n42
Daughter's Return, The (Rody), 122
Davis, Laura, xiv–xv, 75
Debord, Guy, 22, 75
Defoe, Daniel, 243n2
delayed-discovery rules, 100, 112
Denning, Michael, 157, 158, 170
deployments, 35, 36, 37, 41, 134, 225
"Der Familienroman der Neurotiker"
(Freud), 12–13
de Saussure, Ferdinand, 33
desire, 18, 29–30, 41, 135, 139–44, 147,
182; childhood, 84; familial, 210; lust
and, 212; oedipal, 180; unspeakable,
212

Desire and Domestic Fiction (Armstrong), 159

Devlin, Rachel, 56, 249n40

Diagnostic and Statistical Manual of Mental Disorders (DSM-III), 81, 82, 83

Diedrich, Susan, 43

Dillon v. Legg (1968), 108, 255n56

Dimock, Wai Chee, 229, 230, 231, 236

Diotima, 125, 127

disciplinary childhood: incest and, 47–54

discipline, 41, 52, 53, 56

Doane, Janice, xx, 88, 214, 215

"Does Childhood Sexual Abuse Cause Adult Psychiatric Disorders?" (Pope and Hudson), 206

domesticity, 112, 122, 132, 133, 139, 225, 233

Donzelot, Jacues, 48

Douglass, Frederick, 257n23

droit, 36, 37, 38, 40, 59

Durkheim, Émile, 29

dysfunction, 36, 205–6, 261n20

EchoHawk, Larry, 233

Economic Opportunity Act (1964), 251n12

Edwards, Brent, 16, 245n22

Elementary Structures of Kinship, The (Lévi-Strauss), 126

Elliott, J. F., 66, 206

Ellison, Ralph, 1, 115

empire, 23, 28, 112, 126, 233

Empire (Hardt and Negri), 6

End of History and the Last Man, The (Fukuyama), 71, 244n6

Epistemology of the Closet (Sedgwick), 46

Erichsen, John, 252n19

Erickson, Julia A., 203

ethnicity, 4, 14, 20

Evans, David, 65

"Experiencing of Sexual Traumas as a Form of Sexual Activity, The" (Abraham), 55

expert testimony, 102, 107

exploitation, xvi, xviii, 58–59, 61, 80, 198, 233–34, 261n24; harm from, 214; slave owners and, 128

false memory, xiv, xviii, 88–93, 95, 98–99, 101–2, 232, 253n33

false memory syndrome (FMS), 89, 90, 115, 232, 253n34

False Memory Syndrome Foundation (FMSF), 89, 90, 92, 101, 254n41

familialism, 71, 72, 111, 157, 209, 211

family: as agency of control, 36; isolation/naturalization of, 54; labor and, 171, 172; language of, 7; marketization of, 207; nation and, xix, 188; neoliberal reformulations of, 167; nuclear, 5, 14, 213; sexuality and, 36, 225

family problems, 205, 206, 226

Family Research Council (FRC), 193

family romance, xix, xx, 4, 17, 18, 117, 141, 158, 180, 181, 182, 217; alternative genealogy of, 129; bastard, 163–68; bourgeois, 155, 159, 160, 164, 179; multicultural, 159; national, 12–15, 23, 24, 146; neoliberal, 21–25; patriarchal, 216; social realism and, 24

"Family Romances" (Freud), 17–18, 179

"Family Secrets, Child Sexual Abuse" (McIntosh), 54

family-state relations, xx, 27, 72, 195

family values, xvi, 7, 132, 134, 190

fantasy, 13, 79, 87, 181, 195, 211, 212, 221, 223, 224; analogy and, 19; as articulation, 15–18, 20, 22, 85, 188; beating, 178, 182, 183, 184; Bone and, 177–78, 179, 182–83, 185; Freudian discourse of, 14, 15; imagination and, 17, 19; incest and, 16, 32, 178, 188, 208, 227; legal, 22, 23; liberalized, 200–208, 224; racial, 141; realized, 179, 182; real-life consequences of, 188; sexual, 84, 141, 252n25

father–daughter incest, xi, xvii, 21, 56, 117, 124, 145, 148, 208; consensual, 213, 215; depicting, 116; memories of, 91–92; recovered memory of, 72; symbol of, 24; universal, 79

Father-Daughter Incest (Herman), 59, 82–83, 145

Father-Daughter Rape (Ward), 58

Father's Days (Brady), 74

father's law, 29, 227

Father's No, 33

Faulkner, William, 1, 244n2

Federal Minor Victim of Sexual Assault Law, 101

Federal Rules of Evidence (1975), 102

Felman, Shoshana, 6–7, 118, 119

feminism, 208, 235. *See also* second-wave feminism

Fighting Back (Bode), 73

Fincher, Kelly, 43

Flammang, C. J., 66

flashbacks, 86, 90, 256n2

Fliess, Wilhelm, 83, 246n3

FMS. *See* false memory syndrome

FMSF. *See* False Memory Syndrome Foundation

"Follow-up Report on Children Who Had Atypical Sexual Experience" (Bender and Grugett), 55

Fontes, Lisa Eronson, 233

force relations, 35, 59, 79, 188

formalism, 155, 228, 231; social, 68, 166

Foucault, Michel, xv, 9, 22, 26, 34, 59, 112, 130, 190, 247n17; biopower and, 38, 40, 41, 44; governmentality and, 46, 47, 48, 67; historical knowledge of struggles and, 12; incest and, 36, 40; incest taboo and, 35, 37, 57, 247n14; racism and, 37, 38, 39; sexual normalization and, 67

Franklin v. Stevenson and Kiniry (1999), 254n40, 254n49

Frazer, James G., 29, 31

freedom, 147–51, 227; sexual, 197, 208; slavery and, 124, 138

Free Speech Coalition v. Reno (1997), 263n2

Freud, Sigmund, 17–18, 22, 24, 68, 69, 92, 95, 119, 130, 252n23; beating fantasy and, 178; childhood sexual experience and, 84; "death" of, 70, 93, 98–99; eugenics and, 247n8; family romance and, 12, 13; fantasy and, 18, 84, 178; father's authority and, 179; genealogical metaphors and, 30; incest taboo and, 29, 30, 32, 34, 35, 37, 66, 178, 246n5; legacy of, 71, 93, 99; oedipus complex and, 252n26; phantasy and, 16–17, 18; psychoanalysis and, 29, 90, 107; on reality/unconscious, 85; return to, 32–33; seduction hypothesis and, 83; wounding of the mind and, 81

"Freud in Our Midst" (Adler and Underwood), 70

Freyd, Jennifer, 89, 253n29

Freyd, Pamela, 89, 253n29

Friedman, Arnold, ix–x, xiii–xiv, xvi

Friedman, David, xix

Friedman, Ellen G., 214, 223

Friedman, Howard, xiii–xiv

Friedman, Jesse, ix, x, xiii, 243n1

Friedman, Milton, 243n4

Fromm, Erich, 27

Frost, Laura, 214, 215, 216

Frye v. United States (1923), 102, 103, 106

Fukuyama, Francis, 5, 71, 244n6

Galasso, Frances, xiii

Gallagher, Cathy, 157, 186

Gardner, Richard, 90

gatekeeping function, 103, 105, 107

Gavigan, Melody, 91–92

Gavin-Reposa, Patricia, 106, 255n52

gender, 15, 60, 226; as difference, 14, 116, 133, 205, 261n18; as identity, 28, 203–4, 206

genealogy, 4, 21, 30, 118, 122, 130, 131

"Geography of the Apocalypse, The" (Keizer), 118

Gilman, Sander, 30

Gilmore, Leigh, 163, 167, 179

Gilroy, Paul, 120

globalization, xvii, 5, 6, 170, 262n32; cultural transformations of, 235; neoliberalism and, 171; white labor and, 172

Gordon, Linda, 91

governmentality, 7, 38, 46, 47, 54, 66, 100, 112, 224, 248n25; cultures of, 28, 111; dominant modes of, 236; incest and, 232, 234; neoliberal, 67, 69, 79, 228, 231, 234; postwelfare state, 225; racial, 67; rationalities of, 99; representation and, 231; transformations of, 67; welfare, 22, 27, 48, 87, 111

graded offenses: language of, 61, 64

Gray, Laura, 73

Gray, Paul, 70

Grewal, Inderpal, 191

Grinker, Roy, 252n21

Grisham, John, 216

Groff, William, 104

Grove, William, 255n52
Grugett, A. E., 55

Haag, Pamela, 195, 197, 226
Haaken, Janice, x, 75, 86, 87, 88, 202,
  205, 208–9, 226; on cultural borders,
  207; political claims and, 203
Hacking, Ian, 53, 89, 92, 232
Hagerman, Amber, 256n62
Hale, Dorothy, 166
Hale, Sir Matthew, 44
Hall, Stuart, 15, 68, 230
hands: image of, 24, 168–71, 172, 174
Hardt, Michael, 6
harm, 53, 65, 66–68, 73, 189, 190, 195,
  202, 214, 224, 232; child sexual abuse
  and, 200, 207; dysfunction and, 206;
  gendered, 259n13; infliction of, 228;
  justice and, 230; legal measurement of,
  229; neoliberal temporalities of, 110;
  protection from, 49, 198, 201;
  psychological, 63, 191, 204; risk and,
  109; willingness and, 205
Harmful to Minors (Levine), 189, 199
Harrison, Kathryn, 2, 24, 209, 214,
  261n22; consensual incest and, 10,
  188–89, 191
Hart, Lynda, 177–78
Hartman, Saidiya, 19, 130, 131, 135, 141,
  147
"Have You Seen Me?" (Ivy), 3
Hayek, Friedrich, 243n4
Helping Children (Levine and Levine),
  49
Hemings, Sally, 258n25
Hennessy, Rosemary, 168, 226
Herdt, Gilbert, 199
Herman, Judith Lewis, xiv, 56, 59, 82–83,
  145, 191
Herron, Carolivia, 10, 23, 114, 115
historical materialism, 17, 18, 76
History of Pleas of the Crown, The, 44
History of Sexuality, The (Foucault), 34,
  35, 38
Hodges, Devon, xx, 88, 214, 215
homosexuality, 36, 63, 193, 194, 219
"Hopeful Grief" (King), 154
Hopkins, Pauline, 1
How I Learned to Drive (Vogel), 2
Hudson, James, 206, 254n48

Hughes, Langston, 223
Human Development (Fischer and
  Lazerson), 205
Hungerford, Joel, 103
Hungerford v. Jones (1995, 1997, and
  1998), 102, 103, 104, 105, 106, 107,
  110
Hunt, Lynn, 13
hypnosis, 105, 254n49
hysteria, x, 28, 29, 83, 84

identification, xviii, 9, 14, 80, 166
If I Should Die before I Wake (Morris),
  74
I Know Why the Caged Bird Sings
  (Angelou), 74, 115
imaginary, 4, 14, 16, 17, 33, 231
Immigration and Naturalization Service,
  62
Immigration Reform and Control Act
  (1996), 70, 251n4
imperialism, 6, 171, 233
incest: as abuse of power, xiii; analytic, 21,
  28; archaeology/archive of, 12, 27;
  backlash against, 88; as child sexual
  abuse, xii, 22, 57–58, 59–68, 83, 232,
  254n57; consensual, 188–89, 191, 199,
  209, 222; crime of, 44, 227; defining/
  titling, 229; disclosing, 77; historical
  function of, 25; images of, 11, 123;
  knowledge about, 101; modernization
  of, 47, 69, 72; nationalization of, 47–
  48, 235; prohibition against, 29, 36,
  43, 44–45, 57, 67, 212; reading, xviii–
  xix, xx, 2, 11, 12, 28; representations
  of, 159, 231; reproductive, 116–17;
  social content of, 59; as structural
  absence, 34; studies of, 27, 55–56, 58.
  See also father–daughter incest
"Incest and Intertextuality in Carolivia
  Herron's *Thereafter Johnnie*" (Breau),
  128
Incest and the Medieval Imagination
  (Archibald), 42
Incest Behavior (Weinberg), 56
incest law, 43, 44, 46, 47, 53, 58, 60, 65,
  67; development of, 42; historical
  archive of, 41; justice and, 229–30;
  public welfare/sexual regulation and,
  48; reform of, 63; statutory role of, 45

incest narratives, xix, 2, 9, 10, 78, 116,
165–66; African American, 147; family
romance tradition and, 4; glut of, 21;
Greeks and, 1; multicultural, 74;
patriarchal rule and, 226; production/
consumption of, 3; reading, 11, 21
incest scene, 18–25, 176, 179–84
incest taboo, xii, xx, 9, 22, 26, 27, 28–34,
40, 41, 54, 57, 58, 59, 66, 67, 103,
147, 195; democracy of, 135; kinship/
sexuality and, 28, 167; law of the
father and, 126; liberal, 132; neoliberal,
224–27; observance of, 128; regulatory
aim of, 166–67; return of, 192; rule of
rules and, 42; universalization of, 66
indecent liberties, 64
Indecent Liberties law (1861), 43
individualism, 5, 13, 51, 70
I Never Told Anyone (Bass and Thornton),
73, 75
infant genital trauma theory, 84
In re Gault (1967), 248n29
Instance of Holocaust, An (Herron), 114
Institute for Advanced Study of Human
Sexuality, 199
International Conference on Incest and
Related Problems, 72
International Monetary Fund (IMF), xvii
In the Break (Moten), 138
"Intrafamilial and Extrafamilial Sexual
Abuse Vulnerability Factors" (Palotta),
205
Invisible Man (Ellison), 1, 115
Isabella, Marche, 108, 255n54
Ivy, Marilyn, 3, 198

James, Henry, 154
Jameson, Fredric, 120, 244n13
Janet, Pierre, 29, 81
Jarecki, Andrew, ix, x, xix
Jaroff, Leon, 91, 92, 93
Jefferson, Thomas, 258n25
Jenkins, Philip, 190, 260n5
Jennifer's Law, 112, 256n62
Johnston, Moira, 110
Jones, Claireece Precious, 217, 224;
education of, 222, 223; Ms. Rain and,
218, 220, 221; writing of, 219–20
Jones, Gayl, 10, 115
Jones, Susan, 254n48

Joseph, Miranda, 170–71
justice, 25; alternative, 228, 230–31;
criminal, 9, 54, 57, 59, 62, 100; desire
for, 182; distributive, 236; fantasy of,
182; harm and, 230; incest and, 228,
229–30; retributive, 163; social, xvii,
154, 155, 180, 187, 236; spectacle of,
184–87

Kaiser, Marvin, 45
Kanka, Megan, 256n62
Kaplan, Amy, 156, 157, 160, 186, 187
Kaplan, Ann, 80
Kaplan, Caren, 191
Kardiner, Abram, 252n21
Katz, Sanford, 136
Kazanjian, David, 16, 245n22
Keating-Owen Act (1916), 249n31
Keeping Up with the Dow Joneses
(Prashad), 224, 235
Keizer, Arlene, 118, 127, 128, 129
Kempe, Henry, 51
Kenan, Randall, 154, 166
Keynesianism, 48, 243n4
Killing the Black Body (Roberts), 40
Kincaid, James, xvi, 198
King, Vincent, 154
Kinsey, Alfred, 55, 199, 204
kinship, 15, 20, 23, 27, 34, 51, 65,
167–68, 247n11; African American,
127, 128, 129, 130; biological/genetic
order of, 28; bourgeois, 164;
deployment of, 36; expansive, 21;
formation/model of, 33, 45, 129–30,
148; generational, 189; hetronormative,
10; incest and, 28, 57, 131; legal
definition of, 46; liberal, 130, 138;
national, 126, 128; neoliberal, 227;
norms, 46; ontology of, 34; political,
130, 132; racialized, xv, 127, 136;
regulating, 45, 163, 167; social order
of, 28; state intervention into, 57;
structures of, 26, 33, 54; studying, 29,
126
Kiss, The (Harrison), 2, 188–89, 191,
192, 222, 223; consent and, 24, 224;
controversy over, 214–15; explicit sex
scenes and, 216, 217; narrator of, 237;
oedipal crisis and, 213; politics of
morality and, 209; reading, 199, 211

Kiss Daddy Goodnight (Armstrong), 74, 115

Klaas, Polly, 256n62

Knapp, Stephen, 117

Kris, Ernst, 252n24

labor, xv, 24, 158, 168, 170–71, 225, 259n19; division of, 59, 233; family and, 171, 172; feminization of, 170; flexibilization of, 10; forced, 27; kinship and, 174; migration, 170, 171; racialization of, 171; reproductive/productive, 13; slave, 222; transnational conditions of, 234; white, 169–70, 172; working-class, 173

Lacan, Jacques, 37, 66, 120, 247n9, 247n10, 252n26; discourse and, 33; incest taboo and, xii, 34; kinship/language and, 247n11; on law of the father, 59

Lamb, Sharon, 202, 203, 205, 207, 208–9

Language of Psycho-Analysis, The (Laplanche and Pontalis), 16, 85

Laplanche, Jean, 16, 85, 253n26

Laub, Dori, 6–7, 118, 119

law, 37, 55, 231; concept of, 36, 40; hermeneutics of, 26; incest as, 41–47; legitimacy of, 230

law of the father, 33–34, 127, 129–34, 167, 168, 180; incest taboo and, 126; kinship and, 131; slavery and, 131; state and, 59

Lawrence v. Texas (2003), 248n24

Lear, Jonathan, 251n2

"Leda and the Swan" (Yeats), 124

Lee, Devon, 43

Lee, Lydia, 231

Levett, Ann, 234–35

Levine, Adeline, 49, 50, 227

Levine, Judith, 188, 189, 190, 199

Levine, Murray, 49, 50, 227

Lévi-Strauss, Claude, 33, 126

Leys, Ruth, 81, 118

liability, 68, 108, 112, 141

liberalism, 5, 10, 207, 209, 257n17

"Lies of the Mind" (Jaroff), 91, 95

Limits of Autobiography, The (Gilmore), 163, 179

literacy, 189, 219, 221, 223

Literary Trauma (Horvitz), xx

literature: African American, 257n9; alternative, 3; autobiography and, 152; commensurability and, 231; incest, 1, 3, 115, 117, 229, 231; justice and, 230; minority, 158; multicultural approach to, 153; sexual assault, 116, 117; survivor, 75, 115

Lloyd, David, 172

Loftus, Elizabeth, 71, 106, 254n48, 255n52

Lolita (Nabokov), 1, 115

Lot, 137, 139

love, 37, 135, 137, 174, 212

Lovrod, Marie, 233

Lowe, Lisa, 121, 172

Luce, Henry, 44

Lukács, Georg, 157

MacFarlane, Kee, 61

Mahurin, Matt, 93, 253n35; illustration by, 94, 96

"Making the Incest Scene" (Roiphe), 1, 215, 216

Male Subjectivity at the Margins (Silverman), 247n11

"Mama's Baby, Papa's Maybe" (Spillers), 148

Maraecek, Jeanne, 86, 87

Marett, R. R., 29

marriage law, 43, 53, 232

Marx, Karl, 19, 71, 257n23

Marxism, 70, 71

Marxism and Literature (Williams), 69, 76

"Marxism and the New Historicism" (Gallagher), 157

Masson, Jeffrey Moussaieff, 83, 84

masturbation, 176, 182, 204, 260n27

McCain, Robert Stacy, 188, 198–99

McClintock, Ann, 14

McDougal, William, 81

McDowell, Deborah, 121, 122, 146

McHugh, Paul, 254n48, 255n52

McIntosh, Mary, 54, 55

McNaron, Toni, 26, 27, 58

Megan's Law, x, 112, 256n62

Melville, Herman, 1

memory, 11, 17, 85, 113, 117, 124, 125, 126, 210, 211; childhood, 210; child sexual abuse and, 89, 92, 114; as crisis,

81; critical, 148; etiological event of, 83; language of, 69, 72; popular culture and, 88; posttraumatic, 82, 86; reliability of, 102, 104; risky, 72; traumatic, 82, 86, 88, 90. *See also* false memory; recovered memory; repressed memory

memory wars, x, xi, 22, 28, 68, 71, 72, 88–93, 95, 98–99, 112, 116, 189, 232; cultural history and, 98; debates about, 88; fantasy and, 93; impact of, 107; neoliberalism and, 69; witchcraft trials and, 93

Memory Wars, The (Crews), 89

Mendez, Gioconda Batres, 233

Mertz, Elizabeth, 108, 109, 255n54, 255n57

"Meta-Analytic Examination of Assumed Properties of Child Sexual Abuse Using College Samples, A" (Rind, Bauserman, and Tromovitch). *See* Rind study

Meyer v. Nebraska (1923), 248n29

military-industrial complex, xviii, 52

Miller, Laura, 1, 3, 10, 11

Mirkin, Harris, 199

miscegenation, 1, 20, 138

"Misnomer of Freud's 'Seduction Theory,' The" (Triplett), 84

Model Penal Code, 60, 197, 250n43

modernity, 26, 81, 121, 158

molestation, xiii, xv, 117, 143, 165, 175, 179

Molien v. Kaiser Foundation Hospitals (1980), 108

Moll Flanders (Defoe), 243n2

Money, John, 199

Moon, Daniel, 44

Morahan, John A., 103

moral panic, ix, xv, xvi, 190

morality, 194, 207, 208, 209, 212

Morgan, Yarrow, 26, 27, 58

Morris, Michelle, 74

Morrison, Toni, 10, 74, 115, 147, 183

Moses and Monotheism (Freud), 119

Moten, Fred, 19, 138, 257n23

Moynihan report (1965), 52

Mullahy, Patrick, 66

multiculturalism, 7, 76, 153, 158

Muth, Allen, 248n24

Muth, Patricia, 248n24

Myers, Charles S., 81

Myers, John, 43

Nabokov, Vladimir, 1, 115

Name-of-the-Father, 33

narratives, 78, 87, 120, 123, 126, 155, 158; fetishism of, 172–75; oedipal, 224; political, 202; postpatriarchal, 223; sexual assault, 256n5; survivor, 233; trauma, 7; white middle-class, 75. *See also* incest narratives

nation, xix, 2, 23, 47–48, 132, 147, 188, 235

National Association on Research and Therapy of Homosexuality (NARTH), 260n8

National Center on Child Abuse and Neglect, 61

National Child Protection Act (1993), 260n13

nationalism, 14, 27, 28, 157; black, 122; bourgeois, 4; cultural, 69, 224, 225, 227, 235; imaginative relations of, 13; neoliberalism and, xviii; political, xviii, 69; racial, 20

National Law Center for Children and Families, 260n8

"Nation Form, The" (Balibar), 14

nativisms, 170, 171

Negri, Antonio, 6

neoconservatives, 170, 207

neoliberalism, 52, 72, 160, 172, 192, 194, 199, 207, 223, 226; ascendancy/contents of, xviii, 11, 70, 71, 228; child sexual abuse and, xvii, 22; cultural logics of, xvii, 7, 22, 88, 113, 228; false consciousness of, 99; globalization and, 171; impact of, 5; incest and, 8–9, 25, 227, 229, 231, 232; memory wars and, 69; political economies of, 67; pressures/processes of, 6, 235; privatization and, 5; welfare and, 188

"New Imperialism, The" (Bamyeh), 112

"New" Police, The (Elliott), 66

Newsweek, 70, 75, 93, 95; photo from, 97

New York Society for the Prevention of Cruelty to Children, 248n28

New York v. Feber (1982), 262n1

Nixon, Richard M., 249n36

No More Secrets (Ristock), 73
normalization, xii, 47, 52, 53, 219;
    childhood, 49–50; political, 226;
    sexual, 35, 51, 64, 67, 190, 198
norms, xv, 46, 53, 202; moral, 64, 109,
    110, 199, 212; social reproduction of,
    36
North American Man/Boy Love
    Association, 193
"Notes on Gridlock" (Povinelli), 132

oedipalization, 18, 212
oedipal struggle, 14–15, 213
Oedipus, 1, 66, 165, 209, 223
oedipus complex, 30, 31, 32, 67, 85, 120,
    252n23, 252n26
Oedipus: Myth and Complex (Mullahy),
    66
Of One Blood (Hopkins), 1
Ofsche, Richard, 71, 106, 255n52
Olsen v. Hooley (1993), 254n40
OneVoice/ACAA, 260n8
orthogonal articulation, 39, 40, 42, 46,
    55, 67, 111, 247n16; incest and, 35,
    66
Osborne v. Ohio (1990), 262n1

Paidika: The Journal of Pedophilia, 193
panic, x, xi, 93. *See also* moral panic; sex
    panic
parens patriae, 49, 58, 248n29, 249n31,
    249n36
parental alienation syndrome, 90, 254n41
parental authority, 53, 65, 196
parental rights, 136, 198, 248n29
"Paris, Capital of the Nineteenth Century"
    (Benjamin), 98
Parshall, Janet, 193
Pateman, Carole, 166, 167, 196
paternal authority, 132, 135, 138, 180
patriarchal conspiracy, 58, 59
patriarchalism, 24, 73, 192, 233
patriarchal law, 57, 126, 146
patriarchal property, 129, 136, 138
patriarchal right, incest as, 54–59
patriarchal rule, 5, 22, 23, 28, 129, 131,
    133, 140; incest narratives and, 226
patriarchy, 28, 77, 130, 131, 145, 186,
    223; diminution of, 214; experiences
    of, 86; liberal, 132, 136; political

    legitimation of, 167; romantic rewriting
        of, 156
Patterson, Laura, 185
Pavlov, Ivan, 252n19
Pearl, Mrs., 184
Pearl, Shannon, 176, 180–83, 184
pedophiles, xvi, 67, 193, 208, 260n10
pedophilia, x, xi, xiii, xiv, xv, xviii, 195
"Pedophilia and the Culture Wars"
    (Zuriff), 194, 208
Pellegrini, Anne, 30
Pelton, Leroy H., 52, 249n37
People v. Martinez (1995), 63
Perez, Emma, 233
"Permanent Obliquity of an In[pha]llibly
    Straight, The" (Spillers), 126, 147
Personal Responsibility and Work
    Opportunity Reconciliation Act (1994),
    70
phallus, 24, 33, 34, 168, 208, 225
phantasy, 16, 17, 18, 245n24
Phillips, Lynn M., 203
Phipps, Charles A., 64, 65
Pierce v. Society of Sisters (1925),
    248n29
Pierre (Melville), 1
Pillar of Salt (Haaken), x, 75
pivot, 38, 41, 160, 167, 179, 192; incest
    as, 36, 40, 180
Police and the Underprotected Child, The
    (Flammang), 66
Policing of Families, The (Donzelot), 48
political economy, 35, 67, 159
political right, 28, 37, 38, 40, 59, 60, 126,
    197
Political Unconscious, The (Jameson), 8,
    120, 244n13
politics, 48, 80, 97, 120, 122, 150, 170,
    198; cultural, 121, 236; ethics and,
    230; family model of, 13; identity, 73,
    76; incest, 21, 155, 228; sexual, 194,
    195, 207, 208
"Politics and the Study of Discourse"
    (Foucault), 26
"Politics of Child Sexual Abuse Research,
    The" (Haaken and Lamb), 202
*Politics of Culture in the Shadow of
    Capital, The* (Lloyd and Lowe), 172
Politics of Survivorship, The (Champagne),
    xx

popular culture, xii, 8, 74, 99, 229, 231,
234; domains of, 190; incest literature
and, 3; reconstruction of, 72; traumatic
memories and, 88
population: biopolitics of, 9, 38, 39
pornography, child, x, ix, 231–32, 262n1,
263n2
possession, 124, 164, 174, 212; domestic,
134–39; paternal, 136, 212; patriarchal,
151; testimonial, 122–25
"Postpatriarchal Endings in Recent U.S.
Fiction" (Friedman), 214
poststructuralist theory, 156, 245n21
post-traumatic stress disorder (PTSD), xv,
81, 86, 87, 200; child sexual abuse and,
xiii, 83; fantasy and, 85; intrusive
phenomena of, 90; memory and, 82
poverty, xvi, 50, 155, 192, 198, 203, 217,
218, 224, 225; child sexual abuse and,
153; incest and, 24; Southern white,
153; war on, 51, 52, 77, 88
Povinelli, Elizabeth, 126, 132
power, 34–41, 43, 66; abuse of, xiii;
gendered analysis of, 67–68; incest
taboo and, 37; self-, 219, 220, 223
Prashad, Vijay, 224, 227, 235
President's Daughter, The (Brown),
258n25
preterition, 53, 55, 60, 64, 67
Prince, Morton, 81
Prince v. Massachusetts (1944), 248n29
print culture, 9, 16, 74, 121, 231, 233,
236
prison-industrial complex, xviii, 52
privacy, 5, 99, 126, 164, 193
privatization, 5, 9, 20, 194, 199
ProjectMuse, 253n34
promiscuity, 36, 57
"Promoting Pedophilia" (McCain), 188,
198–99
property, 19, 134, 136, 139, 140, 225;
erotic enjoyment of, 131; genealogy of,
20; kinship and, 130, 131; patriarchal
systems of, 36
property rights, 132, 134, 136, 145
"Prosecution of Child Sexual Abuse in the
United States" (Myers et al.), 43
Proulx, Annie, 2, 10
psychoanalysis, 56, 59, 84, 105, 120;
Freudian, 12–14, 16–18, 29–32, 95;

history of sexuality and, 37; Lacanian,
33–34
psychology, 27, 29, 33, 54, 58, 117, 231
PTSD. *See* post-traumatic stress disorder
public safety, 47, 52, 113
"Pulling Together II: Surviving Stopping
Incest" (conference), 73
Punishment of Incest Act (1908), 42
Push (Sapphire), 2, 189, 191, 199, 219,
222; as articulation of value, 220; black
pathology and, 192; consent and, 24,
224; explicit sex scenes and, 216, 217;
pedagogy and, 223; poverty and, 217
Puwar, Nirmal, 166

"Q and A with Judith Levine" (Levine),
188
Quattrocchi, John, 103, 254n46
Queen of America, The (Berlant), 79
queer theory, 24

race, 12, 22, 23, 27, 40, 74, 79;
articulating principle of, 15–16; as
blood quantum, 20; new concept of,
39; reproduction and, 41; war and,
112
"Race, Articulation, and Societies
Structured in Dominance" (Hall), 15,
230
racial formations, 20, 21, 54, 118, 121,
221, 246n29, 258n8
racialization, 20, 38, 129, 233, 234
racism, 9, 42, 59, 77, 79, 135, 146, 183,
223; appearance of, 40, 41; biological,
39, 41, 247n8; body/sex and, 37,
40; child sexual abuse and, 78;
civilizational, 32; killing and, 39;
reproductive, 38, 41; state, 35, 37, 66
Rain, Blue, 218, 219, 220, 221
Ramona, Gary, 108, 255n54
Ramona, Holly, 108, 110, 255n54
Ramona, Stephanie, 108
Ramona v. Isabella (1994), 107, 108
Ramona v. Ramona (1990 and 1991),
102, 103, 108, 109
rape, 44, 65, 124, 146, 149, 185, 189,
202; analogy of, 60, 62; father-
daughter, 58; genealogy of, 221; law,
60, 63; sexuality and, 141; statutory,
42–43, 63, 65; stranger, 62

Rauch, Jonathan, 194
"Reactions of Children to Sexual
 Relations with Adults, The" (Bender
 and Blau), 55
"Reading Family Matters" (McDowell),
 121
Reagan, Ronald, xvi
realism, 14, 95, 166, 172, 176, 177, 179,
 184, 187; bourgeois, 13, 157, 159, 165,
 168; cultures of, 155–60; fantasy and,
 178; formal, 124, 157; incest, 86, 165;
 legal, 161, 162, 163; literary, 155, 156,
 159–60, 180; magical, 158, 258n7;
 minority, 153, 158; populist, 169;
 regional, 154, 156; social, 8, 23, 24,
 155, 157, 158, 159, 186; social justice
 and, 155; survivor, 153, 155, 159, 160,
 186; working-class, 23, 160, 162, 163,
 172, 175
reality, 17, 79, 166, 224; fantasy and, 84,
 177, 178, 226, 227; unconscious and,
 85
"Recasting Consent" (Phillips), 203
recovered memory, xiv, xviii, 68, 70, 72,
 88, 92, 99, 100, 101, 105, 108, 109,
 232, 253n33, 254n40; acceptance of,
 89, 102, 103, 106; cases about, 102–3;
 dismissal of, 95, 106; fantasy and, 23;
 hysteria, 71; legitimacy of, 102,
 255n53; popular/legal adjudication of,
 188; potential falsehood of, 89; public
 disclosure of, 114; Satan and, 93;
 testimony based on, 104
recovery, 75, 92; trauma and, 79–80
Reddy, Chandan, 171, 225, 226
"Relationship of Child Sexual Abuse
 and Family Violence to Adult
 Adjustment, The" (Higgins and
 McCabe), 205
Remembering Generations (Rushdy),
 146
representation, xviii, 41, 229; modes of,
 110, 119, 160, 231
repressed memory, xiv, xviii, 70, 91, 92,
 106; processes of, 104–5; scientific
 theory of, 101, 104
reproduction, xvi, 13, 21, 147; biological,
 36; ideological, 22; incestuous, 23, 45;
 race and, 41; social, 22, 36, 37, 225,
 259n25; visual, 213

Residues of Justice (Dimock), 229, 236
responsibility, 47, 189; civic, 199; family,
 48; parental, 52; personal, 77; sexual
 abuse and, 186; state, 52
Rethinking History in a Global Age
 (Bender), 119
Rewriting the Soul (Hacking), 92, 232
Rind, Bruce, 188, 191, 201
Rind study, 205, 206, 208, 211, 224;
 childhood sexual contact and, 192;
 child sexual abuse and, 201–2; consent
 and, 204, 212; fantasy and, 212; gender
 roles and, 203–4; incestuous trauma
 and, 207; normative policy claims and,
 200, 214; political narratives of, 202;
 psychological harm and, 191; response
 to, 193–94, 195, 198, 199, 203; sex
 radicals and, 194
Rise of the Novel (Watt), 157
risk, 51, 71, 111, 112, 189; assessment,
 103, 109, 112; harm and, 109; legal
 measurement of, 229; neoliberal
 discourses of, 68, 110
"River of Names" (Allison), 163–64
Roberts, Dorothy, 40
Rocking the Cradle of Sexual Politics
 (Armstrong), 58
Rody, Caroline, 122
Roiphe, Katie, 1, 10, 221, 243n2; incest
 stories and, 165–66, 215; on *Push*, 2,
 217; on Sapphire, 216
"Rome Discourse" (Lacan), 252n26
Rose, Richard, 108
Rowe, Michael, 154, 259n13
Rule 104, 103
Rule 702 (1975), 102, 103, 255n50
Rush, Florence, 2, 56
Rushdy, Ashraf, 52, 146
Russell, Diana, 2, 56
Ruth Anne. *See* Bone

Sacco, Lynn, 56
Salem witchcraft trials: memory wars and,
 93
Salpêtrière, 29, 246n2
Sane Society, The (Fromm), 27
Sapphire, 2, 10, 24, 189, 216
Sarat, Austin, 161
Sargant, William, 252n21
Satter, Beryl, 56

scandal, 216–24, 226, 260n6; sex, 3, 10, 194, 195, 198, 199
"Scenes of Misrecognition" (Anagnost), 225
Scenes of Subjection (Hartman), 130, 141
Schlessinger, Laura, 193, 260n8
second-wave feminism, x, xiv, xvi, 2, 56, 122; adult survivors and, 61; child sexual abuse and, xii; gendered analysis of power and, 67–68; incest and, 59; PTSD and, xv
"Secrets and Lies" (Jarecki), xix
Secret Survivors (Blume), 86
Secret Trauma, The (Russell), 2
security, 9, 54, 66, 71, 111, 112
Sedgwick, Eve Kosofsky, 46
seduction, 60, 61, 123, 124, 141, 145, 146, 196, 211, 261n24; childhood, 85; hypothesis, 29, 68, 83; power/property relations of, 43
self: creation through language, 69, 78, 218; disclosure, spectacle of, 75; interpretive technologies of, 99; knowledge of, 3, 31, 95, 189, 218; textualization of, 219
self-determination, xv, xvi, 122, 194
self-empowerment, 111, 219, 220, 223
self-esteem, 76–77, 251n12, 261n17
self-help, xiii, 3, 9, 77
self-representation, xv, xix, 12, 180, 214, 216, 218; national, 9–10; public, 115; survivor, 73, 115; working-class, 175
Seminar of Jacques Lacan, Book VII, The, 33
Sentencing Reform Act (1984), 251n13
sex: adult-child, 191, 193, 194, 208; articulation of, 40, 63; intergenerational, 189, 193, 200; politicization of, 38; violence and, 174
Sex Crimes Unit, xiii
sexism, 9, 59, 146, 223
sex offenders, 112, 190, 256n62
sex panic, x, 91, 190, 198, 203, 207, 260n5, 260n10; appearance of, 191; child endangerment and, 194; child sexual abuse and, xvi
sex radicals, 194, 207, 227
sexual abuse, xi, 67, 73, 86, 189, 191, 203, 218, 254n47; adolescent, 191–92;

black women and, 116; child protection and, 54; false memories of, 71; as gendered norm, 58; history, xv, 91–92; public risk of, 72; responsibility and, 186; working-class realism and, 163. *See also* child sexual abuse
"Sexual Abuse, Family Environment, and Psychological Symptoms" (Briere and Elliott), 206
"Sexual Abuse" (Watson), 75
sexual agency, 141, 146, 151, 169, 197, 199, 207–8, 213, 216, 224
sexual assault, 60, 61, 251n4, 256n5
"Sexual Assault and Mental Disorders in a Community Population" (Burnam et al.), 206
"Sexual Assault and Restorative Justice" (Daly), 230
Sexual Behavior in the Human Female (Kinsey), 55
Sexual Behavior in the Human Male (Kinsey), 204
Sexual Citizenship (Evans), 65
Sexual Citizen, The (Bell and Binnie), 199
sexual conduct, xii, 60, 63, 197; harm and, 189; nonnormative, 212, 255; political/moral regulation of, 195; racialized/class-restrictive norms of, xv; stigmatized, 195
sexual contact, 61, 63, 65; childhood, 192, 200, 201
Sexual Contract, The (Pateman), 166
sexual experience, 206; childhood, 55, 56, 84, 85, 198–99
sexuality, 128, 132, 141, 145, 149, 189, 203; child, 64, 190, 236; deployment of, 35, 36, 37, 38–39, 41, 134, 225; legitimate/illegitimate, 199; liberal, 130, 133–34; marketization of, 226; political/economic relations of, 225; regulating, 163, 167
"Sexual Liberation's Last Frontier" (Erickson), 194, 203
sexual minorities, 194, 195, 198
sexual predation, x, 84, 190
sexual regulation, xii, 20, 22, 48
sexual relations, 54, 64–65, 141, 142–43, 204, 212, 226; age-inappropriate, 45; policing, 65

"Sexual Rights of Children" (Institute for Advanced Study of Human Sexuality), 199
sexual violation, 142, 143, 144
sexual violence, 2, 6, 20, 21, 28, 60, 91, 131, 168, 185, 234; African American, 128; childhood vulnerability to, 233; feminist accounts of, 76; genealogy of, 127; publications about, 11; redressing, 4; slavery and, 23; women's speech about, xv
Shakespeare, William, 1
Shattered Subjects (Henke), xx
Shelley, Mary, 116
"Shifting Contexts, Shaping Experiences" (Lovrod), 233
Shipping News, The (Proulx), 2
Silverman, Kaja, 245n21
Simon, Jonathan, 161
Simpson, O. J., 253n35
Skelton, Martha Wayles, 258n25
Skin (Allison), 258n1
slavery, xix, 8, 114, 116–18, 123, 127, 133, 141, 144, 222; formations of, 19; freedom and, 124, 138; incest and, 146; law of the father and, 131; patriarchal materialism and, 128; violence of, 23, 117, 128, 146
Smiley, Jane, 2, 10
Smith v. Doe (2003), 256n63
Snowdon, Camille, 117, 123, 144, 149; John Christopher and, 132, 133, 134; Patricia and, 150; X shape and, 145
Snowdon, Cynthia Jane (Janie), 117, 125, 140, 148, 149, 237
Snowdon, Eva, 117, 122, 123, 125, 149
Snowdon, John Christopher, 123, 129, 137, 142–43, 144, 145, 257n21; Camille and, 132, 133, 134; daughter's song and, 138–39; digital rape by, 146; liberal paternity and, 134, 135; patriarchal authority and, 133, 136, 139, 143; Patricia and, 116, 117, 124, 125, 127, 131–32, 138, 140, 141, 142–43, 149; sexual relationship and, 142–43; social forms and, 137
Snowdon, Kristen Dolores (Johnnie), 116, 117, 123, 124, 125, 138, 144, 149; on mother, 147

Snowdon, Patricia, 237; adult incest and, 144; incest taboo and, 147; John Christopher and, 116, 117, 124, 125, 127, 131–32, 138, 140, 141, 142–43, 149; nicknames for, 142; seduction by, 123, 124, 146; sexual relationship and, 140, 142–43; X shape and, 145, 150
social, 4, 29, 34, 48, 49, 76, 196, 227; antagonism of, 80–81, 112; bureaucratization of, 55; change, 3, 78, 157, 231; difference, 14, 41, 80; familial relations and, 49; financial relations of, 111; formation, 48, 76, 137, 159; justice, xvii, 154, 155, 180, 187, 236; problems, xvi, 2, 47, 52, 100, 162; struggle, 7, 8, 12, 79, 157, 236
social realism, 8, 23, 155, 157, 158, 186; family romance and, 24; traditional forms of, 159
social relations, 7, 12, 14, 35, 79, 111, 119, 155, 156, 158, 159, 168–69, 176, 186, 207; analysis of, 80–81; culture/representation and, 157, 187; financialization of, 111; normative, 135; psychic relations and, 15; sentimental discourse of, 80
Social Security Act (1935), 249n32
social welfare, 27, 47, 48, 170
Society Must Be Defended (Foucault), 39, 40, 112
Society of the Spectacle, The (Debord), 79
sociology, 27, 56, 57, 58, 59
sodomy, ix, 248n24
"Something about Amelia" (movie), 75
Sound and the Fury, The (Faulkner), 1
speak-outs, x, 73
spectacle, 77, 79, 184
Spectral Evidence (Johnston), 110
Spiegel, John, 252n21, 261n16, 261n20
Spillers, Hortense, 127, 132, 245n21; on African American incest, 147, 148; kinship and, 129–30; nuclear family and, 126; on X, 147–48
state: civil society and, 227; governmentalization of, 55; legitimacy, 233; as mythicized abstraction, 38; political relation between, 167
State of Rhode Island's Daubert Hearing Brief (1998), 255n52

States of Injury (Brown), 133–34, 226, 249n35, 257n17

State v. Chamley (1997), 44, 248n21

State v. Hungerford (1994), 103–4

State v. Kaiser, 46

State v. Quattrocchi (1994, 1996, 1999, and 2001), 102, 103, 104, 106, 107, 110, 254n46

Statute 18 Elizabeth, 43

statute of limitations, 100, 101, 254n37

Stein, Gertrude, 10

Steinberg, Sybil, 154

stereotype, 78, 163–64

Stern, Rachel, 43

Stogner v. California (2003), 256n63

storytelling, 169, 180, 214, 259n19; cultural resistance and, 162; romanticization of, 163, 259n13; tribe, 125, 127; working-class, 156, 162, 164, 184

"Subaltern Studies in a U.S. Frame" (Cherniavsky), 21, 232, 234

subjection, 19, 130, 141, 144

subjectivity, 28, 76, 131; civil, 191, 225; trauma and, 81, 110

"Subject of True Feeling, The" (Berlant), 80

Sullivan, Kathleen, 109

Sullivan v. Cheshier (1993, 1994, and 1995), 102, 103, 107, 109, 256n59

Summit, Roland, 61–62, 107, 111, 250n45

"Survivor Discourse" (Alcoff and Gray), 73

survivors, xiii, 8, 75, 83, 99–100, 222, 234; disqualified knowledges of, 12; emergence of, 72, 73; literary approaches to, 114; mobilization of, 61, 76; public interest in, 89; radicalism of, 77; as spectacle, 77; testimony of, 78, 82; trauma and, 79; voice of, 74, 78, 79

"Survivors of Child Sexual Abuse" statement, 72

symbolic, 33, 34, 41, 127

"Symposium: Defining Incest" (Bienen), 42, 44, 60, 63, 228, 229, 250n50

taboo, 195, 215, 226; conscious rationalization and, 31; Freudian

accounts of, 12; function of, 32, 37; incest as, xii, xx, 9, 22, 26, 27, 28–34; myth of, 74; as trauma, 27; women's discourse and, 28

Tal, Kali, xx, 116

Tarasoff v. Regents of the Univ. of Cal. (1976), 255n57

Tavris, Carol, 203

Telling Incest (Doane and Hodges), xx, 74, 75

Terdiman, Richard, 81

Terrorist Assemblages (Puar), 235

testimony, 78, 82, 119, 126; traumatic, 121; in trials, 99–111

Testimony (Felman and Laub), 6–7, 119

textualism, 120, 121

Theory of the Novel (Lukàcs), 157

therapy, 9, 85, 86–87, 89, 92, 93, 105–7, 108–10; feminization of, 232

Thereafter Johnnie (Herron), 2, 116–18, 129, 130, 136, 140, 147; African American kinship and, 127; familial nation and, 122; father–daughter incest and, 124; genealogical shock and, 122; incest in, 118, 131–32, 141; routine violence and, 150; trauma and, 23, 118, 119, 126

"Theses on the Philosophy of History" (Benjamin), 257n14

third-party liability, 108, 109

Thornton, Louise, 75

Thousand Acres, A (Smiley), 2

Three Strikes bill (1994), 112, 256n62

time: cursed, 130; indexical, 129; narrative, 126; national, 126

Time magazine, 70, 91, 93; illustration from, 94, 96; Simpson mug shot and, 253n35

tort law: economic liability and, 111

Totem and Taboo (Freud), 30–31, 32, 33, 247n7, 247n10

trafficking, 61, 233

transfiguration: politics of, 120, 122, 150

Trash (Allison), 152, 187

trauma, 6, 8, 79–88, 112, 113, 126, 155, 159; incest, xiii, 9, 27, 86, 122, 207, 232; literary theories of, 118, 119, 120–21; media representations of, 83; medicalized determinations of, 87;

national, 21, 80; neoliberal, 7, 10, 11; as psychic wound, 81; recovery and, 79–80; repression, 105–6; subjectivity and, 81, 110; temporality of, 113; textualization of, 120; women's experiences of, 3, 88
Trauma and Recovery (Herman), xiv, 83, 145
Trauma and Survival in Contemporary Fiction (Vickroy), xx
Trauma Cinema (Walker), xx
Trauma: Explorations in Memory (Caruth), 6
Trauma: Genealogy of a Concept (Leys), 81
Triplett, Hall, 84, 252n23
Tromovitch, Philip, 188, 191
trope, 75, 87, 244–45n14; dominant, 69; historical, 16; incest, 4, 5, 11, 15, 19, 20, 21, 232, 235
Tubman, Harriet, 219
Two or Three Things I Know for Sure (Allison), 258n1
Tylor, E. B., 29
Tyson, Dwight Robert, 254n37
Tyson, Nancy Louise, 254n37
Tyson v. Tyson (1986), 100–101, 103, 105, 254n37

Unclaimed Experience (Caruth), 6
Uncle Tom's Cabin (Stowe), 183
unconscious, 18; reality and, 85
Underwood, Anne, 70, 251n2
Ungentlemanly Acts (Barnett), 44
United States Immigration Act (1990), 171
universal particular, 72–88
"'Unnatural Fathers and Vixen Daughters'"(Moon), 44
"Uproar over 'Sexual Abuse' and Its Findings, The" (Tavris), 203
U.S. House of Representatives: Rind study and, 193
U.S. Supreme Court, 102, 263n2
U.S. v. Hilton (1998), 231, 263n2

value, 44, 225; articulation of, 220; capitalization and, 219; social, 220; valorization of, 224–27
Van Derbur, Marilyn, 2

van der Kolk, Bessel A., 254n48
Vermont statute: incest and, 43
victimization, x, 91, 92, 149, 207, 234
Victims of Child Abuse Laws (VOCAL), 254n41
Vienna Psychoanalytic Society, 12
Vienna Society for Neurology and Psychiatry, 107
violence, 4, 51, 57, 119, 150, 179, 220; aesthetics of, 23; consent and, 195; documentary, 181; domestic, 76, 83, 173–74; family, 23, 192, 205; gendered, 6, 74, 208; historical, 126–29, 151; nonsexual forms of, 198; patriarchal, 6, 145, 185–86; racial, 6, 183; sex and, 174; against women, xiv, 111, 171; working-class, 175, 176. *See also* sexual violence
Violence Against Women Act (VAWA), 70, 251n4
Violent Crime Control and Law Enforcement Act (1994), 251n4
Voices in the Night (Morgan), 26, 73, 74
"Vulnerability to Sexual Assault" (Ageton), 206

Waddell, Glen (Daddy Glen): accountability of, 175, 180; Anney and, 184, 185; beating of, 184; Bone and, 166, 173–74, 177, 185, 186; hands of, 168–69, 172, 173–75; kinship and, 167–68; patriarchy and, 164, 165, 166, 167, 174, 175; privacy and, 164–65; rape scene and, 185; responsibility of, 186; sexual agency of, 169, 173; sexual violence of, 165, 185
Walker, Alice, xx, 10, 74, 219
Wall, Barry, 255n52
Ward, Elizabeth, 58
war on drugs, 52, 77, 251n13
War on Poverty, 51, 52, 77, 88
Washington Consensus, xvii
"Washington's Other Sex Scandal" (Rauch), 194
Washington Times, 198–99
Watt, Ian, 157
Watters, Ethan, 71, 102
Wayward Reproductions (Weinbaum), 30, 244n4
Weinbaum, Alys Eve, 30, 41, 244n4

Weinberg, S. Kirson, 55–56
welfare, 4, 10, 58, 66, 111, 228; neoliberal governance and, 188; public, 47,
  48, 52, 54, 249n32; reform, 171, 222;
  social, 27, 47, 48, 170
Welfare Reform Act, 251n4
welfare state, xviii, 5, 7, 46, 47, 69, 100,
  111–13, 225, 237; child protection/
  sexual regulation, 22; residual cultural
  logics of, 172
"What Is Our Bane, That Alone We Have
  in Common" (Cahill), 44–45
White House Conference on Child
  Dependency, 249n31, 249n33
white supremacy, 115, 121
white trash, 23, 172, 175
"'Who Owns the Child?'" (Woodhouse),
  136
Wieland (Brown): incest in, 1
Williams, Patricia, 123
Williams, Raymond, 17, 68, 69, 72, 76,
  251n8
Williamson, John, xvii
willingness, 202, 206, 214; consent and,
  203, 204; harm and, 205
Will to Empower, The (Cruikshank), 47,
  77
Wilson, Melba, 233
Winfrey, Oprah, 2, 3

witch hunts, x, 69, 88, 93, 99, 253n28
women: child sexual abuse and, 99–100;
  heteronormative access to, 167; incest
  and, 21, 27, 67, 78, 235; violence
  against, xiv, 111, 171. *See also* black
  women
women's movements, xiv, 73
Women Who Hate Me (Allison), 152
Woodhouse, Barbara Bennett, 135, 136
Woodward, Kathy, 92
Woolf, Virginia, 116
Wordsworth, William, 262n27
workfare, 10, 191, 192, 222, 223
Worlds of Hurt (Tal), xx, 116
wounding of the mind, 81

X shape, 142, 143, 147–48; domination
  and, 144; patriarchy and, 145, 146;
  repudiation and, 150–51; sexual
  violation and, 144

Yeats, William Butler, 124
Young, Allan, 81, 82, 89, 90
Young, Elizabeth, 153–54
Yukins, Elizabeth, 122, 147

Zaretsky, Eli, 253n28
Žižek, Slavoj, 245n21
Zuriff, G. E., 194, 208

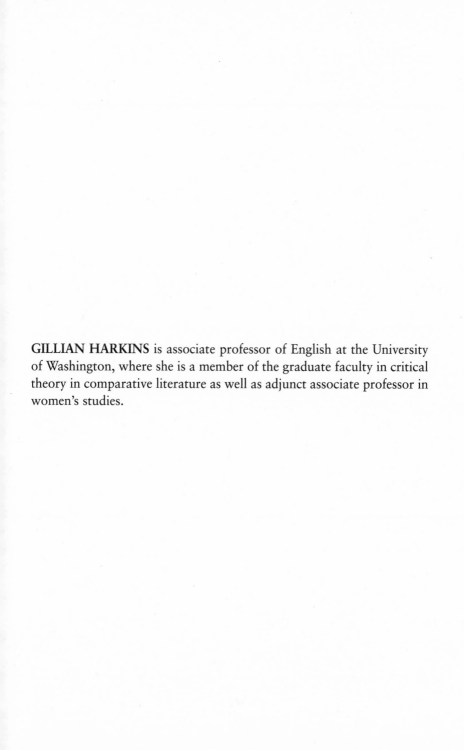

GILLIAN HARKINS is associate professor of English at the University of Washington, where she is a member of the graduate faculty in critical theory in comparative literature as well as adjunct associate professor in women's studies.